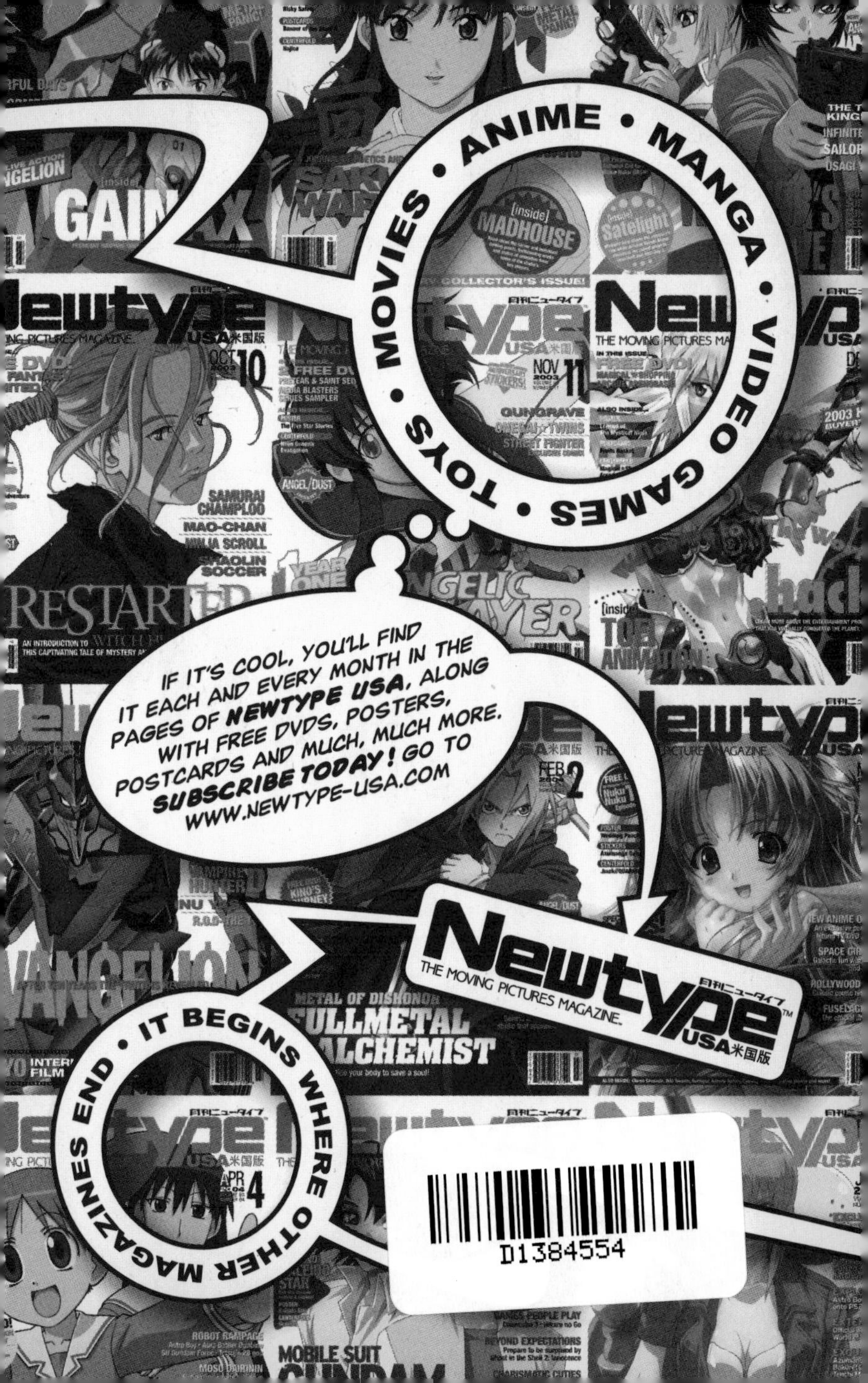
ANIME • MANGA • VIDEO GAMES • TOYS • MOVIES •
IF IT'S COOL, YOU'LL FIND IT EACH AND EVERY MONTH IN THE PAGES OF NEWTYPE USA, ALONG WITH FREE DVDS, POSTERS, POSTCARDS AND MUCH, MUCH MORE. SUBSCRIBE TODAY! GO TO WWW.NEWTYPE-USA.COM
Newtype
THE MOVING PICTURES MAGAZINE.
USA 米国版
IT BEGINS WHERE OTHER MAGAZINES END •
D1384554

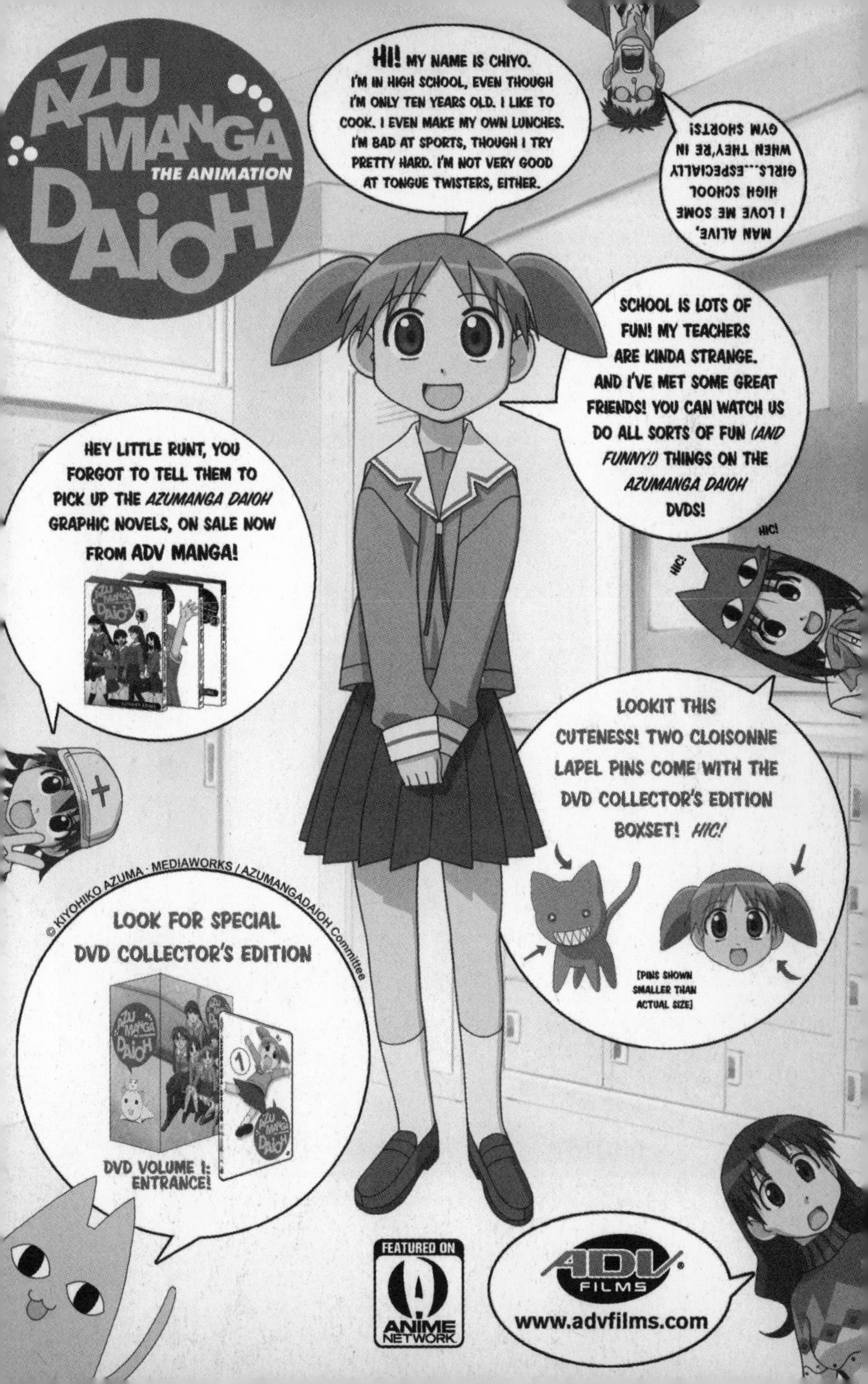
AZUMANGA DAIOH THE ANIMATION
HI! MY NAME IS CHIYO. I'M IN HIGH SCHOOL, EVEN THOUGH I'M ONLY TEN YEARS OLD. I LIKE TO COOK. I EVEN MAKE MY OWN LUNCHES. I'M BAD AT SPORTS, THOUGH I TRY PRETTY HARD. I'M NOT VERY GOOD AT TONGUE TWISTERS, EITHER.
MAN ALIVE, I LOVE ME SOME HIGH SCHOOL GIRLS...ESPECIALLY WHEN THEY'RE IN GYM SHORTS!
SCHOOL IS LOTS OF FUN! MY TEACHERS ARE KINDA STRANGE. AND I'VE MET SOME GREAT FRIENDS! YOU CAN WATCH US DO ALL SORTS OF FUN *(AND FUNNY!)* THINGS ON THE *AZUMANGA DAIOH* DVDS!
HIC!
HIC!
HEY LITTLE RUNT, YOU FORGOT TO TELL THEM TO PICK UP THE *AZUMANGA DAIOH* GRAPHIC NOVELS, ON SALE NOW FROM ADV MANGA!
LOOKIT THIS CUTENESS! TWO CLOISONNE LAPEL PINS COME WITH THE DVD COLLECTOR'S EDITION BOXSET! *HIC!*
[PINS SHOWN SMALLER THAN ACTUAL SIZE]
© KIYOHIKO AZUMA · MEDIAWORKS / AZUMANGADAIOH Committee
LOOK FOR SPECIAL DVD COLLECTOR'S EDITION
DVD VOLUME 1: ENTRANCE!
FEATURED ON ANIME NETWORK
ADV FILMS
www.advfilms.com

Welcome to Spring

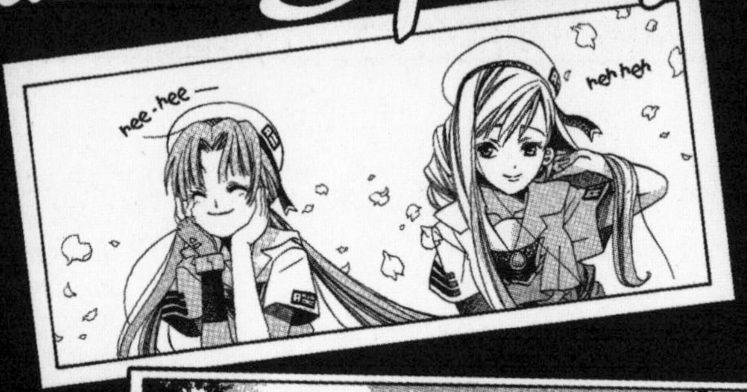
hee-hee—
heh heh

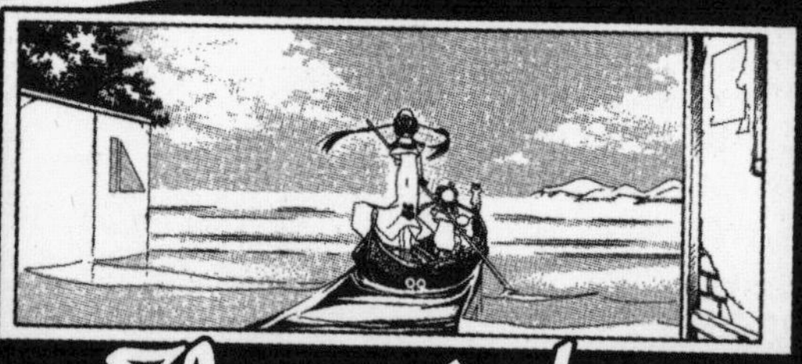

in Neo-Venezia!

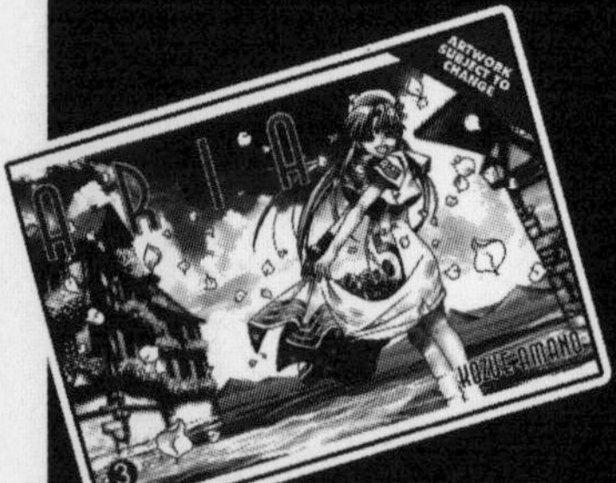
ARTWORK SUBJECT TO CHANGE
ARIA
KOZUE AMANO
3

ARIA ③

Follow Akari and her friends as they uncover hidden treasures in ARIA vol. 3!

Be sure you start at the beginning!

ARIA vol. 1 ISBN 1-4139-0040-2, $9.99

ARIA vol. 2 ISBN 1-4139-0071-2, $9.99

AVAILABLE NOW!

ADV Manga™

www.adv-manga.com

THE ADVENTURE CONTINUES IN

The First King Adventure 2

The challenges become more difficult as Prince Varumu continues his journey to become the king. Keeping his companions safe won't be easy, but the appearance of two meddling kids may lead to answers about their troubles with the spirit masters. And what will Varumu do when he meets a spirit master looking for him?! More fantastic surprises lie ahead, as the journey resumes in *The First King Adventure*, Volume 2!

COMING SOON FROM ADV MANGA!

The First King Adventure Vol. 01

 PG. 83 ***Teru teru bouzu***

On this page, Matsuri sings about a "sunny angel." The term in Japanese was *teru teru bouzu*, which is actually a sort of ghostlike figure hung outside school buildings, usually before important outdoor events, field trips, etc. It serves to ward off rain. (But, if it is hung upside-down, the effect is to *invite* rainy weather.) In terms of appearance, the *teru teru bouzu* is something akin to the "lollypop ghosts" that American students often make on Halloween by wrapping a napkin around a lollypop and painting a scary face on the head.

 PG. 120 **Shoes**

One thing you would likely notice upon entering just about any Japanese school would be rows and rows of cubbies holding children's shoes. In Japan, elementary, middle, and high school students all have separate shoes that they wear inside the school building. Their "inside" shoes are school-issued, like the uniforms, and are kept in the lockers or cubbies when the students are outside or at home. Upon entering and leaving the school building, students switch their shoes accordingly. Incidentally, guests visiting the schools will be offered a pair of slipper-like footwear (kind of like a sandal with a closed front and no straps).

 PG. 170 **Tone**

"Tone" is what artists use to create patterns and shading in manga. It is used when a manga author wants a pattern over some part of an illustration (for example, on someone's clothes, like a plaid shirt or pinstripe suit). Tone is sold in sheets and is cut to size then applied over an illustration to produce the pattern. The same technique can be used to create a gradient in shading, or for some background elements, like clouds and water.

the FiRSt King Adventure ◆1

© Moyamu Fujino 2002
All rights reserved.
First published in 2002 by MAG Garden Corporation.
English translation rights arranged with MAG Garden Corporation.

Translator **KAY BERTRAND**
Lead Translator/Translation Supervisor **JAVIER LOPEZ**
ADV Manga Translation Staff **JOSH COLE, AMY FORSYTH, BRENDAN FRAYNE,**
HARUKA KANEKO-SMITH, EIKO McGREGOR AND MADOKA MOROE

Print Production/Art Studio Manager **LISA PUCKETT**
Pre-press Manager **KLYS REEDYK**
Art Production Manager **RYAN MASON**
Sr. Designer/Creative Manager **JORGE ALVARADO**
Graphic Designer/Group Leader **SHANNON RASBERRY**
Graphic Designer **HEATHER GARY**
Graphic Artists **SHANNA JENSCHKE, KERRI KALINEC, GEORGE REYNOLDS**
Graphic Intern **MARK MEZA**

International Coordinator **TORU IWAKAMI**
International Coordinator **ATSUSHI KANBAYASHI**

Publishing Editor **SUSAN ITIN**
Assistant Editor **MARGARET SCHAROLD**
Editorial Assistant **VARSHA BHUCHAR**
Proofreaders **SHERIDAN JACOBS AND STEVEN REED**
Editorial Intern **JENNIFER VACCA**

Research/Traffic Coordinator **MARSHA ARNOLD**

Executive VP, CFO, COO **KEVIN CORCORAN**

President, CEO & Publisher **JOHN LEDFORD**

Email: editor@adv-manga.com
www.adv-manga.com
www.advfilms.com

For sales and distribution inquiries please call 1.800.282.7202

ADV MANGA™ is a division of A.D. Vision, Inc.
10114 W. Sam Houston Parkway, Suite 200, Houston, Texas 77099

English text © 2004 published by A.D. Vision, Inc. under exclusive license.
ADV MANGA is a trademark of A.D. Vision, Inc.

ISBN: 1-4139-0194-8
First printing, December 2004
10 9 8 7 6 5 4 3 2 1
Printed in Canada

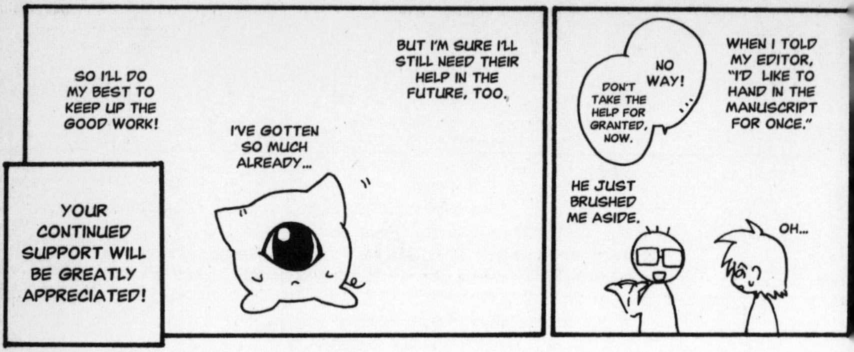
WHEN I TOLD MY EDITOR, "I'D LIKE TO HAND IN THE MANUSCRIPT FOR ONCE."
NO WAY!
DON'T TAKE THE HELP FOR GRANTED, NOW.
...
OH...
HE JUST BRUSHED ME ASIDE.
BUT I'M SURE I'LL STILL NEED THEIR HELP IN THE FUTURE, TOO.
I'VE GOTTEN SO MUCH ALREADY...
SO I'LL DO MY BEST TO KEEP UP THE GOOD WORK!
YOUR CONTINUED SUPPORT WILL BE GREATLY APPRECIATED!

THANK YOU FOR READING THIS TO THE END.
HOPE TO SEE YOU NEXT TIME!

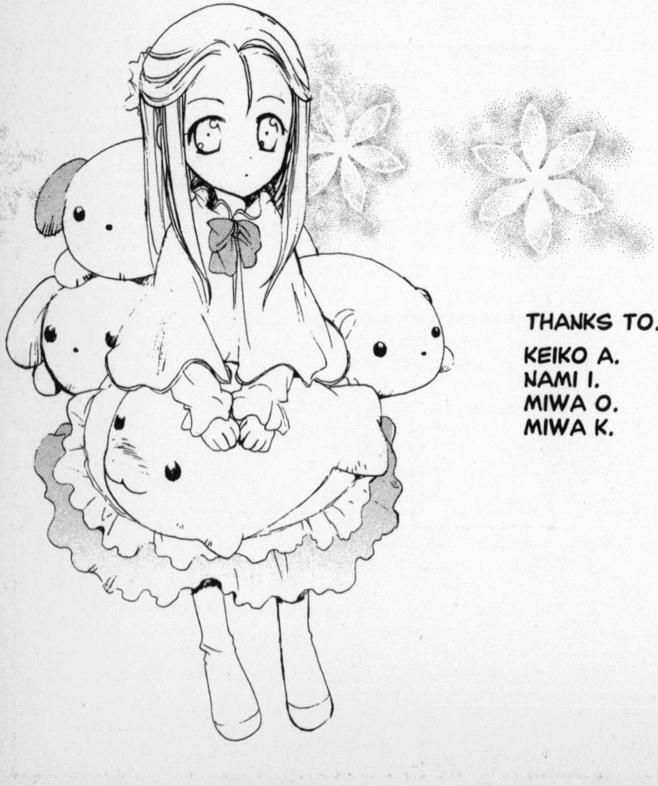

THANKS TO...

KEIKO A. TOMOKO T.
NAMI I. MAMI H.
MIWA O. YU-KI M.
MIWA K. YUMI M.

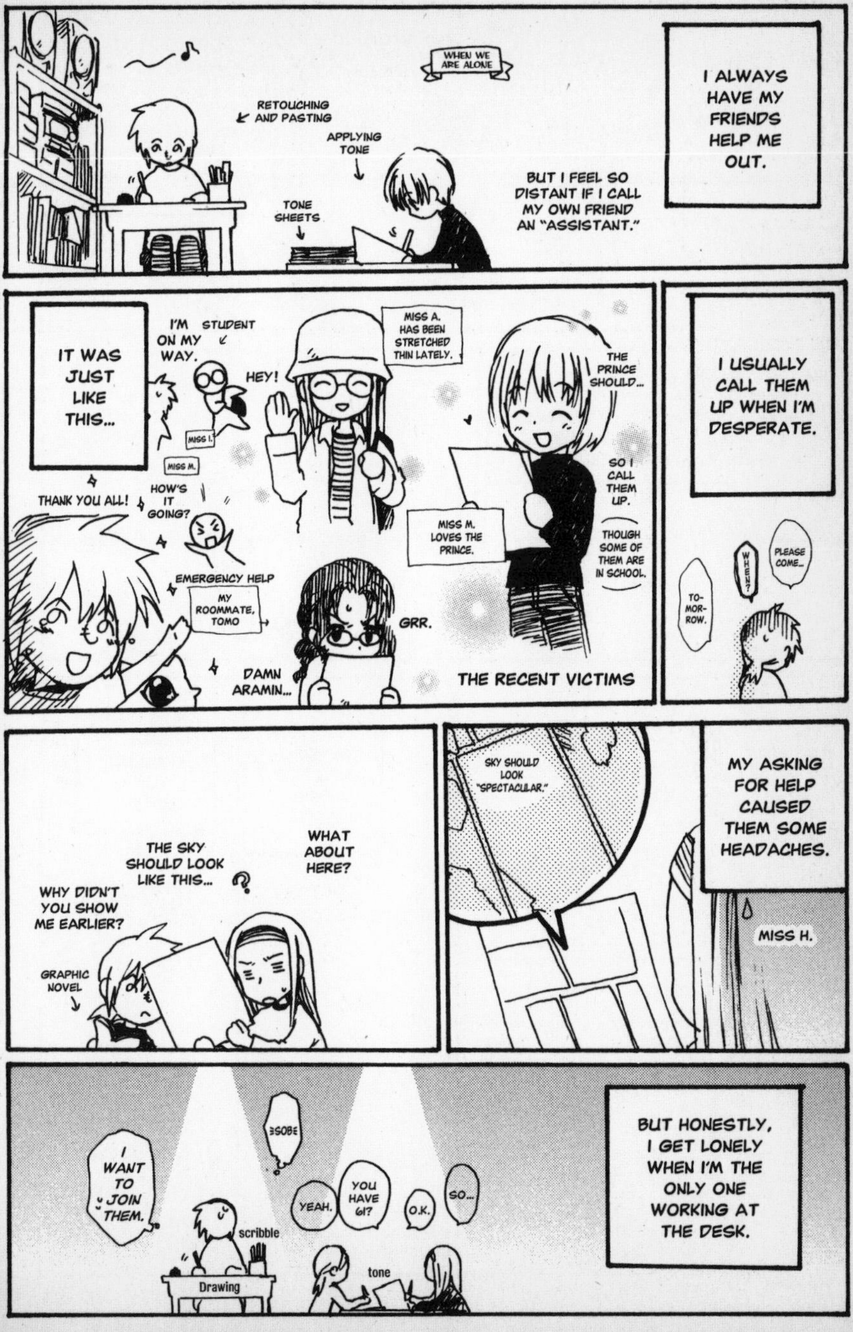
I ALWAYS HAVE MY FRIENDS HELP ME OUT.
BUT I FEEL SO DISTANT IF I CALL MY OWN FRIEND AN "ASSISTANT."
WHEN WE ARE ALONE
APPLYING TONE
TONE SHEETS
RETOUCHING AND PASTING
I USUALLY CALL THEM UP WHEN I'M DESPERATE.
PLEASE COME...
WHEN?
TO-MOR-ROW.
THE PRINCE SHOULD...
SO I CALL THEM UP.
THOUGH SOME OF THEM ARE IN SCHOOL.
THE RECENT VICTIMS
MISS A. HAS BEEN STRETCHED THIN LATELY.
MISS M. LOVES THE PRINCE.
GRR.
DAMN ARAMIN...
I'M ON MY WAY.
STUDENT
HEY!
MISS I.
MISS M.
IT WAS JUST LIKE THIS...
HOW'S IT GOING?
THANK YOU ALL!
EMERGENCY HELP
MY ROOMMATE, TOMO
MY ASKING FOR HELP CAUSED THEM SOME HEADACHES.
MISS H.
SKY SHOULD LOOK "SPECTACULAR."
WHAT ABOUT HERE?
THE SKY SHOULD LOOK LIKE THIS...
WHY DIDN'T YOU SHOW ME EARLIER?
GRAPHIC NOVEL
BUT HONESTLY, I GET LONELY WHEN I'M THE ONLY ONE WORKING AT THE DESK.
SO...
O.K.
YOU HAVE 61?
YEAH.
I WANT TO JOIN THEM.
scribble
Drawing
tone

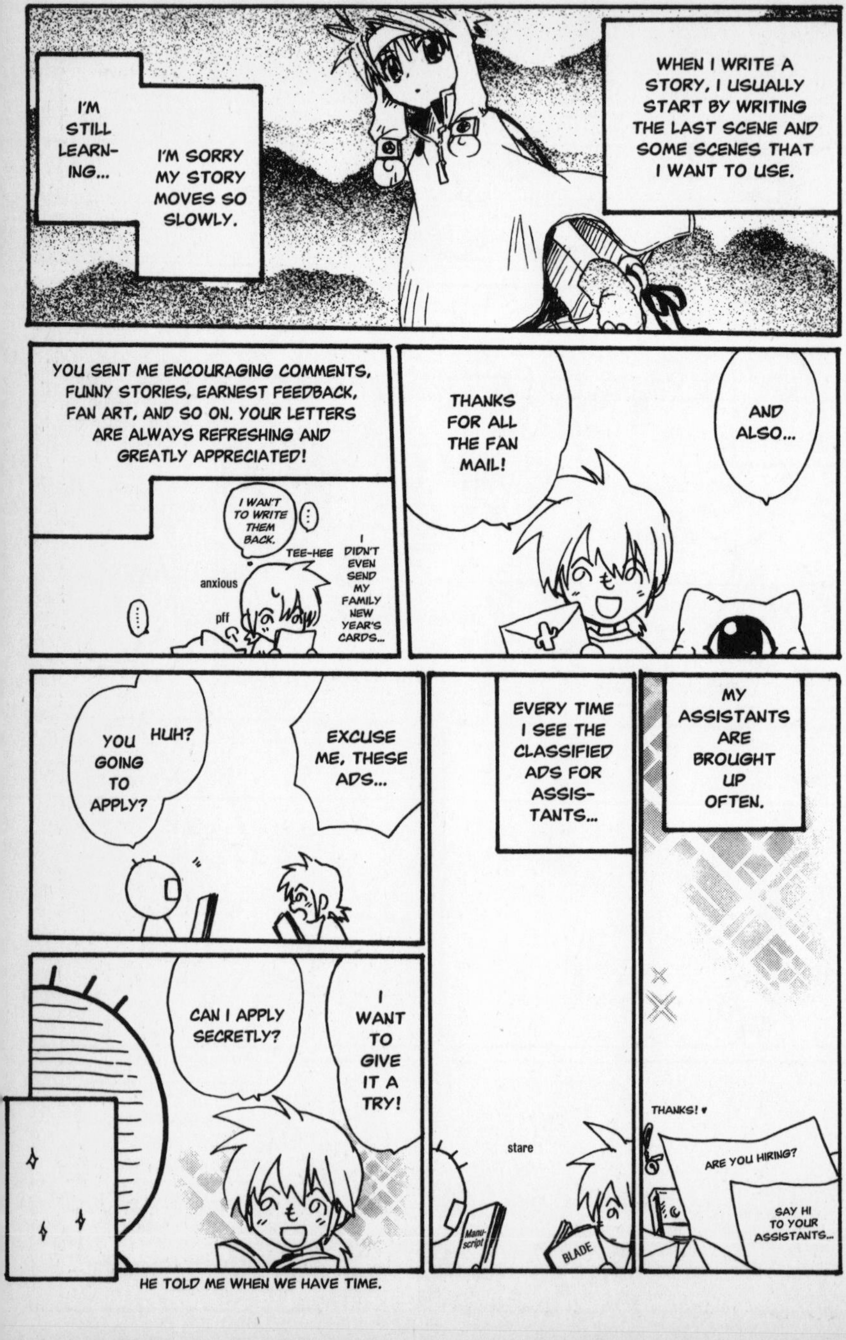
WHEN I WRITE A STORY, I USUALLY START BY WRITING THE LAST SCENE AND SOME SCENES THAT I WANT TO USE.
I'M SORRY MY STORY MOVES SO SLOWLY.
I'M STILL LEARN-ING...
AND ALSO...
THANKS FOR ALL THE FAN MAIL!
YOU SENT ME ENCOURAGING COMMENTS, FUNNY STORIES, EARNEST FEEDBACK, FAN ART, AND SO ON. YOUR LETTERS ARE ALWAYS REFRESHING AND GREATLY APPRECIATED!
I DIDN'T EVEN SEND MY FAMILY NEW YEAR'S CARDS...
...
I WAN'T TO WRITE THEM BACK.
TEE-HEE
anxious
pff
...
MY ASSISTANTS ARE BROUGHT UP OFTEN.
EVERY TIME I SEE THE CLASSIFIED ADS FOR ASSIS-TANTS...
EXCUSE ME, THESE ADS...
HUH?
YOU GOING TO APPLY?
THANKS! ♥
ARE YOU HIRING?
SAY HI TO YOUR ASSISTANTS...
stare
Manu-script
BLADE
I WANT TO GIVE IT A TRY!
CAN I APPLY SECRETLY?
HE TOLD ME WHEN WE HAVE TIME.

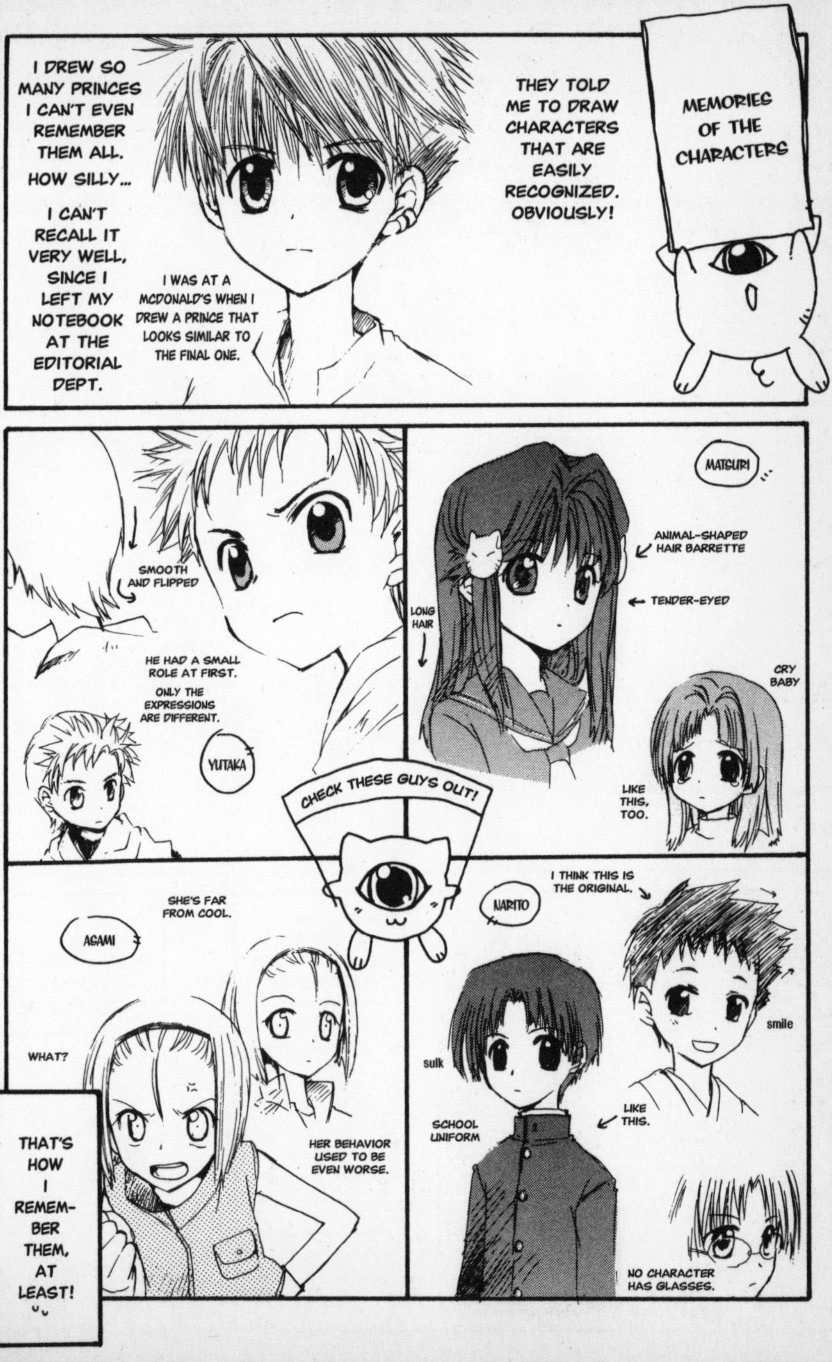
MEMORIES OF THE CHARACTERS
THEY TOLD ME TO DRAW CHARACTERS THAT ARE EASILY RECOGNIZED. OBVIOUSLY!
I DREW SO MANY PRINCES I CAN'T EVEN REMEMBER THEM ALL. HOW SILLY...
I CAN'T RECALL IT VERY WELL, SINCE I LEFT MY NOTEBOOK AT THE EDITORIAL DEPT.
I WAS AT A MCDONALD'S WHEN I DREW A PRINCE THAT LOOKS SIMILAR TO THE FINAL ONE.
MATSURI
ANIMAL-SHAPED HAIR BARRETTE
TENDER-EYED
LONG HAIR
CRY BABY
LIKE THIS, TOO.
SMOOTH AND FLIPPED
HE HAD A SMALL ROLE AT FIRST.
ONLY THE EXPRESSIONS ARE DIFFERENT.
YUTAKA
CHECK THESE GUYS OUT!
NARITO
I THINK THIS IS THE ORIGINAL.
smile
sulk
LIKE THIS.
SCHOOL UNIFORM
NO CHARACTER HAS GLASSES.
SHE'S FAR FROM COOL.
ASAMI
WHAT?
HER BEHAVIOR USED TO BE EVEN WORSE.
THAT'S HOW I REMEMBER THEM, AT LEAST!

THE STORY USED TO BE LIKE THIS...PART 2

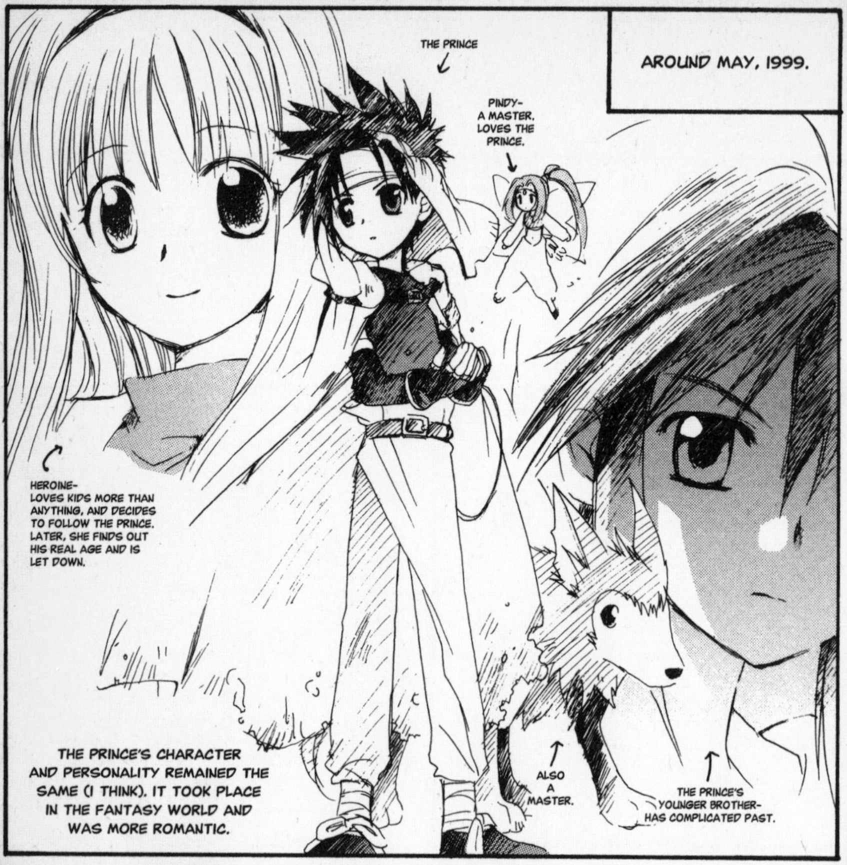

AROUND MAY, 1999.
THE PRINCE
PINDY- A MASTER. LOVES THE PRINCE.
HEROINE- LOVES KIDS MORE THAN ANYTHING, AND DECIDES TO FOLLOW THE PRINCE. LATER, SHE FINDS OUT HIS REAL AGE AND IS LET DOWN.
THE PRINCE'S CHARACTER AND PERSONALITY REMAINED THE SAME (I THINK). IT TOOK PLACE IN THE FANTASY WORLD AND WAS MORE ROMANTIC.
ALSO A MASTER.
THE PRINCE'S YOUNGER BROTHER- HAS COMPLICATED PAST.

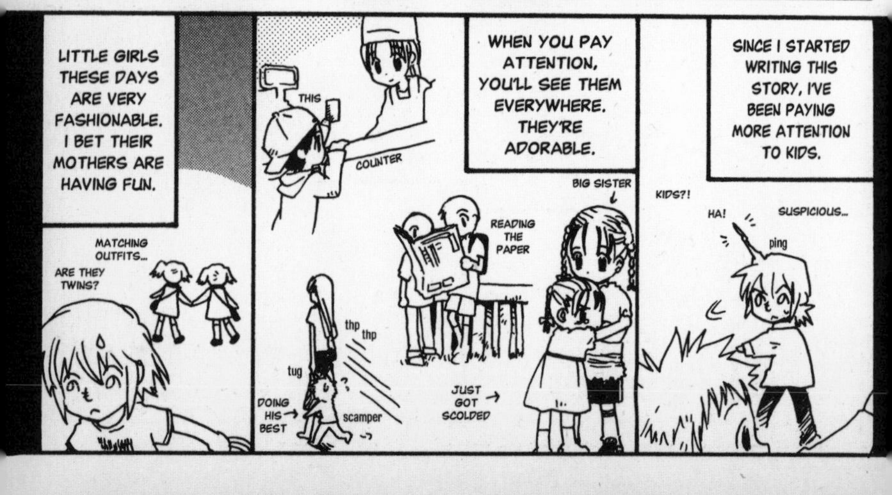

SINCE I STARTED WRITING THIS STORY, I'VE BEEN PAYING MORE ATTENTION TO KIDS.
WHEN YOU PAY ATTENTION, YOU'LL SEE THEM EVERYWHERE. THEY'RE ADORABLE.
THIS
COUNTER
LITTLE GIRLS THESE DAYS ARE VERY FASHIONABLE. I BET THEIR MOTHERS ARE HAVING FUN.
KIDS?!
HA!
SUSPICIOUS...
ping
BIG SISTER
READING THE PAPER
JUST GOT SCOLDED
thp thp
tug
DOING HIS BEST
scamper
MATCHING OUTFITS...
ARE THEY TWINS?

THE STORY USED TO BE LIKE THIS...PART I

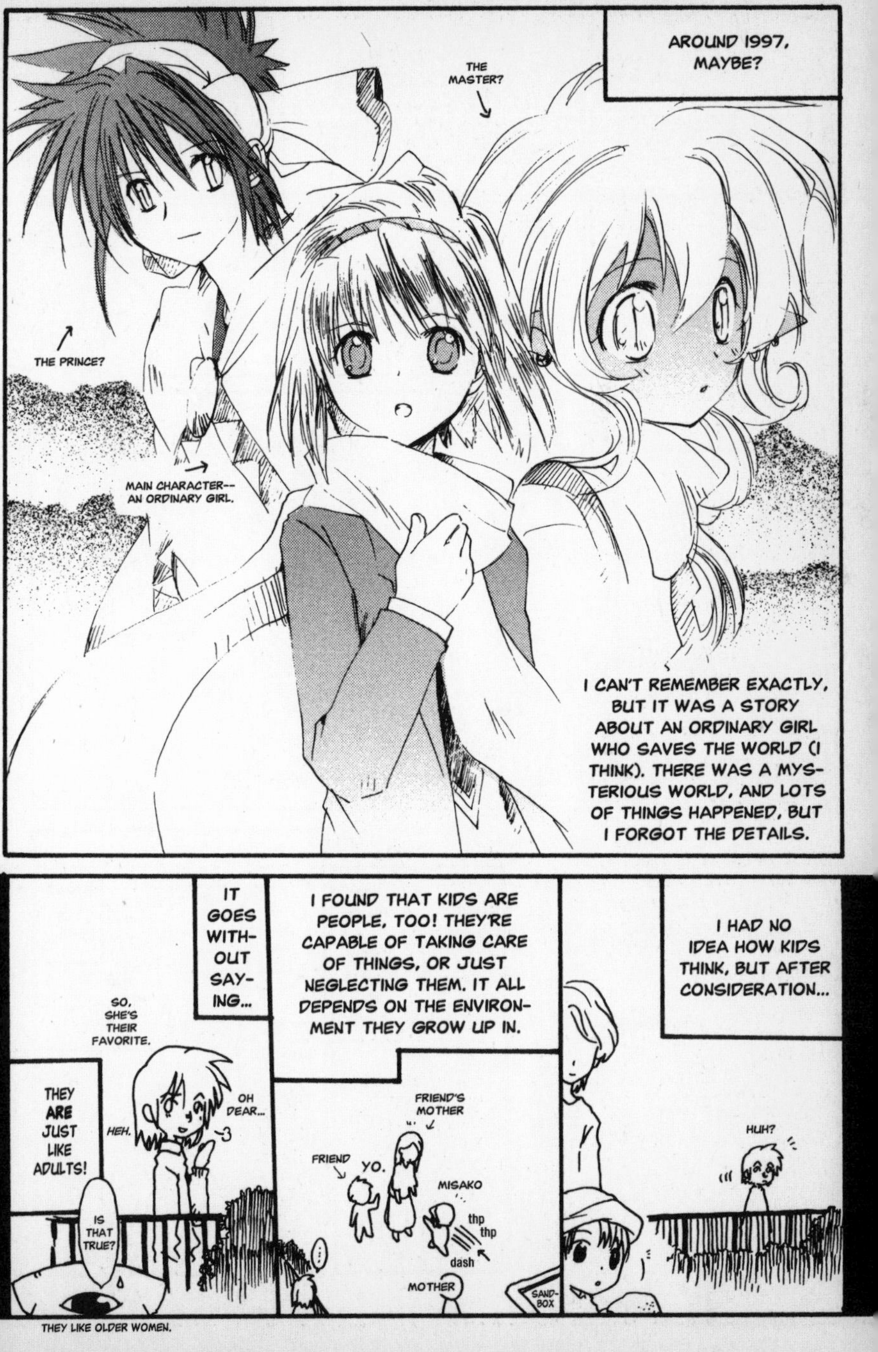
AROUND 1997, MAYBE?
THE MASTER?
THE PRINCE?
MAIN CHARACTER-- AN ORDINARY GIRL.
I CAN'T REMEMBER EXACTLY, BUT IT WAS A STORY ABOUT AN ORDINARY GIRL WHO SAVES THE WORLD (I THINK). THERE WAS A MYS-TERIOUS WORLD, AND LOTS OF THINGS HAPPENED, BUT I FORGOT THE DETAILS.
I HAD NO IDEA HOW KIDS THINK, BUT AFTER CONSIDERATION...
HUH?
SAND-BOX
I FOUND THAT KIDS ARE PEOPLE, TOO! THEY'RE CAPABLE OF TAKING CARE OF THINGS, OR JUST NEGLECTING THEM. IT ALL DEPENDS ON THE ENVIRON-MENT THEY GROW UP IN.
FRIEND'S MOTHER
FRIEND
YO.
MISAKO
thp thp
dash
MOTHER
IT GOES WITH-OUT SAY-ING...
SO, SHE'S THEIR FAVORITE.
OH DEAR...
HEH.
THEY **ARE** JUST LIKE ADULTS!
IS THAT TRUE?

THEY LIKE OLDER WOMEN.

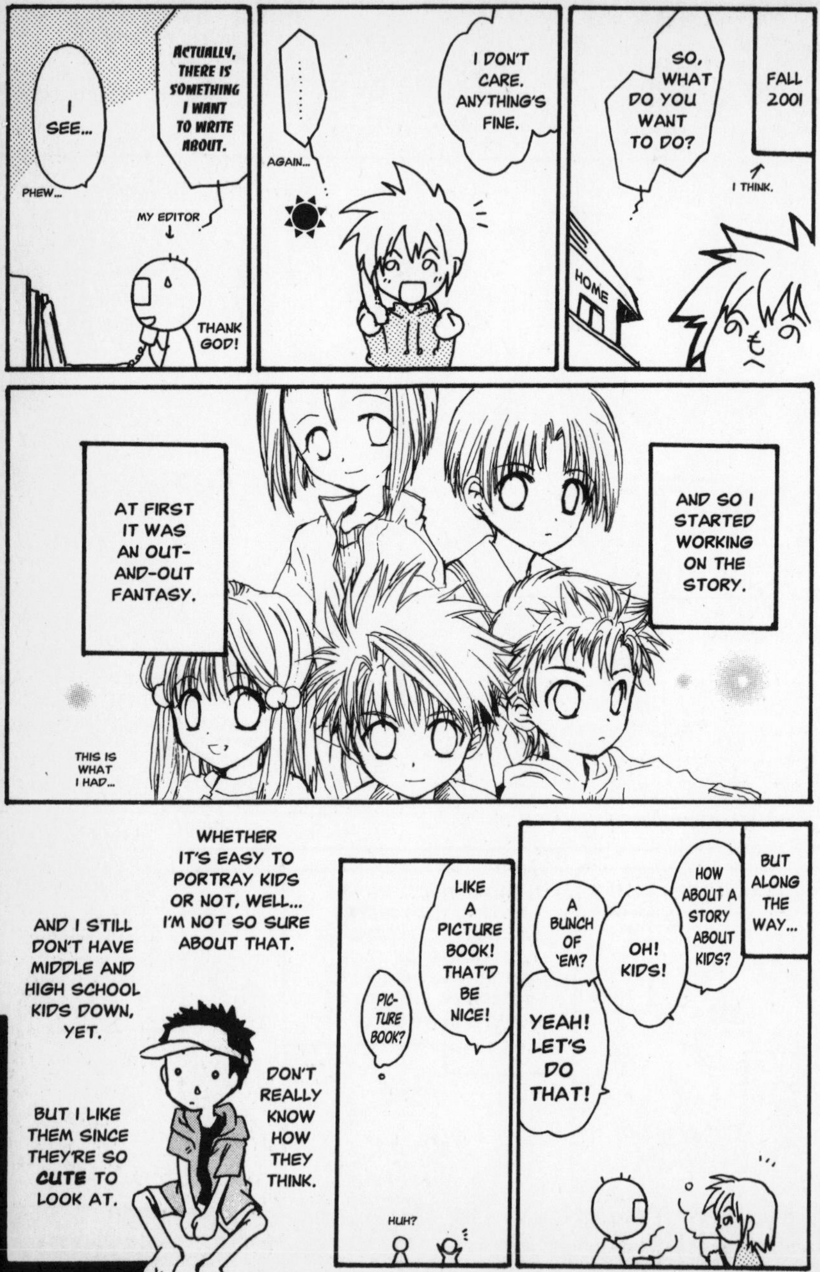

FALL 2001
I THINK.
SO, WHAT DO YOU WANT TO DO?
HOME
I DON'T CARE. ANYTHING'S FINE.
......
AGAIN...
ACTUALLY, THERE IS SOMETHING I WANT TO WRITE ABOUT.
I SEE...
PHEW...
MY EDITOR
THANK GOD!
AND SO I STARTED WORKING ON THE STORY.
AT FIRST IT WAS AN OUT-AND-OUT FANTASY.
THIS IS WHAT I HAD...
BUT ALONG THE WAY...
HOW ABOUT A STORY ABOUT KIDS?
OH! KIDS!
A BUNCH OF 'EM?
YEAH! LET'S DO THAT!
LIKE A PICTURE BOOK! THAT'D BE NICE!
PIC-TURE BOOK?
HUH?
WHETHER IT'S EASY TO PORTRAY KIDS OR NOT, WELL... I'M NOT SO SURE ABOUT THAT.
AND I STILL DON'T HAVE MIDDLE AND HIGH SCHOOL KIDS DOWN, YET.
DON'T REALLY KNOW HOW THEY THINK.
BUT I LIKE THEM SINCE THEY'RE SO CUTE TO LOOK AT.

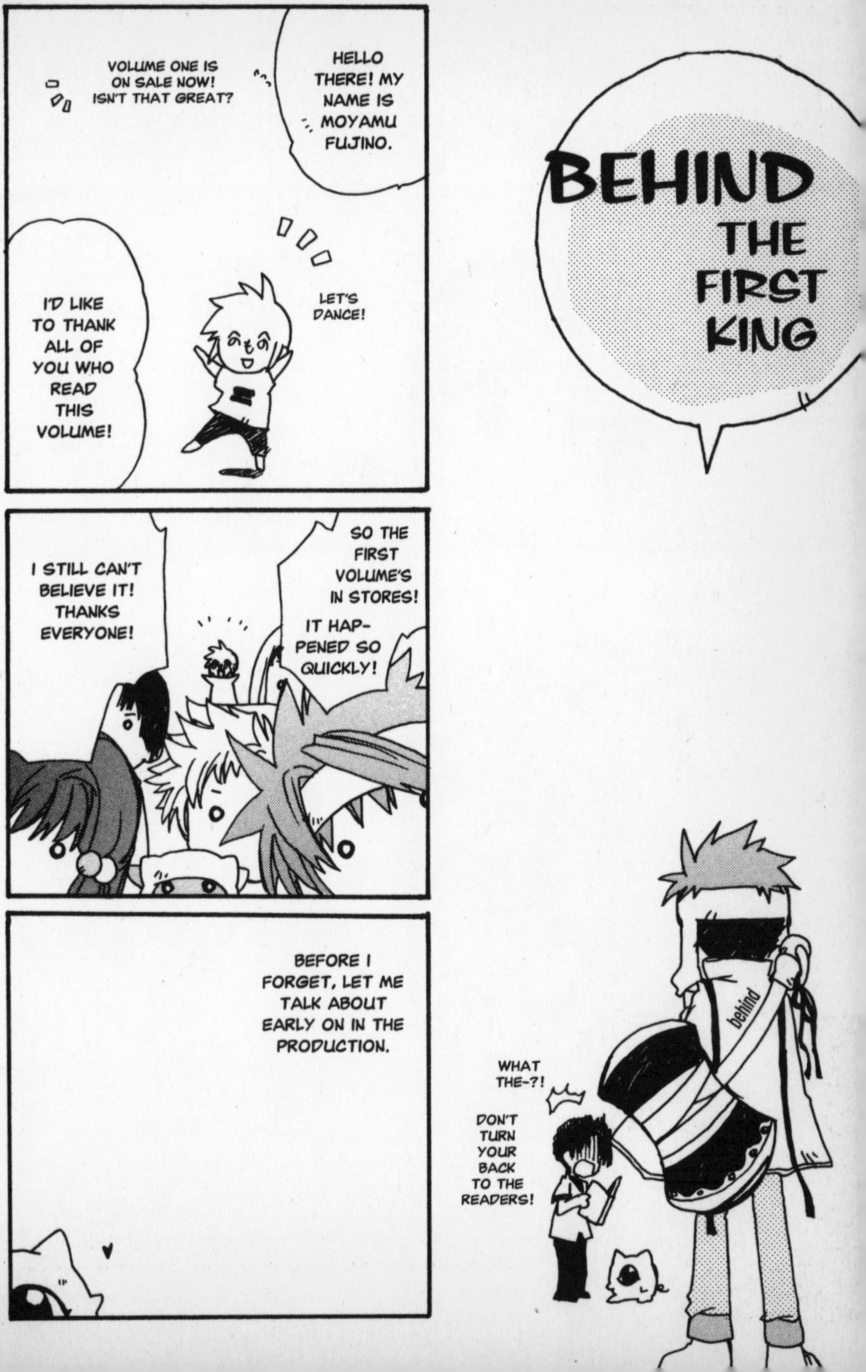
BEHIND THE FIRST KING
HELLO THERE! MY NAME IS MOYAMU FUJINO.
VOLUME ONE IS ON SALE NOW! ISN'T THAT GREAT?
LET'S DANCE!
I'D LIKE TO THANK ALL OF YOU WHO READ THIS VOLUME!
SO THE FIRST VOLUME'S IN STORES!
IT HAPPENED SO QUICKLY!
I STILL CAN'T BELIEVE IT! THANKS EVERYONE!
BEFORE I FORGET, LET ME TALK ABOUT EARLY ON IN THE PRODUCTION.
behind
WHAT THE-?!
DON'T TURN YOUR BACK TO THE READERS!

The FIRST KING Adventure

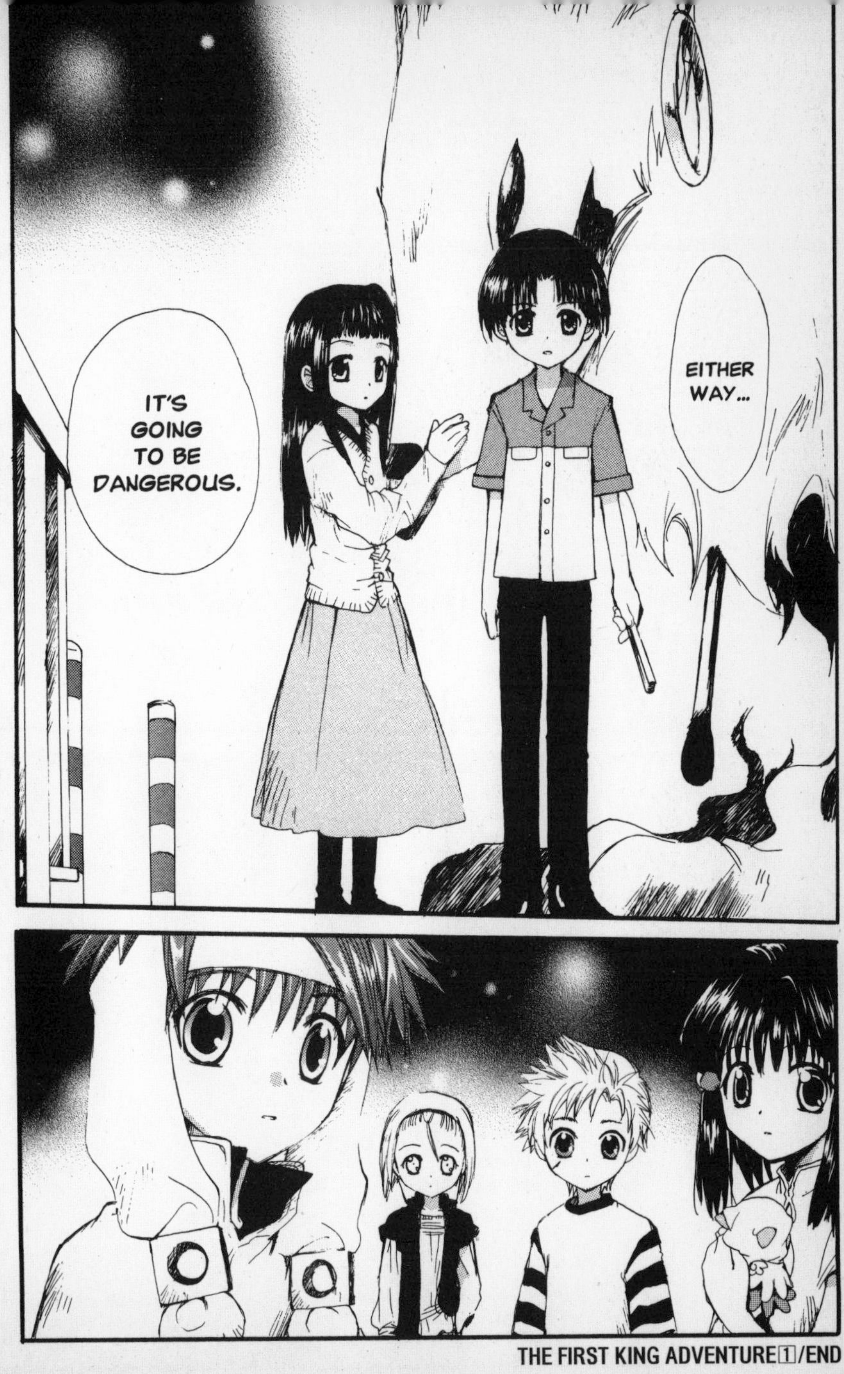
EITHER WAY...
IT'S GOING TO BE DANGEROUS.

THE FIRST KING ADVENTURE 1 /END

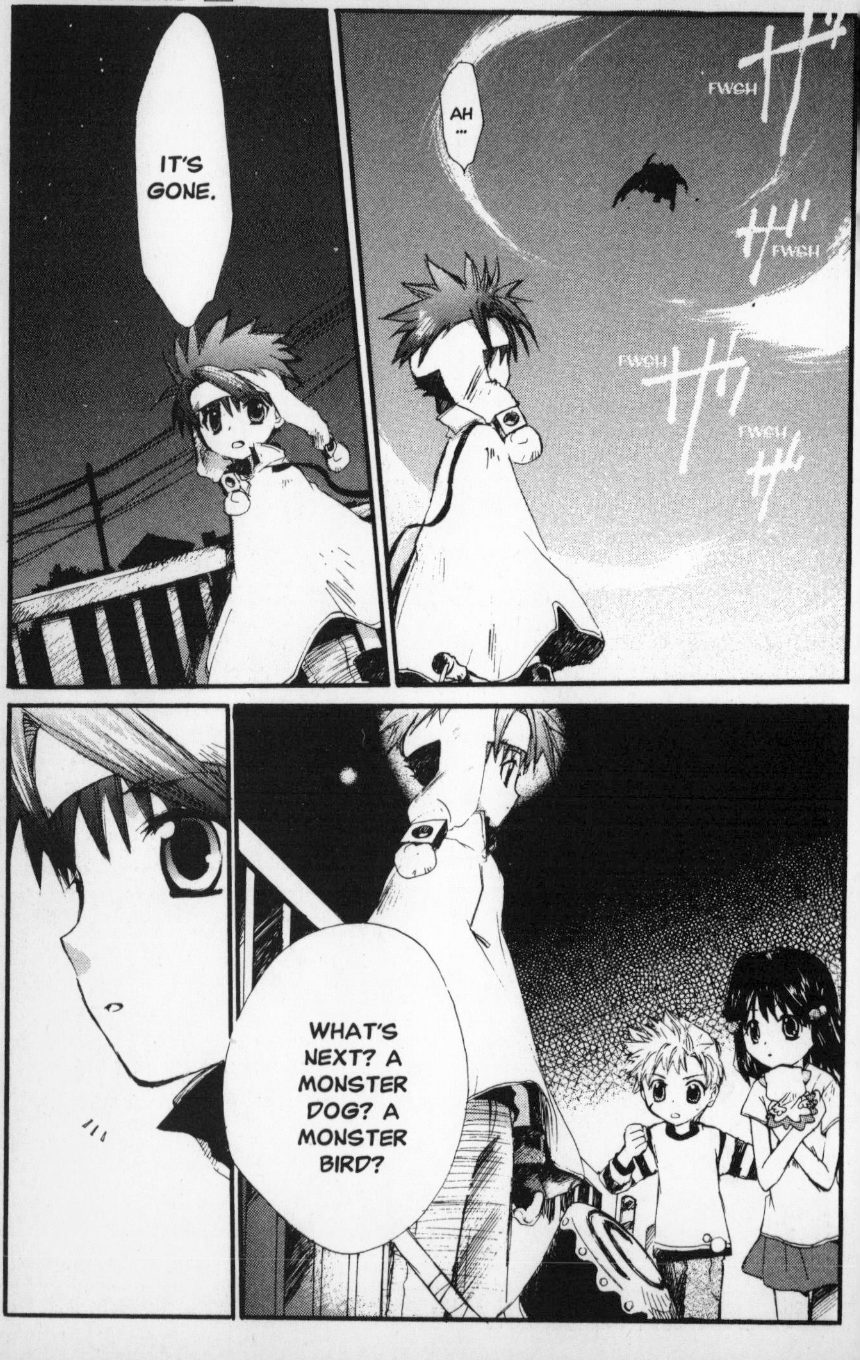
AH ...
FWSH
FWSH
FWSH
FWSH
IT'S GONE.
WHAT'S NEXT? A MONSTER DOG? A MONSTER BIRD?

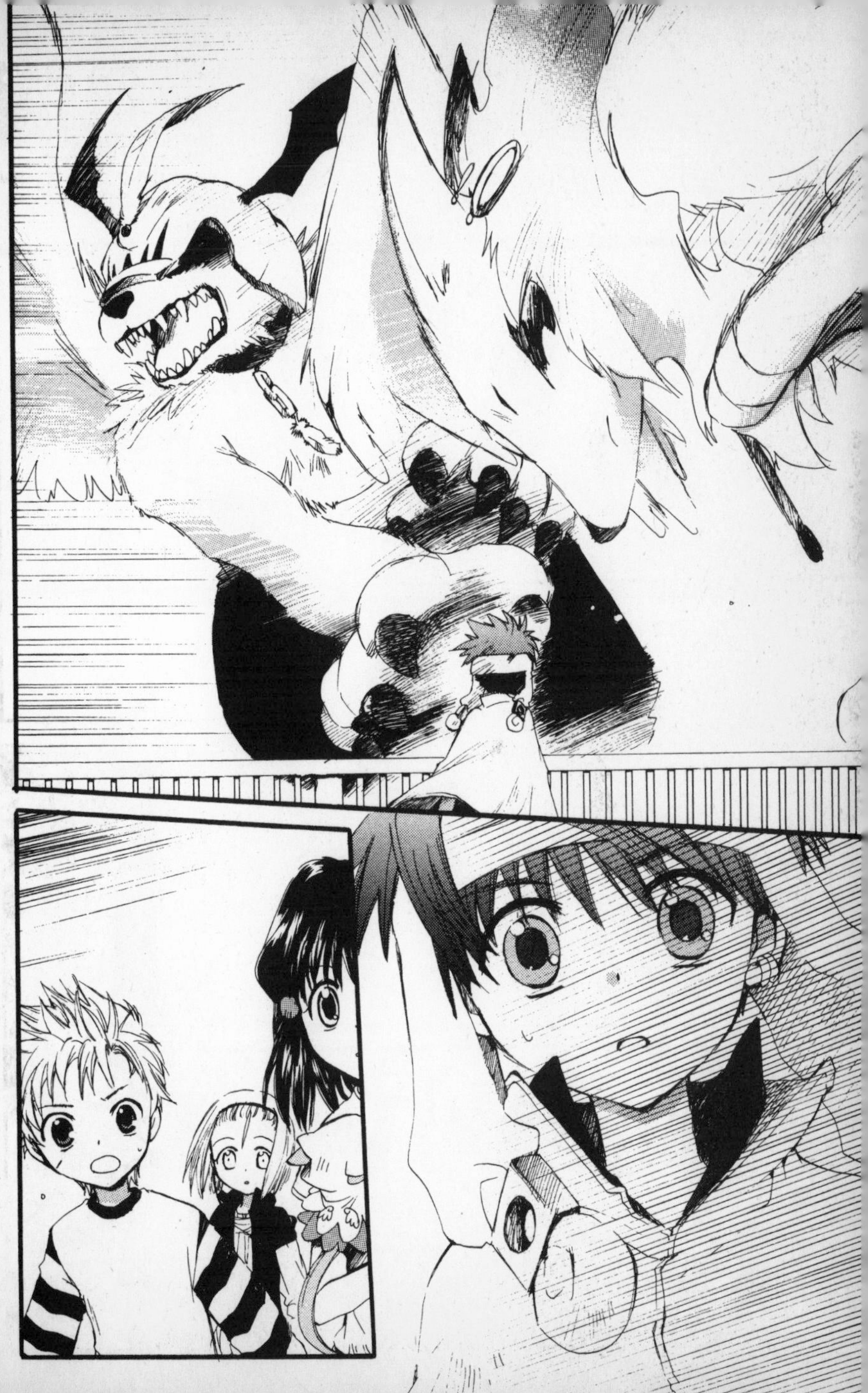

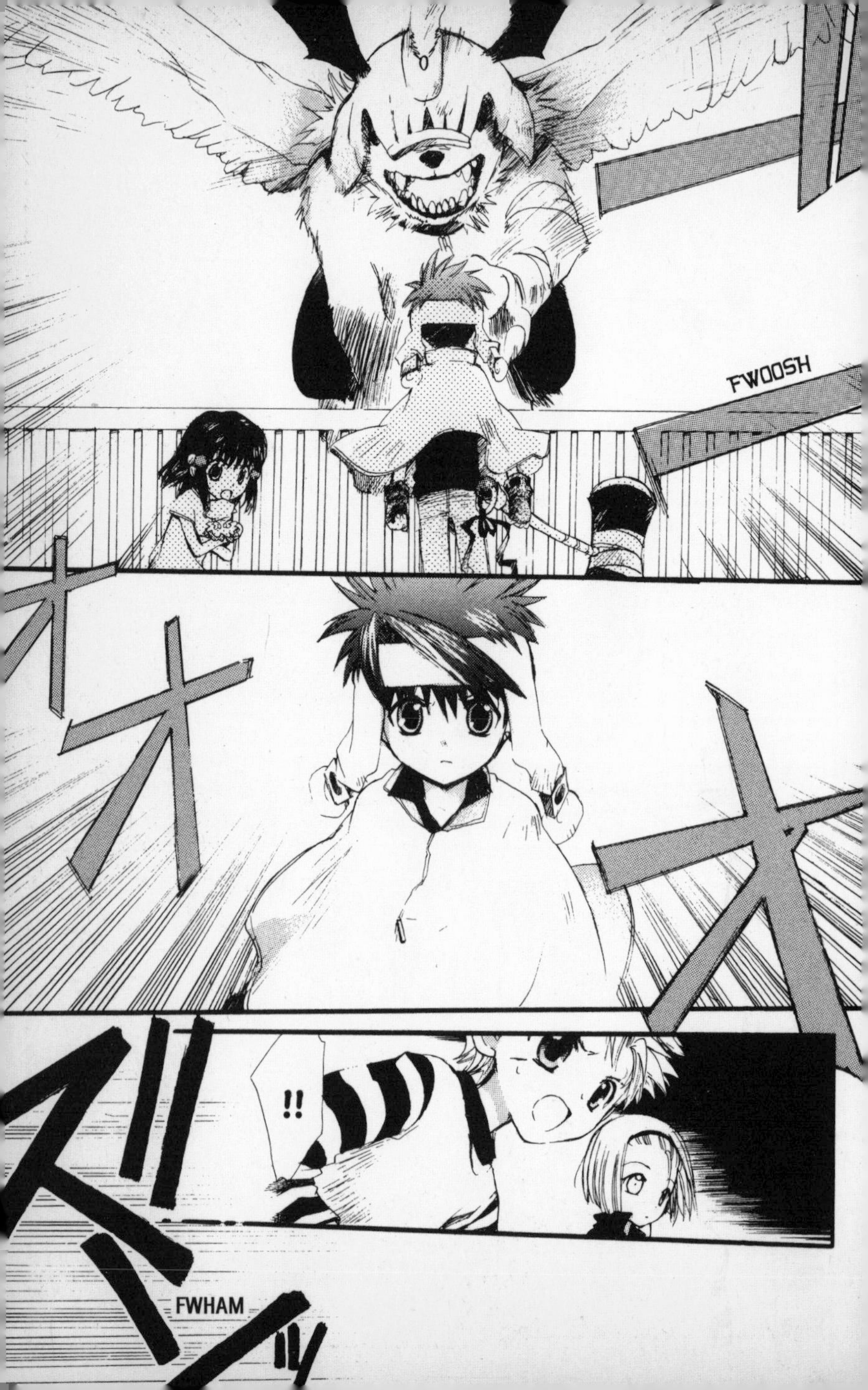
FWOOSH
!!
FWHAM

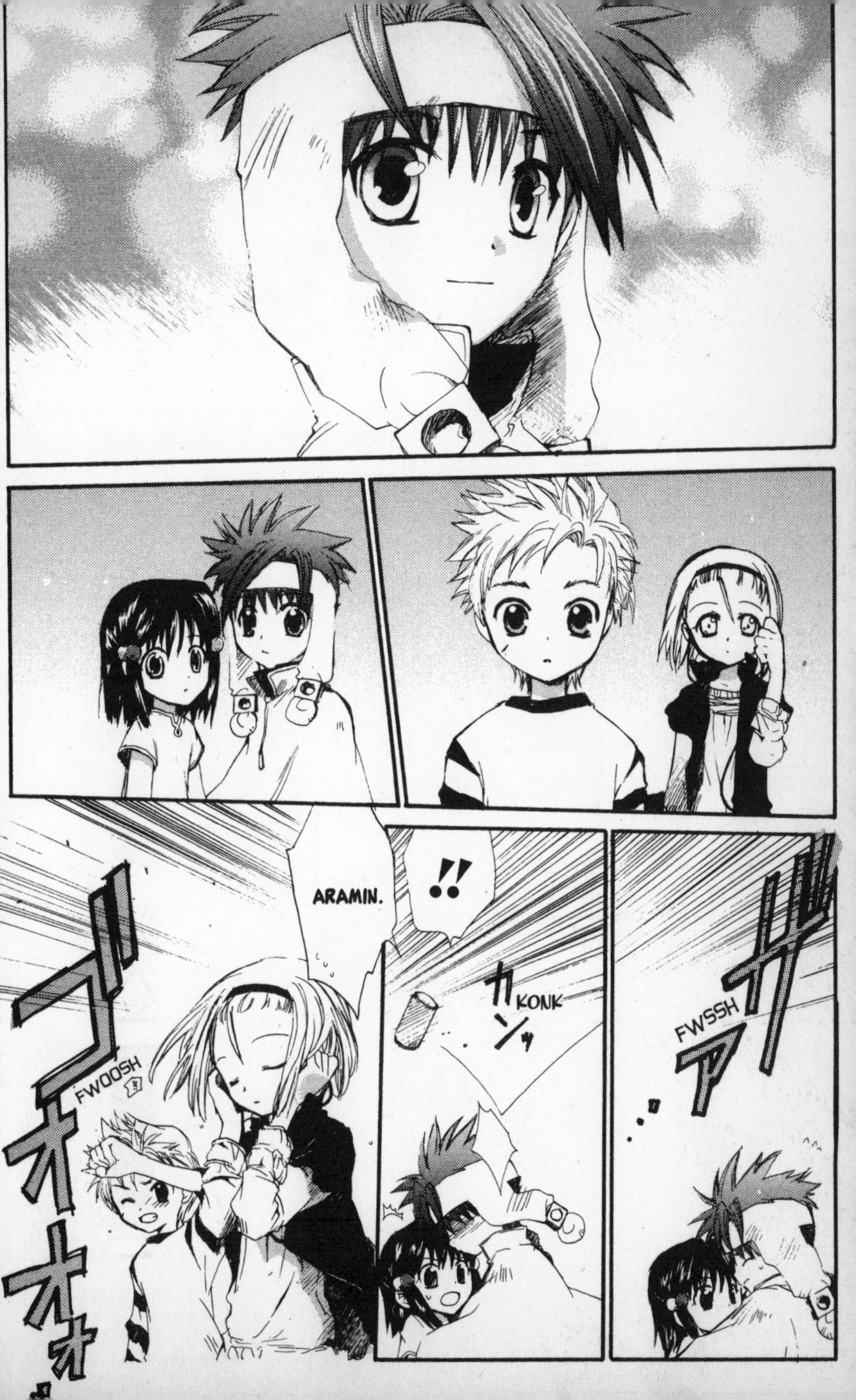
FWSSH
KONK
!!
ARAMIN.
FWOOSH

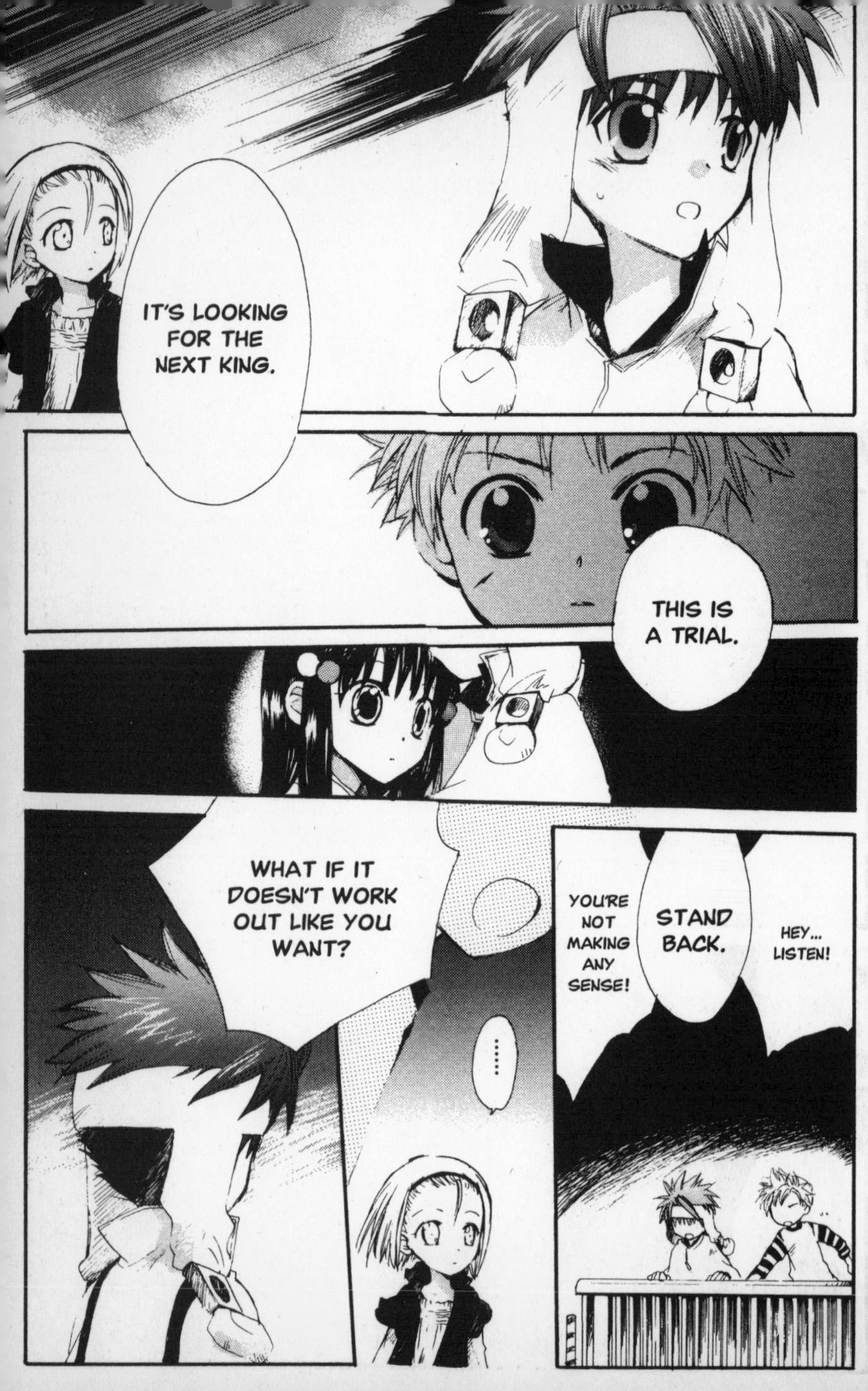
IT'S LOOKING FOR THE NEXT KING.
THIS IS A TRIAL.
HEY... LISTEN!
STAND BACK.
YOU'RE NOT MAKING ANY SENSE!
WHAT IF IT DOESN'T WORK OUT LIKE YOU WANT?
......

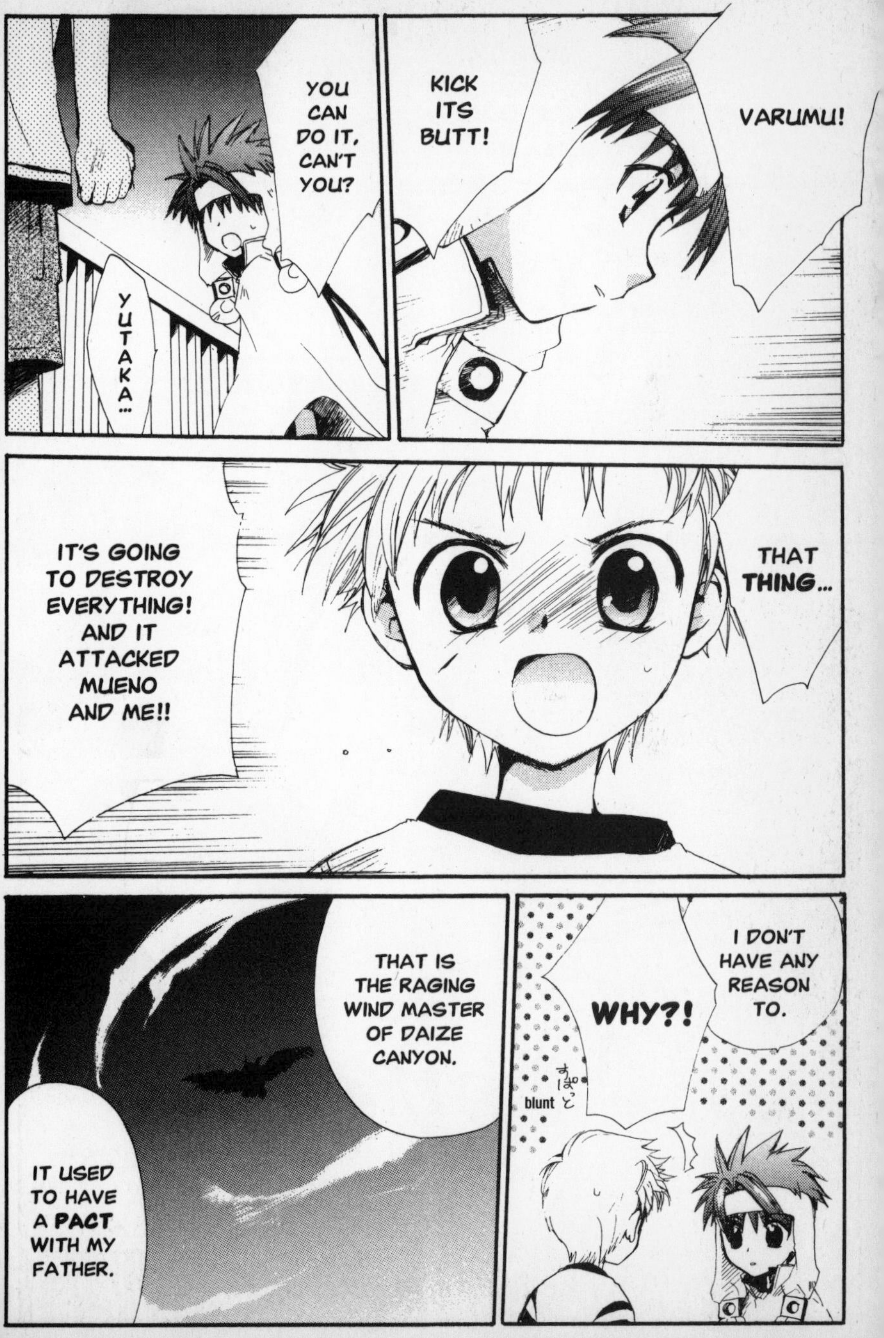

VARUMU!
KICK ITS BUTT!
YOU CAN DO IT, CAN'T YOU?
YUTAKA...
THAT THING...
IT'S GOING TO DESTROY EVERYTHING! AND IT ATTACKED MUENO AND ME!!
I DON'T HAVE ANY REASON TO.
WHY?!
blunt
THAT IS THE RAGING WIND MASTER OF DAIZE CANYON.
IT USED TO HAVE A PACT WITH MY FATHER.

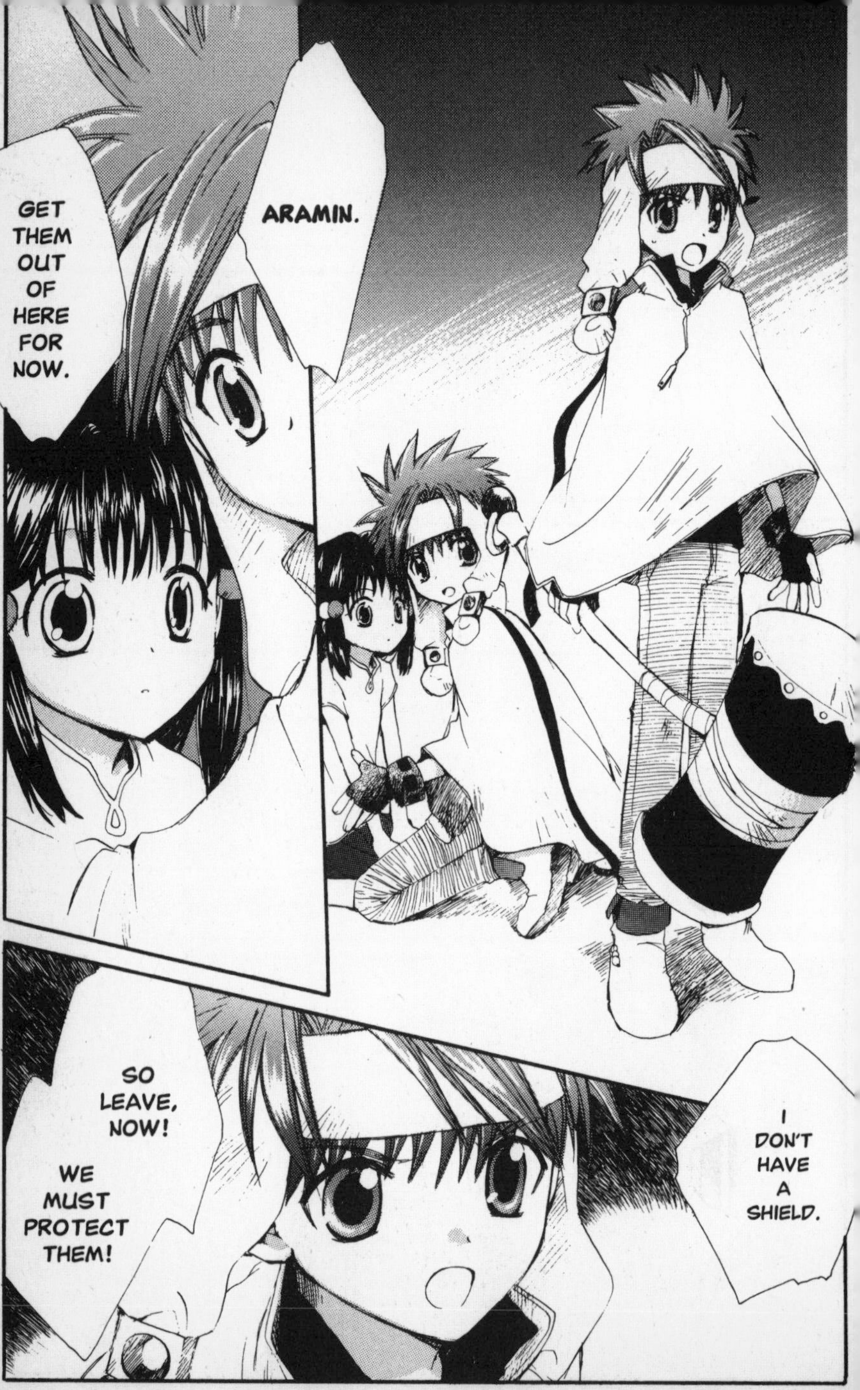
ARAMIN.
GET THEM OUT OF HERE FOR NOW.
I DON'T HAVE A SHIELD.
SO LEAVE, NOW!
WE MUST PROTECT THEM!

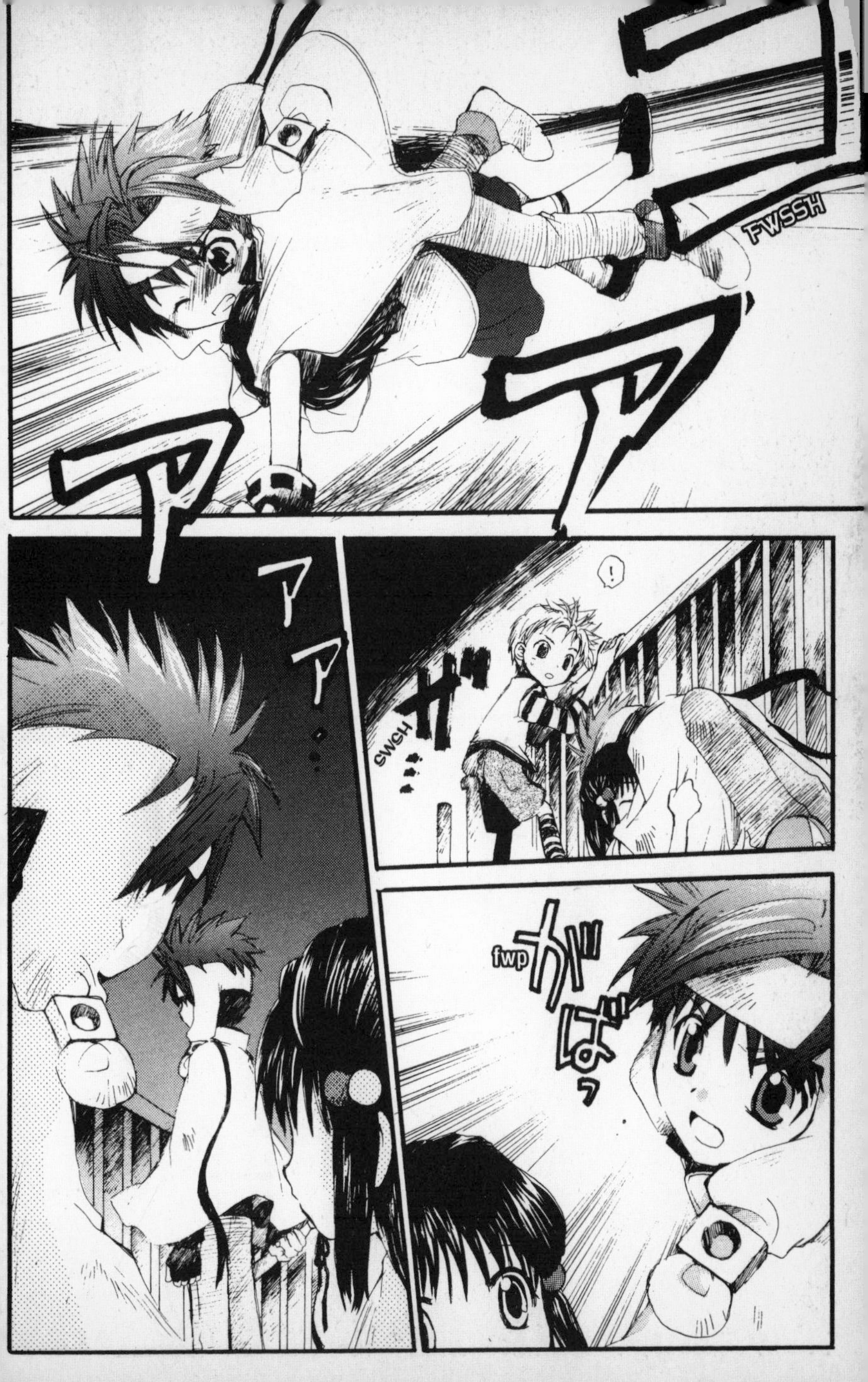
FWSSH
アアアァ…
!
ザ
swsh
fwp がばっ

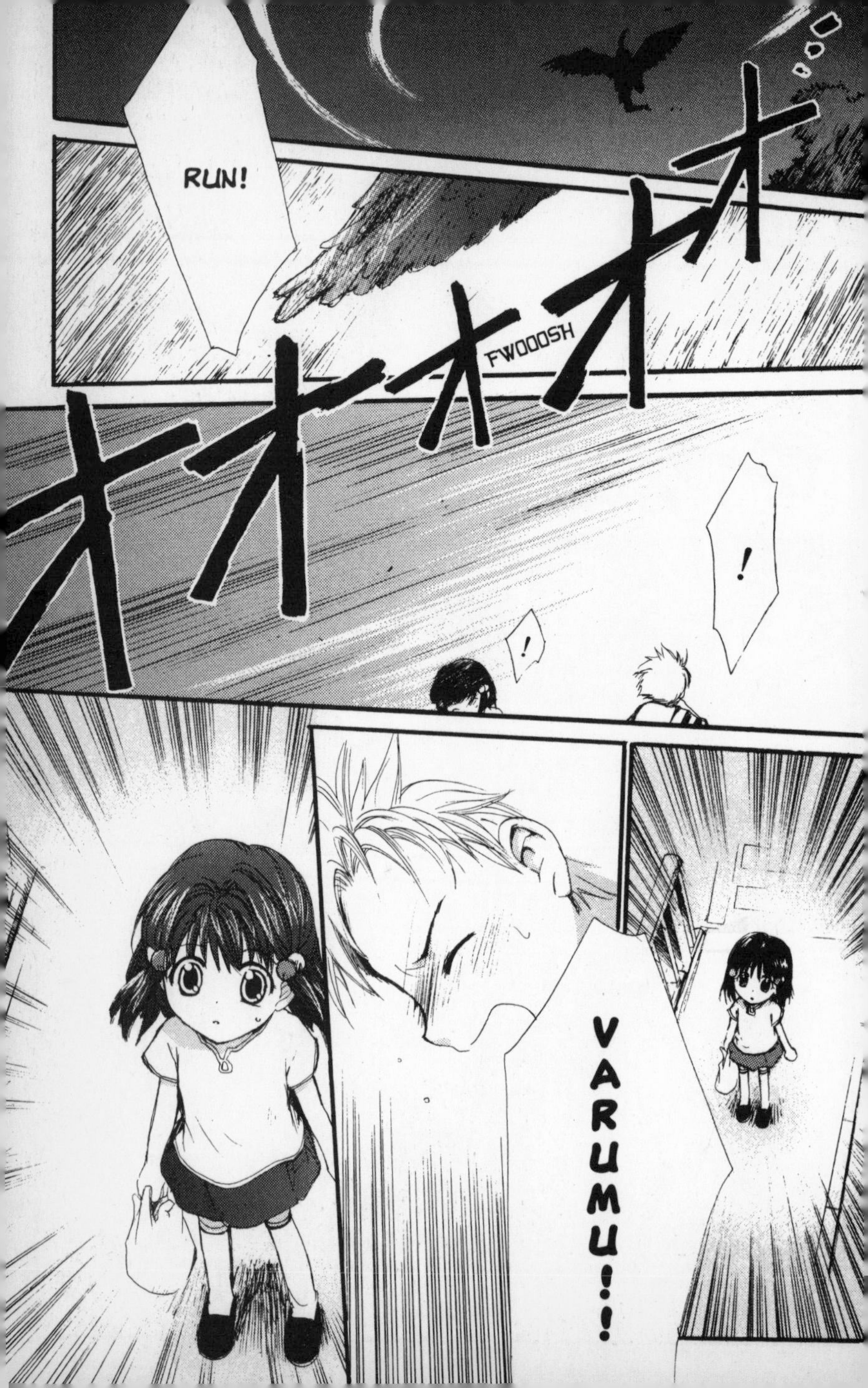
RUN!
オオオオ
FWOOOSH
!
!
VARUMU!!!

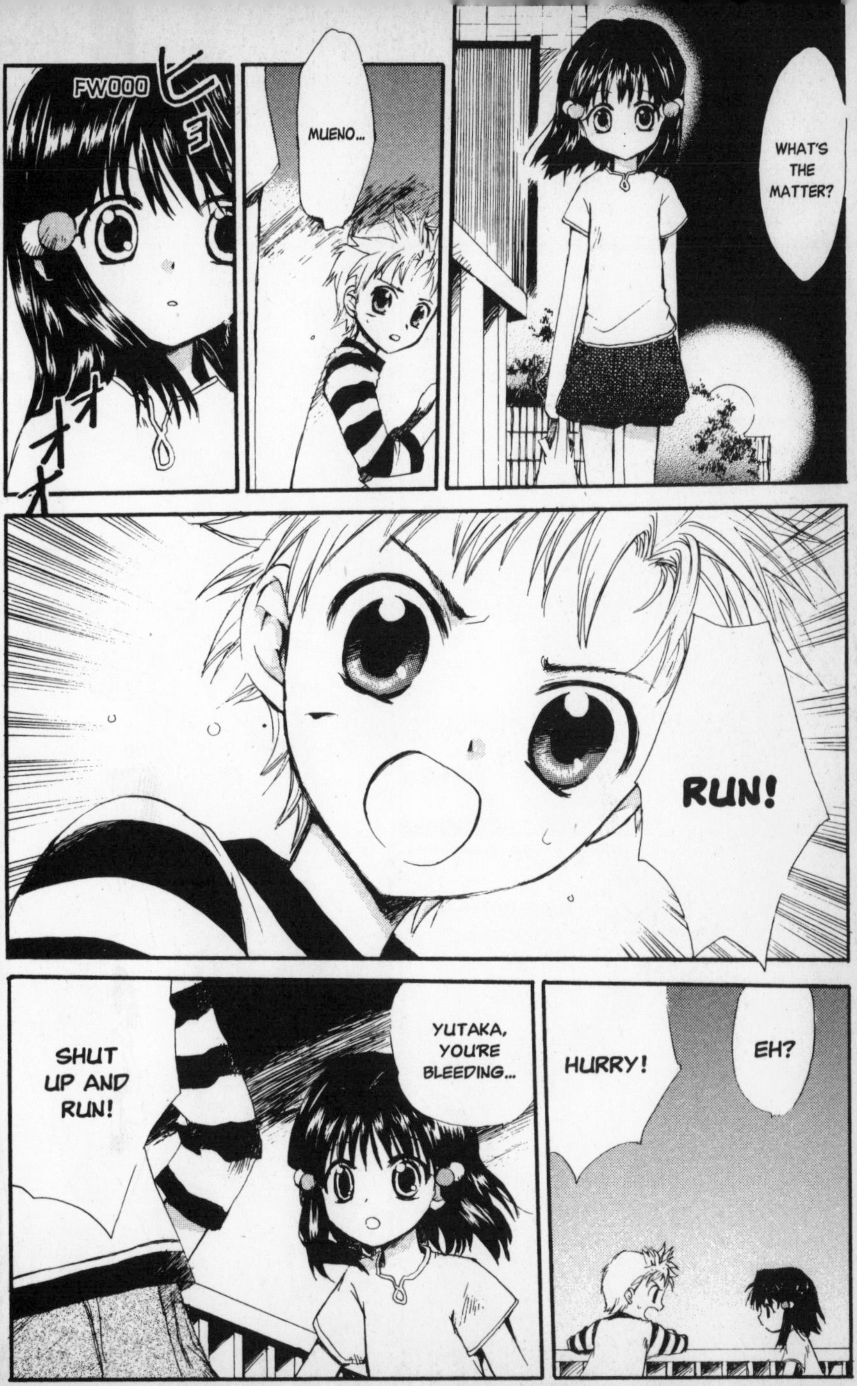
WHAT'S THE MATTER?
MUENO...
FWOOO
ヒョ
オオオ
RUN!
EH?
HURRY!
YUTAKA, YOU'RE BLEEDING...
SHUT UP AND RUN!

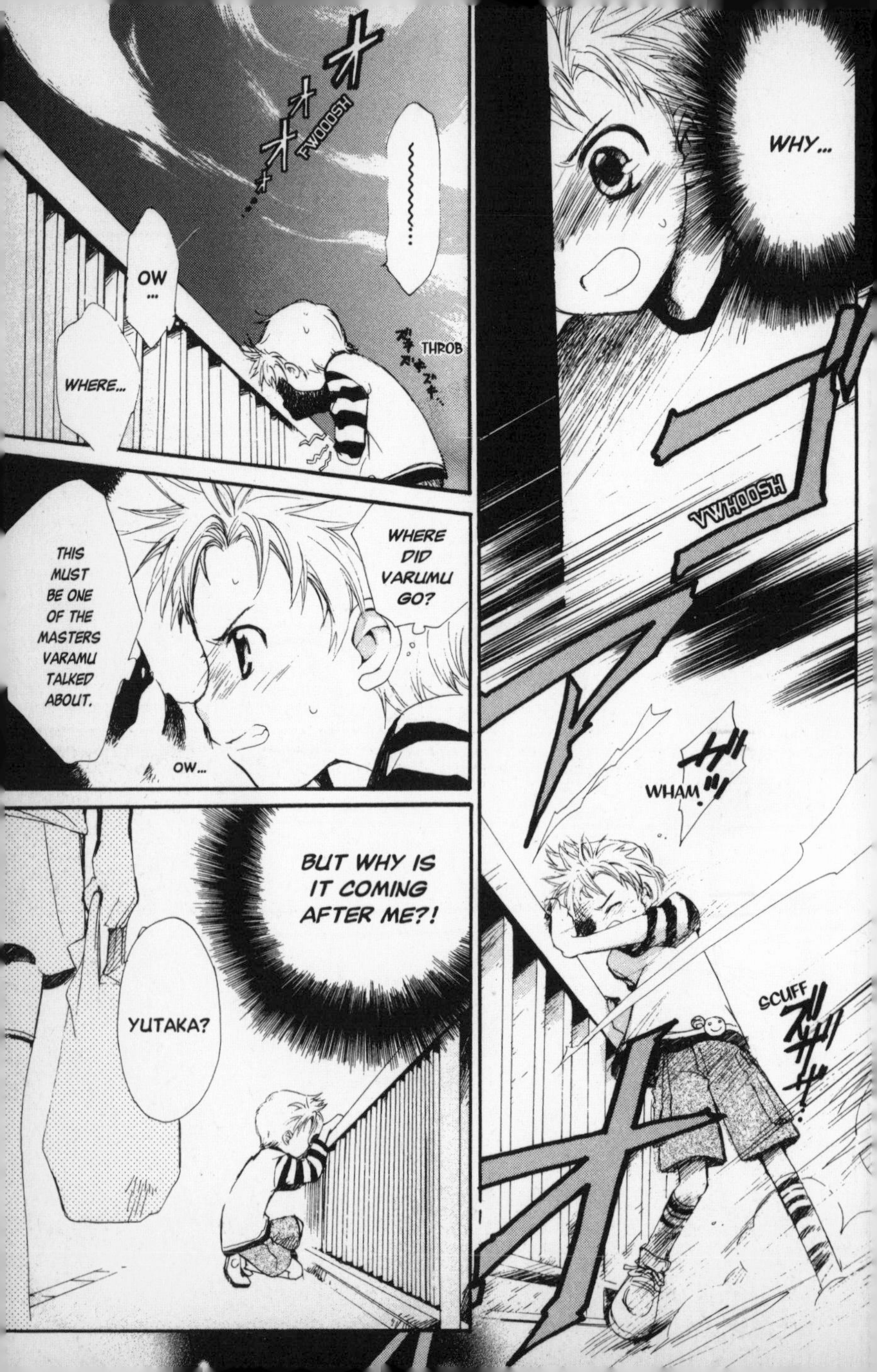
WHY...
VWHOOSH
WHAM!
SCUFF
FWOOOSH
......
OW ...
THROB
WHERE...
WHERE DID VARUMU GO?
THIS MUST BE ONE OF THE MASTERS VARAMU TALKED ABOUT.
OW...
BUT WHY IS IT COMING AFTER ME?!
YUTAKA?

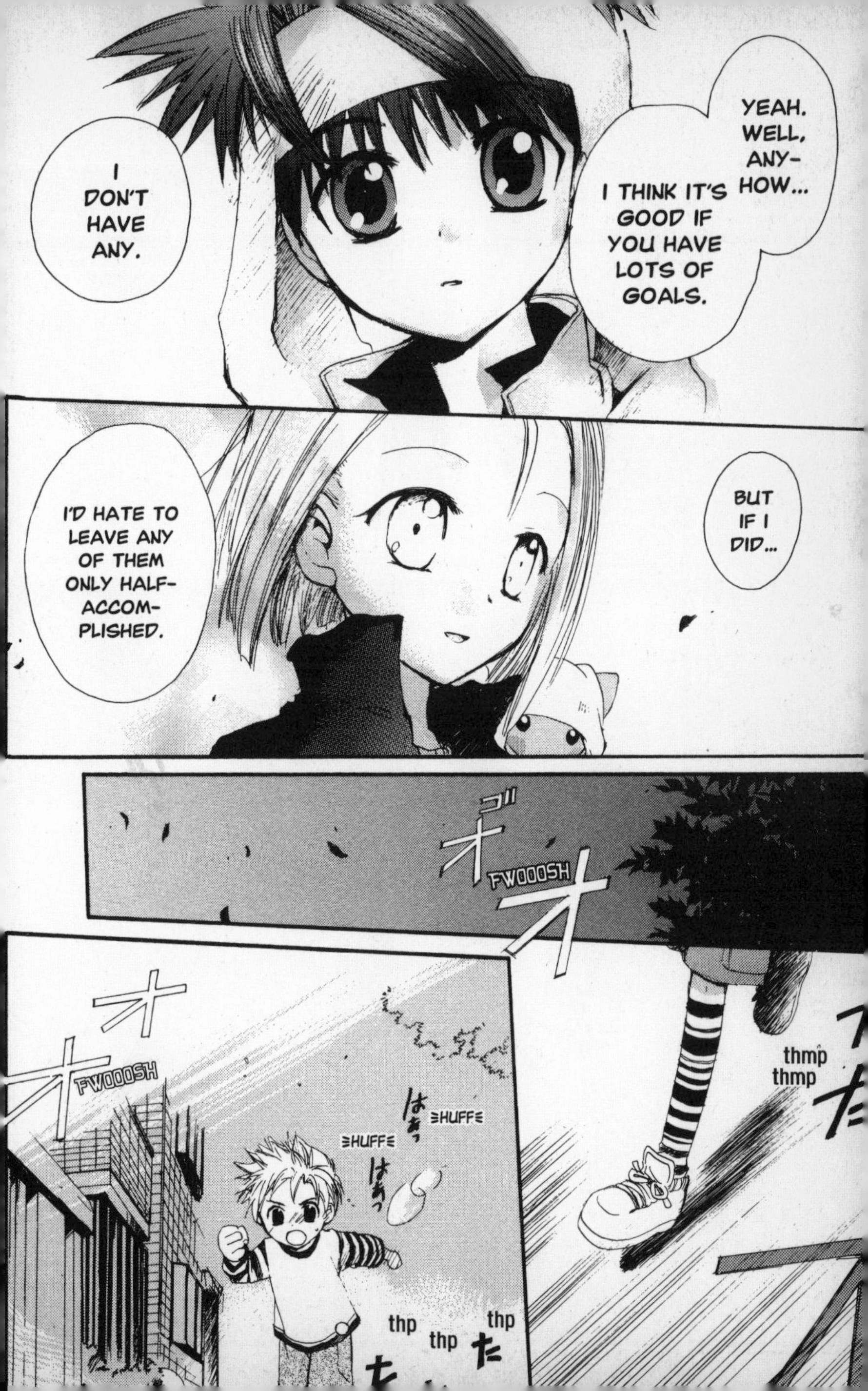
YEAH. WELL, ANYHOW...
I THINK IT'S GOOD IF YOU HAVE LOTS OF GOALS.
I DON'T HAVE ANY.
BUT IF I DID...
I'D HATE TO LEAVE ANY OF THEM ONLY HALF-ACCOMPLISHED.
ゴオ
FWOOOSH
thmp thmp
たっ
オオ
FWOOOSH
はあっ
HUFF
はあっ
HUFF
thp thp thp
たたっ

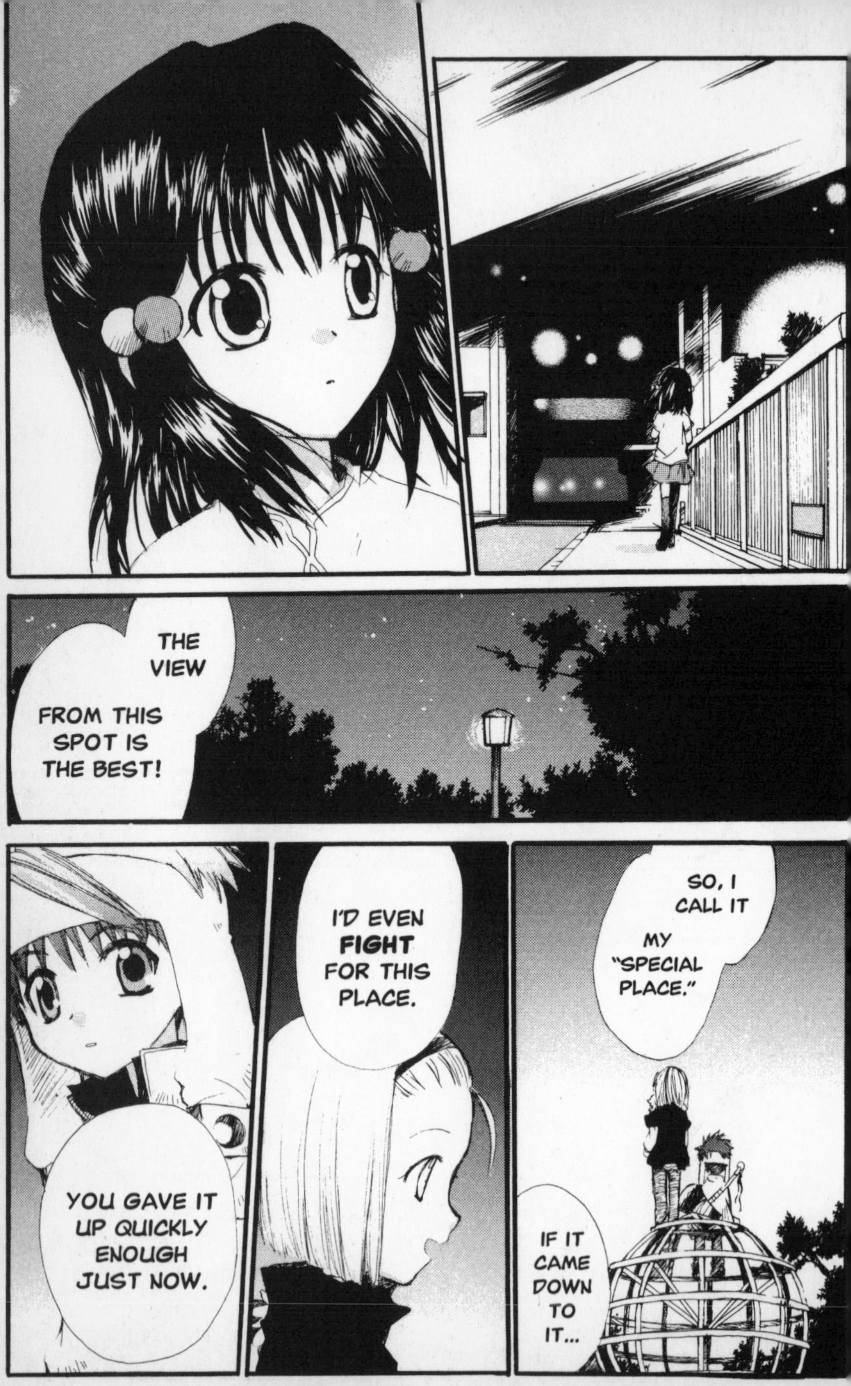
THE VIEW FROM THIS SPOT IS THE BEST!
SO, I CALL IT MY "SPECIAL PLACE."
IF IT CAME DOWN TO IT...
I'D EVEN **FIGHT** FOR THIS PLACE.
YOU GAVE IT UP QUICKLY ENOUGH JUST NOW.

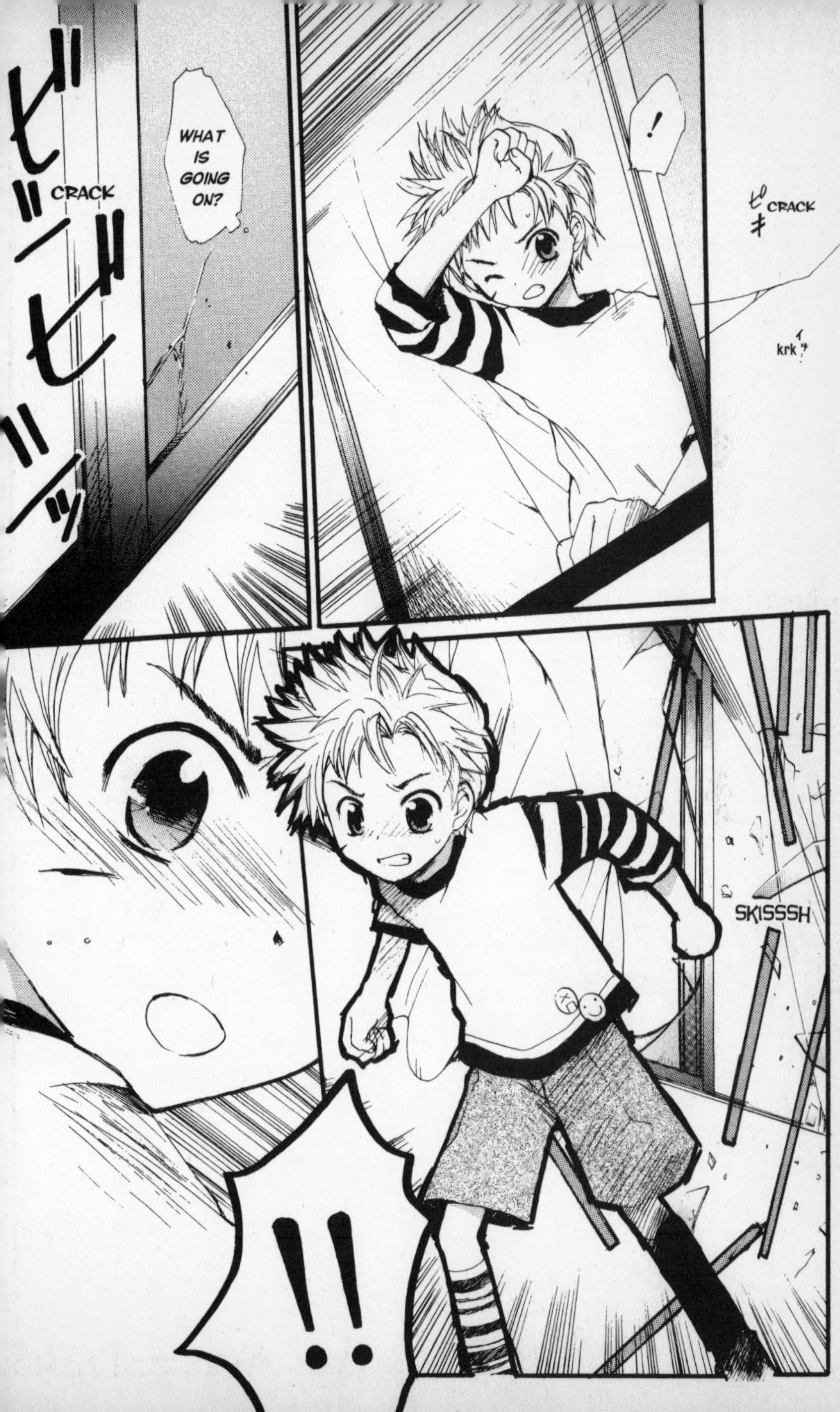
!
CRACK
krk
WHAT IS GOING ON?
CRACK
SKISSSH
!!

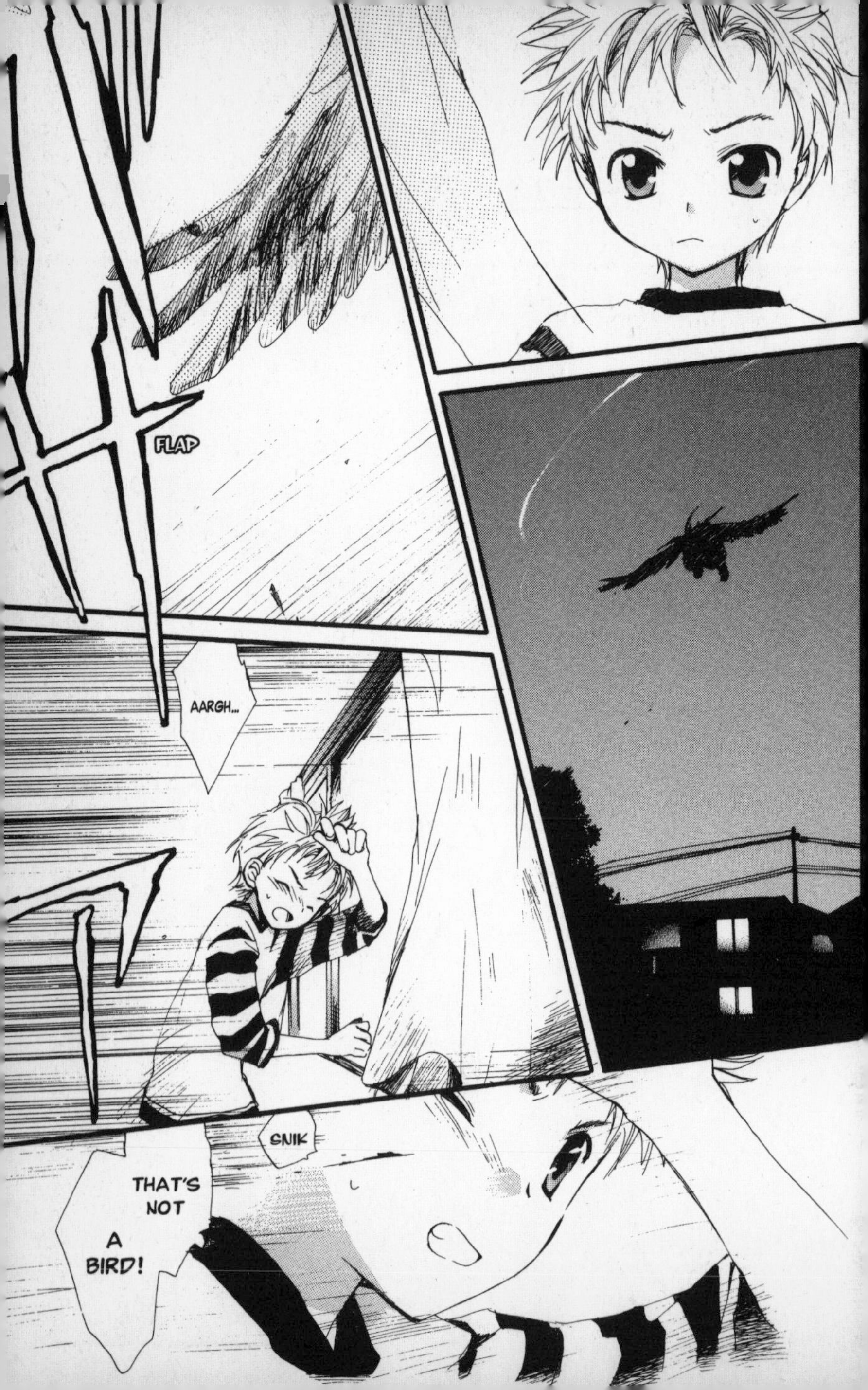
FLAP
AARGH...
SNIK
THAT'S NOT A BIRD!

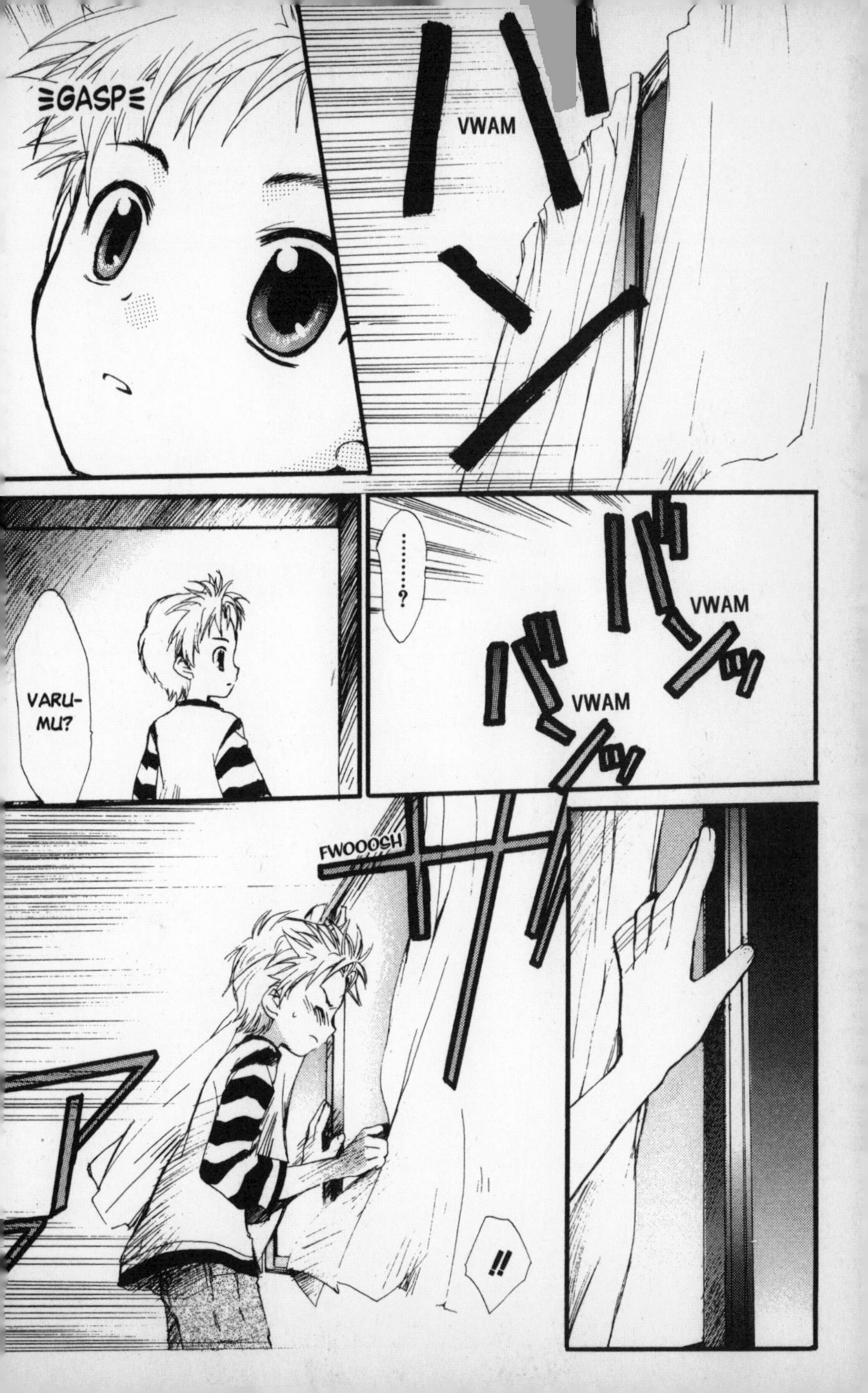
VWAM
GASP
VWAM
VWAM
......?
VARU-MU?
FWOOOSH
!!

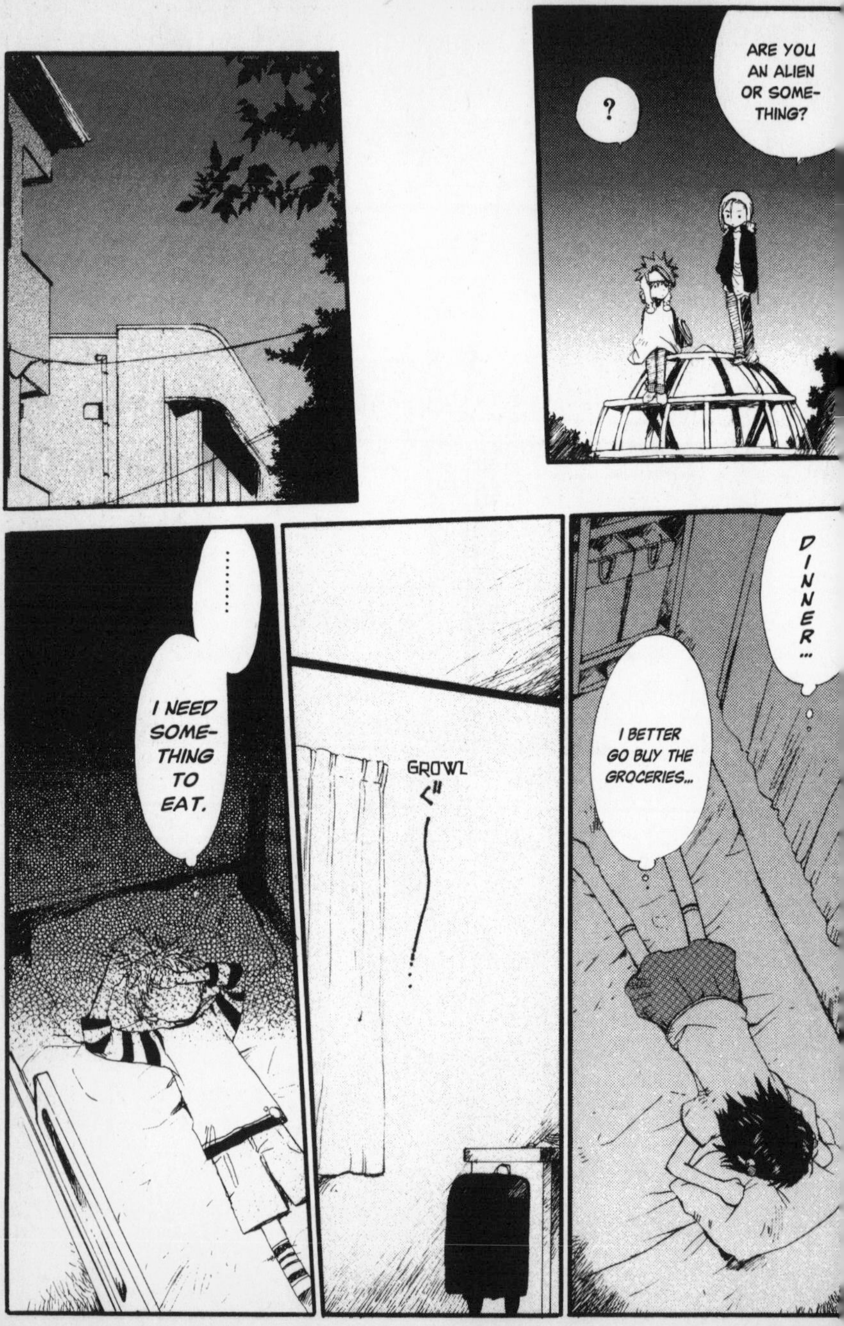
ARE YOU AN ALIEN OR SOME-THING?
?
DINNER...
I BETTER GO BUY THE GROCERIES...
GROWL
......
I NEED SOME-THING TO EAT.

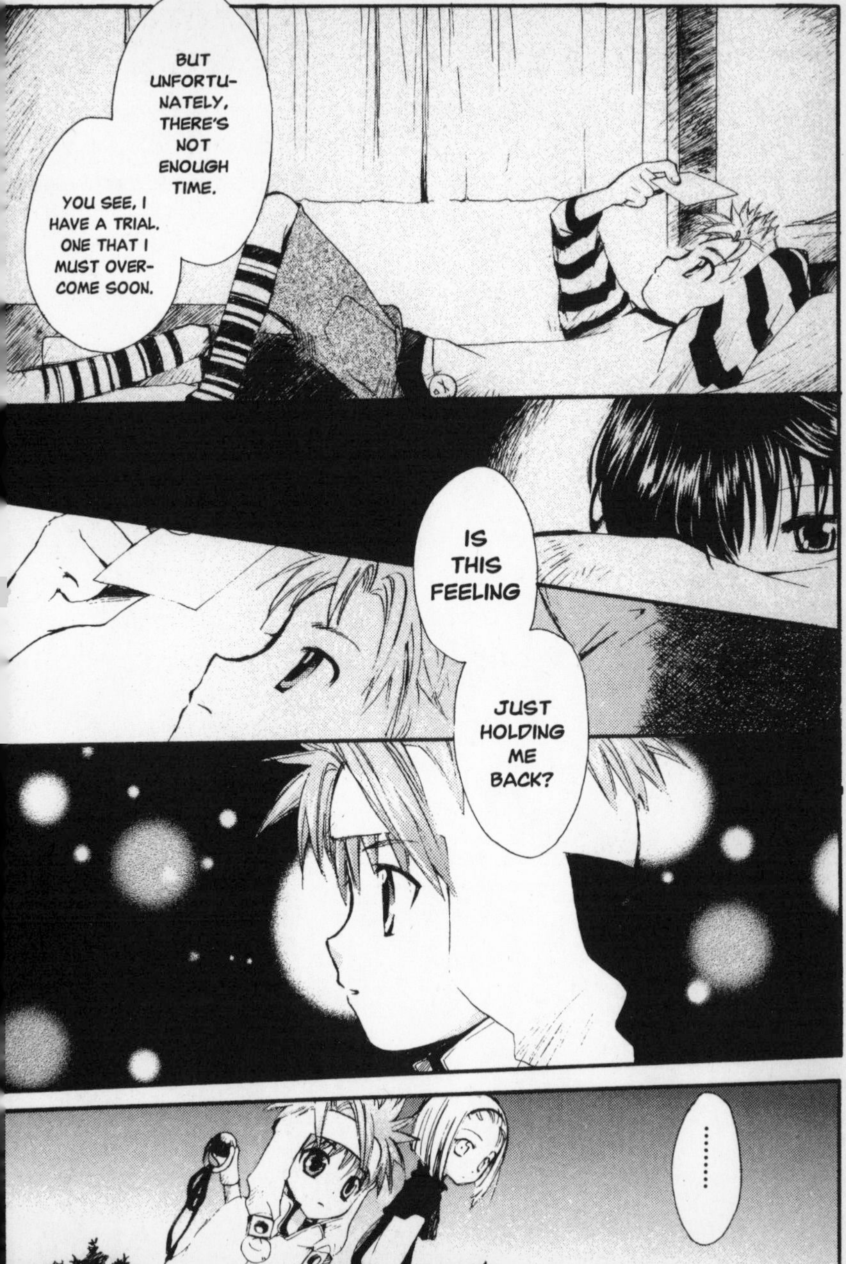
BUT UNFORTU- NATELY, THERE'S NOT ENOUGH TIME.
YOU SEE, I HAVE A TRIAL. ONE THAT I MUST OVER- COME SOON.
IS THIS FEELING
JUST HOLDING ME BACK?
....

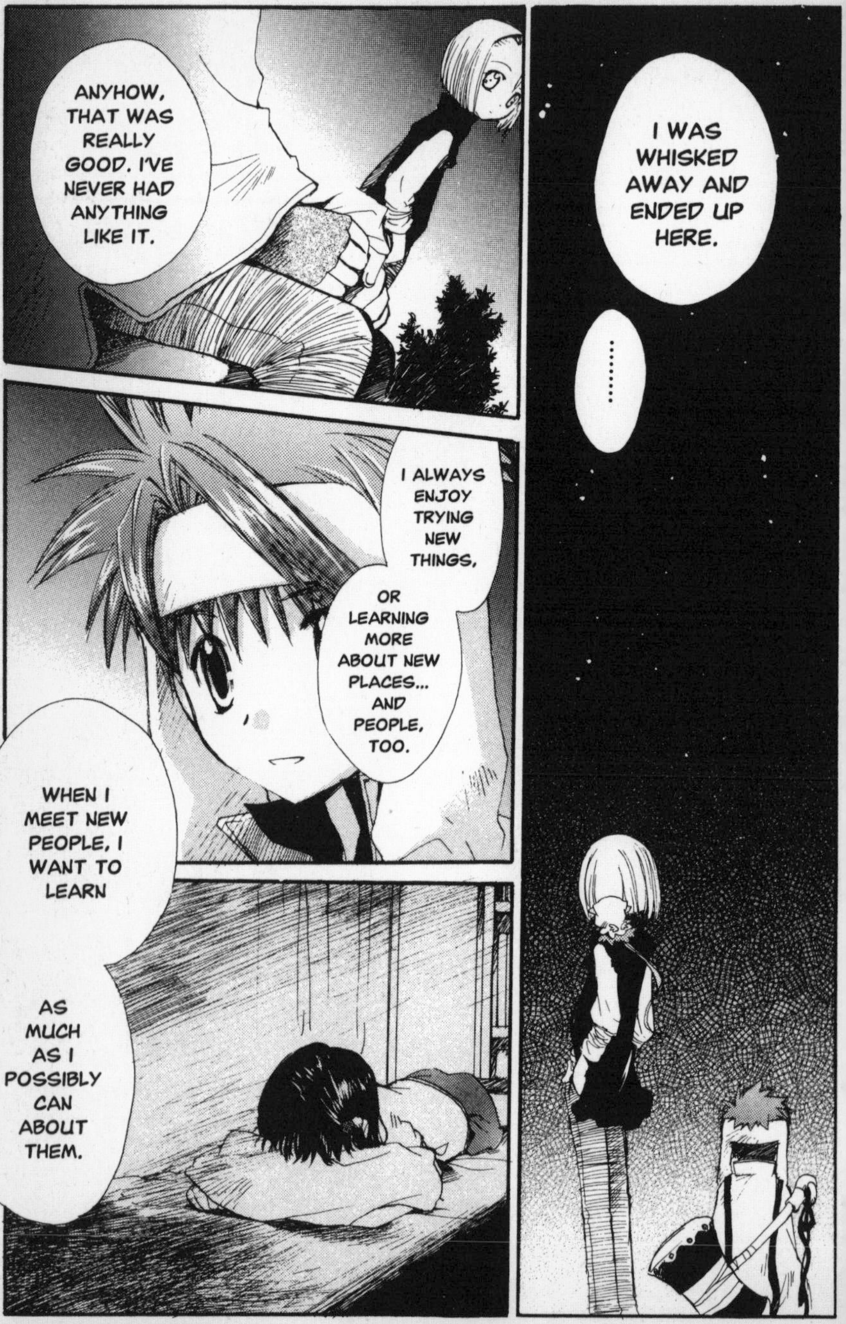
I WAS WHISKED AWAY AND ENDED UP HERE.
......
ANYHOW, THAT WAS REALLY GOOD. I'VE NEVER HAD ANYTHING LIKE IT.
I ALWAYS ENJOY TRYING NEW THINGS,
OR LEARNING MORE ABOUT NEW PLACES... AND PEOPLE, TOO.
WHEN I MEET NEW PEOPLE, I WANT TO LEARN
AS MUCH AS I POSSIBLY CAN ABOUT THEM.

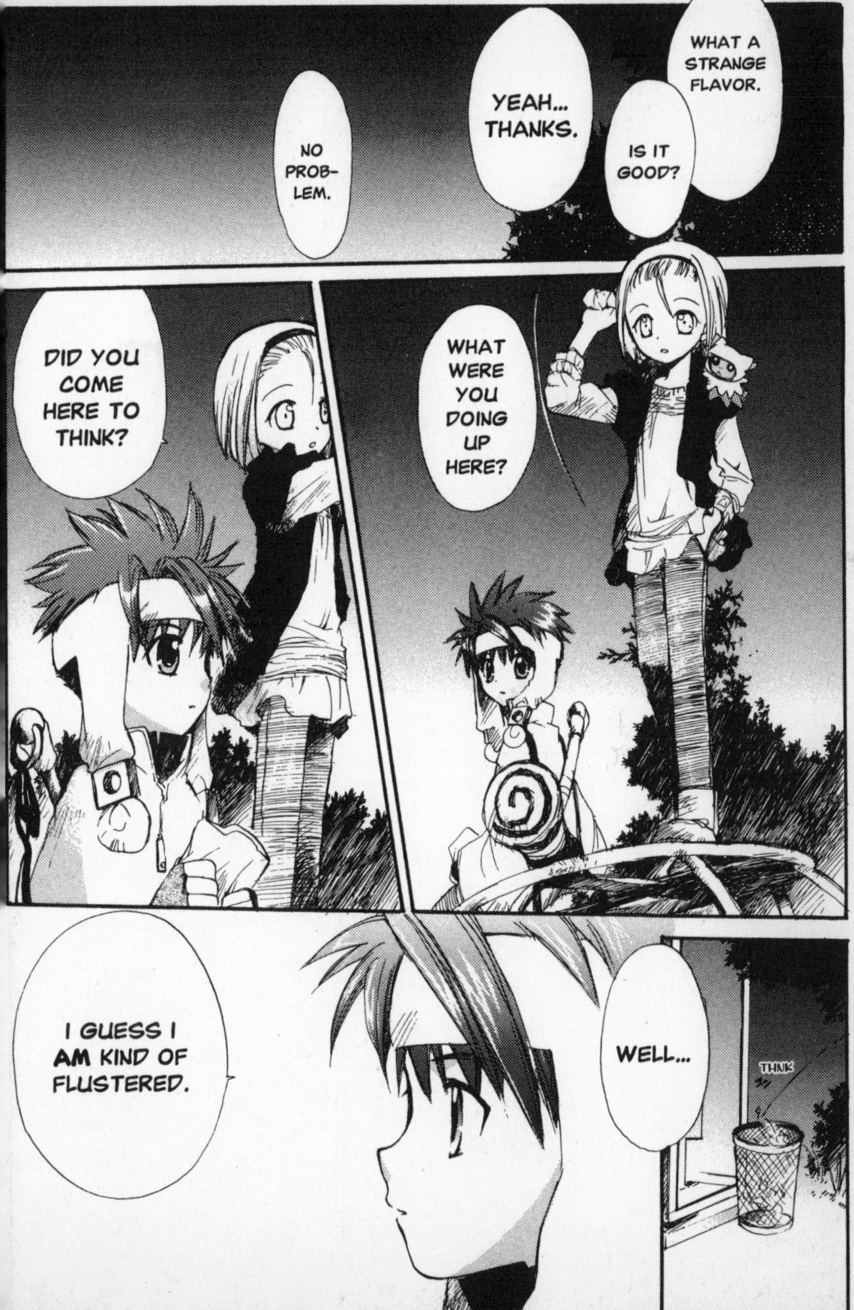
WHAT A STRANGE FLAVOR.
IS IT GOOD?
YEAH... THANKS.
NO PROB-LEM.
WHAT WERE YOU DOING UP HERE?
DID YOU COME HERE TO THINK?
WELL...
THNK
I GUESS I **AM** KIND OF FLUSTERED.

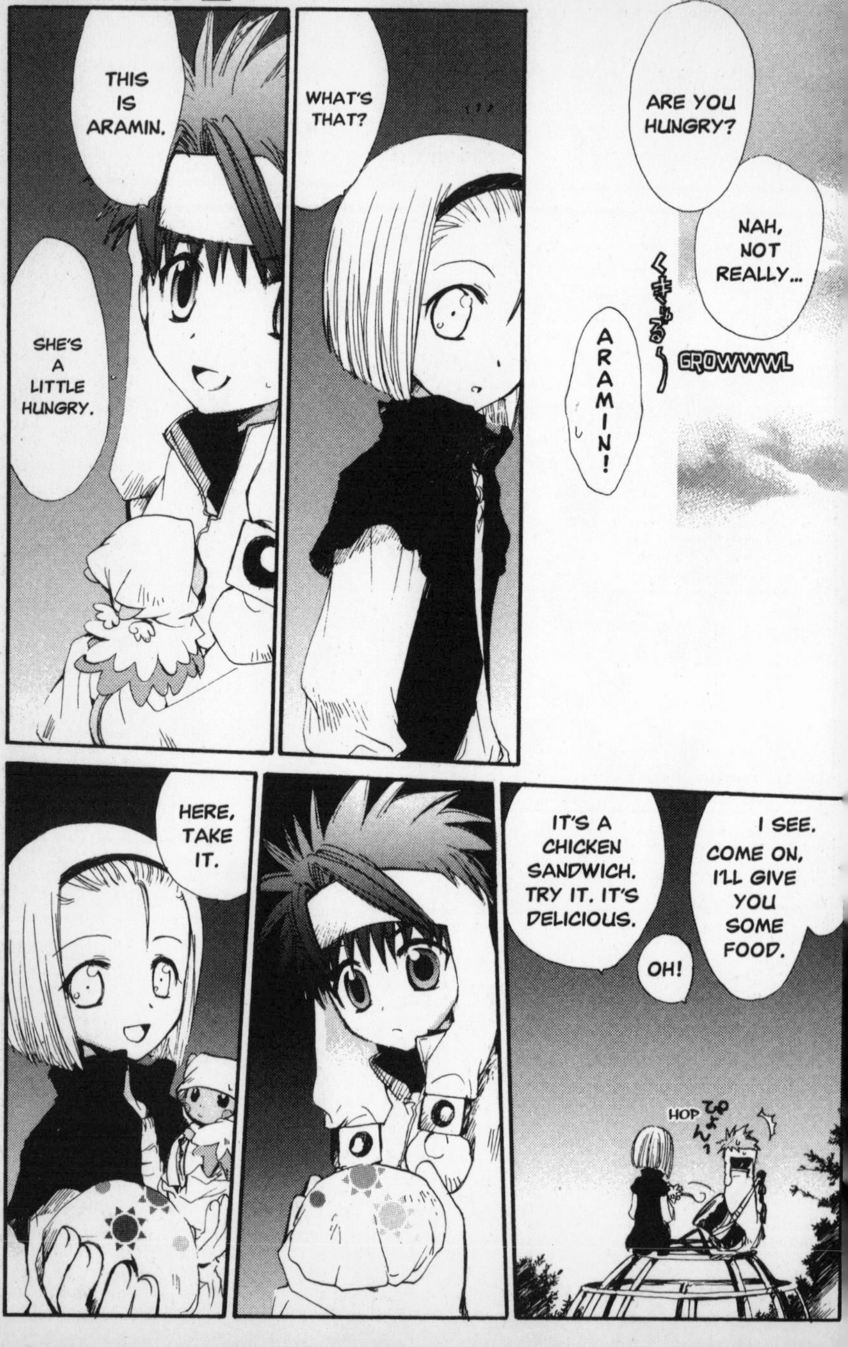
ARE YOU HUNGRY?
NAH, NOT REALLY...
ARAMIN!
GROWWWL
WHAT'S THAT?
THIS IS ARAMIN.
SHE'S A LITTLE HUNGRY.
I SEE. COME ON, I'LL GIVE YOU SOME FOOD.
OH!
HOP
IT'S A CHICKEN SANDWICH. TRY IT. IT'S DELICIOUS.
HERE, TAKE IT.

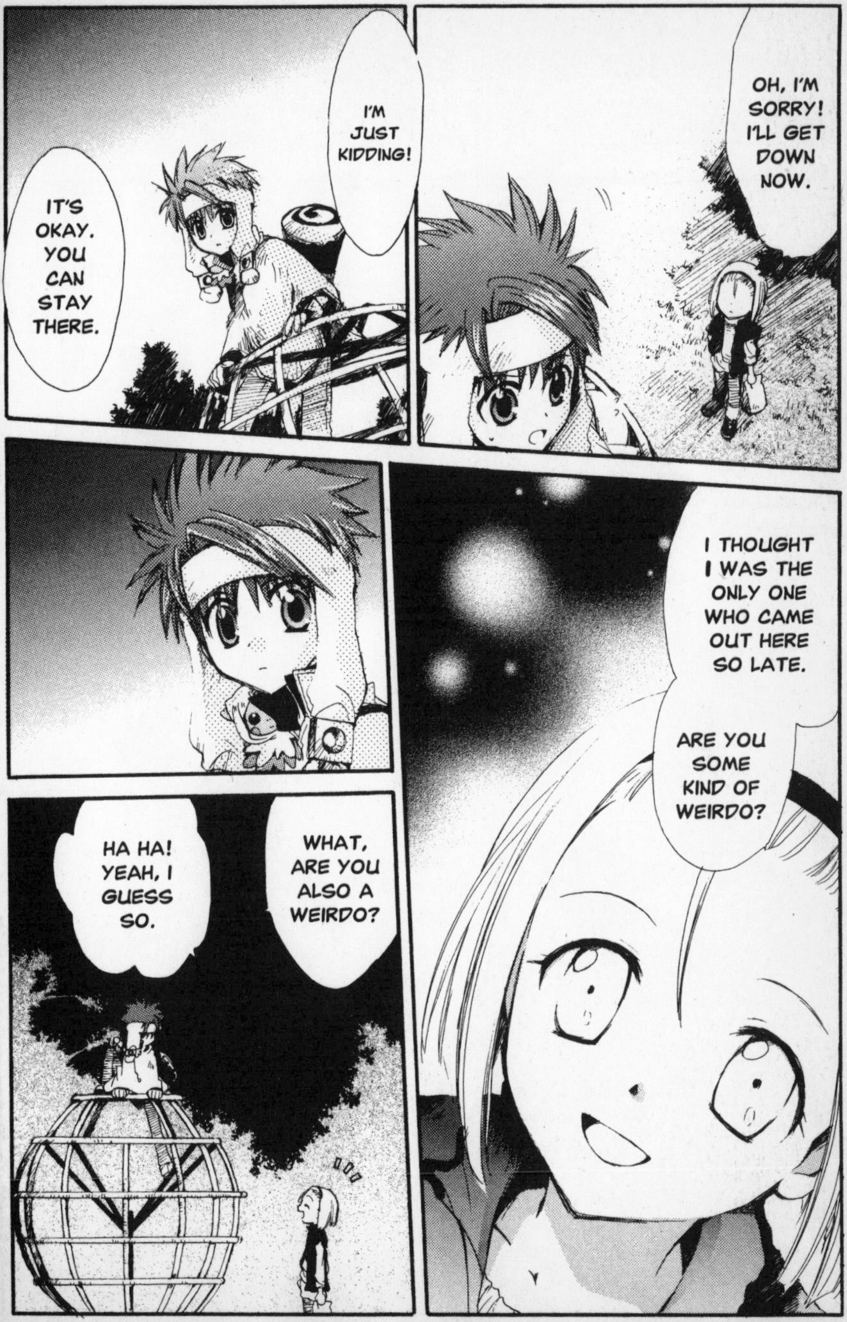
OH, I'M SORRY! I'LL GET DOWN NOW.
I'M JUST KIDDING!
IT'S OKAY. YOU CAN STAY THERE.
I THOUGHT I WAS THE ONLY ONE WHO CAME OUT HERE SO LATE.
ARE YOU SOME KIND OF WEIRDO?
WHAT, ARE YOU ALSO A WEIRDO?
HA HA! YEAH, I GUESS SO.

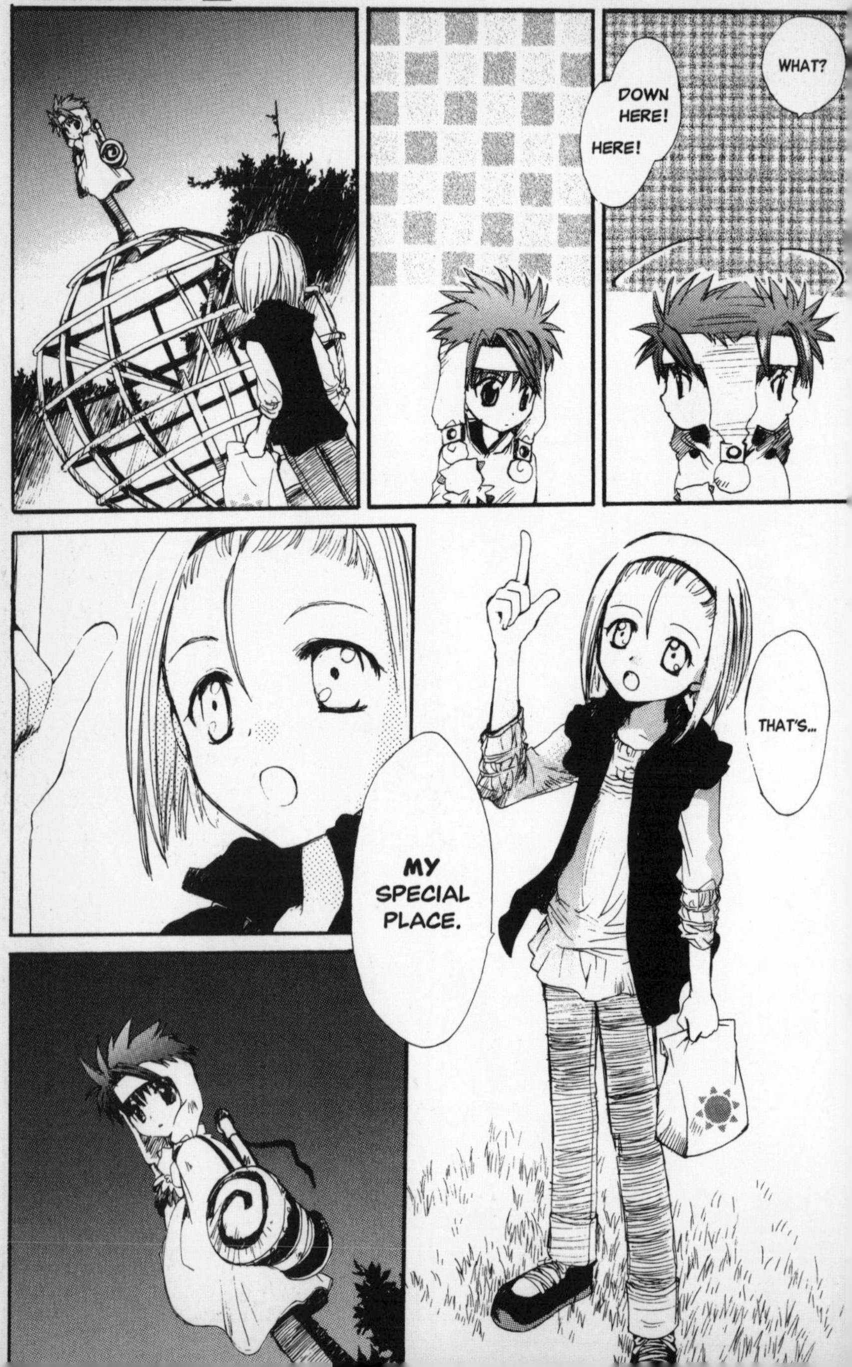
DOWN HERE!
HERE!
WHAT?
THAT'S...
MY SPECIAL PLACE.

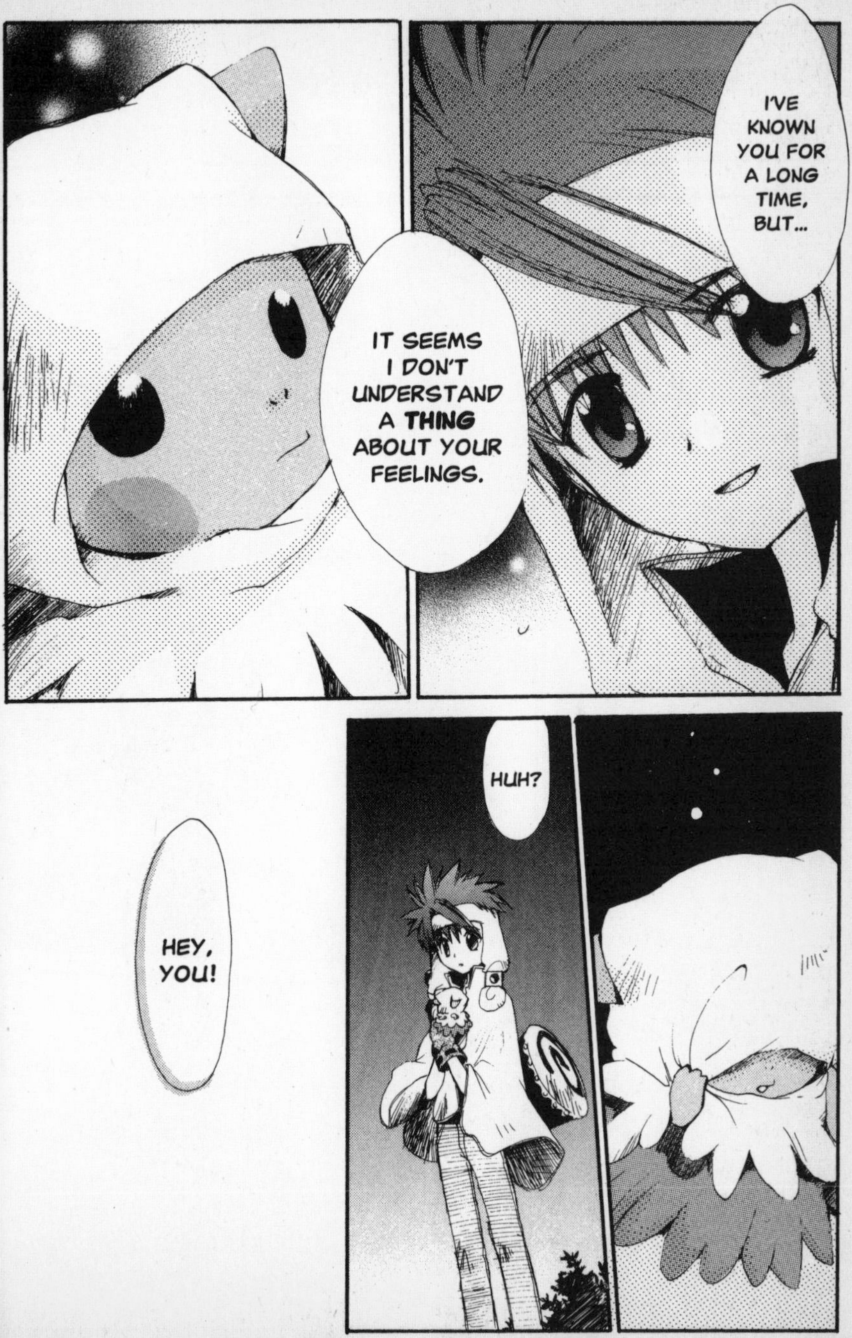

I'VE KNOWN YOU FOR A LONG TIME, BUT...
IT SEEMS I DON'T UNDERSTAND A **THING** ABOUT YOUR FEELINGS.
HUH?
HEY, YOU!

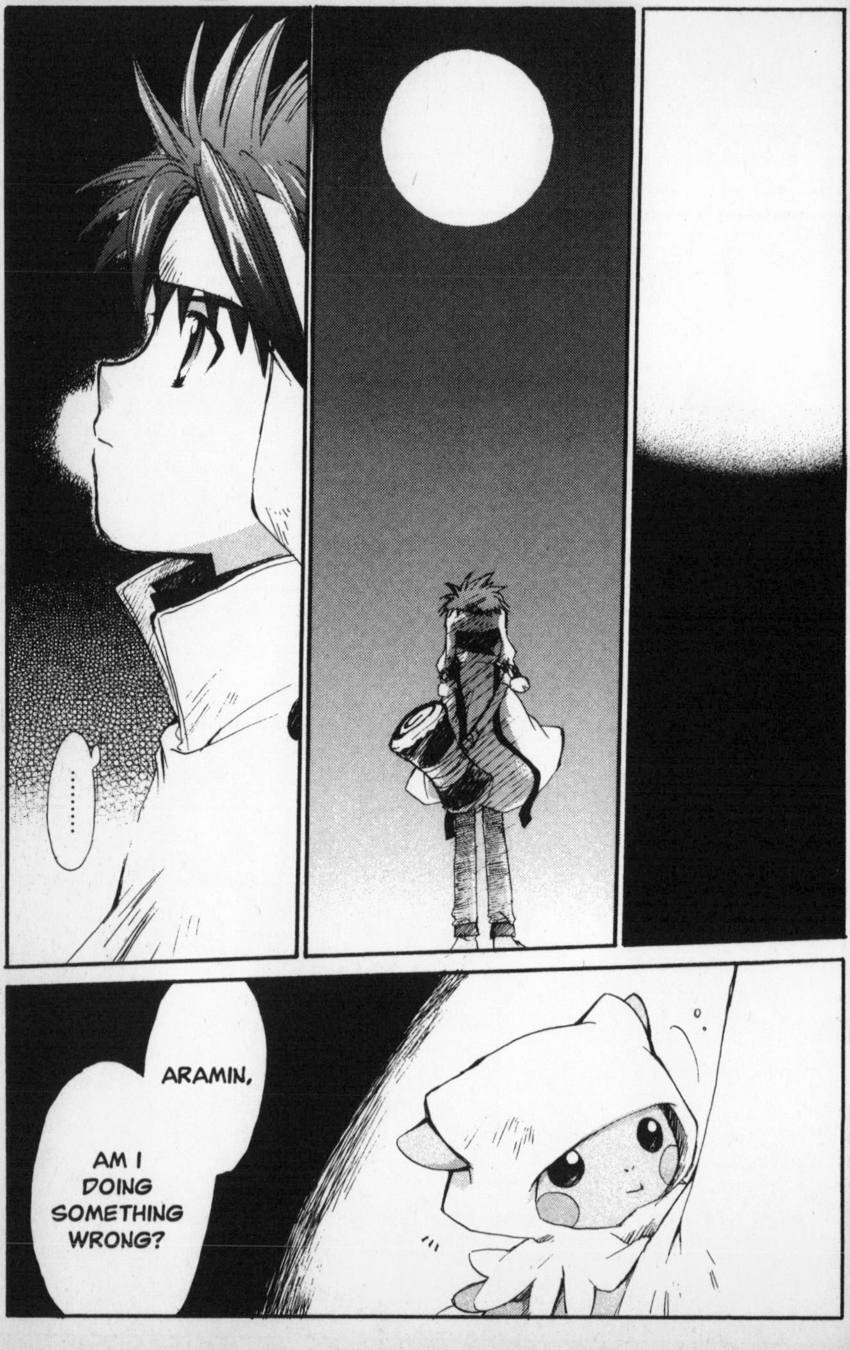
....
ARAMIN,
AM I DOING SOMETHING WRONG?

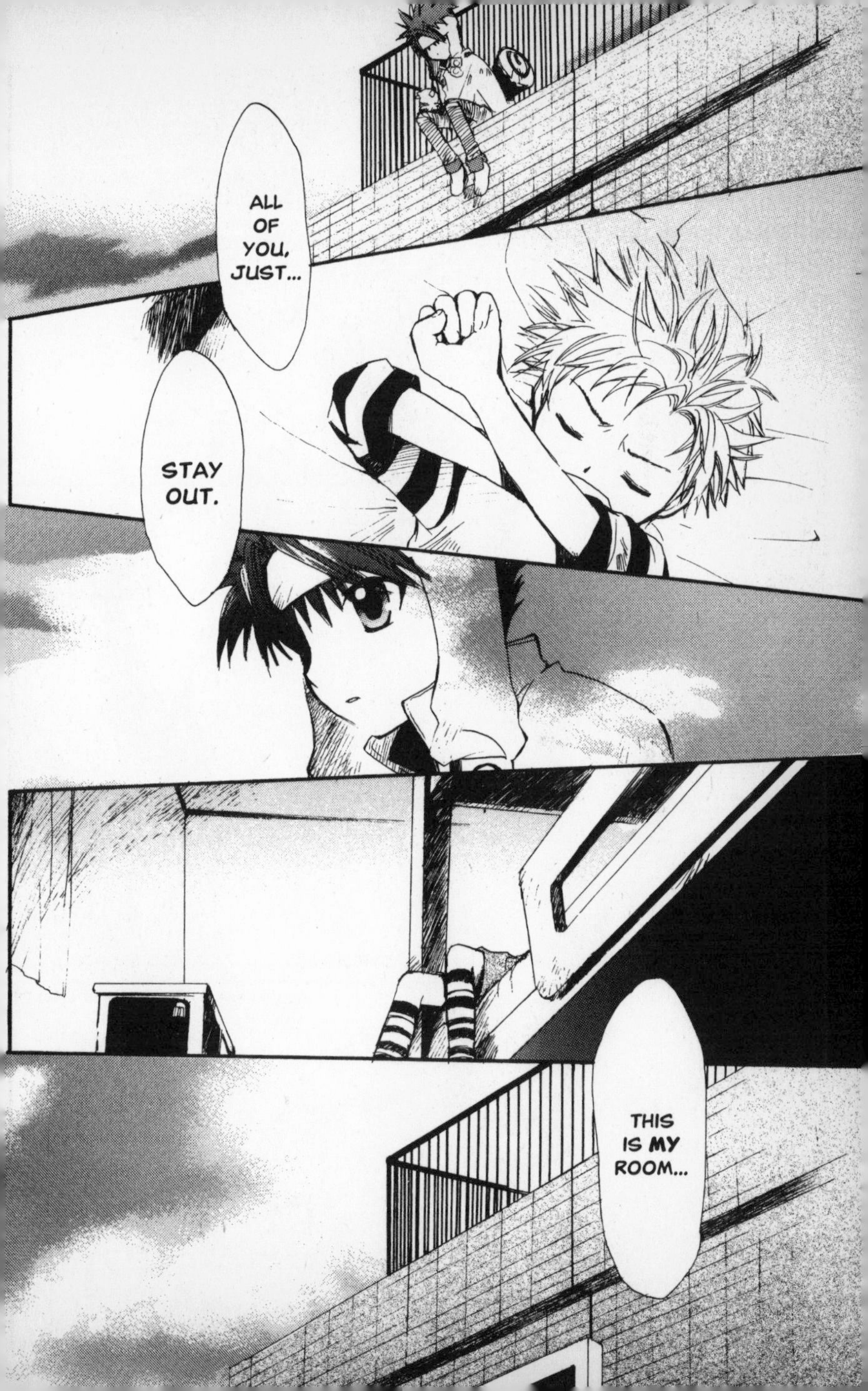
ALL OF YOU, JUST...
STAY OUT.
THIS IS MY ROOM...

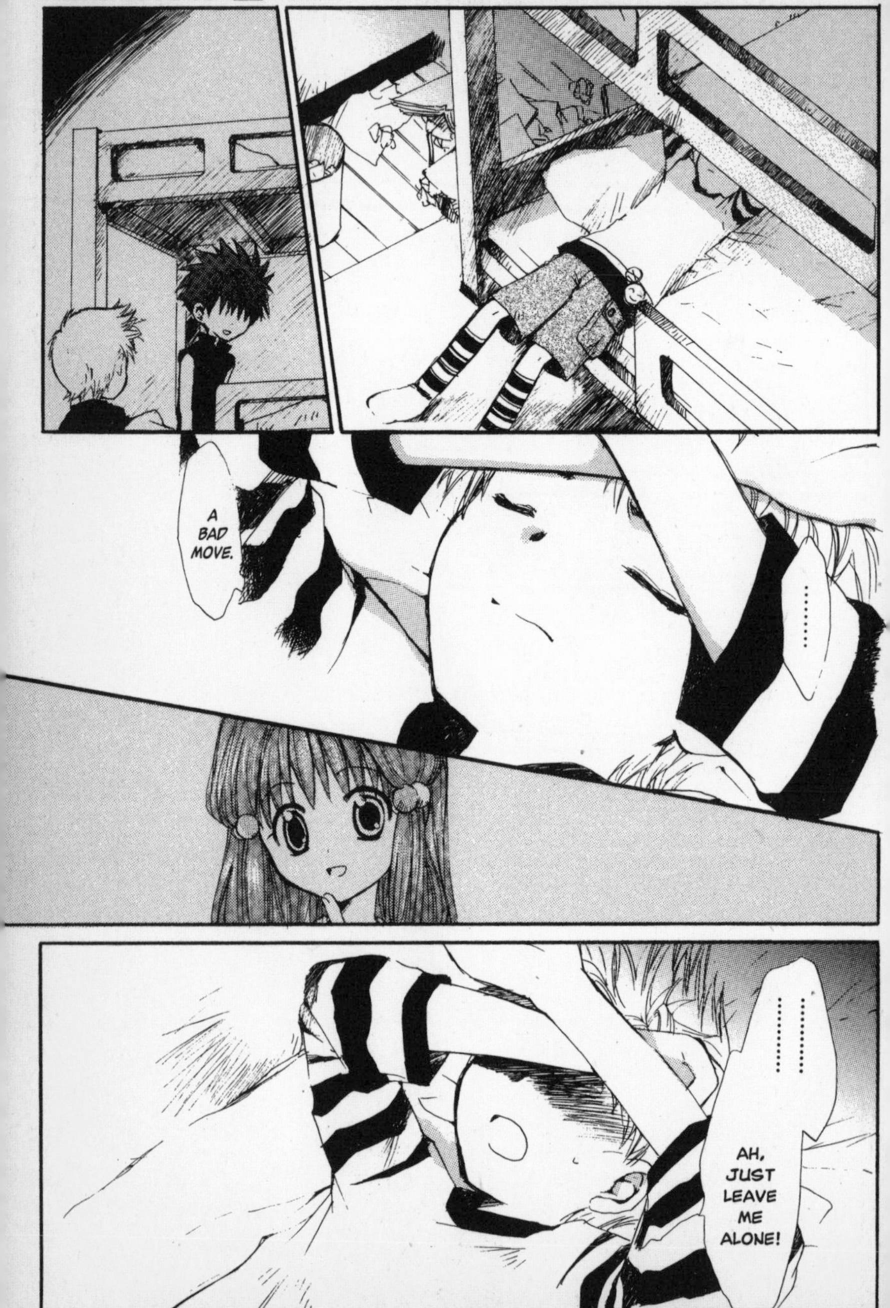
A BAD MOVE.
......
......
AH, JUST LEAVE ME ALONE!

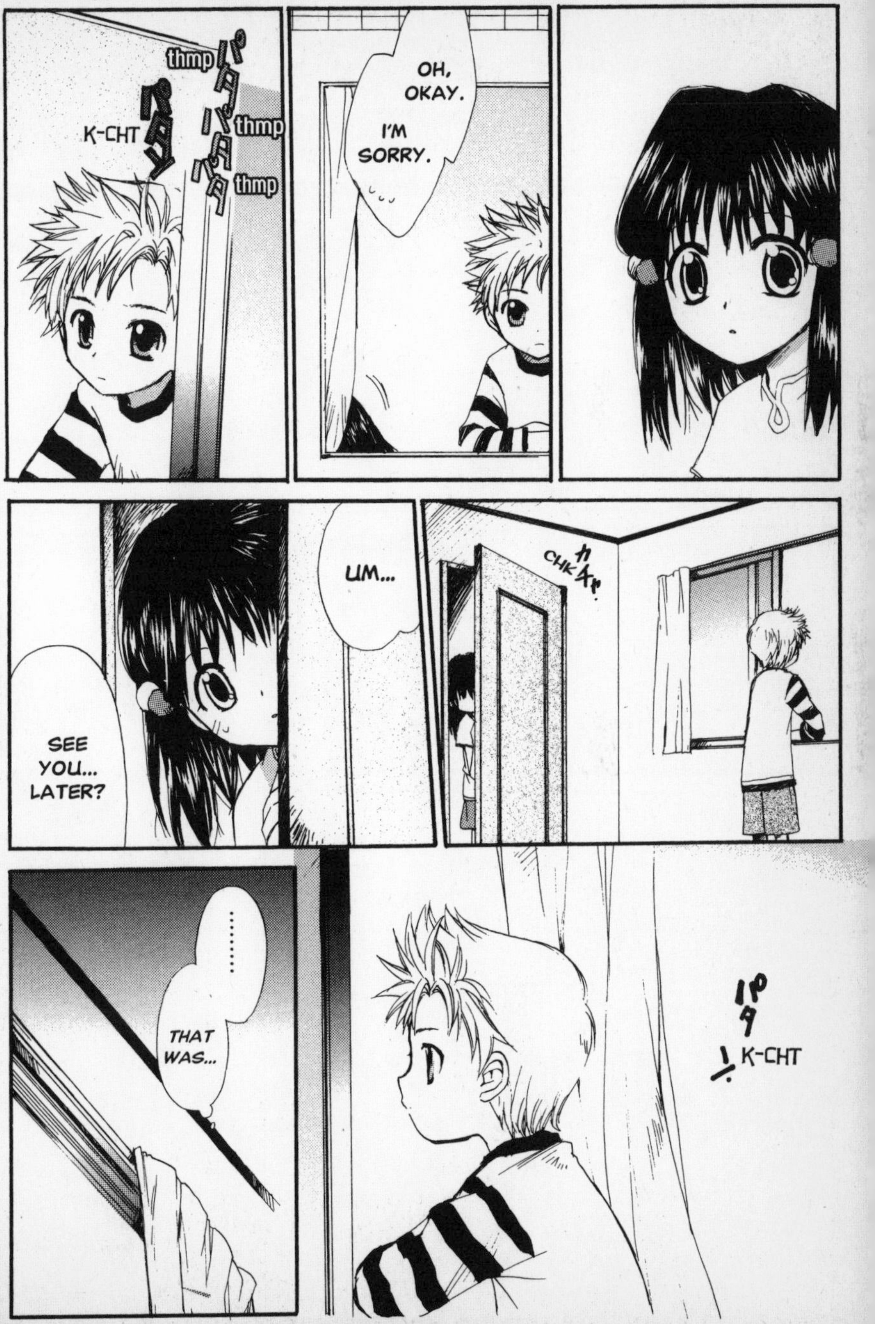
OH, OKAY.
I'M SORRY.
thmp
thmp
thmp
K-CHT
CHK
UM...
SEE YOU... LATER?
K-CHT
....
THAT WAS...

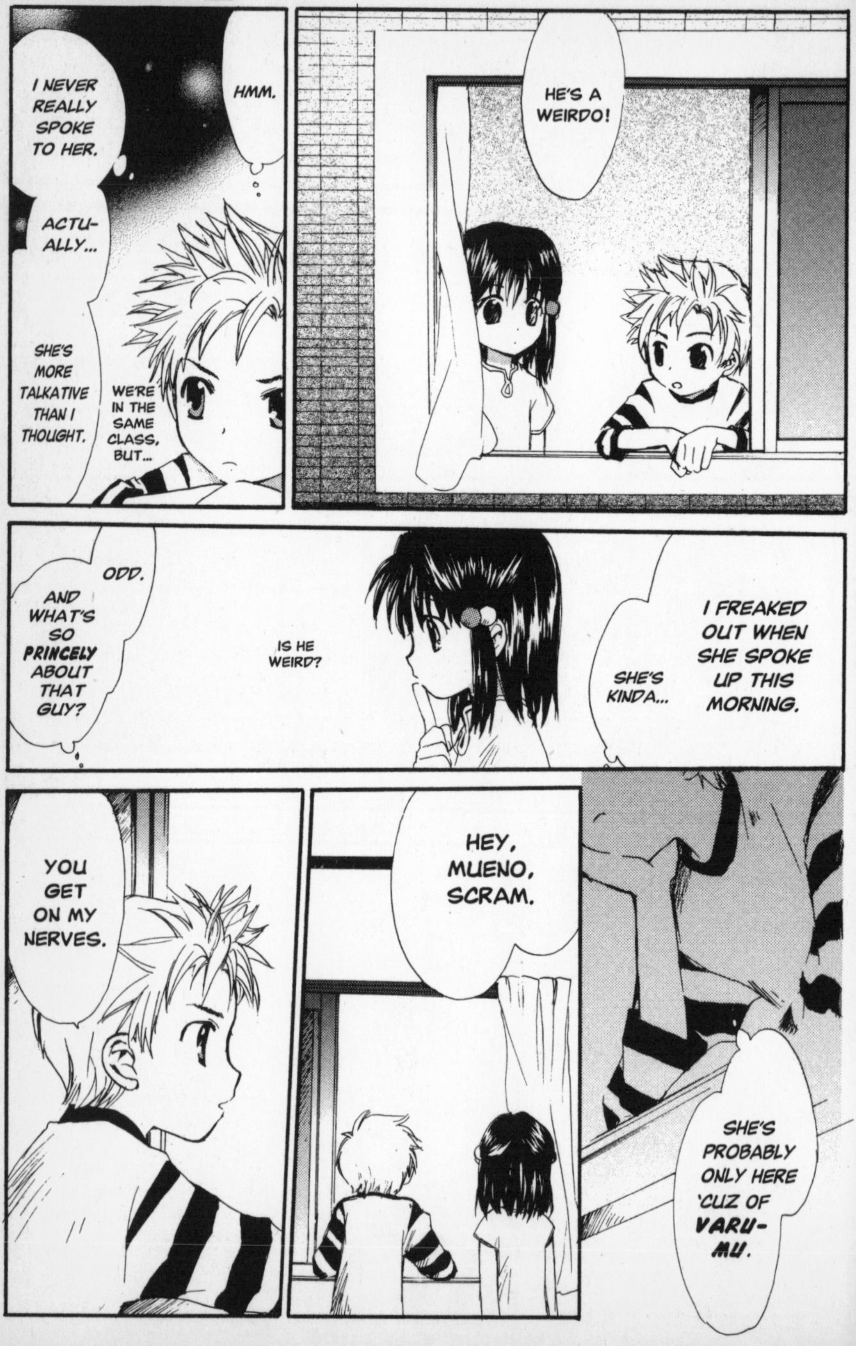
HE'S A WEIRDO!
HMM.
I NEVER REALLY SPOKE TO HER.
WE'RE IN THE SAME CLASS, BUT...
ACTU-ALLY...
SHE'S MORE TALKATIVE THAN I THOUGHT.
I FREAKED OUT WHEN SHE SPOKE UP THIS MORNING.
SHE'S KINDA...
IS HE WEIRD?
ODD.
AND WHAT'S SO PRINCELY ABOUT THAT GUY?
SHE'S PROBABLY ONLY HERE 'CUZ OF VARU-MU.
HEY, MUENO, SCRAM.
YOU GET ON MY NERVES.

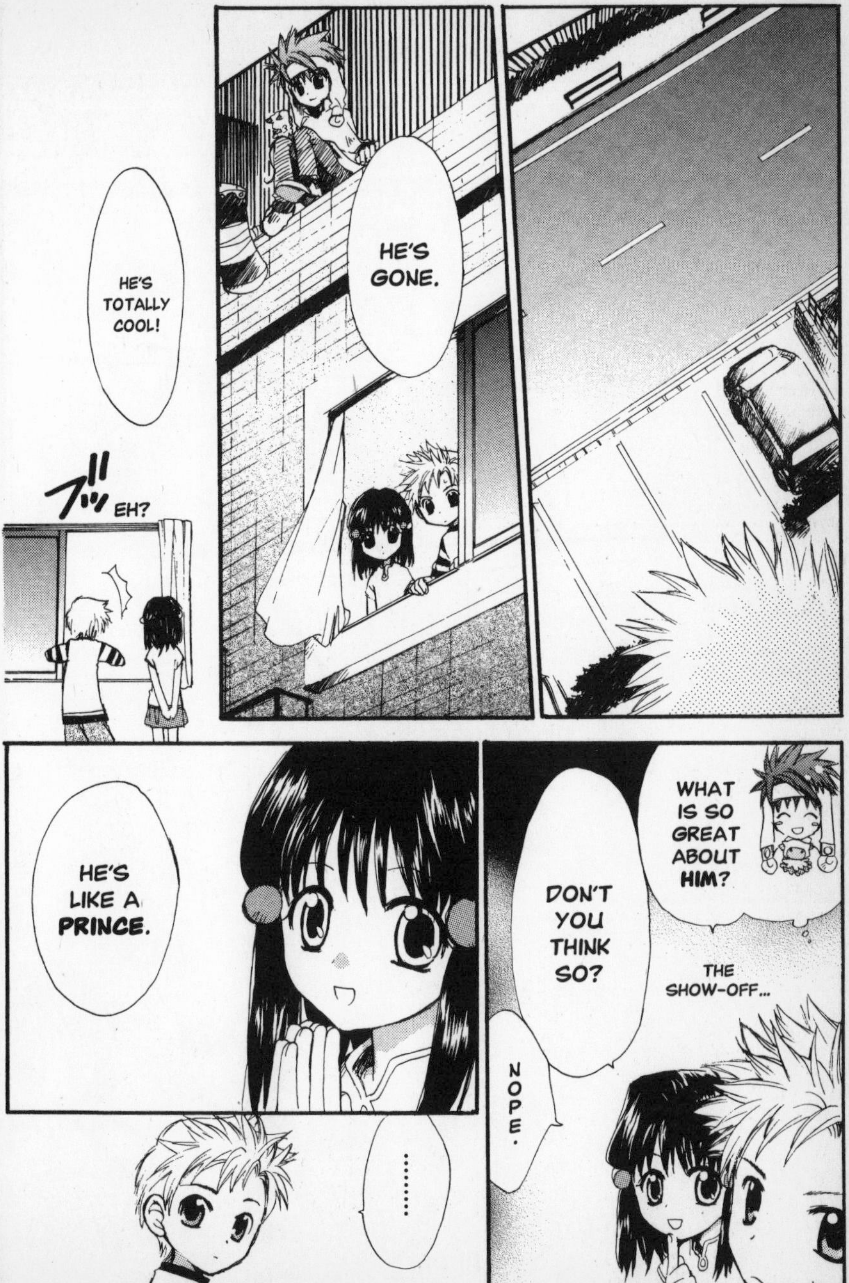
HE'S GONE.
HE'S TOTALLY COOL!
ブッ
EH?
HE'S LIKE A PRINCE.
DON'T YOU THINK SO?
NOPE.
WHAT IS SO GREAT ABOUT HIM?
THE SHOW-OFF...
......

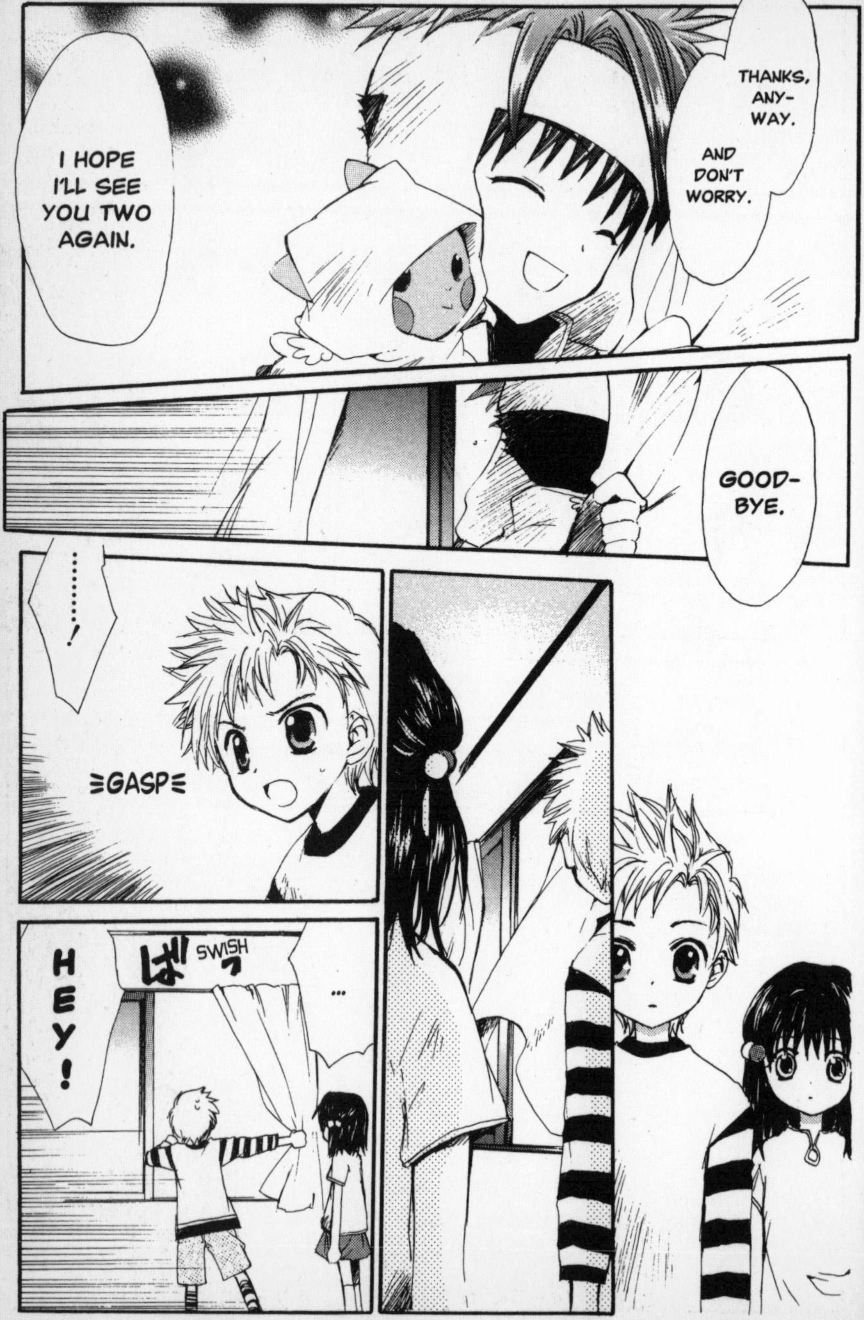
THANKS, ANY-WAY.
AND DON'T WORRY.
I HOPE I'LL SEE YOU TWO AGAIN.
GOOD-BYE.
......!
GASP
SWISH
...
HEY!

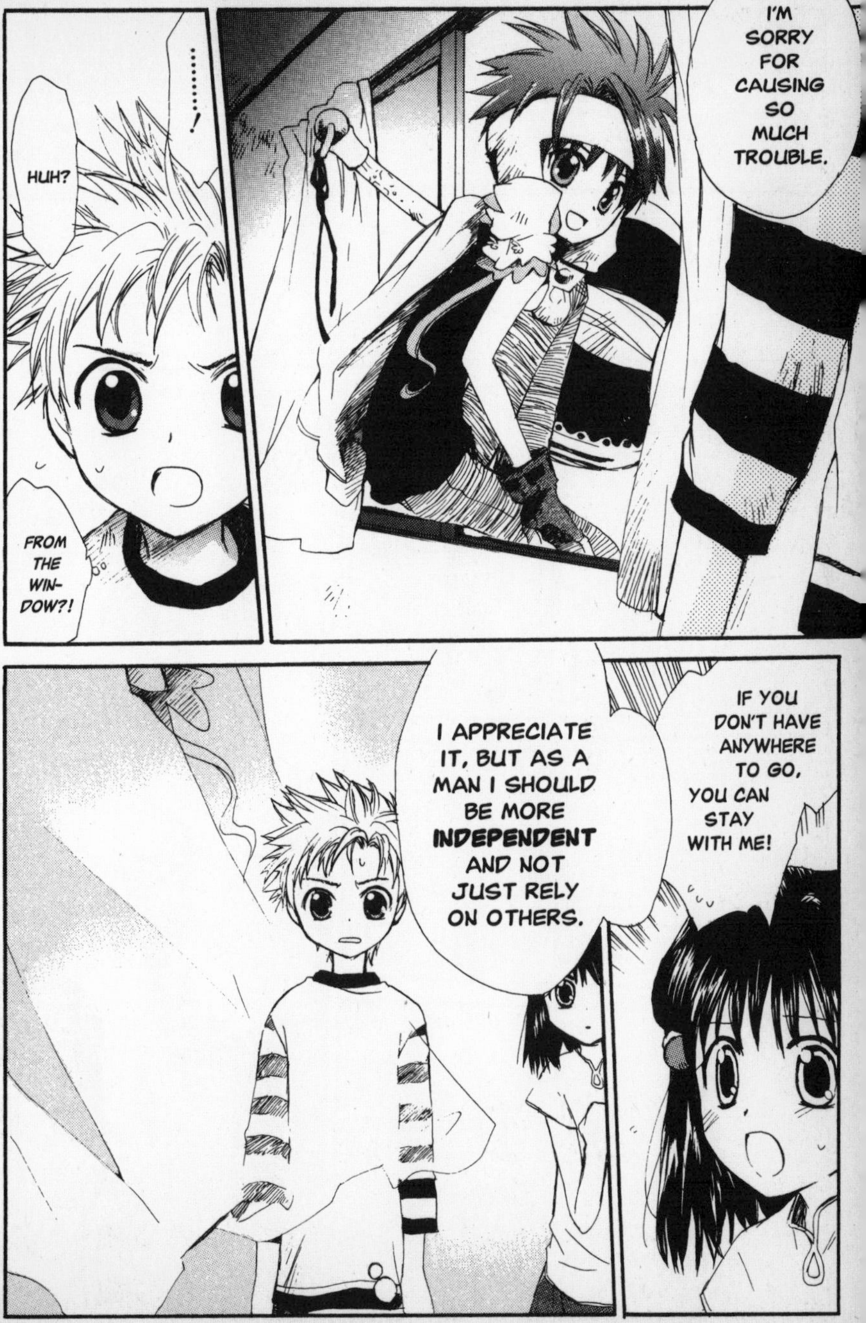
I'M SORRY FOR CAUSING SO MUCH TROUBLE.
......!
HUH?
FROM THE WIN-DOW?!
IF YOU DON'T HAVE ANYWHERE TO GO, YOU CAN STAY WITH ME!
I APPRECIATE IT, BUT AS A MAN I SHOULD BE MORE **INDEPENDENT** AND NOT JUST RELY ON OTHERS.

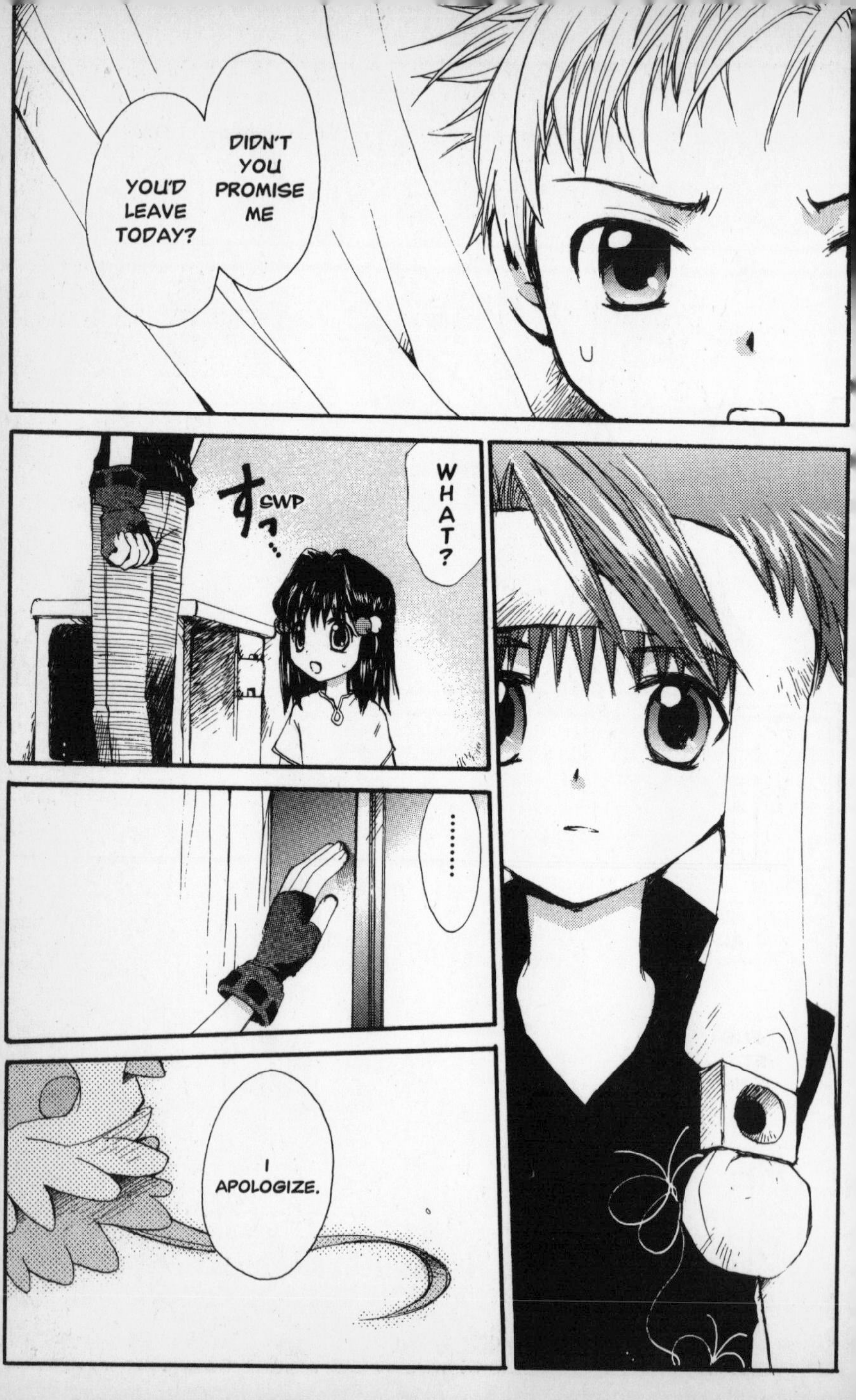
DIDN'T YOU PROMISE ME
YOU'D LEAVE TODAY?
WHAT?
SWP
....
I APOLOGIZE.

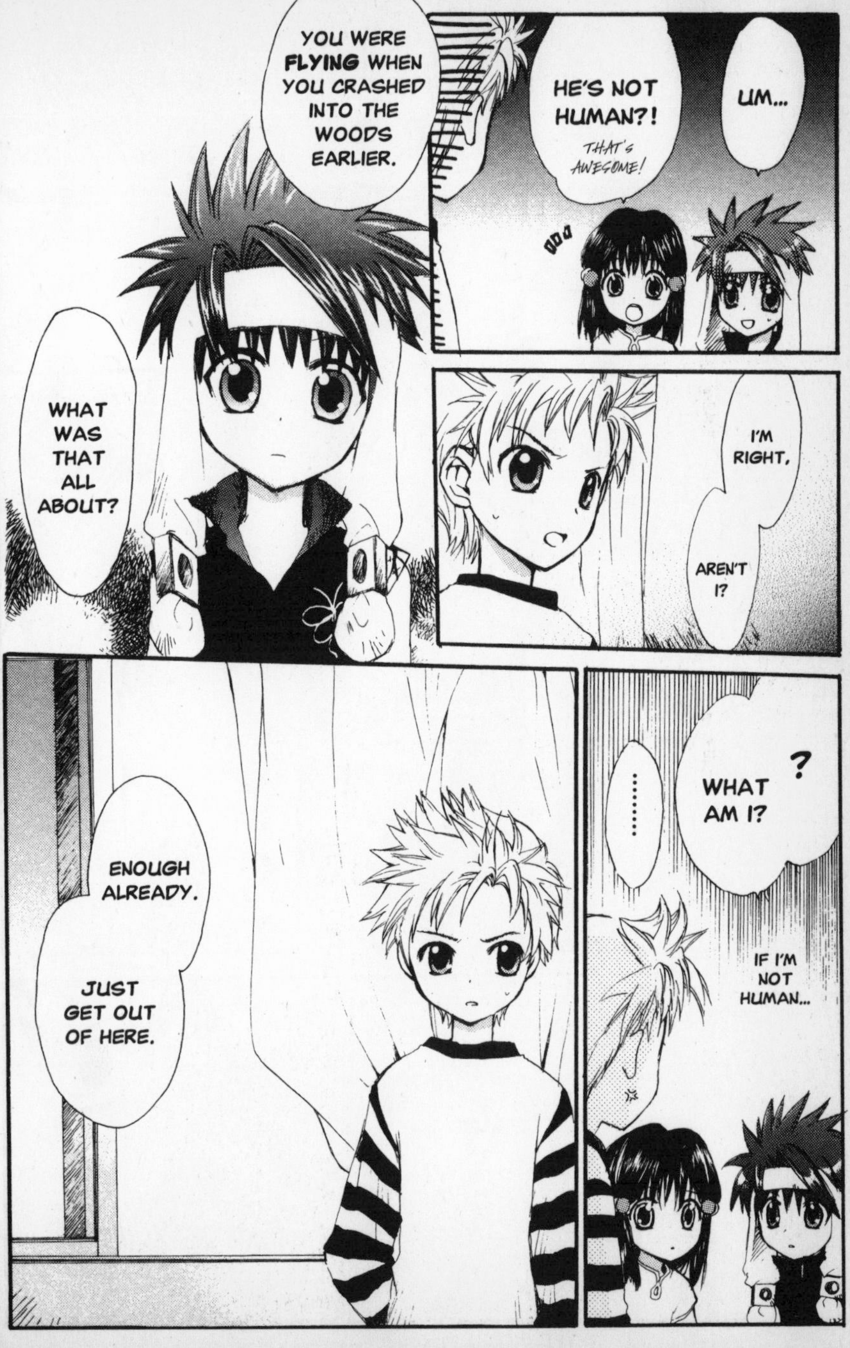
UM...
HE'S NOT HUMAN?!
THAT'S AWESOME!
YOU WERE FLYING WHEN YOU CRASHED INTO THE WOODS EARLIER.
WHAT WAS THAT ALL ABOUT?
I'M RIGHT,
AREN'T I?
WHAT AM I?
IF I'M NOT HUMAN...
....
ENOUGH ALREADY.
JUST GET OUT OF HERE.

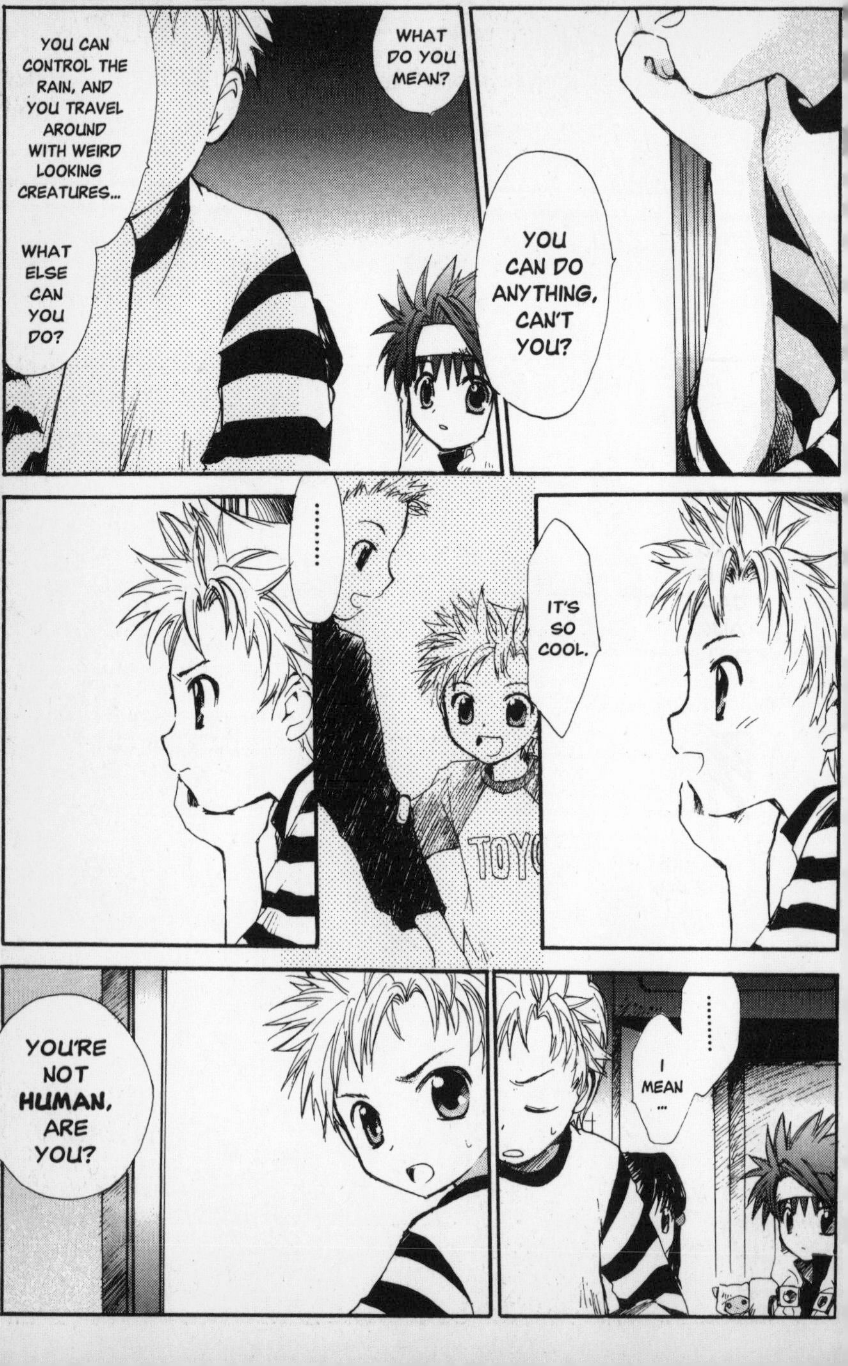
YOU CAN CONTROL THE RAIN, AND YOU TRAVEL AROUND WITH WEIRD LOOKING CREATURES...
WHAT ELSE CAN YOU DO?
WHAT DO YOU MEAN?
YOU CAN DO ANYTHING, CAN'T YOU?
......
IT'S SO COOL.
TOYO
YOU'RE NOT **HUMAN**, ARE YOU?
......
I MEAN ...

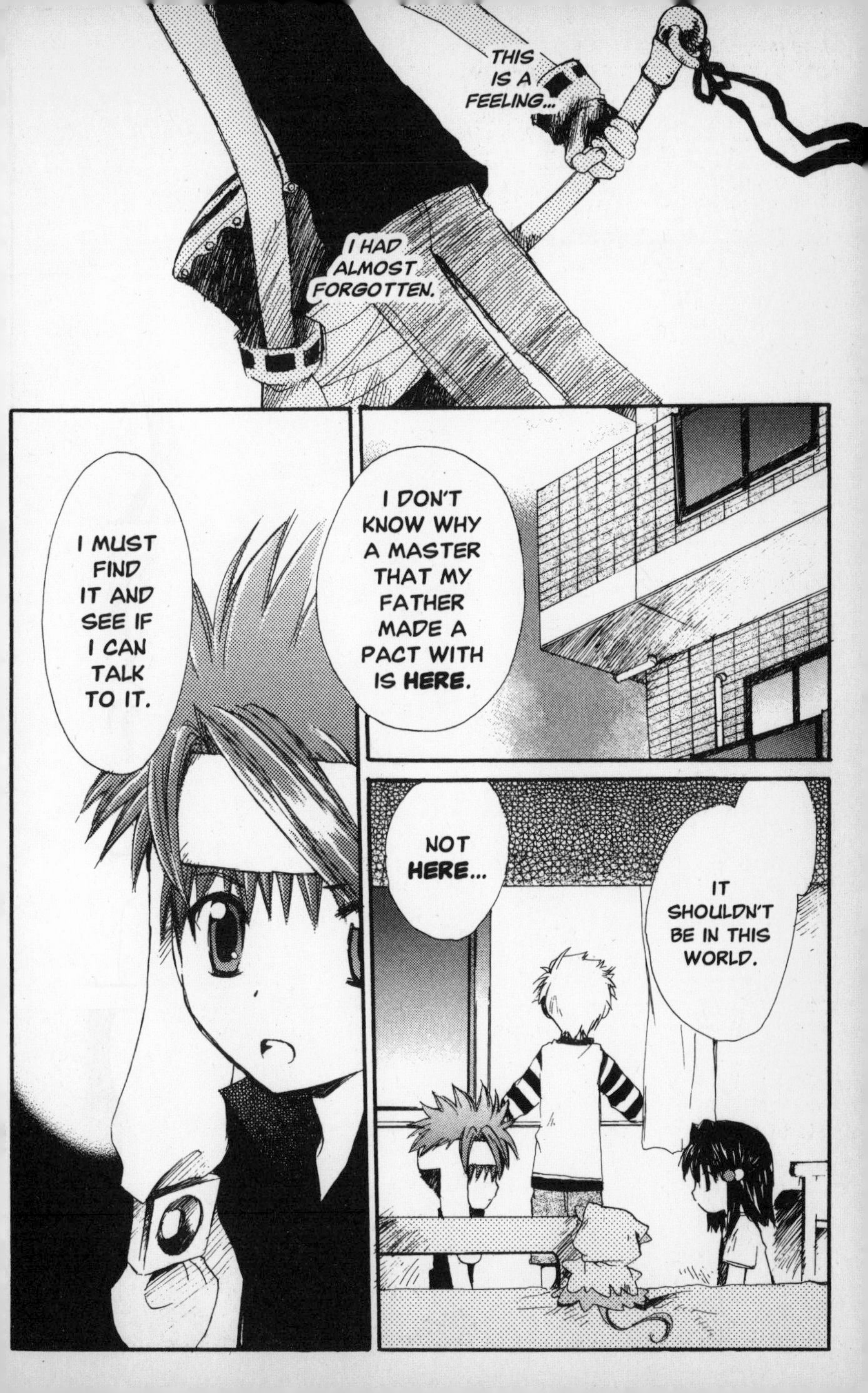
THIS IS A FEELING...
I HAD ALMOST FORGOTTEN.
I DON'T KNOW WHY A MASTER THAT MY FATHER MADE A PACT WITH IS HERE.
I MUST FIND IT AND SEE IF I CAN TALK TO IT.
IT SHOULDN'T BE IN THIS WORLD.
NOT HERE...

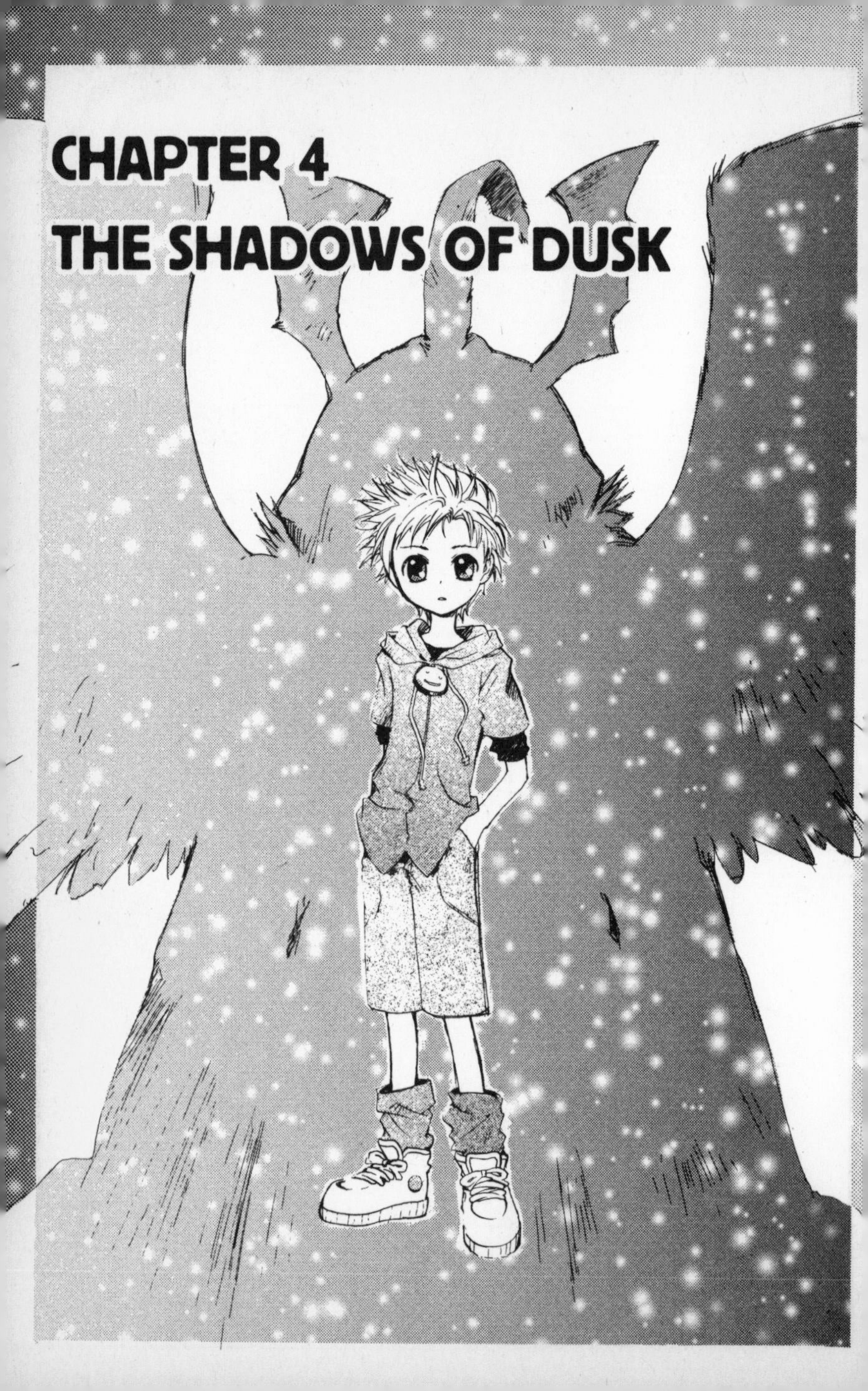
CHAPTER 4
THE SHADOWS OF DUSK

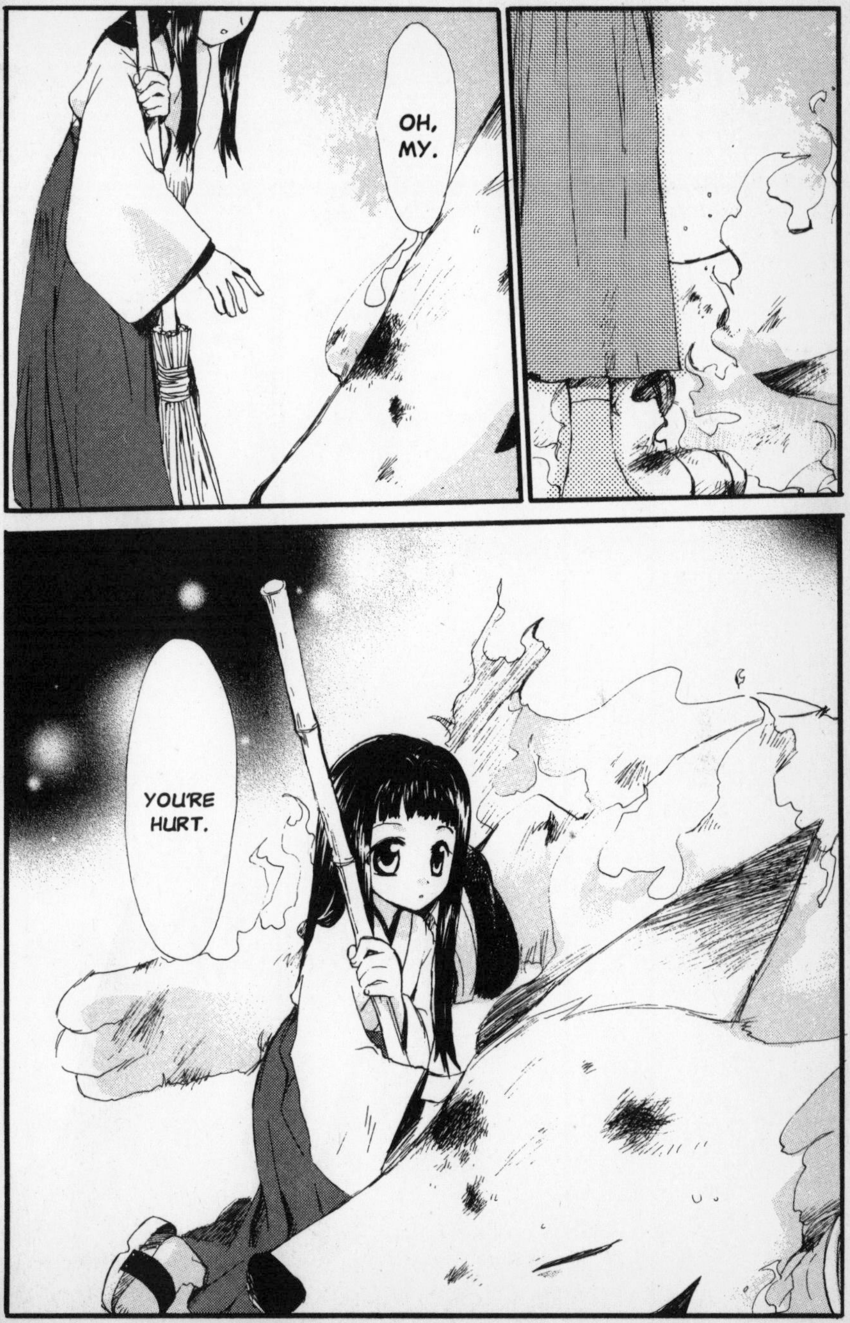
OH, MY.
YOU'RE HURT.

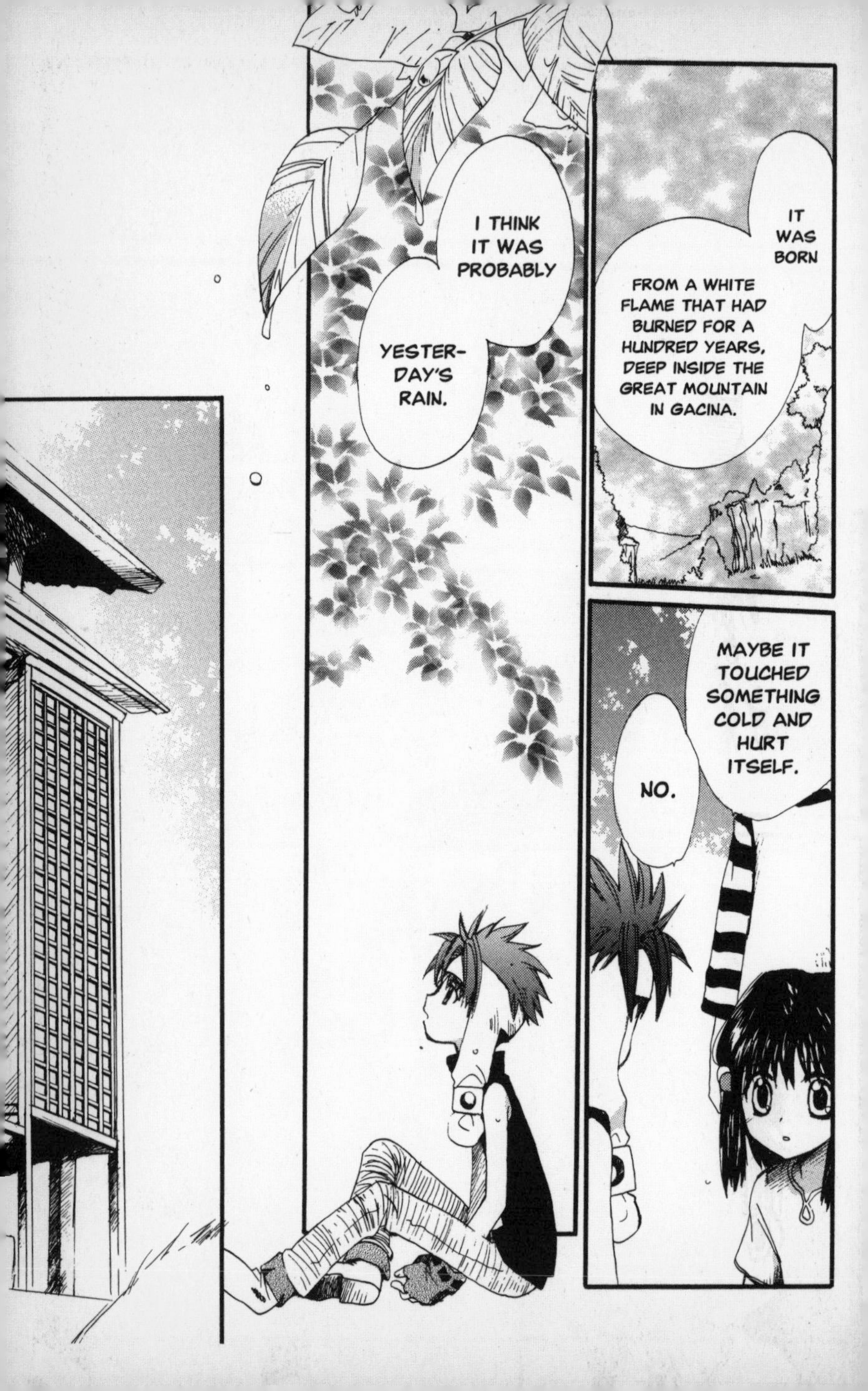
IT WAS BORN
FROM A WHITE FLAME THAT HAD BURNED FOR A HUNDRED YEARS, DEEP INSIDE THE GREAT MOUNTAIN IN GACINA.
MAYBE IT TOUCHED SOMETHING COLD AND HURT ITSELF.
NO.
I THINK IT WAS PROBABLY
YESTER-DAY'S RAIN.

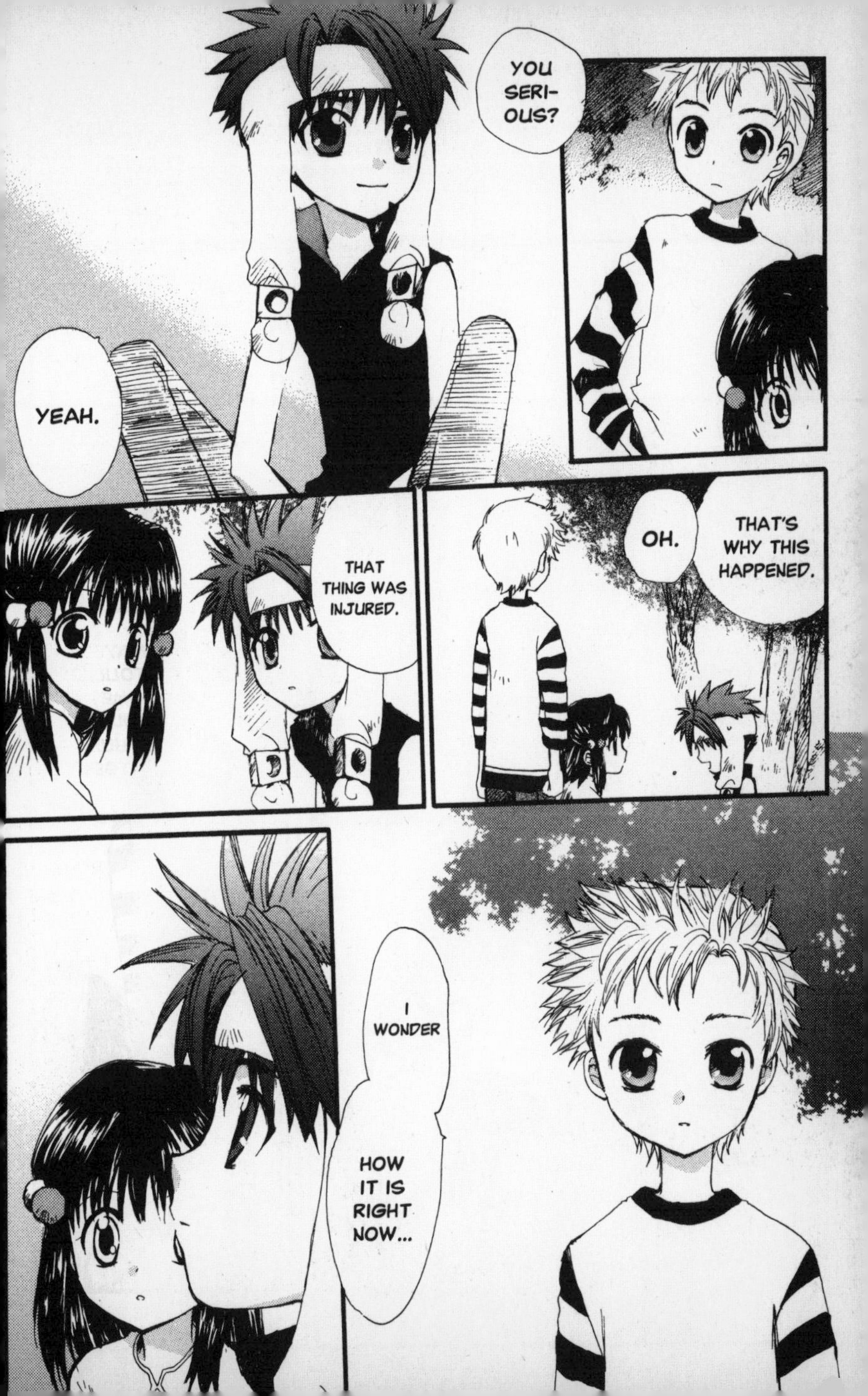
YOU SERIOUS?
YEAH.
THAT THING WAS INJURED.
OH.
THAT'S WHY THIS HAPPENED.
I WONDER
HOW IT IS RIGHT NOW...

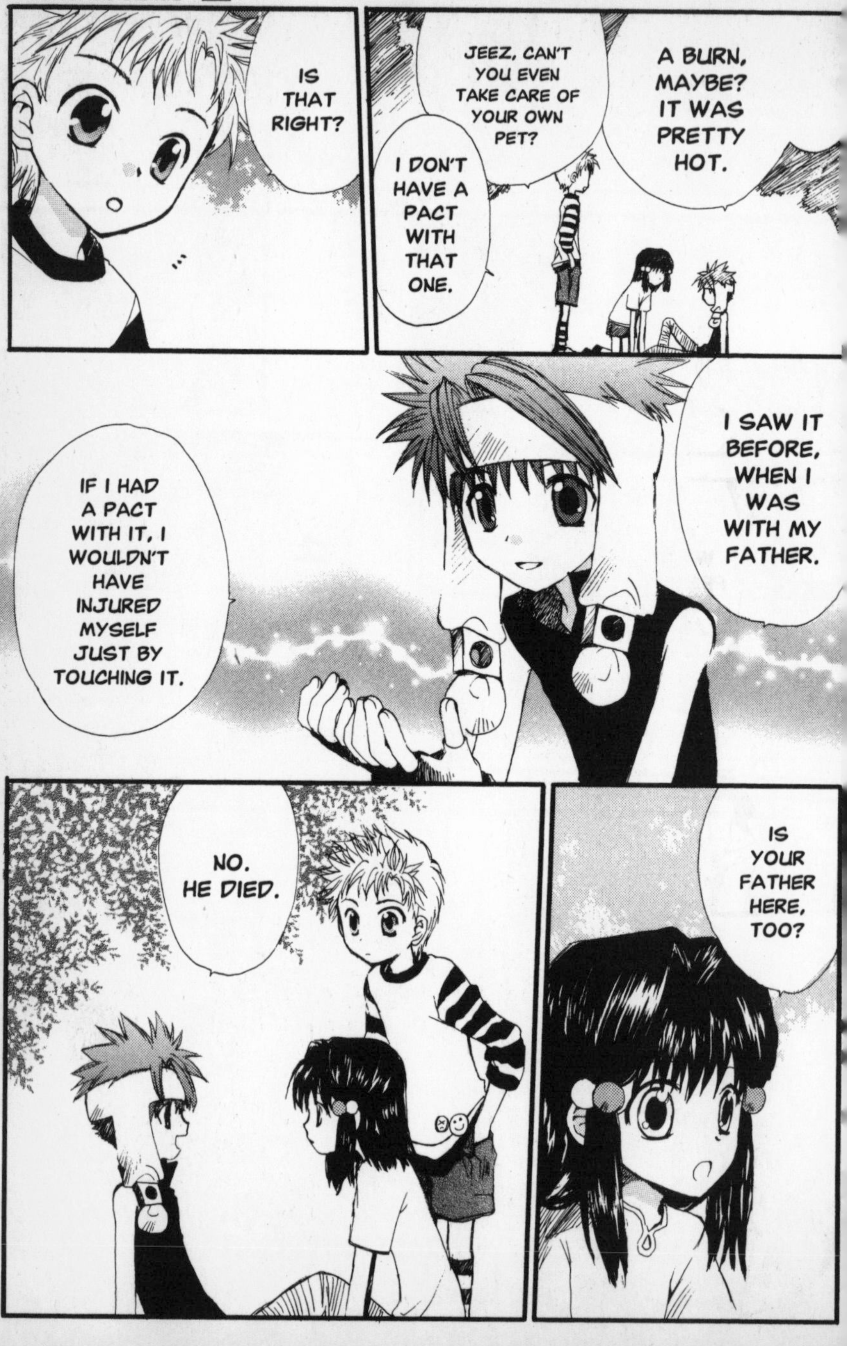
A BURN, MAYBE? IT WAS PRETTY HOT.
JEEZ, CAN'T YOU EVEN TAKE CARE OF YOUR OWN PET?
I DON'T HAVE A PACT WITH THAT ONE.
IS THAT RIGHT?
...
I SAW IT BEFORE, WHEN I WAS WITH MY FATHER.
IF I HAD A PACT WITH IT, I WOULDN'T HAVE INJURED MYSELF JUST BY TOUCHING IT.
IS YOUR FATHER HERE, TOO?
NO. HE DIED.

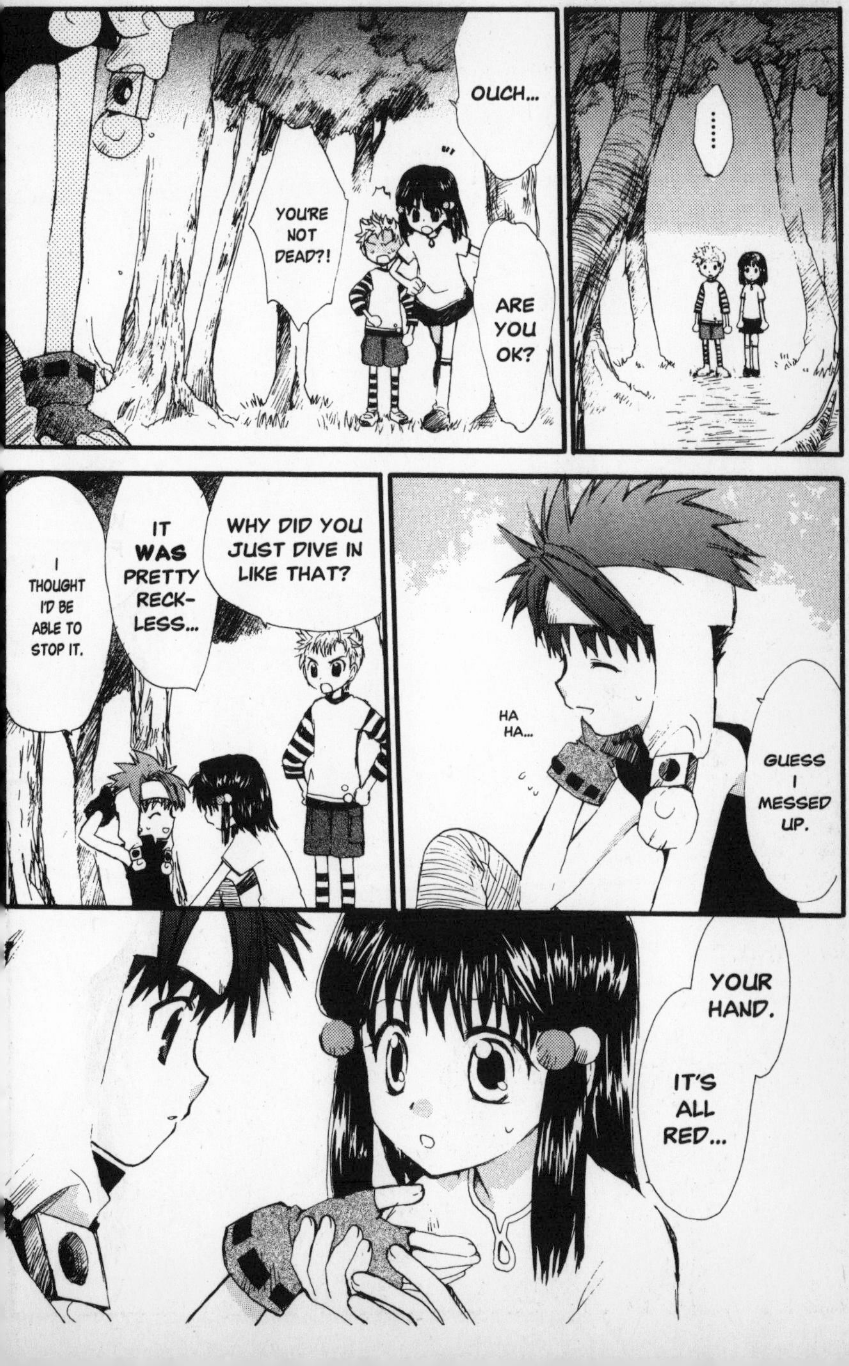
OUCH...
ARE YOU OK?
YOU'RE NOT DEAD?!
......
WHY DID YOU JUST DIVE IN LIKE THAT?
IT **WAS** PRETTY RECKLESS...
I THOUGHT I'D BE ABLE TO STOP IT.
HA HA...
GUESS I MESSED UP.
YOUR HAND.
IT'S ALL RED...

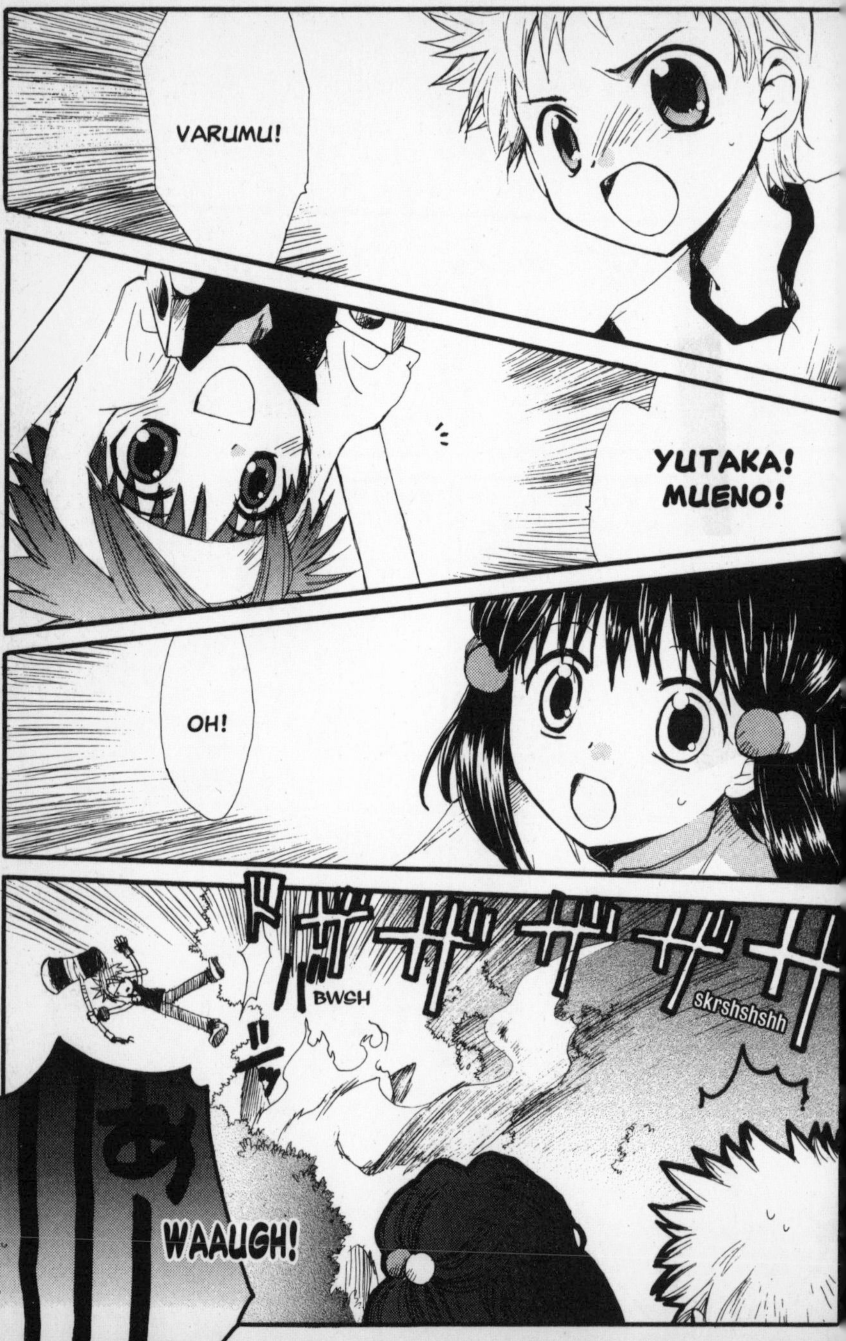

VARUMU!
YUTAKA! MUENO!
OH!
BWSH
skrshshshh
WAAUGH!

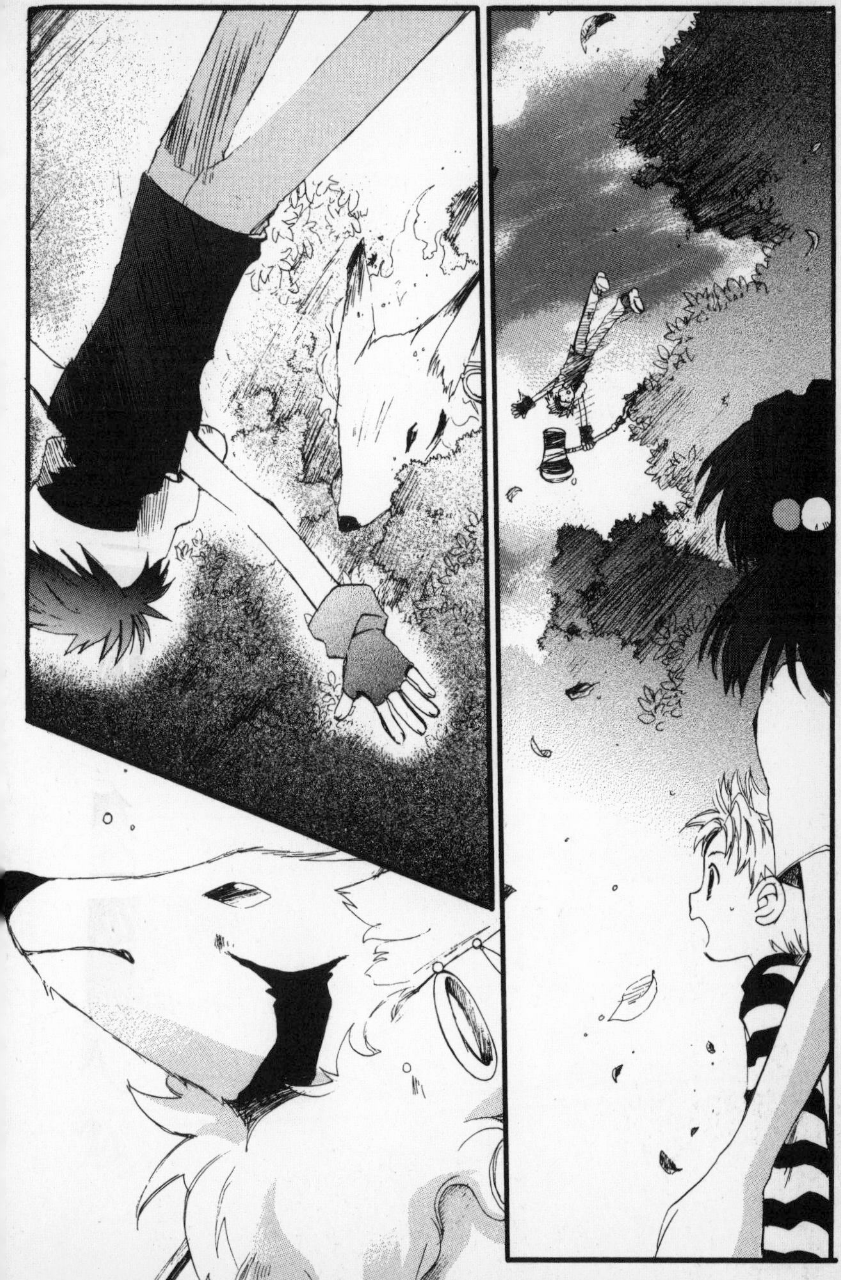

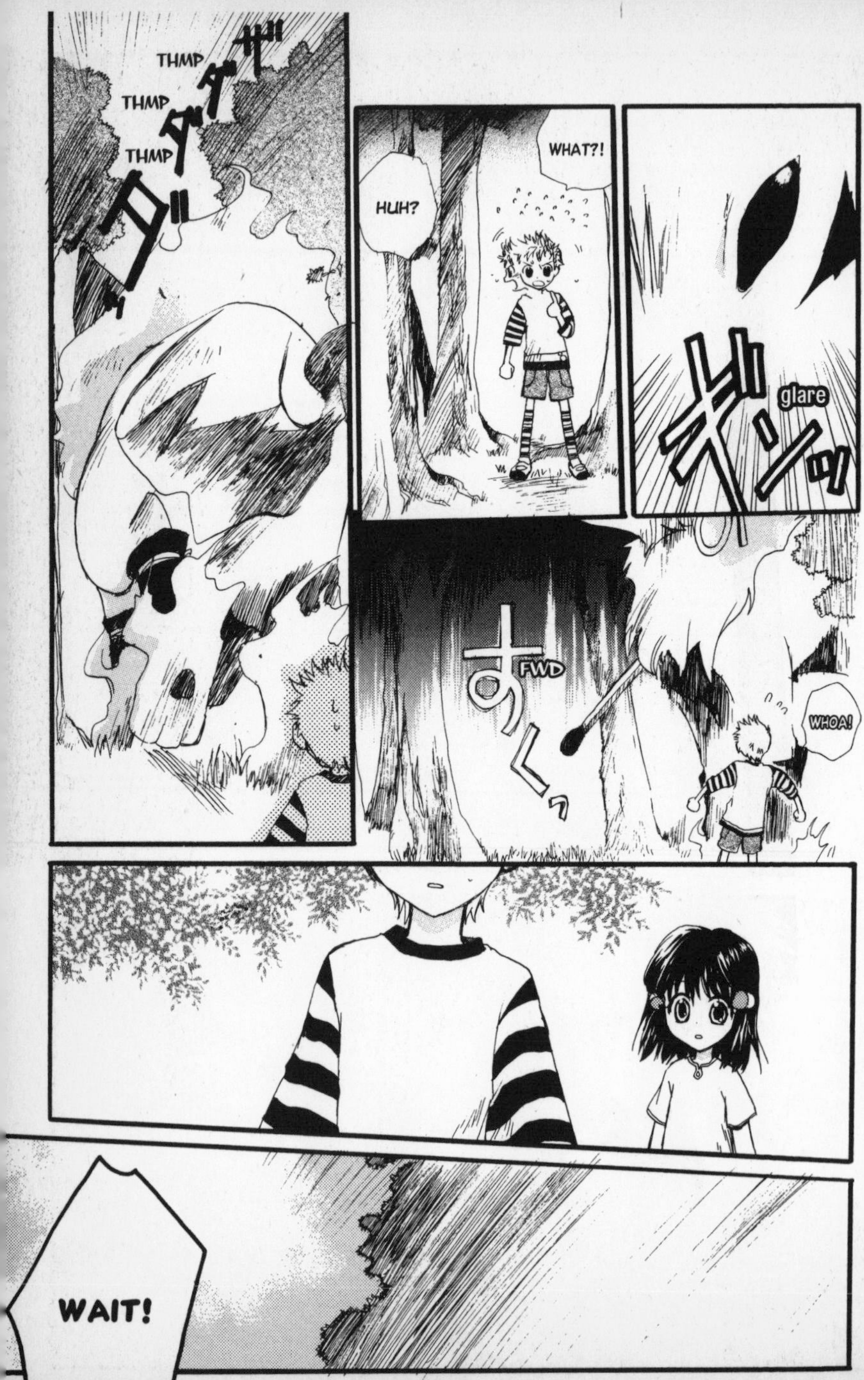
THMP
THMP
THMP
glare
WHAT?!
HUH?
FWD
WHOA!
WAIT!

IS
IT
HURT?

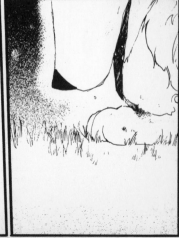

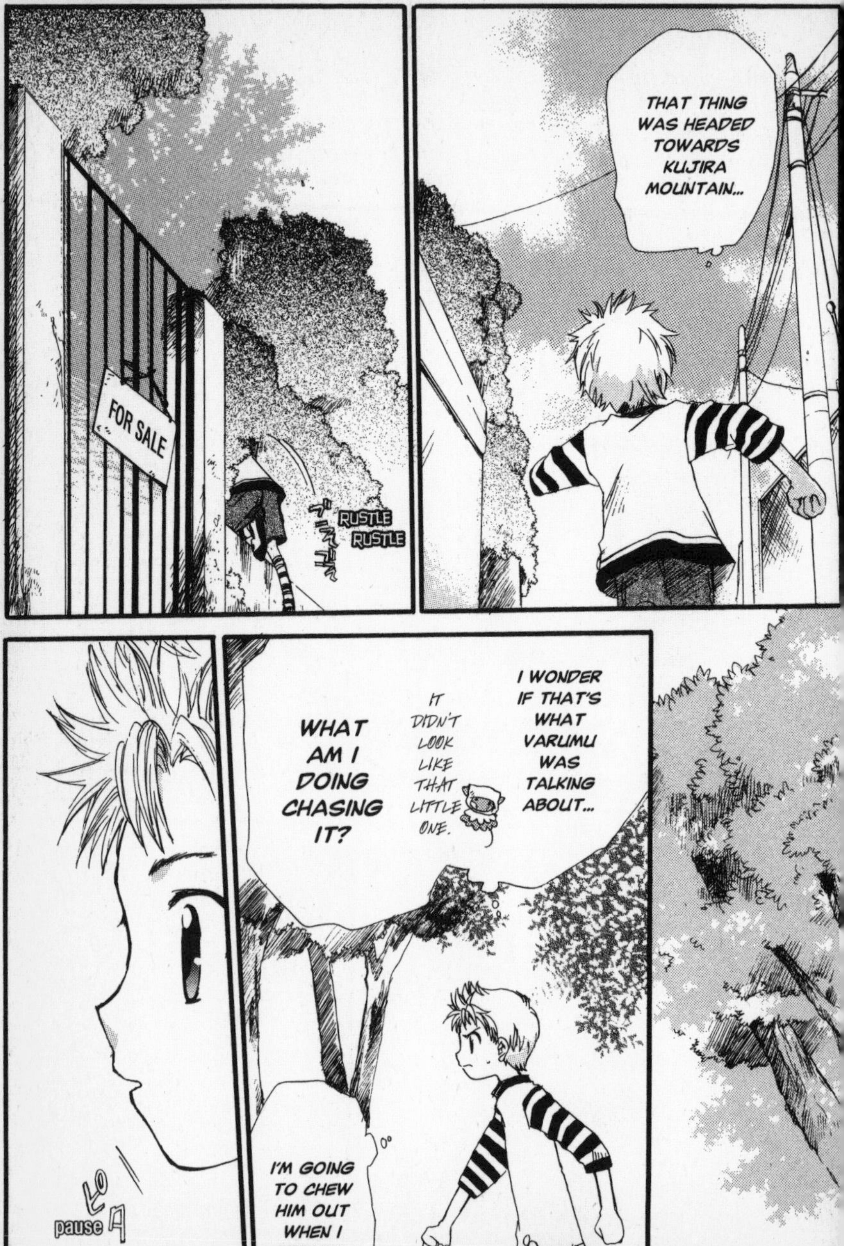
THAT THING WAS HEADED TOWARDS KUJIRA MOUNTAIN...
RUSTLE RUSTLE
I WONDER IF THAT'S WHAT VARUMU WAS TALKING ABOUT...
IT DIDN'T LOOK LIKE THAT LITTLE ONE.
WHAT AM I DOING CHASING IT?
I'M GOING TO CHEW HIM OUT WHEN I SEE HIM...
pause

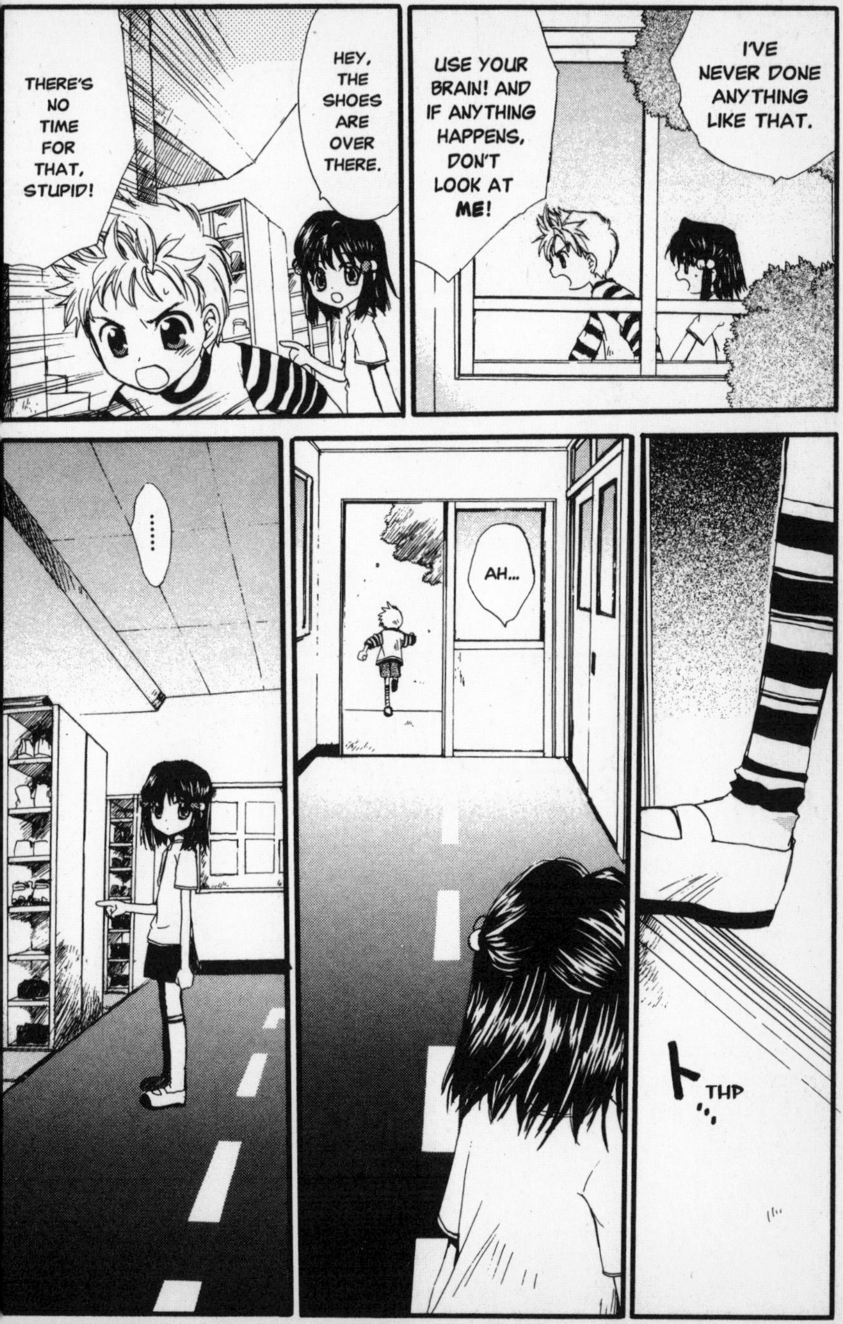
THERE'S NO TIME FOR THAT, STUPID!
HEY, THE SHOES ARE OVER THERE.
USE YOUR BRAIN! AND IF ANYTHING HAPPENS, DON'T LOOK AT ME!
I'VE NEVER DONE ANYTHING LIKE THAT.
......
AH...
THP

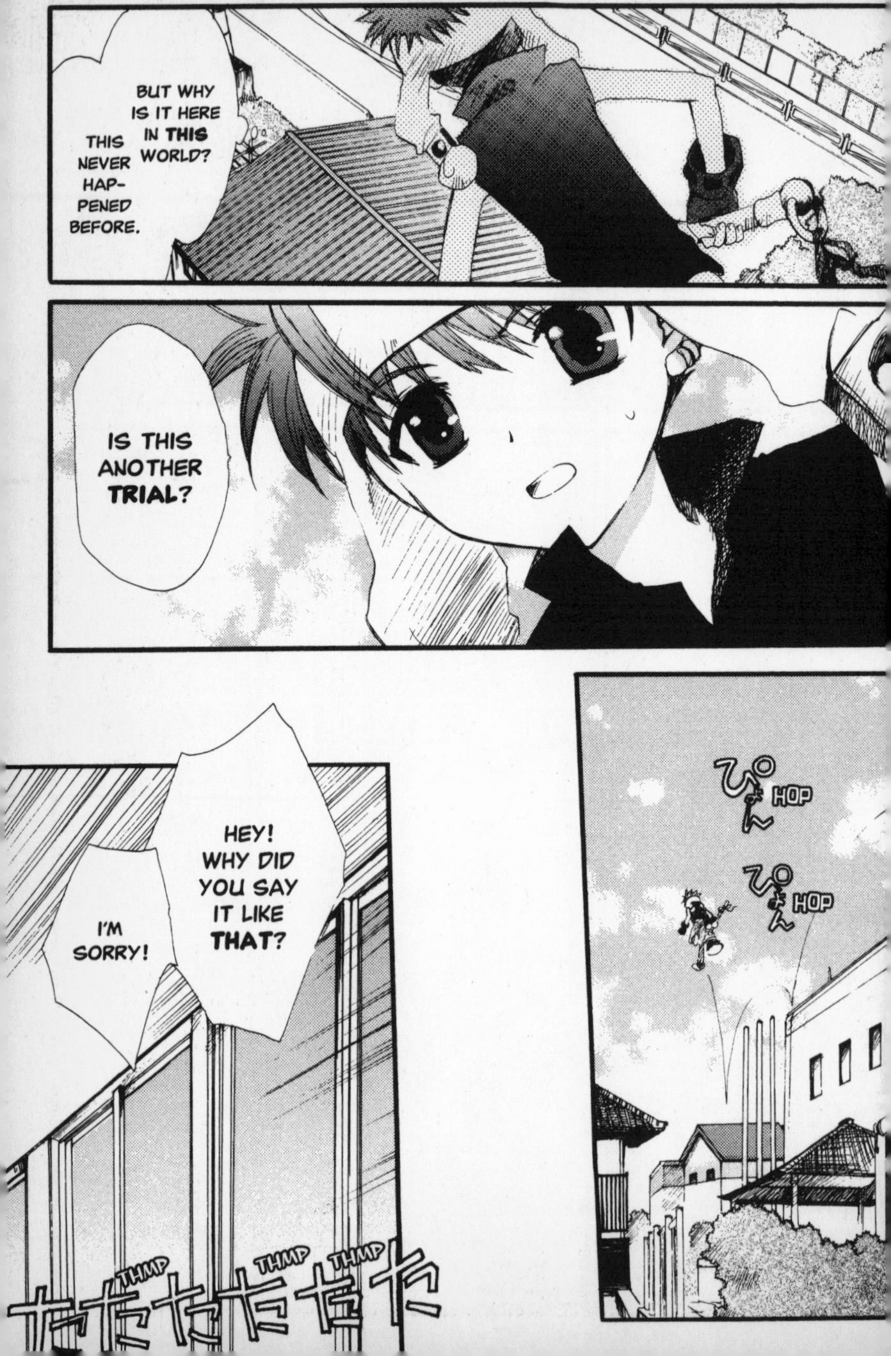
BUT WHY IS IT HERE IN **THIS** WORLD?
THIS NEVER HAP-PENED BEFORE.
IS THIS ANOTHER **TRIAL**?
ぴょん HOP
ぴょん HOP
HEY! WHY DID YOU SAY IT LIKE **THAT**?
I'M SORRY!
THMP THMP THMP

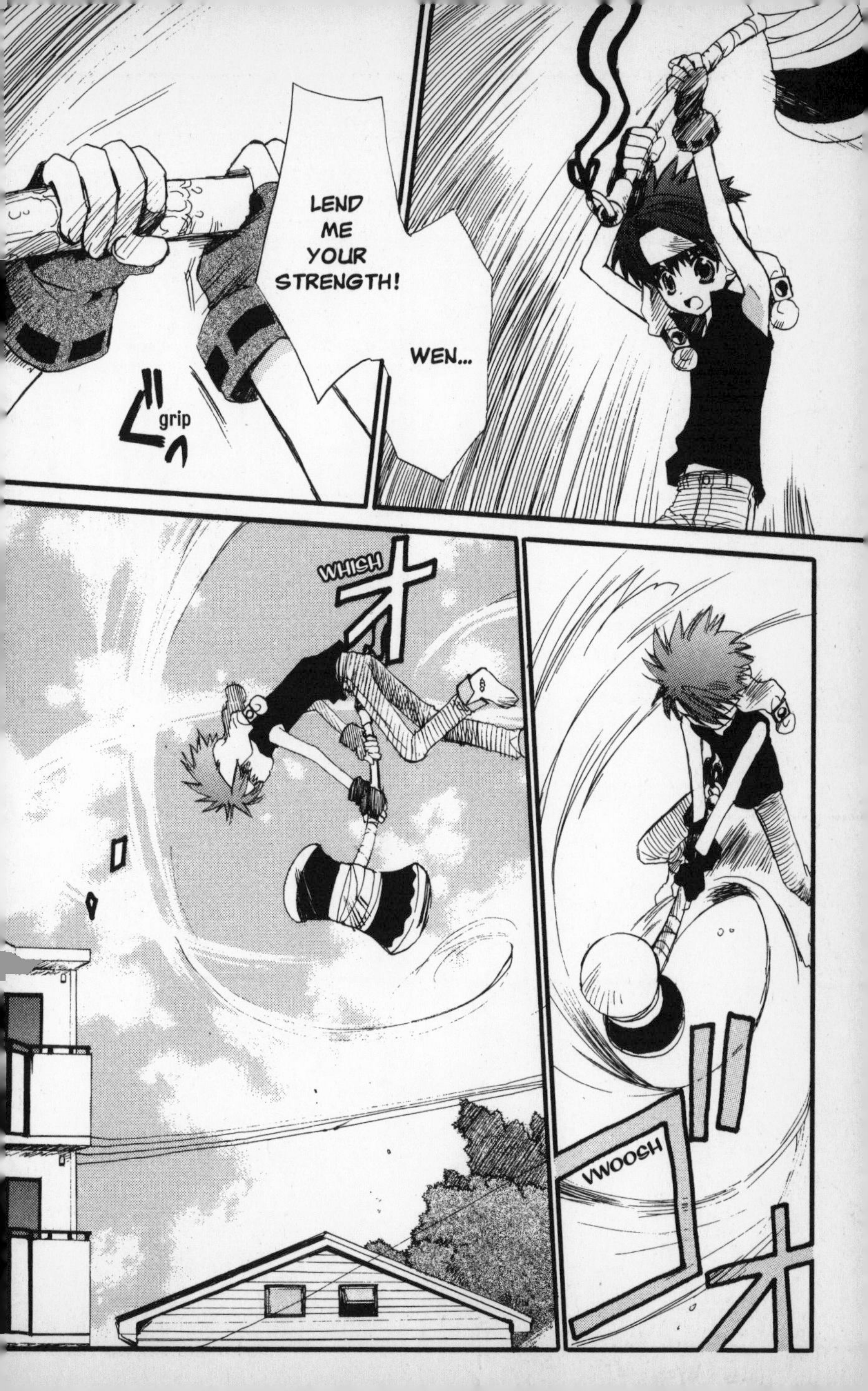
LEND ME YOUR STRENGTH!
WEN...
grip
WHISH
VWOOSH

GO SEE THE NURSE WITH YUTAKA?

CAN I...

SO...

...

WHY?!

5-3

CLAMOR

WHAT?!

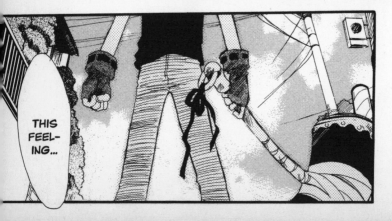

THIS FEEL-ING...

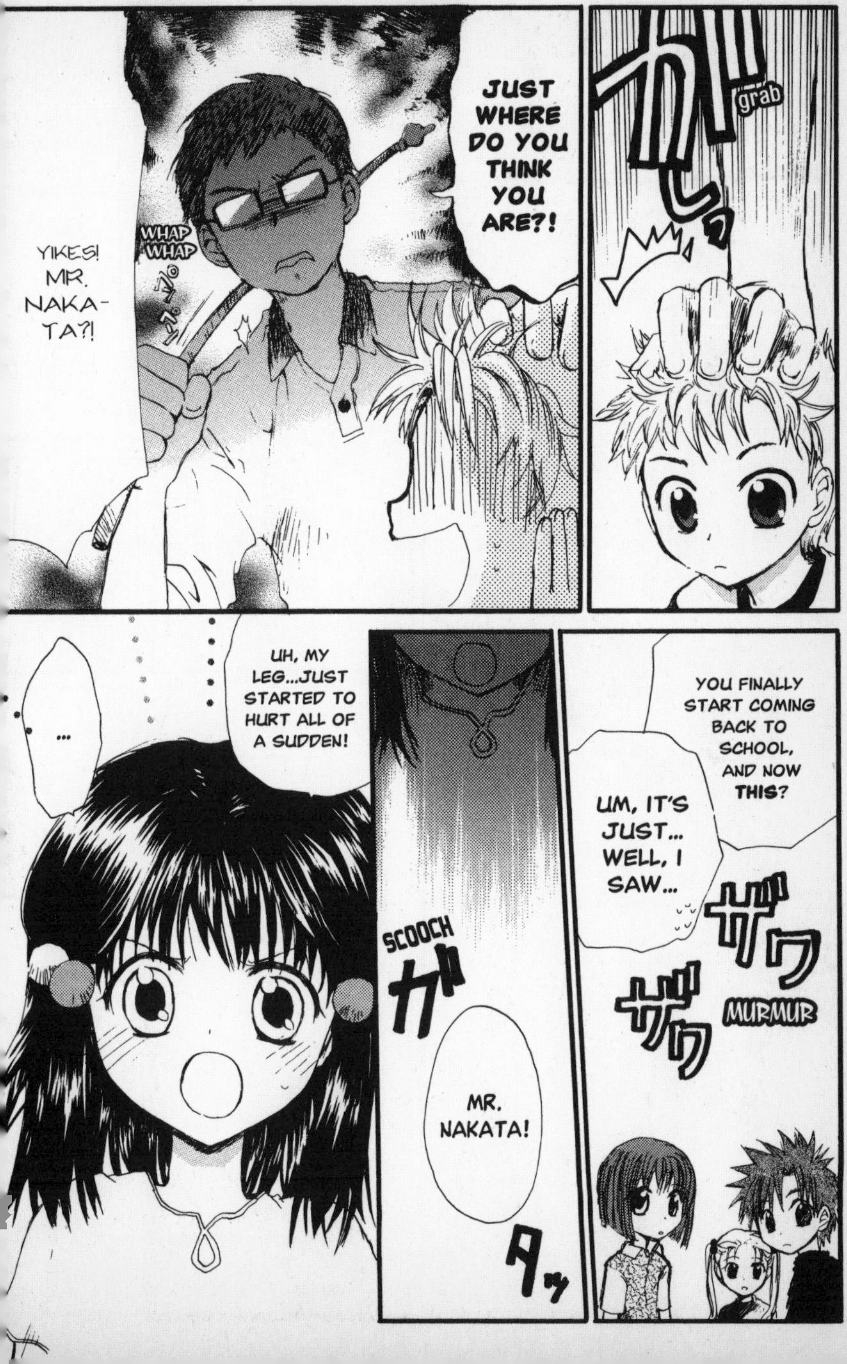
grab
JUST WHERE DO YOU THINK YOU ARE?!
WHAP WHAP
YIKES! MR. NAKA-TA?!
YOU FINALLY START COMING BACK TO SCHOOL, AND NOW THIS?
UM, IT'S JUST... WELL, I SAW...
ザワ ザワ
MURMUR
SCOOCH
MR. NAKATA!
UH, MY LEG...JUST STARTED TO HURT ALL OF A SUDDEN!
...

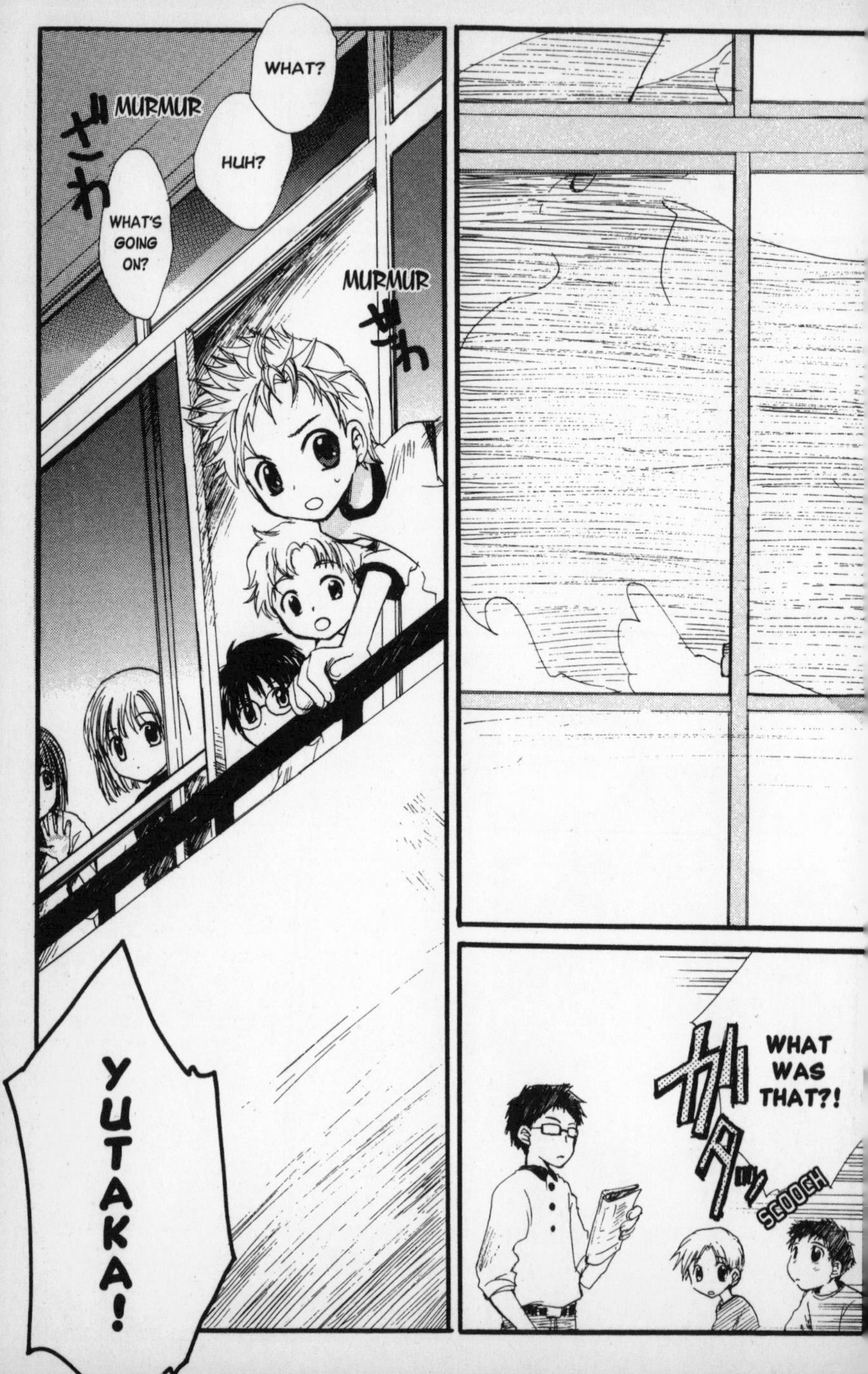
カタッ
SCOOCH
WHAT WAS THAT?!
WHAT?
HUH?
WHAT'S GOING ON?
ざわ
MURMUR
ざわ
MURMUR
YUTAKA!

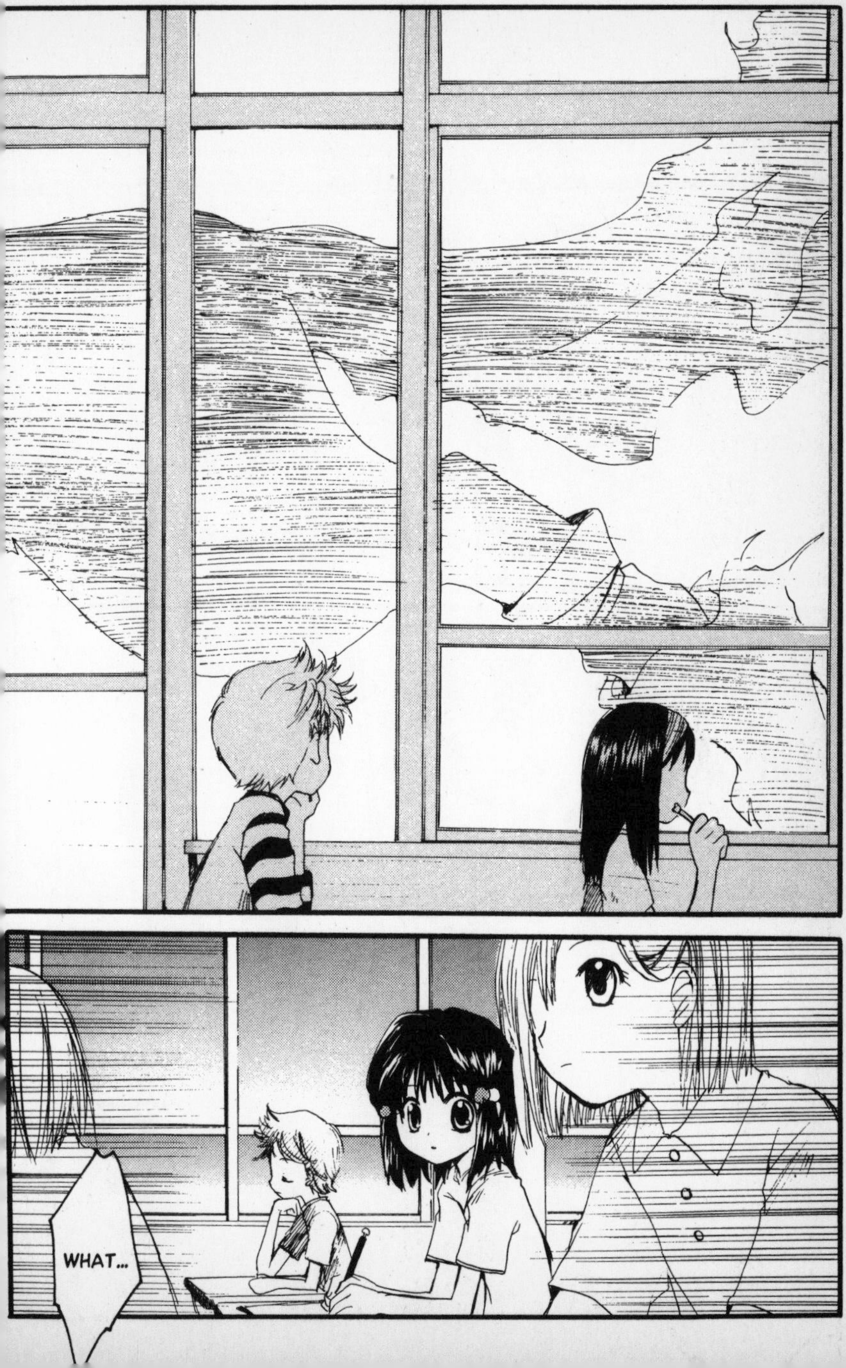
WHAT...

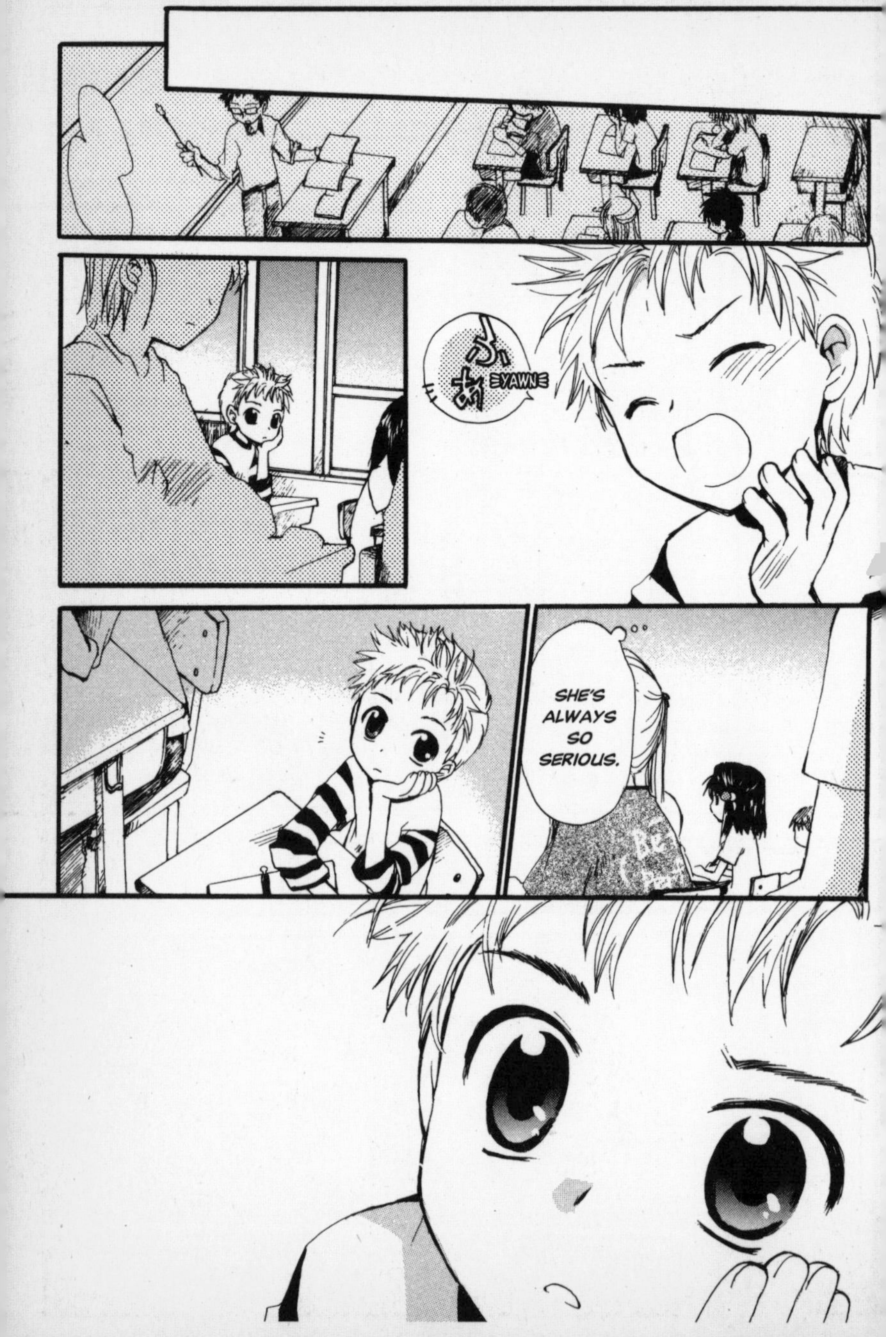
ふぁ
YAWN
SHE'S ALWAYS SO SERIOUS.

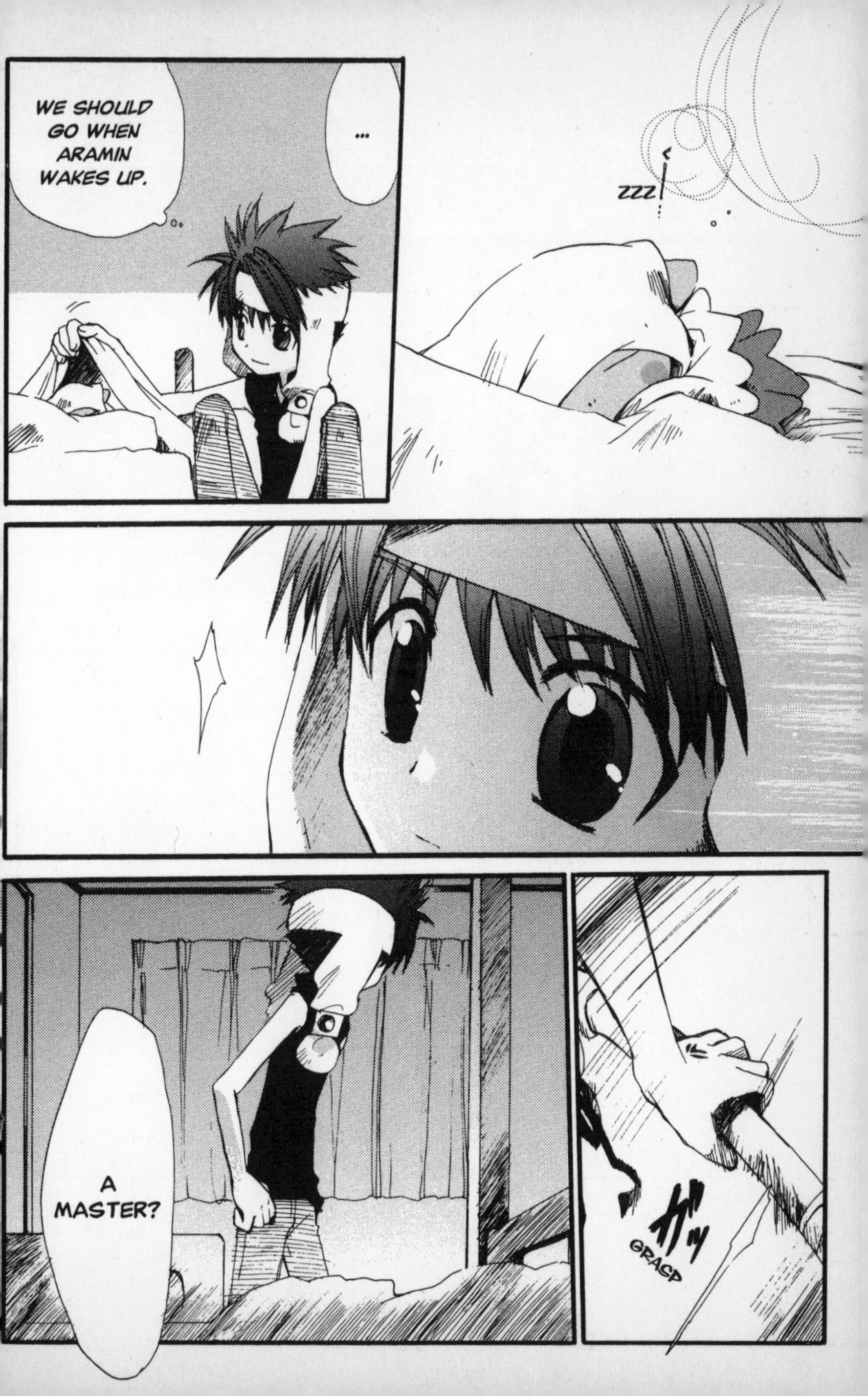
zzz
...
WE SHOULD GO WHEN ARAMIN WAKES UP.
GRASP
A MASTER?

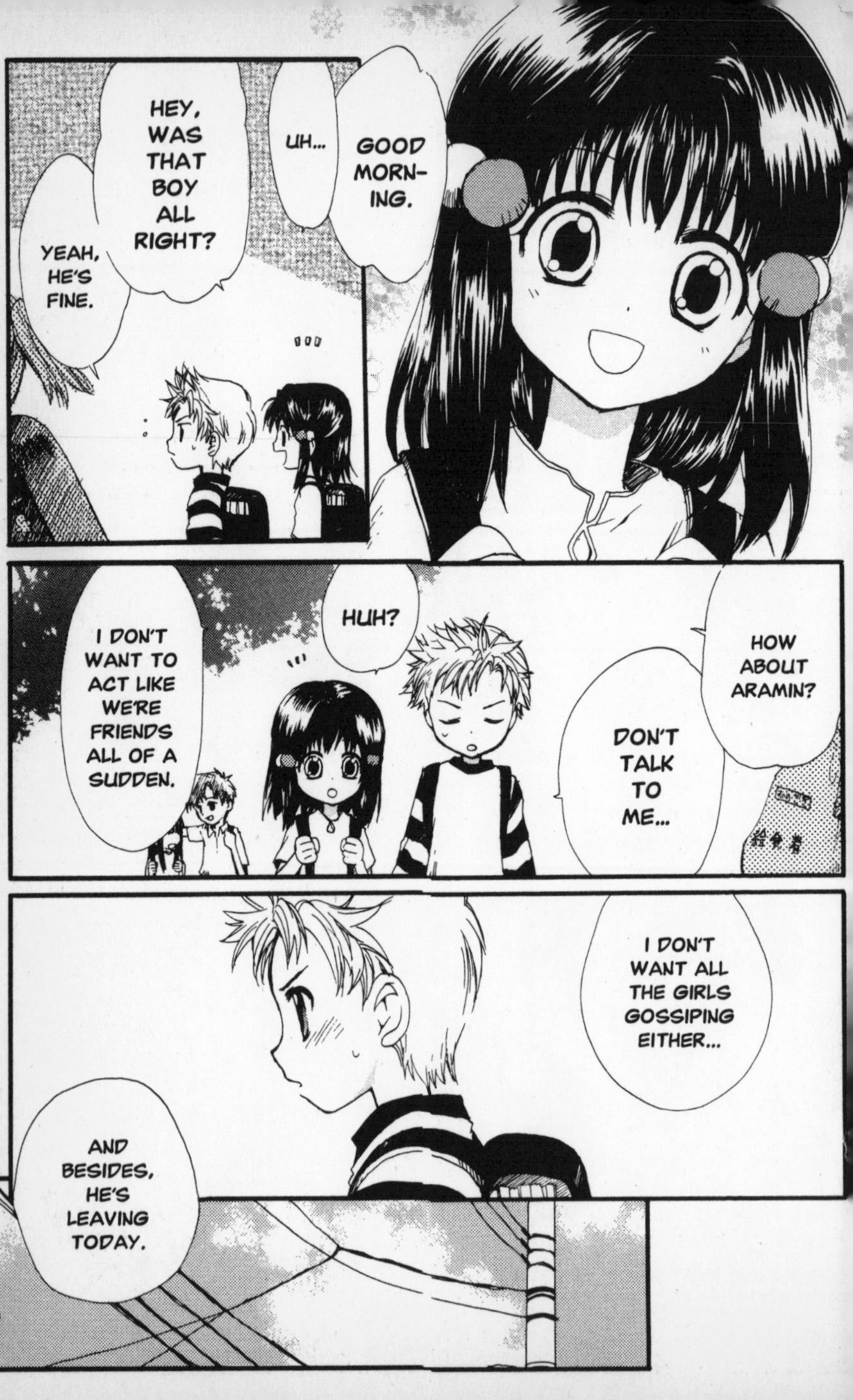
GOOD MORNING.
UH...
HEY, WAS THAT BOY ALL RIGHT?
YEAH, HE'S FINE.
HOW ABOUT ARAMIN?
DON'T TALK TO ME...
HUH?
I DON'T WANT TO ACT LIKE WE'RE FRIENDS ALL OF A SUDDEN.
I DON'T WANT ALL THE GIRLS GOSSIPING EITHER...
AND BESIDES, HE'S LEAVING TODAY.

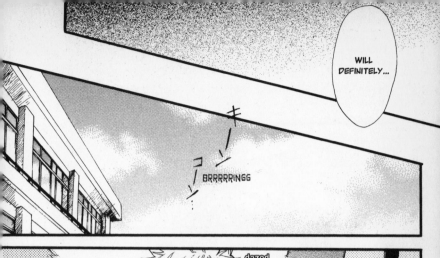

WILL DEFINITELY...

BRRRRRINGG

I DIDN'T SLEEP WELL LAST NIGHT...

dazed

CHATTER

CHATTER

MORNING!

HEY...

YOU CAME TO SCHOOL AGAIN TODAY!

YUTAKA!

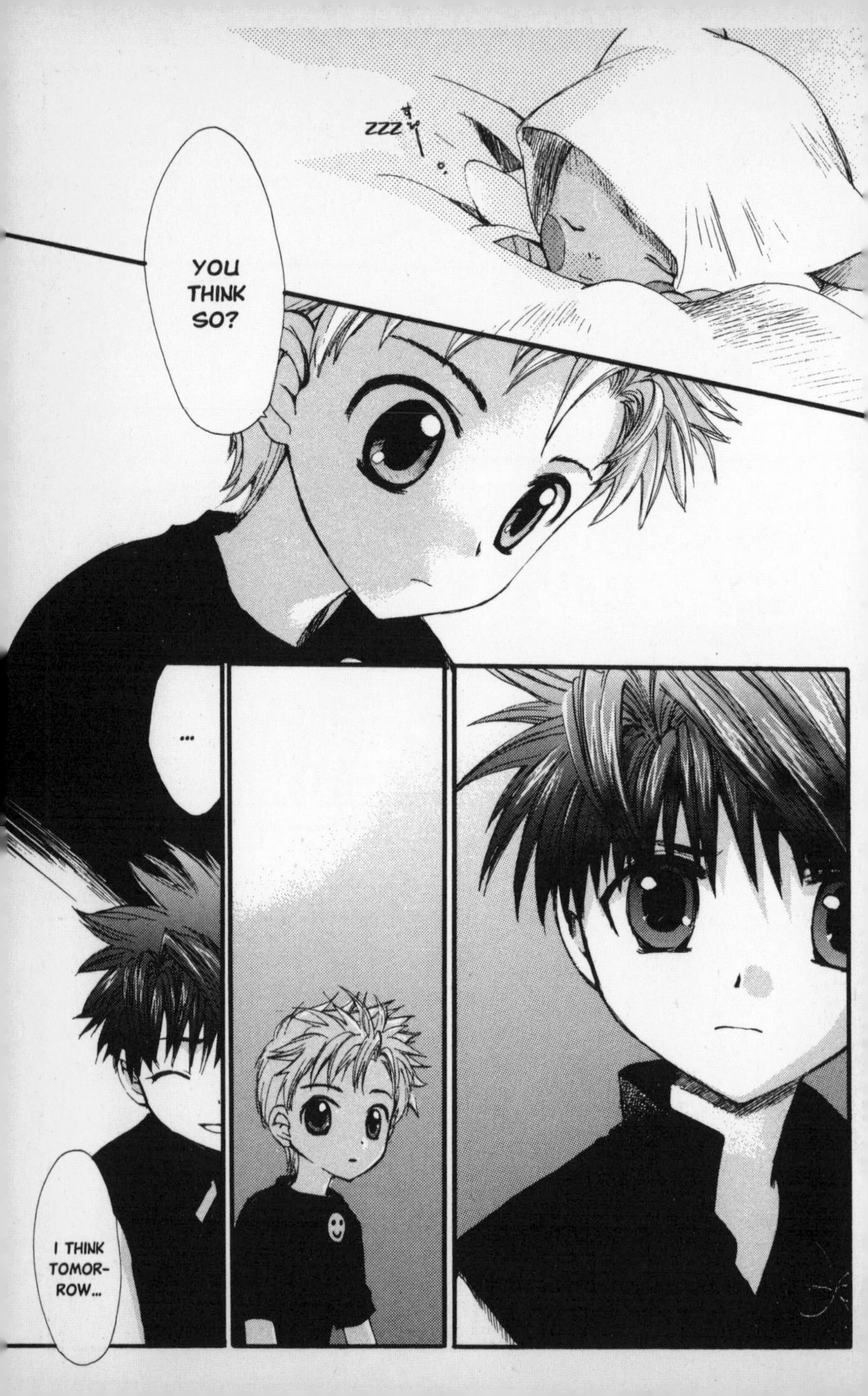
ZZZ
YOU THINK SO?
...
I THINK TOMOR-ROW...

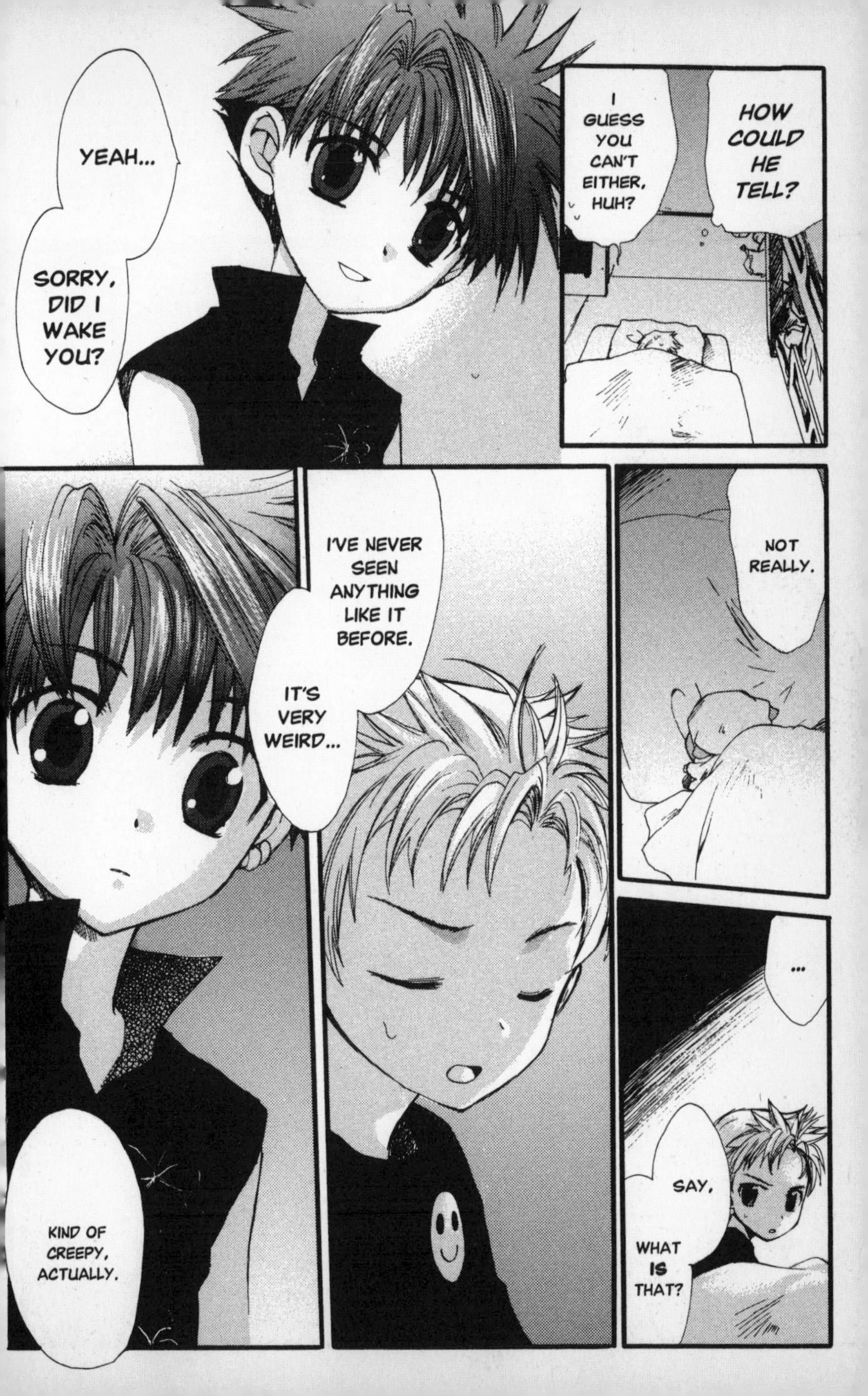
HOW COULD HE TELL?
I GUESS YOU CAN'T EITHER, HUH?
YEAH...
SORRY, DID I WAKE YOU?
NOT REALLY.
...
SAY, WHAT **IS** THAT?
I'VE NEVER SEEN ANYTHING LIKE IT BEFORE.
IT'S VERY WEIRD...
KIND OF CREEPY, ACTUALLY.

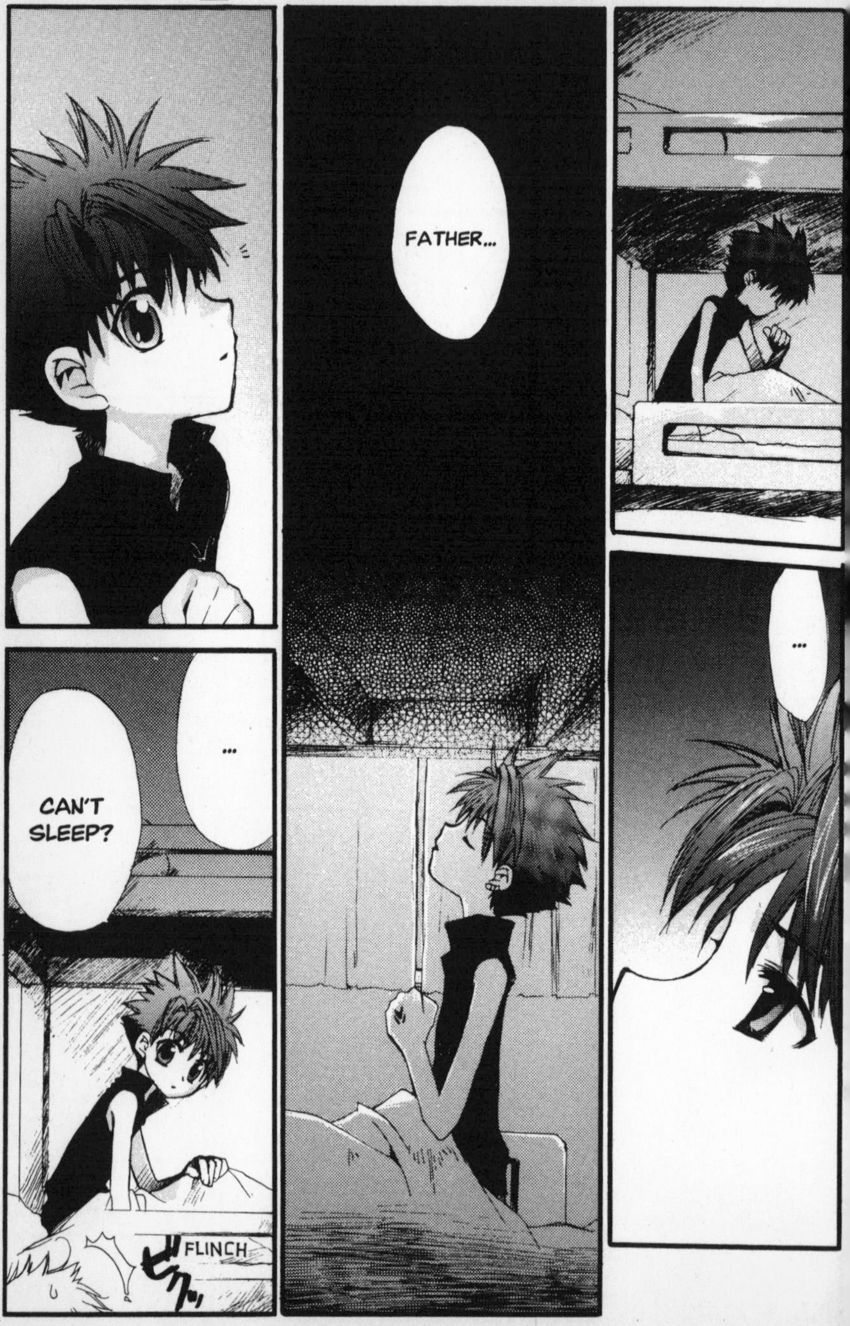
...
FATHER...
...
CAN'T SLEEP?
FLINCH

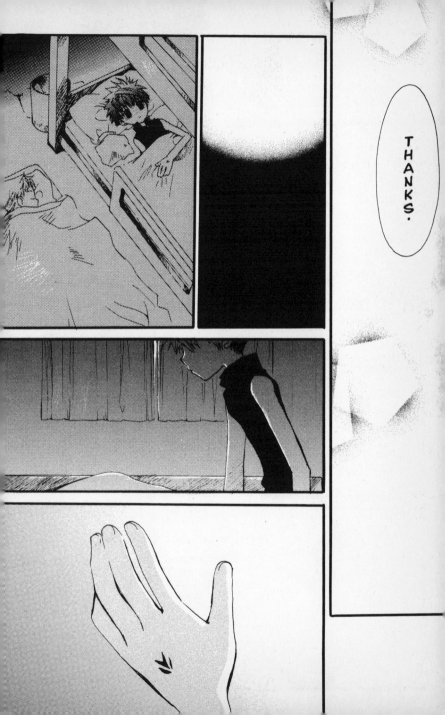

THANKS.

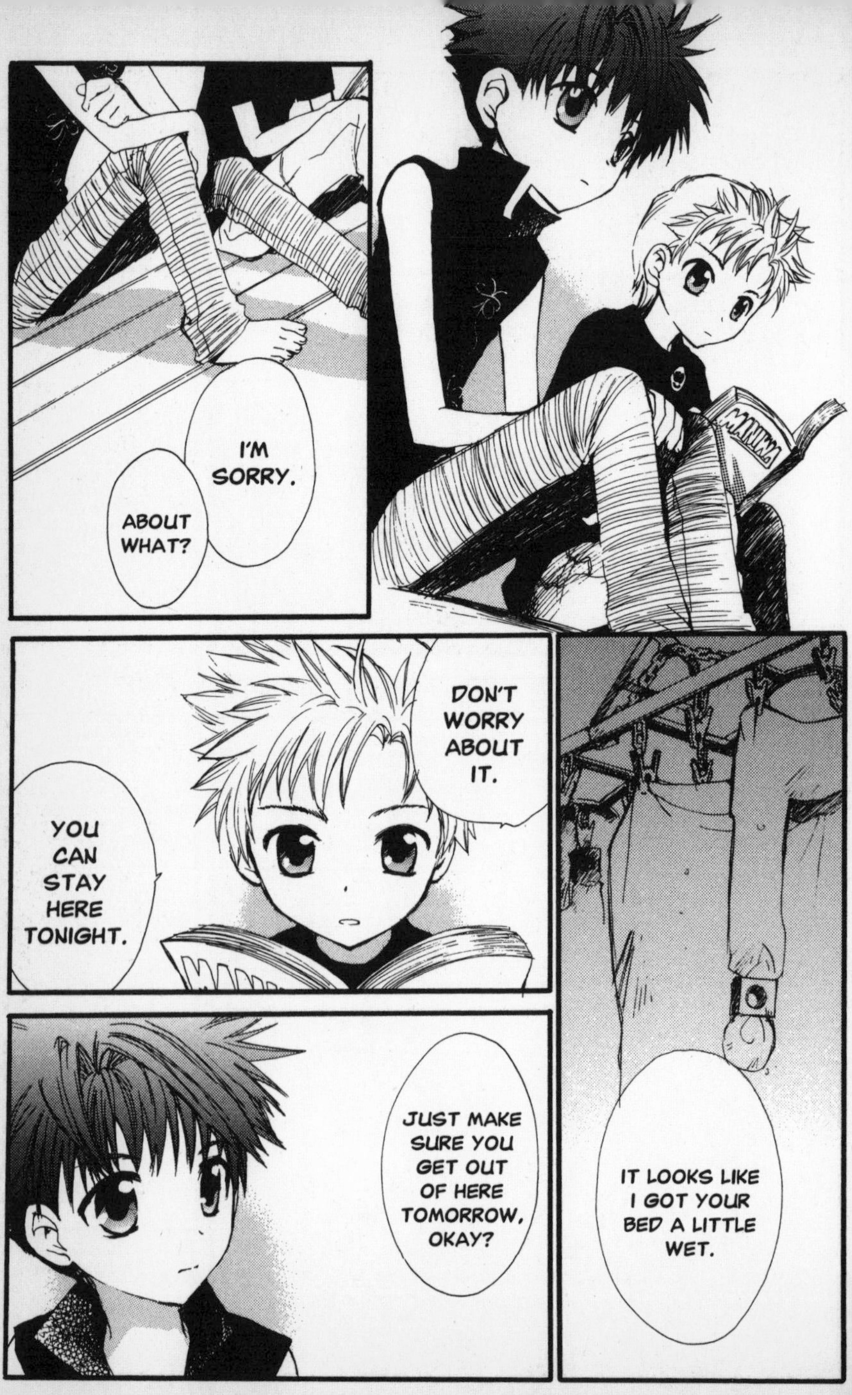
I'M SORRY.
ABOUT WHAT?
IT LOOKS LIKE I GOT YOUR BED A LITTLE WET.
DON'T WORRY ABOUT IT.
YOU CAN STAY HERE TONIGHT.
JUST MAKE SURE YOU GET OUT OF HERE TOMORROW, OKAY?

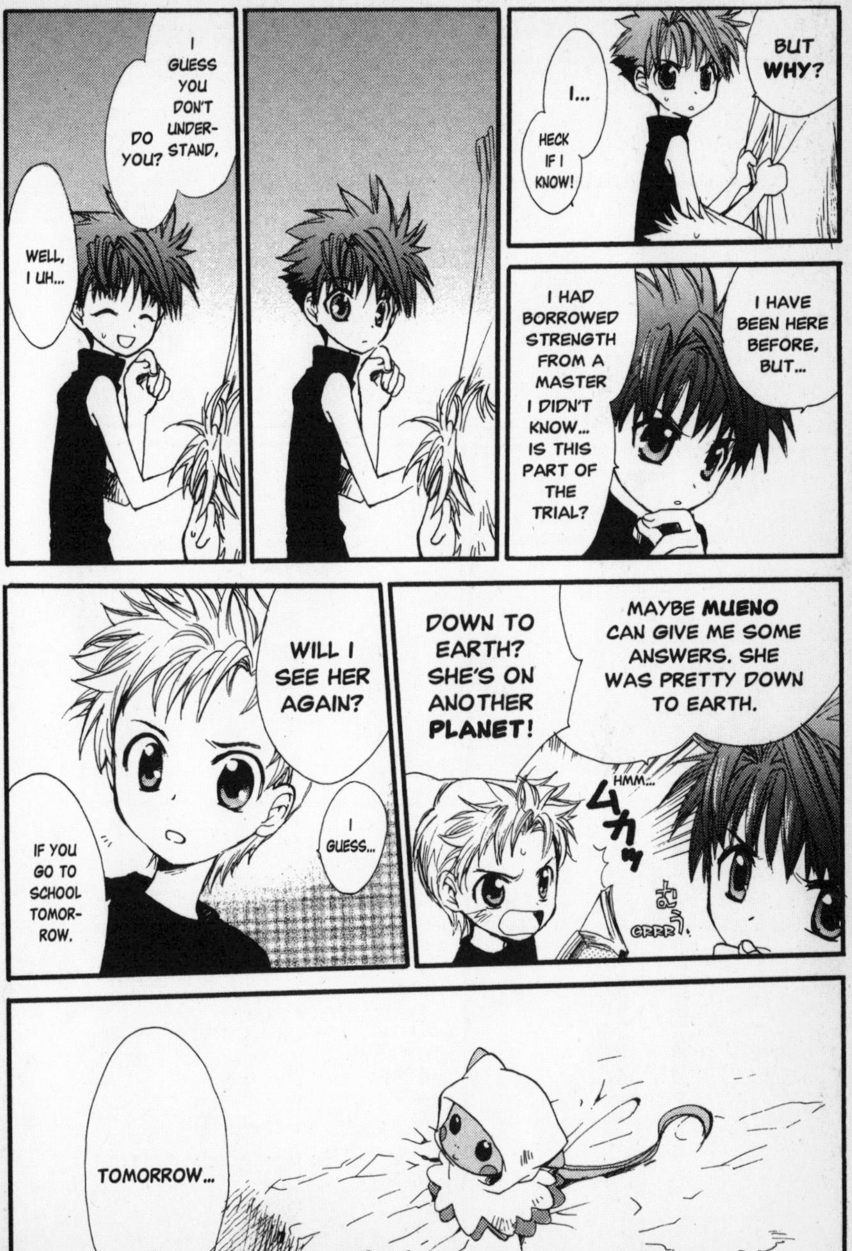
BUT WHY?
I...
HECK IF I KNOW!
I HAVE BEEN HERE BEFORE, BUT...
I HAD BORROWED STRENGTH FROM A MASTER I DIDN'T KNOW... IS THIS PART OF THE TRIAL?
I GUESS YOU DON'T UNDER-STAND,
DO YOU?
WELL, I UH...
MAYBE MUENO CAN GIVE ME SOME ANSWERS. SHE WAS PRETTY DOWN TO EARTH.
DOWN TO EARTH? SHE'S ON ANOTHER PLANET!
HMM...
GRRR
WILL I SEE HER AGAIN?
I GUESS...
IF YOU GO TO SCHOOL TOMOR-ROW.
TOMORROW...

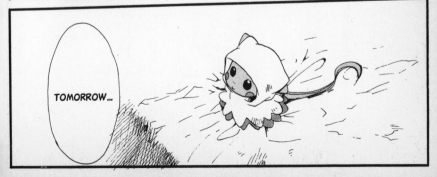

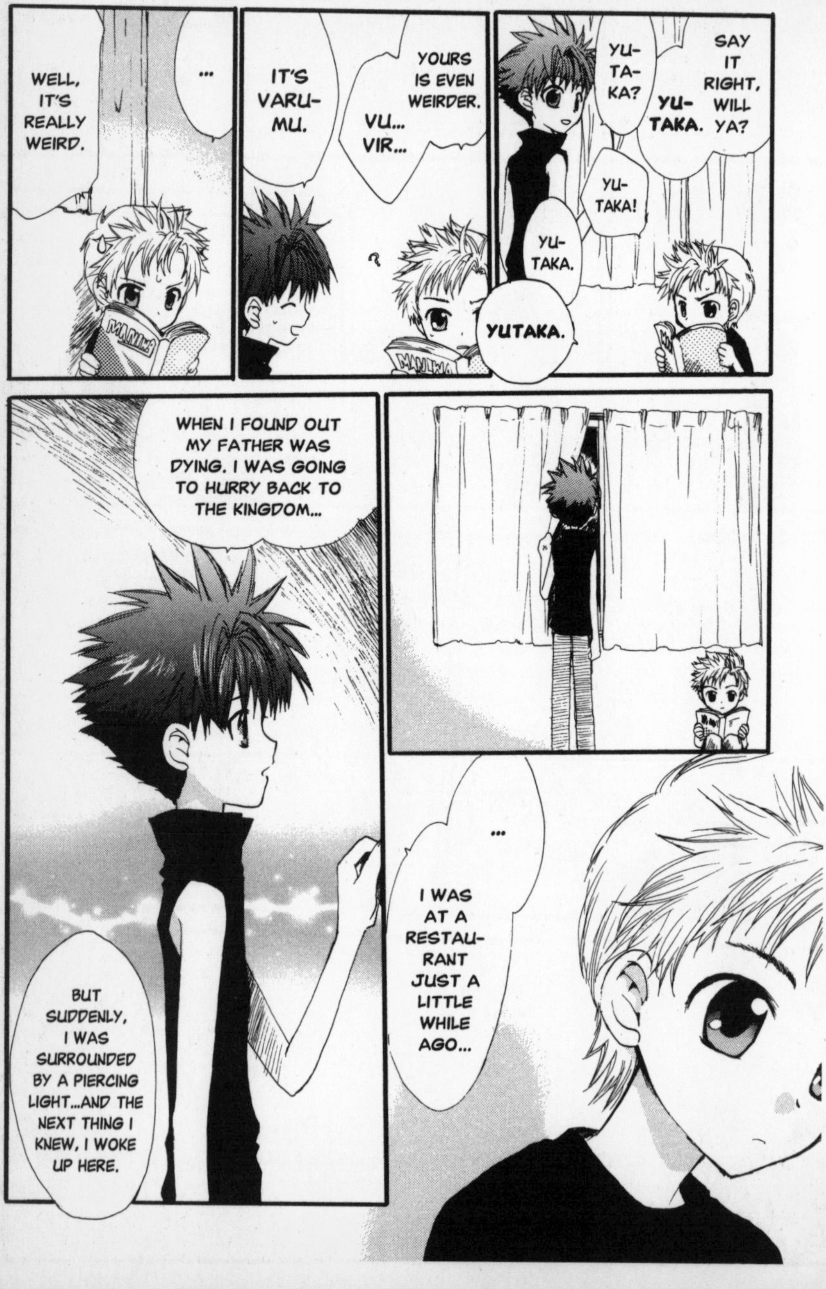
WELL, IT'S REALLY WEIRD.
...
IT'S VARUMU.
VU... VIR...
YOURS IS EVEN WEIRDER.
YUTAKA?
YUTAKA.
SAY IT RIGHT, WILL YA?
YUTAKA!
YUTAKA.
YUTAKA.
WHEN I FOUND OUT MY FATHER WAS DYING, I WAS GOING TO HURRY BACK TO THE KINGDOM...
...
I WAS AT A RESTAURANT JUST A LITTLE WHILE AGO...
BUT SUDDENLY, I WAS SURROUNDED BY A PIERCING LIGHT...AND THE NEXT THING I KNEW, I WOKE UP HERE.

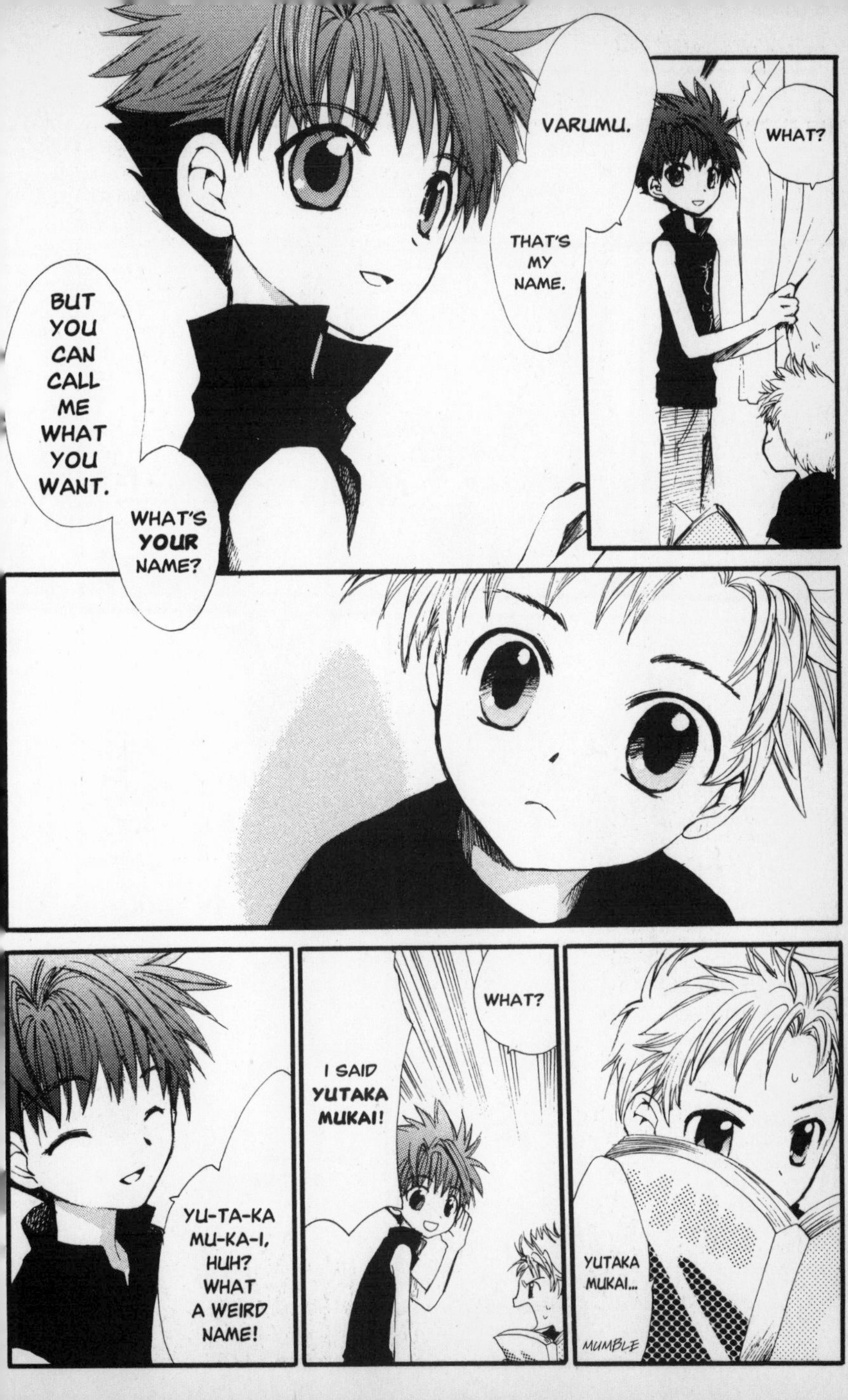

WHAT?
VARUMU.
THAT'S MY NAME.
BUT YOU CAN CALL ME WHAT YOU WANT.
WHAT'S YOUR NAME?
YUTAKA MUKAI...
MUMBLE
WHAT?
I SAID YUTAKA MUKAI!
YU-TA-KA MU-KA-I, HUH? WHAT A WEIRD NAME!

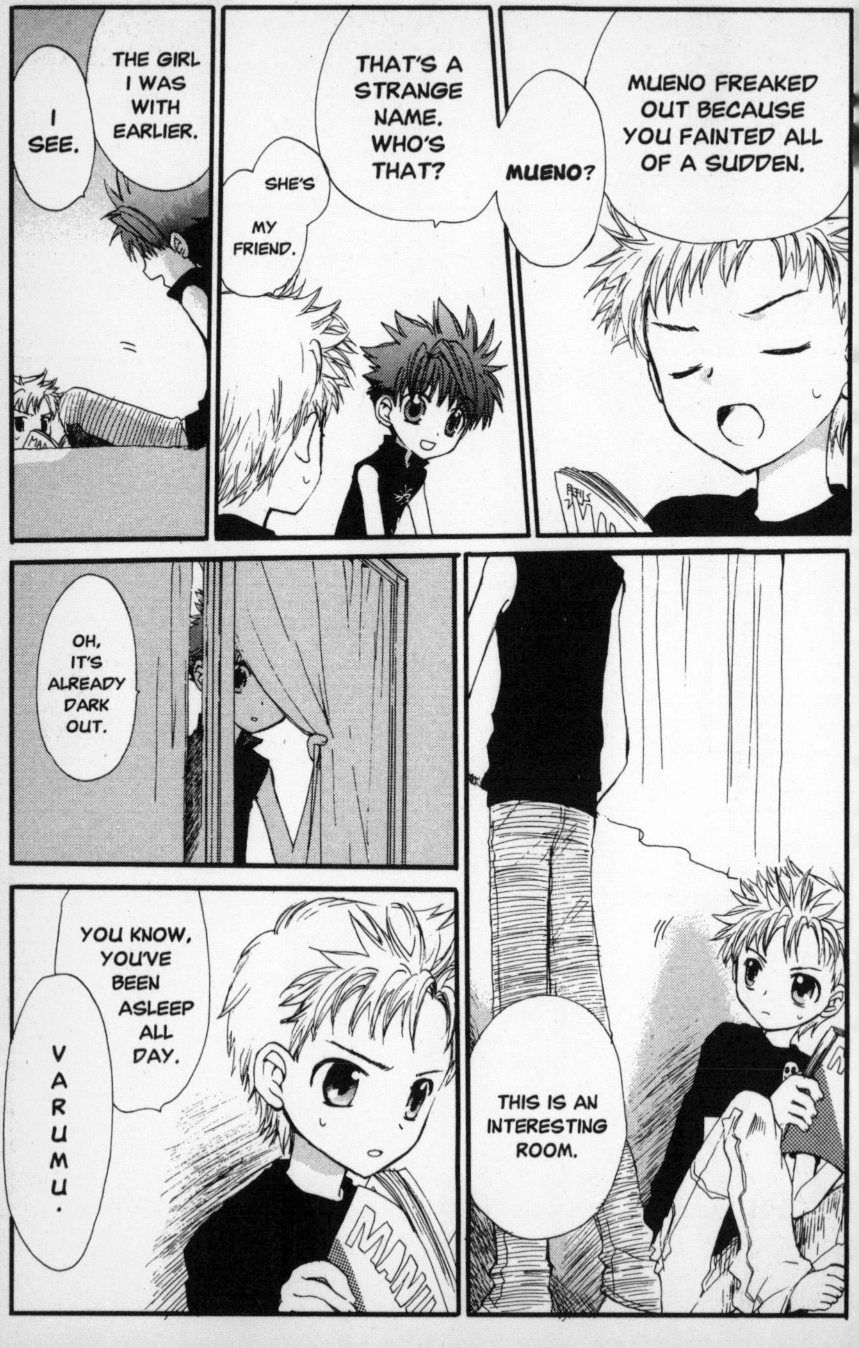
MUENO FREAKED OUT BECAUSE YOU FAINTED ALL OF A SUDDEN.
MUENO?
THAT'S A STRANGE NAME. WHO'S THAT?
SHE'S MY FRIEND.
THE GIRL I WAS WITH EARLIER.
I SEE.
THIS IS AN INTERESTING ROOM.
OH, IT'S ALREADY DARK OUT.
YOU KNOW, YOU'VE BEEN ASLEEP ALL DAY.
VARUMU.

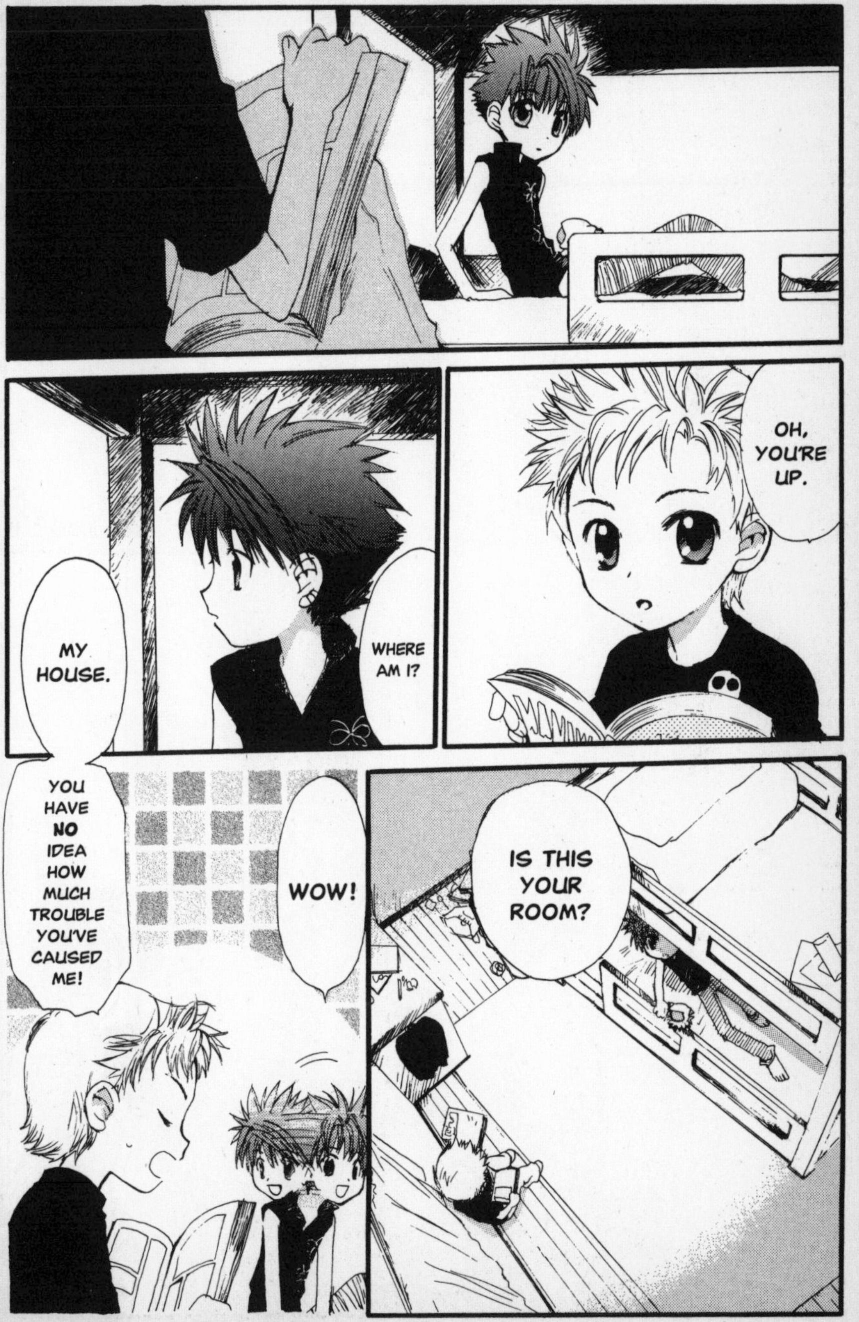

OH, YOU'RE UP.
WHERE AM I?
MY HOUSE.
IS THIS YOUR ROOM?
WOW!
YOU HAVE **NO** IDEA HOW MUCH TROUBLE YOU'VE CAUSED ME!

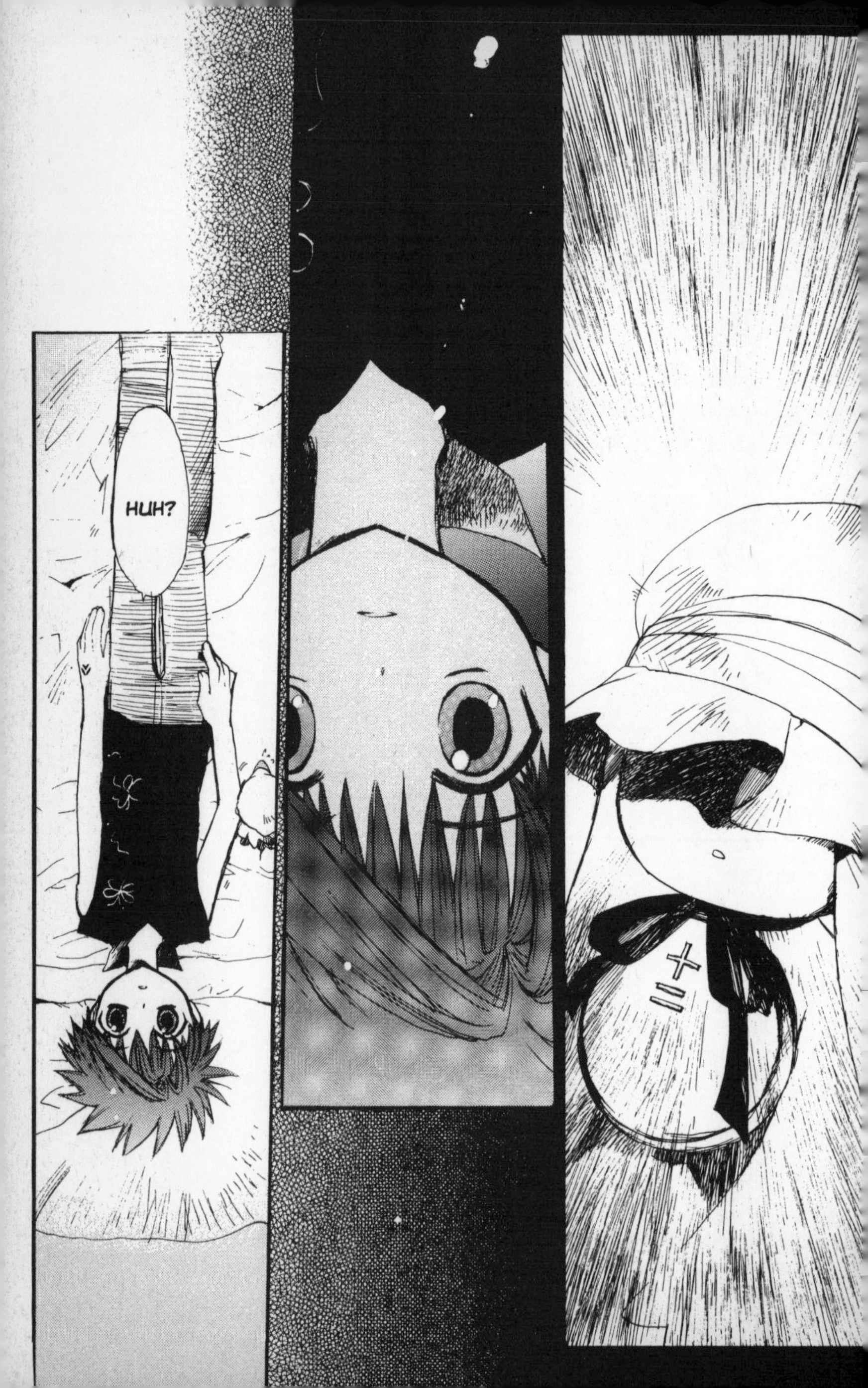
HUH?

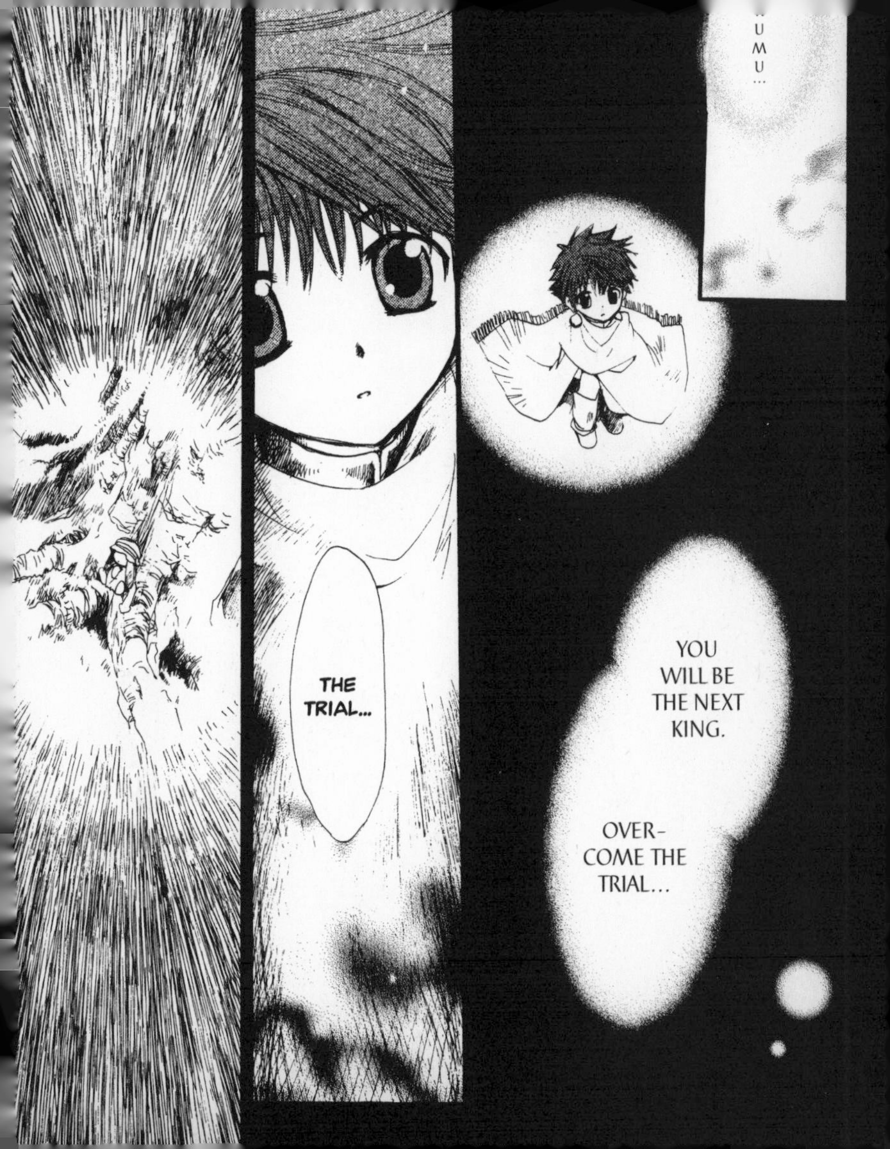
..UMU...
YOU WILL BE THE NEXT KING.
OVER-COME THE TRIAL...
THE TRIAL...

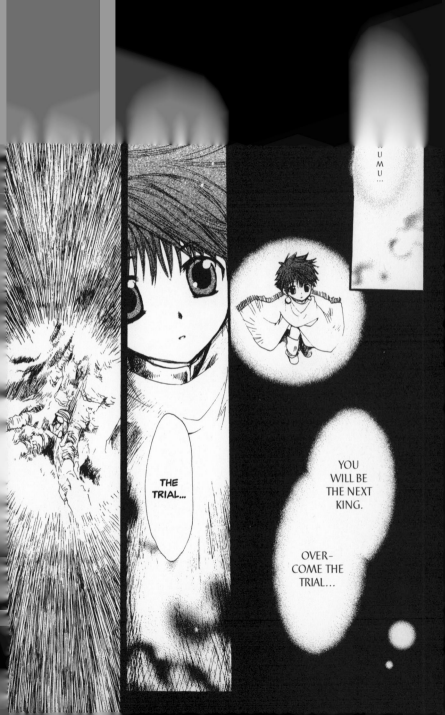

CHAPTER 3
IT BEGINS BY ACCIDENT

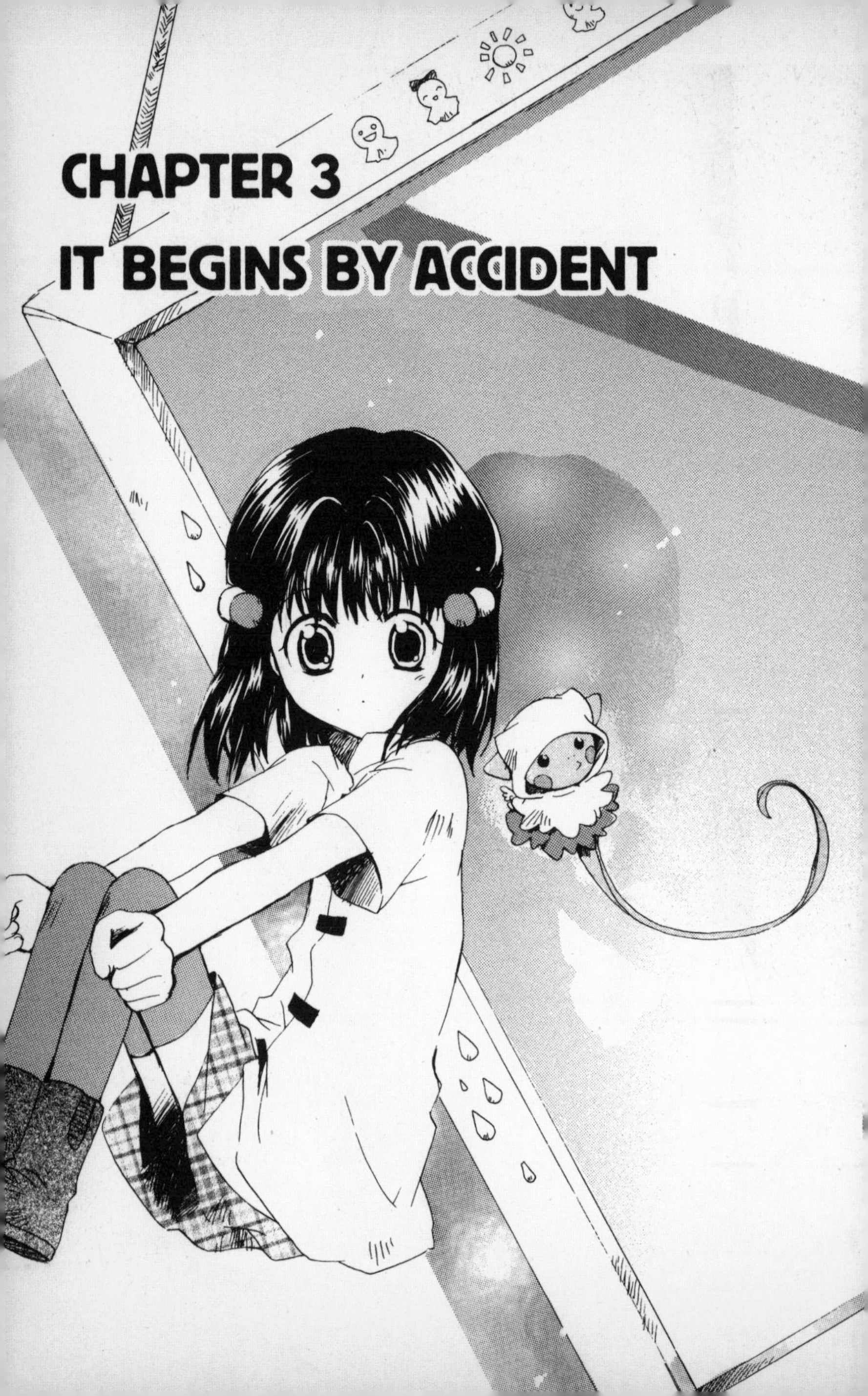

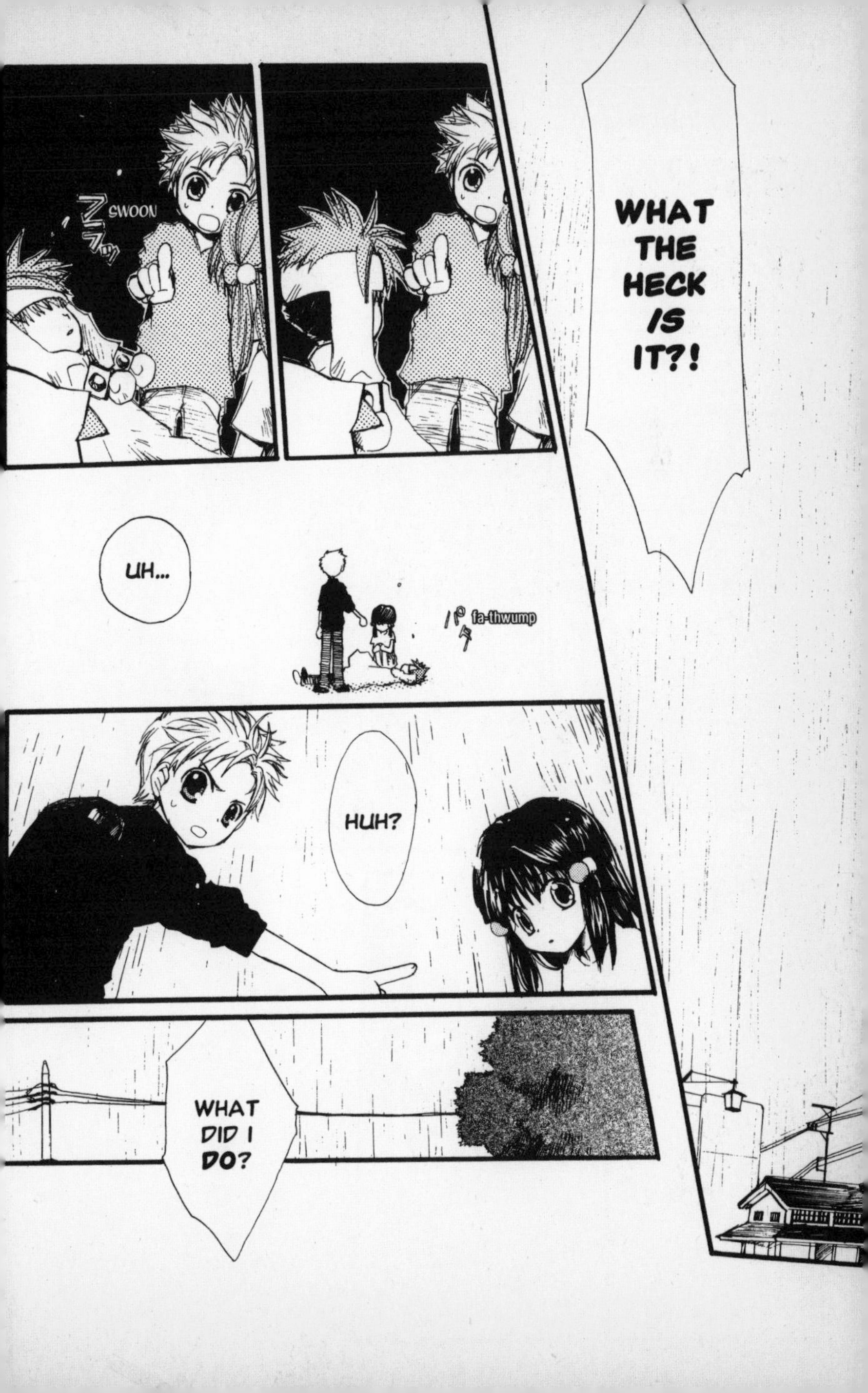
WHAT THE HECK IS IT?!
SWOON
UH...
fa-thwump
HUH?
WHAT DID I DO?

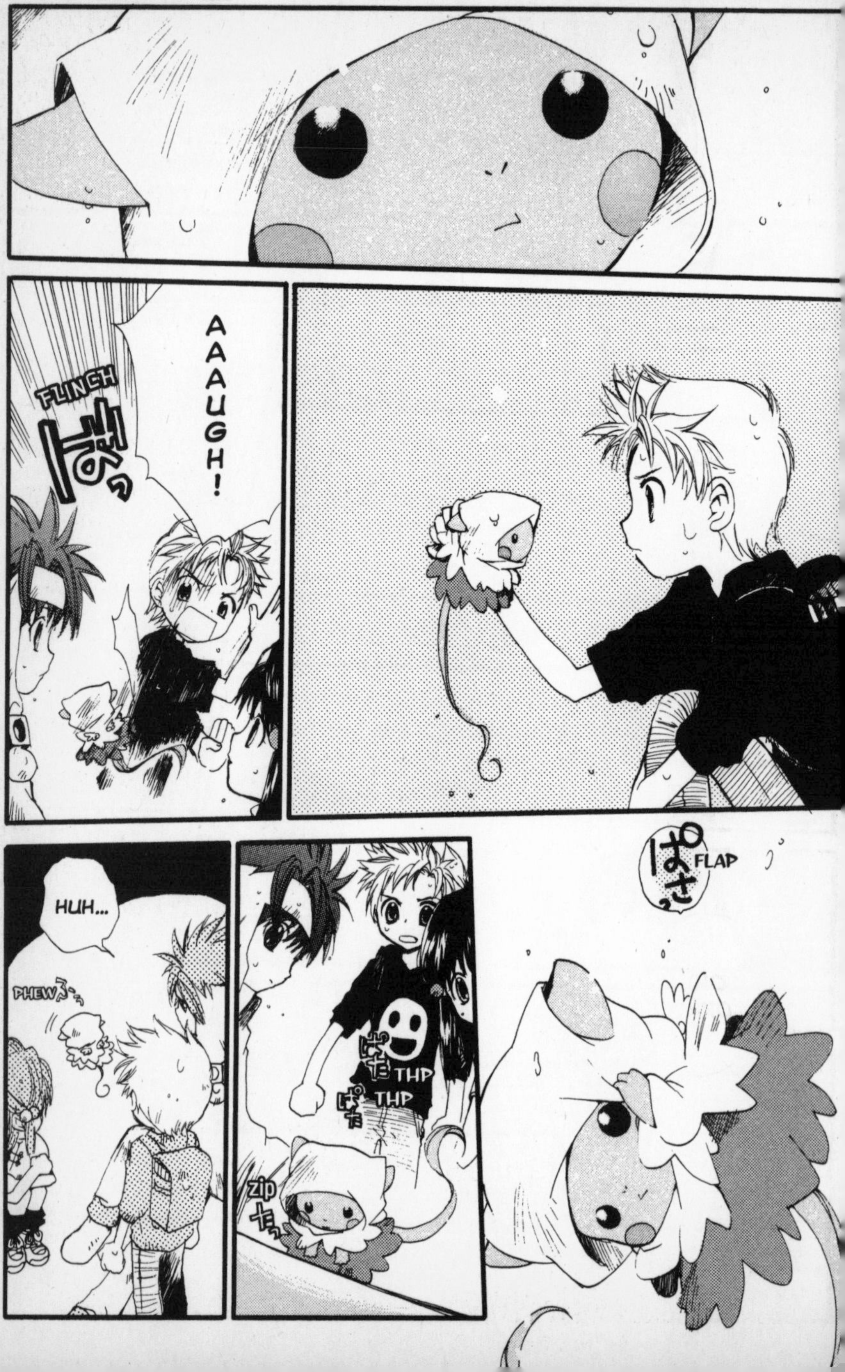
AAAAUGH!
FLINCH ぱっ
ぱさっ FLAP
ぱた THP
ぱた THP
zip たっ
HUH...
PHEW ふ〜っ

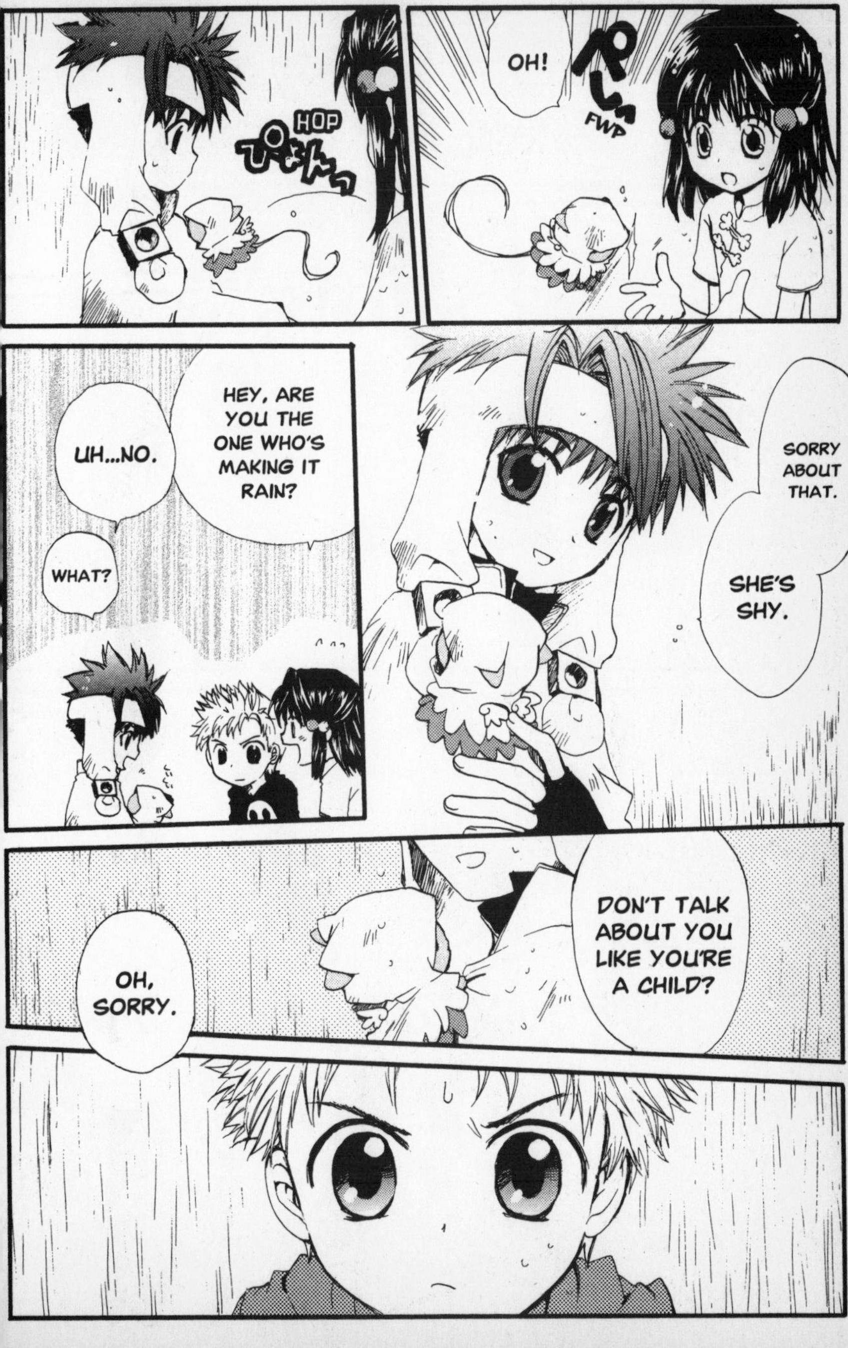
OH!
FWP
HOP
SORRY ABOUT THAT.
SHE'S SHY.
HEY, ARE YOU THE ONE WHO'S MAKING IT RAIN?
UH...NO.
WHAT?
DON'T TALK ABOUT YOU LIKE YOU'RE A CHILD?
OH, SORRY.

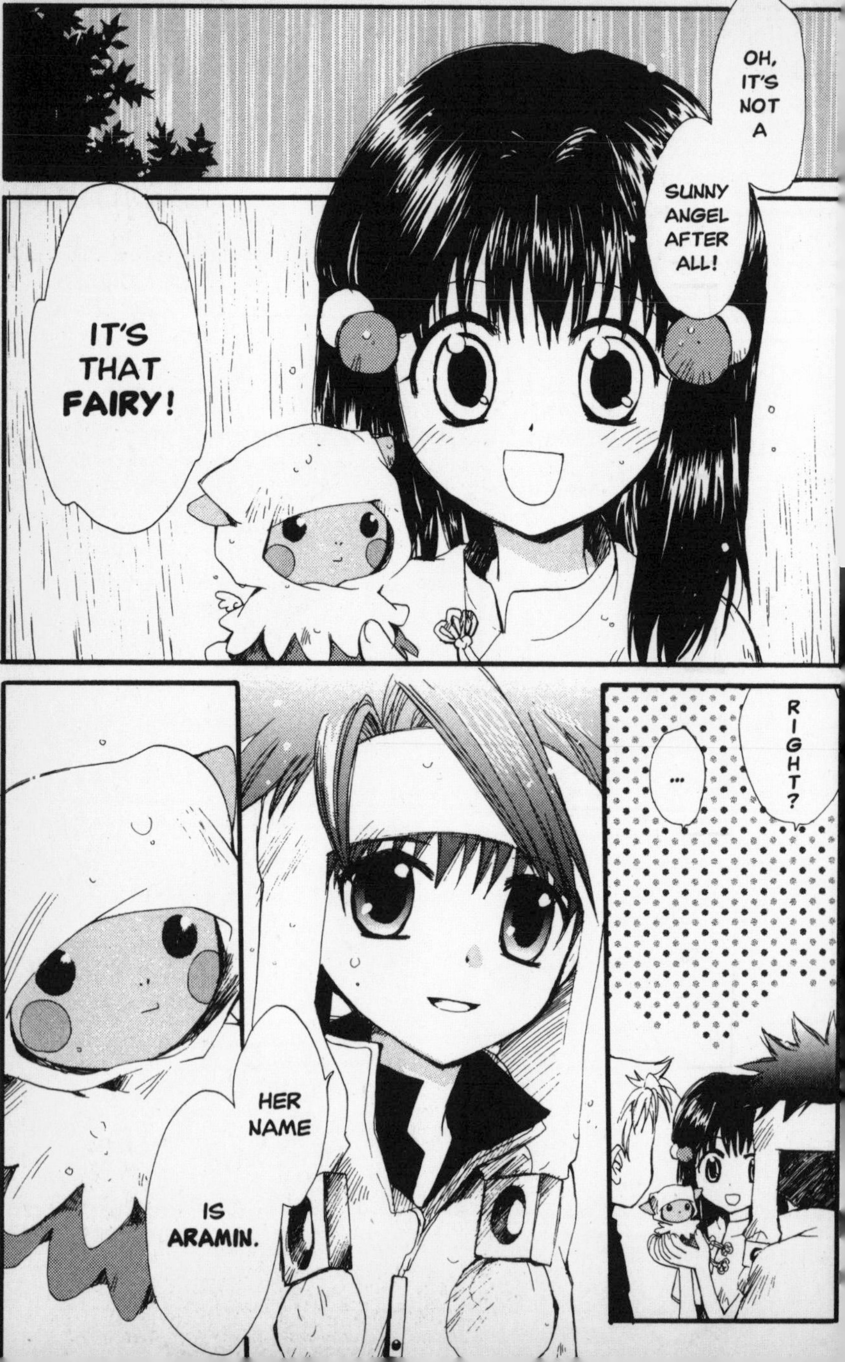
OH, IT'S NOT A SUNNY ANGEL AFTER ALL!
IT'S THAT FAIRY!
RIGHT?
...
HER NAME IS ARAMIN.

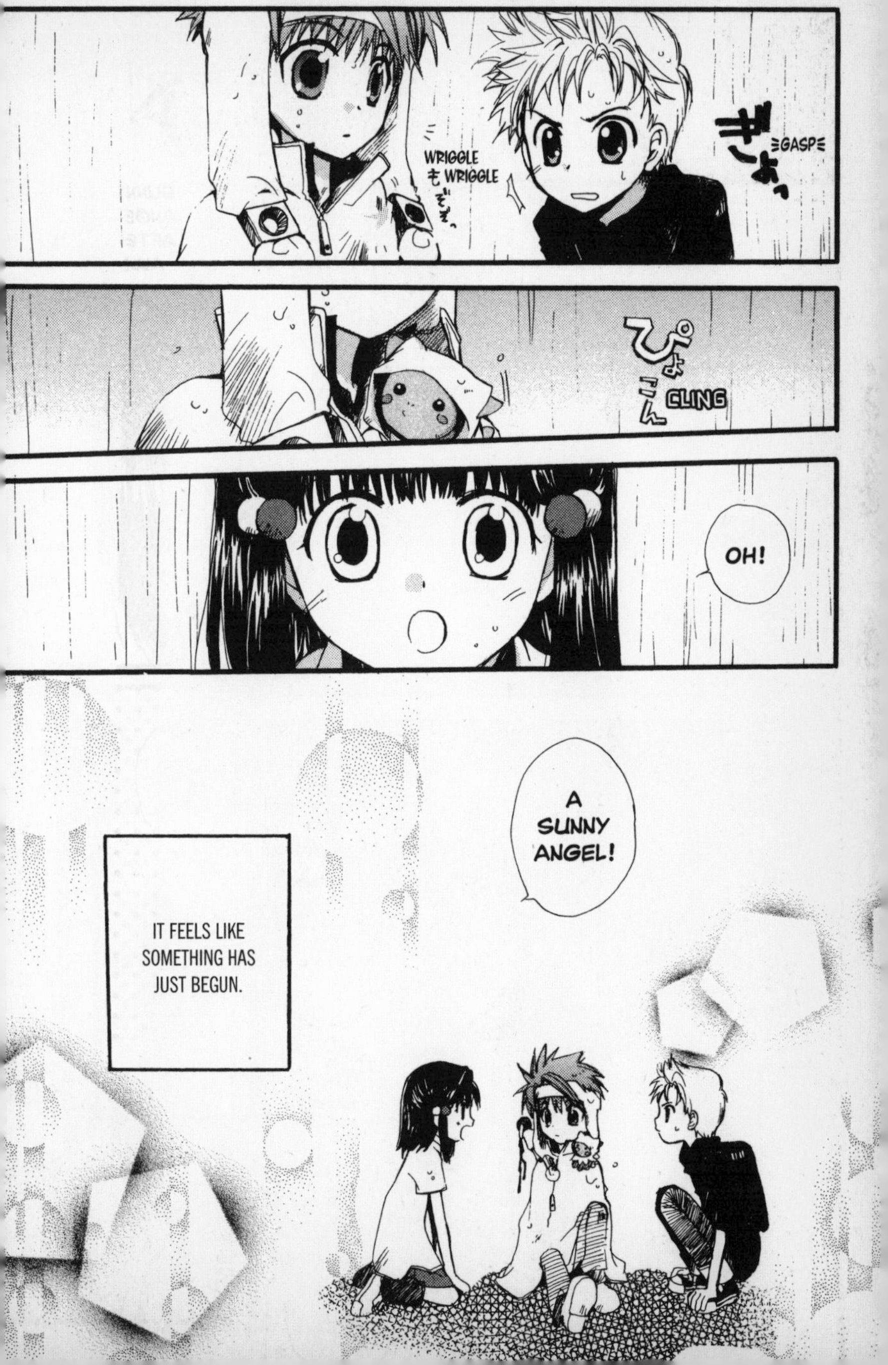
ぎょっ
GASP
WRIGGLE WRIGGLE
もぞもぞ
ぴょこん
CLING
OH!
A SUNNY ANGEL!
IT FEELS LIKE SOMETHING HAS JUST BEGUN.

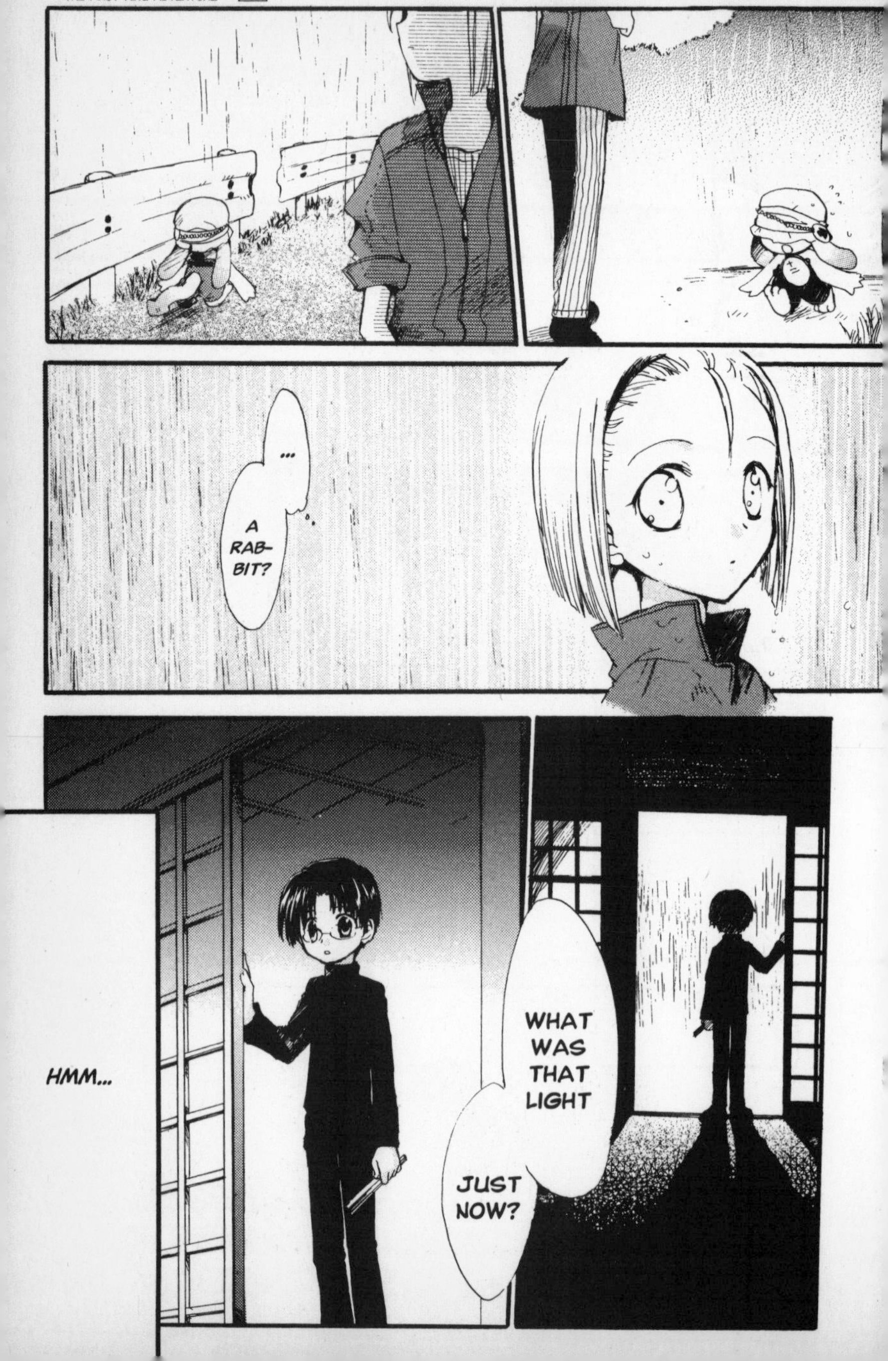
...
A RAB-BIT?
WHAT WAS THAT LIGHT
JUST NOW?
HMM...

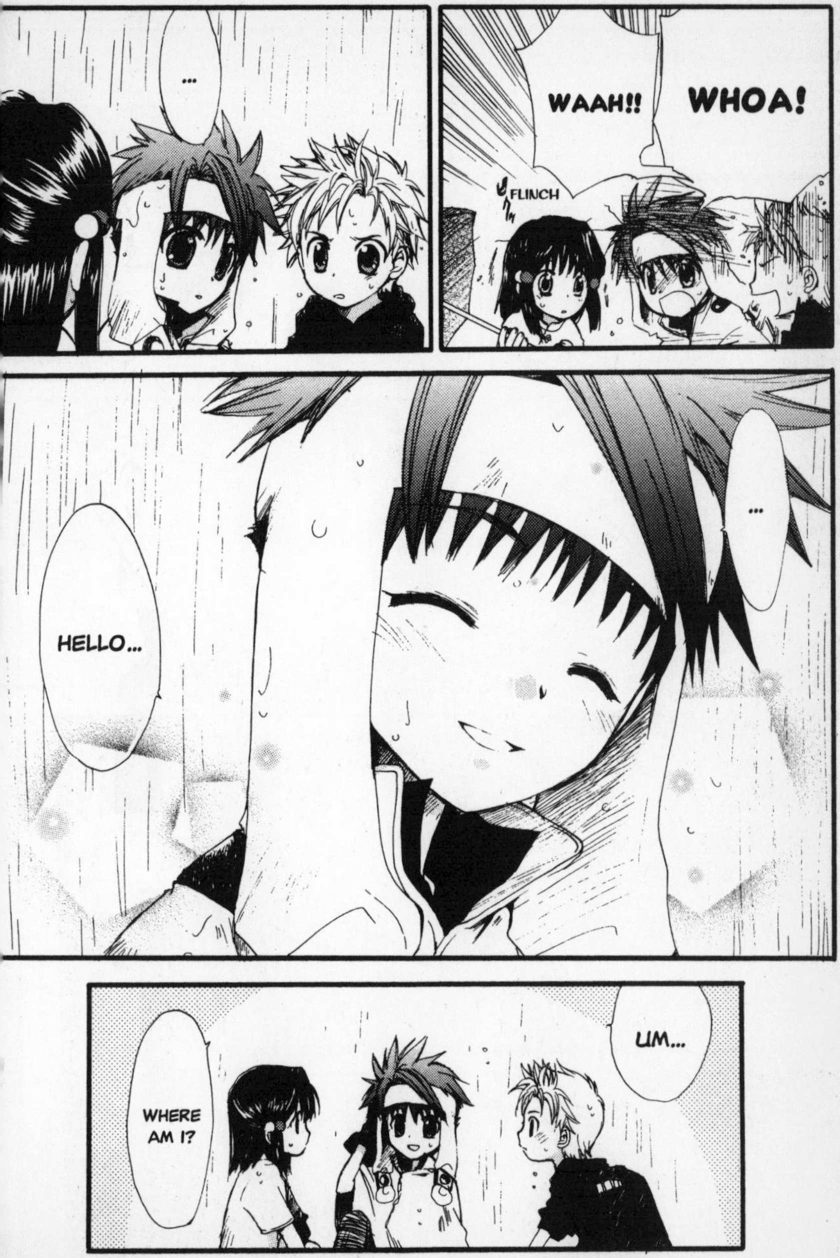
WHOA!
WAAH!!
FLINCH
...
...
HELLO...
UM...
WHERE AM I?

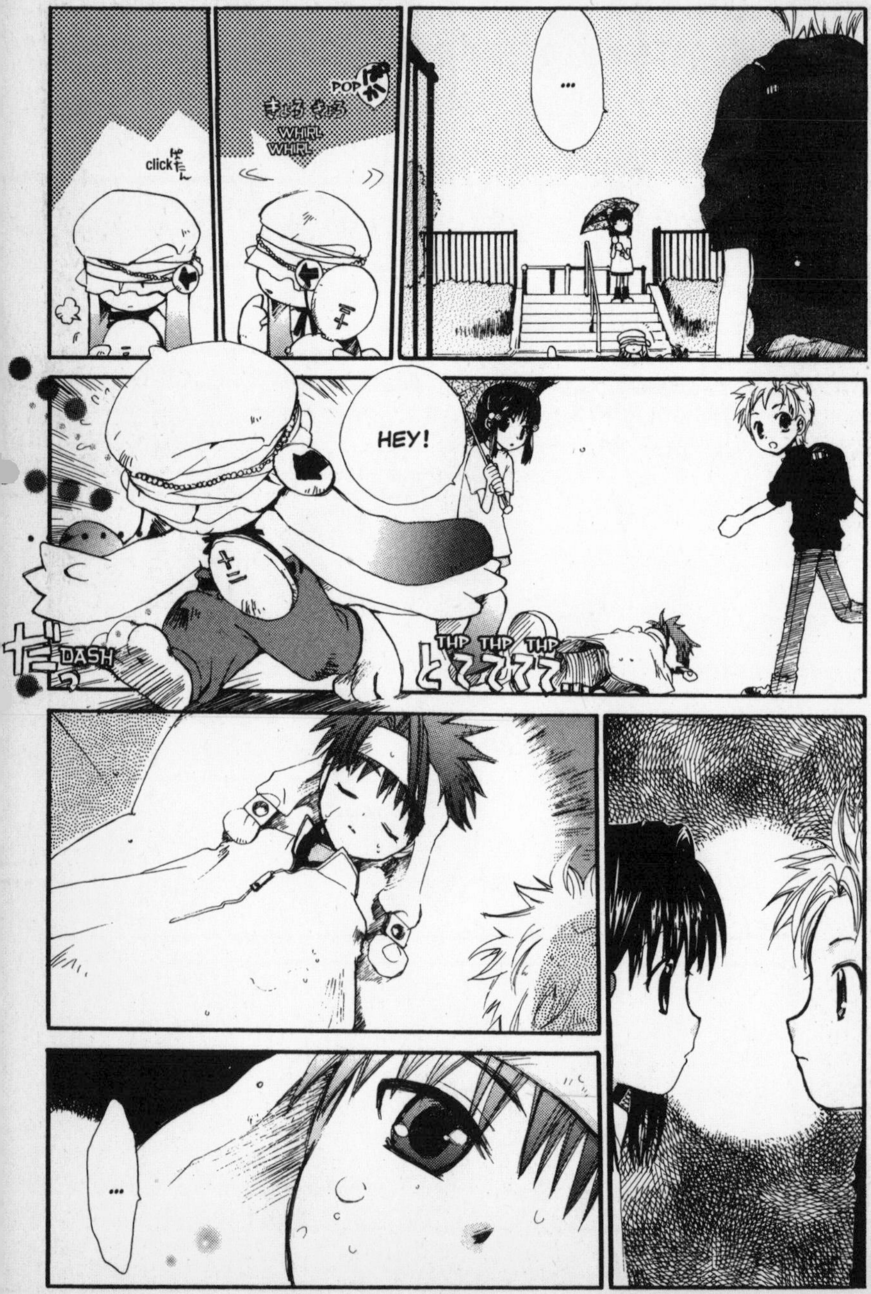
click
WHIRL WHIRL
POP
...
HEY!
DASH
THP THP THP
...

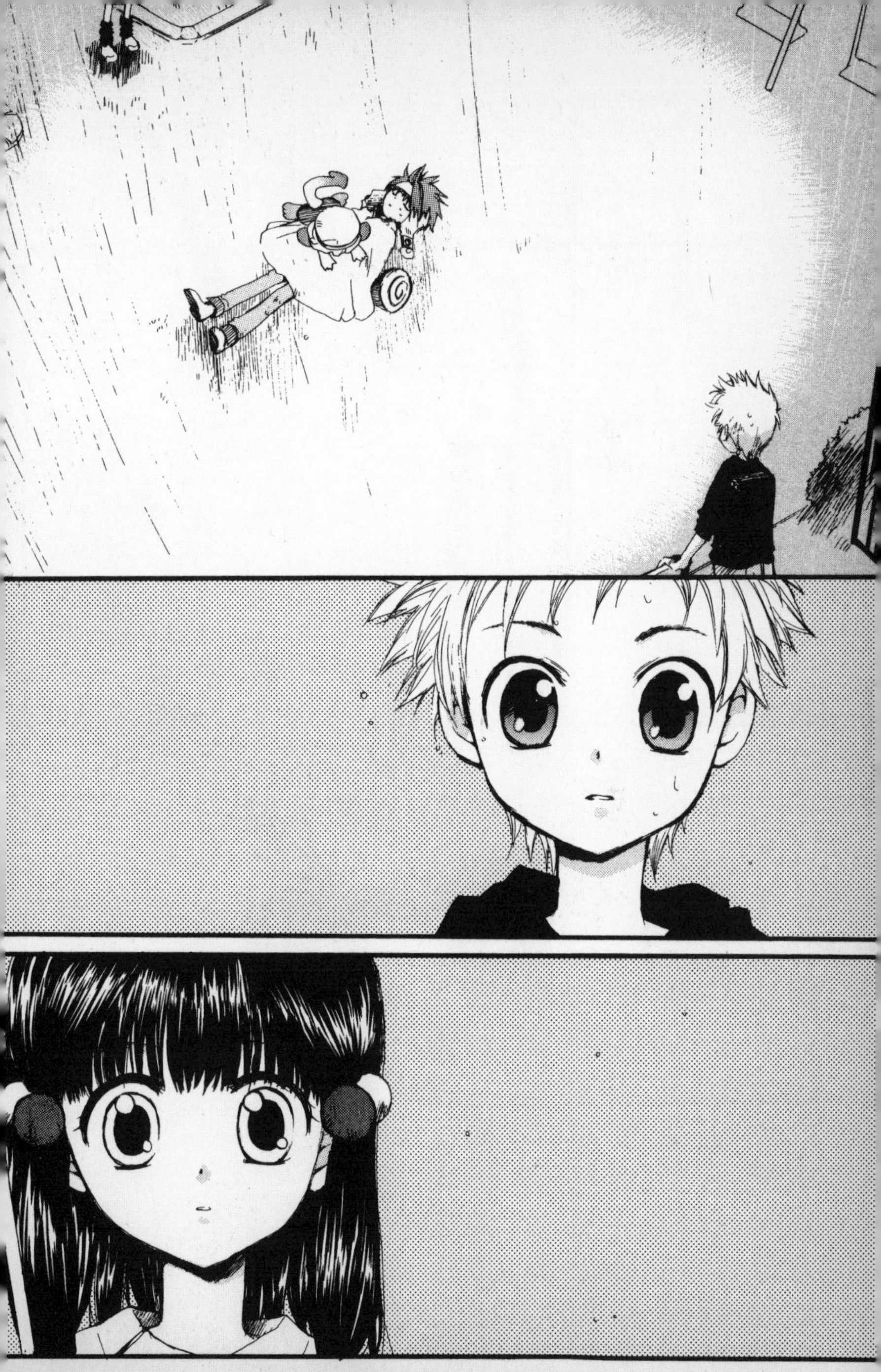

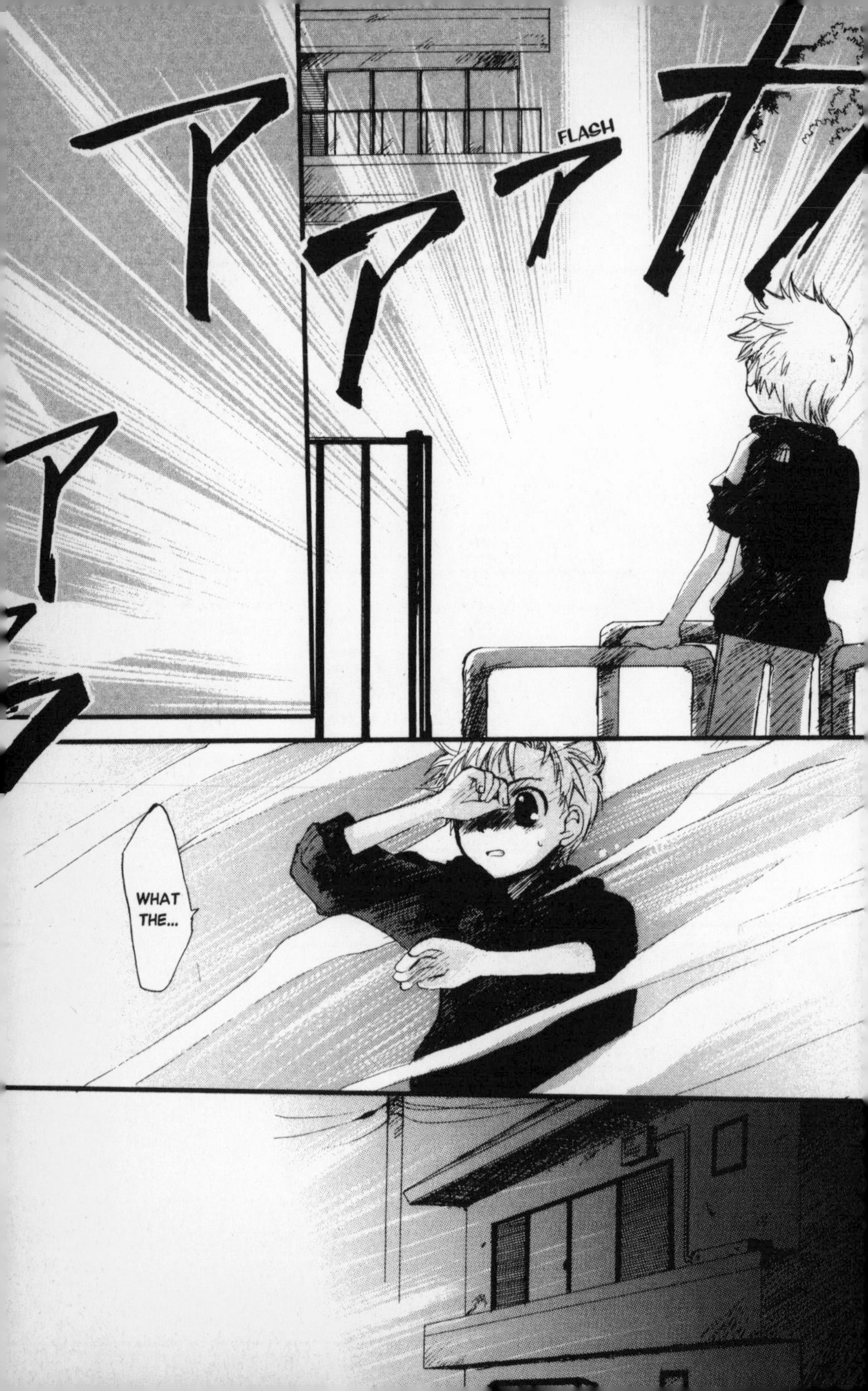

FLASH
WHAT THE...

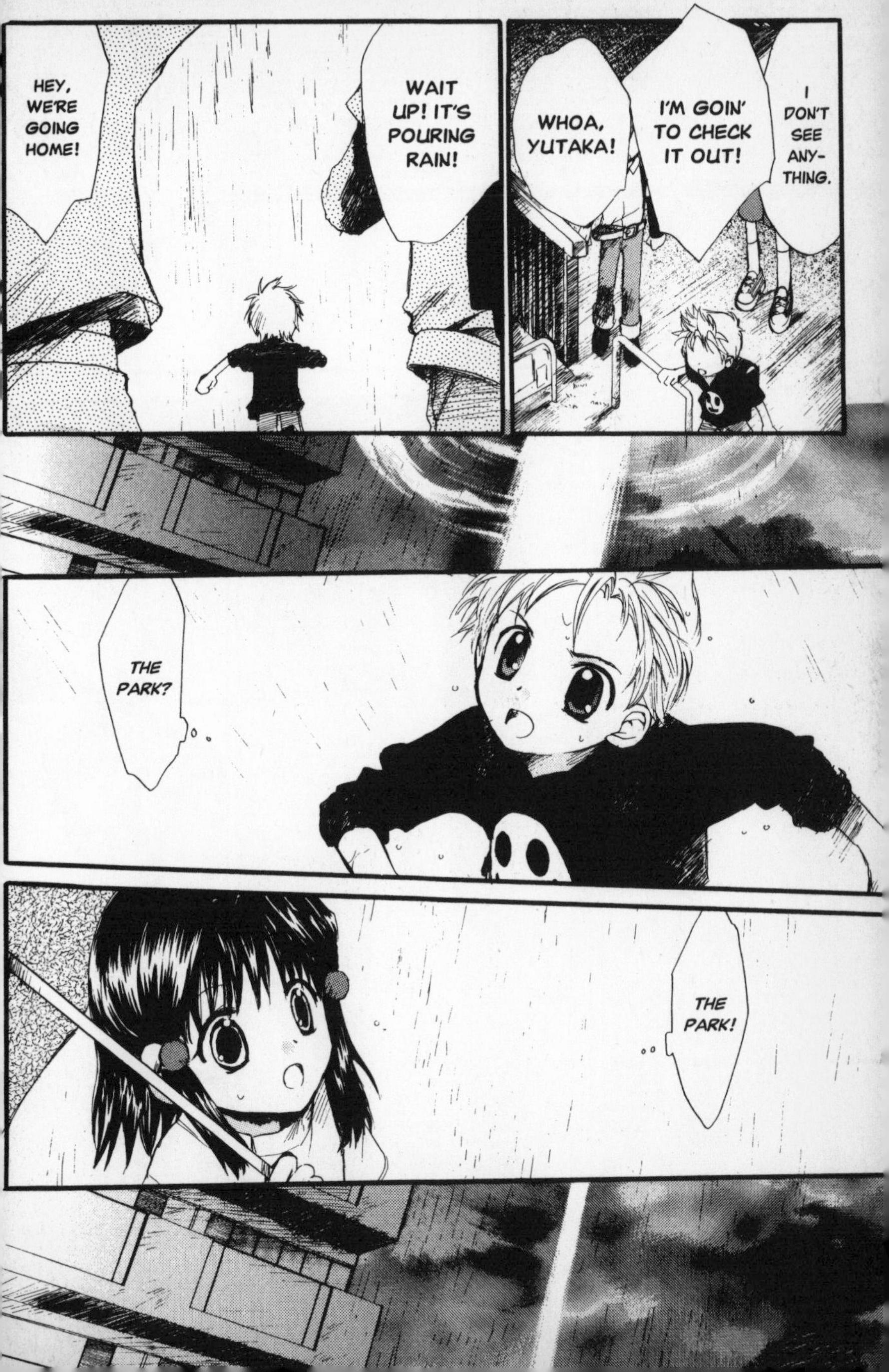
I DON'T SEE ANYTHING.
I'M GOIN' TO CHECK IT OUT!
WHOA, YUTAKA!
WAIT UP! IT'S POURING RAIN!
HEY, WE'RE GOING HOME!
THE PARK?
THE PARK!

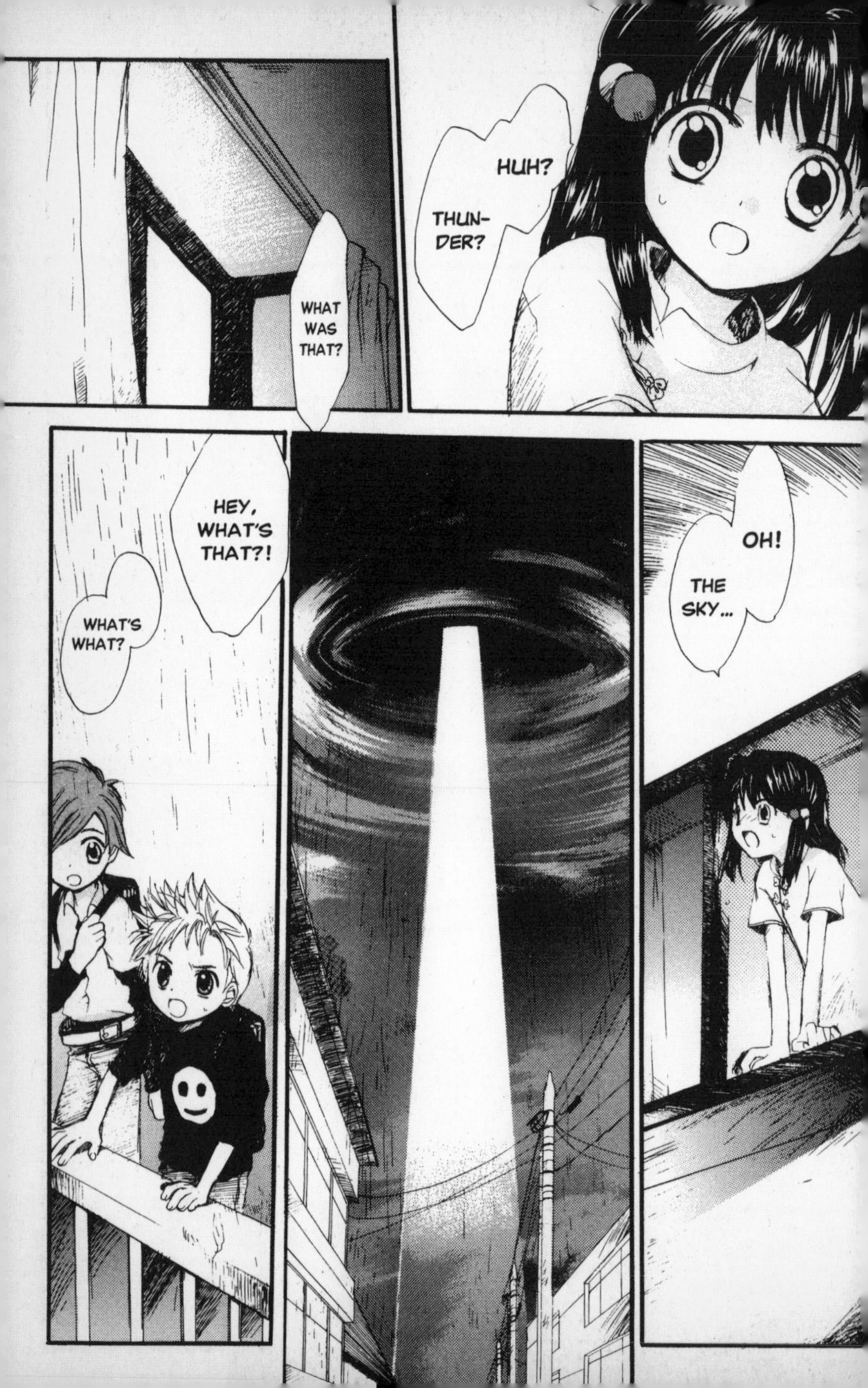
HUH?
THUN-DER?
WHAT WAS THAT?
OH!
THE SKY...
HEY, WHAT'S THAT?!
WHAT'S WHAT?

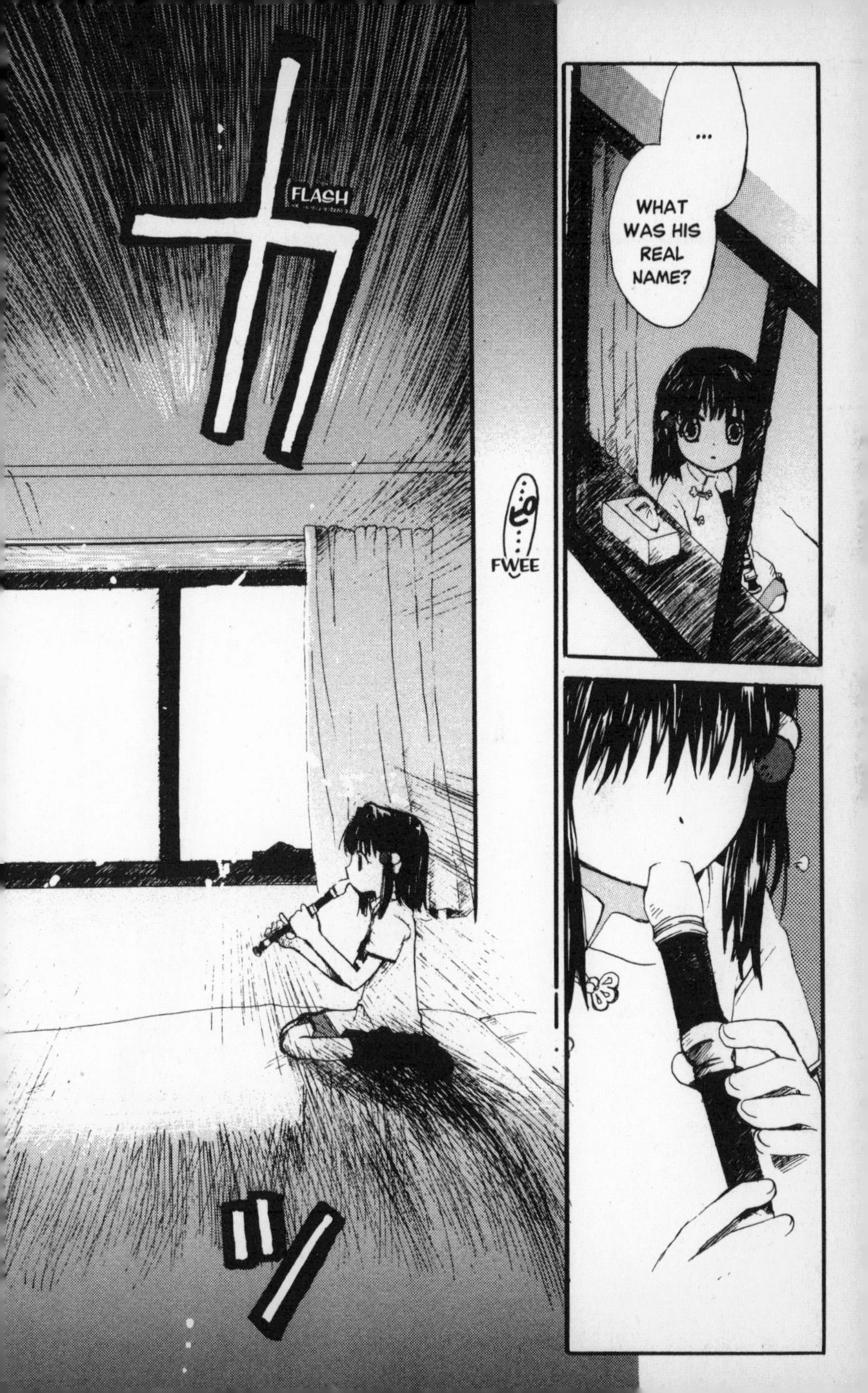
...
WHAT WAS HIS REAL NAME?
FLASH
FWEE

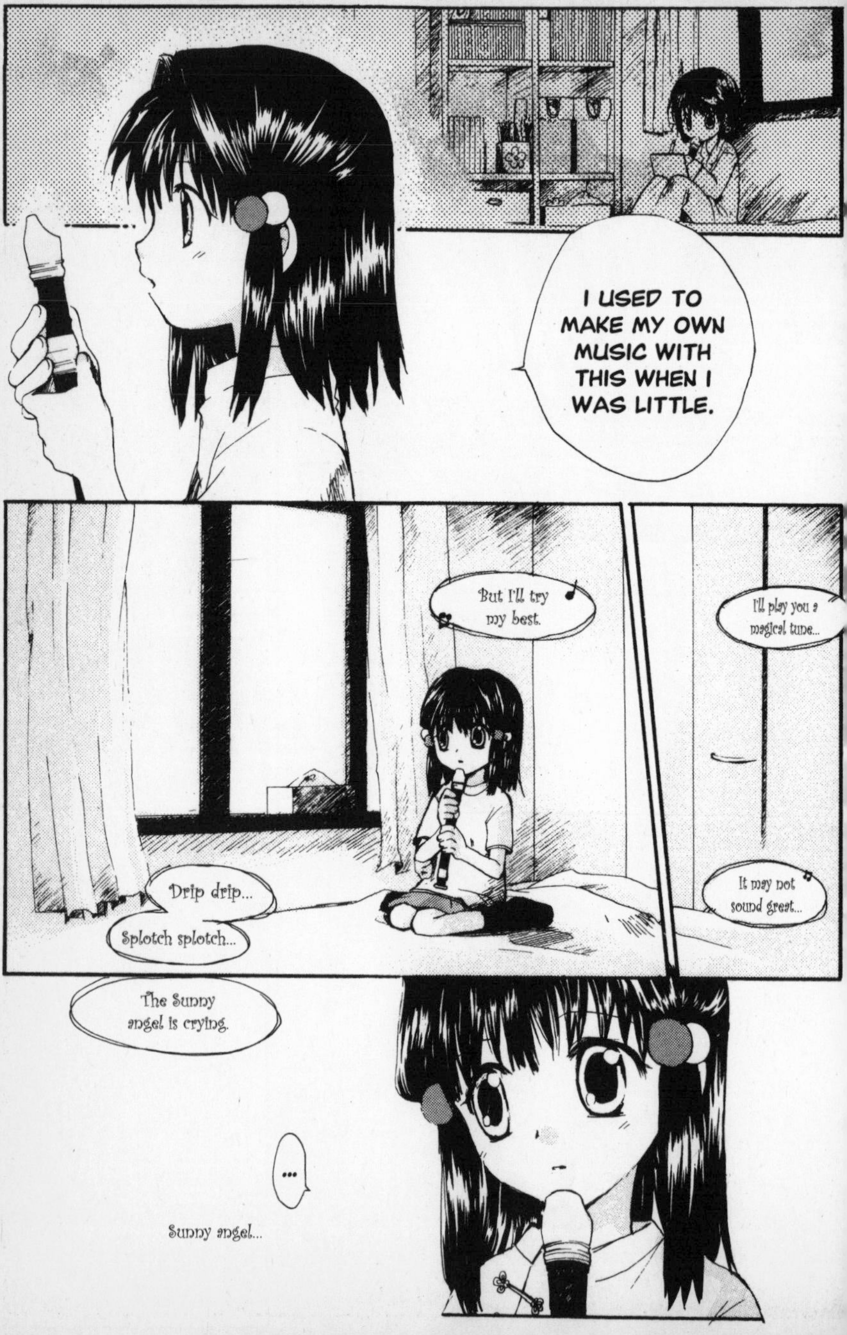
I USED TO MAKE MY OWN MUSIC WITH THIS WHEN I WAS LITTLE.
I'll play you a magical tune...
It may not sound great...
But I'll try my best.
Drip drip...
Splotch splotch...
The Sunny angel is crying.
...
Sunny angel...

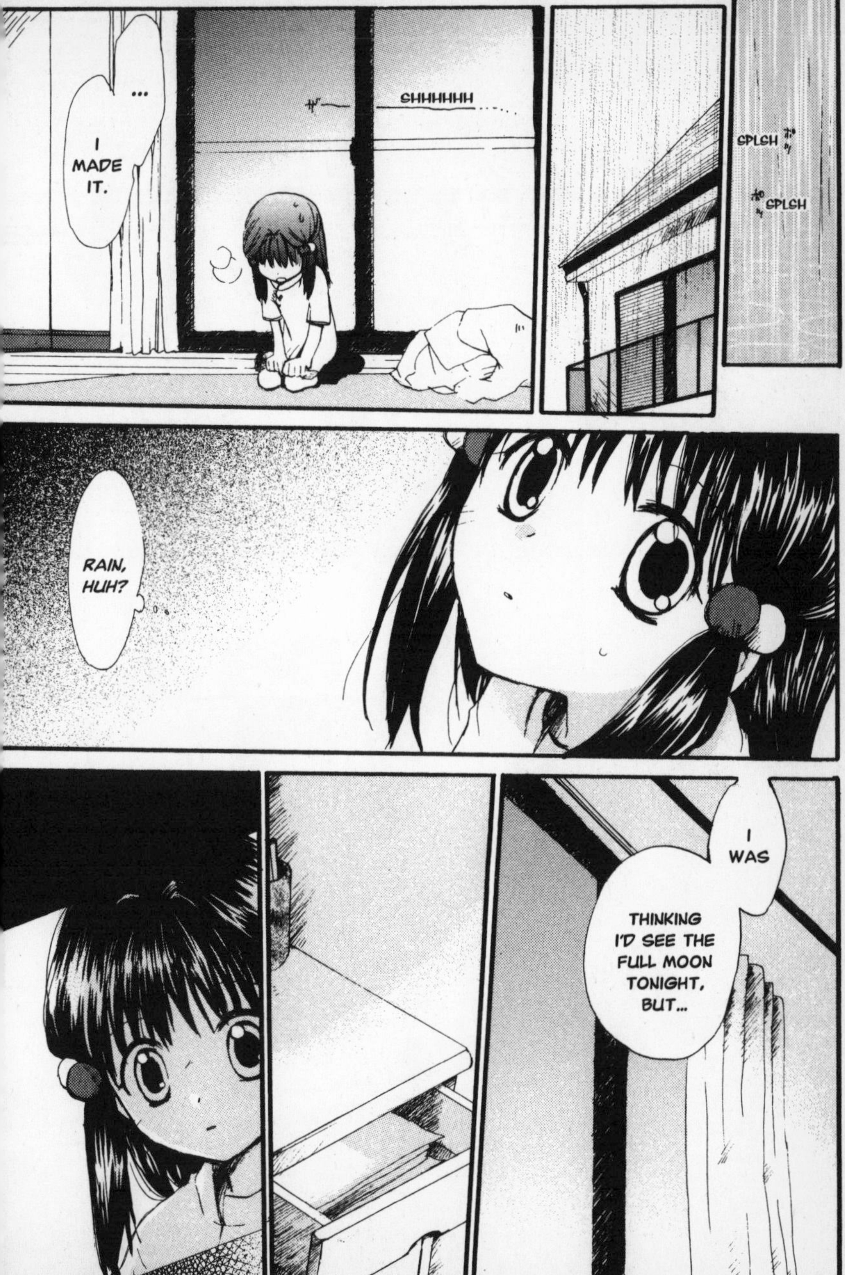
SPLSH
SPLSH
SHHHHHH
...
I MADE IT.
RAIN, HUH?
I WAS
THINKING I'D SEE THE FULL MOON TONIGHT, BUT...

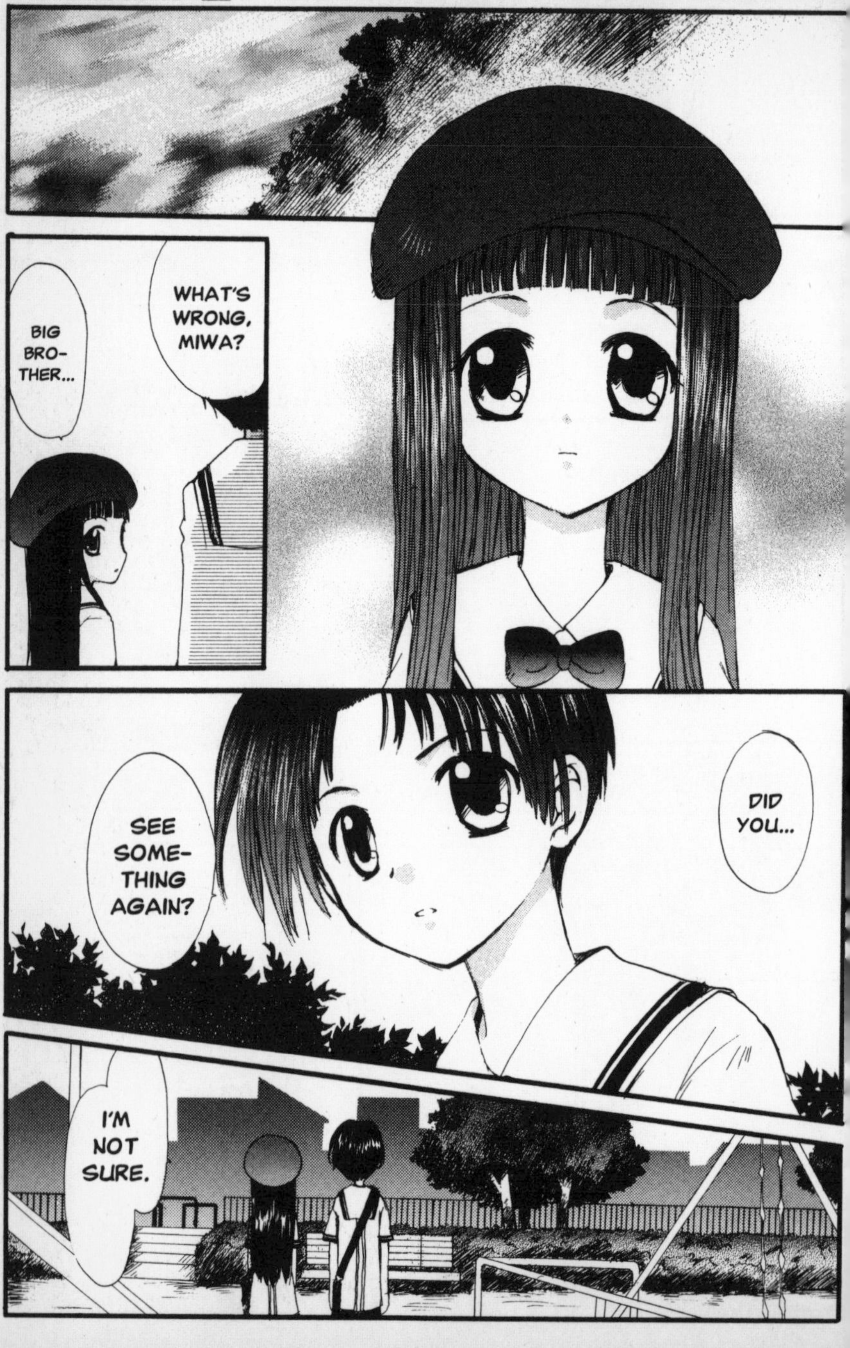
WHAT'S WRONG, MIWA?
BIG BROTHER...
DID YOU...
SEE SOMETHING AGAIN?
I'M NOT SURE.

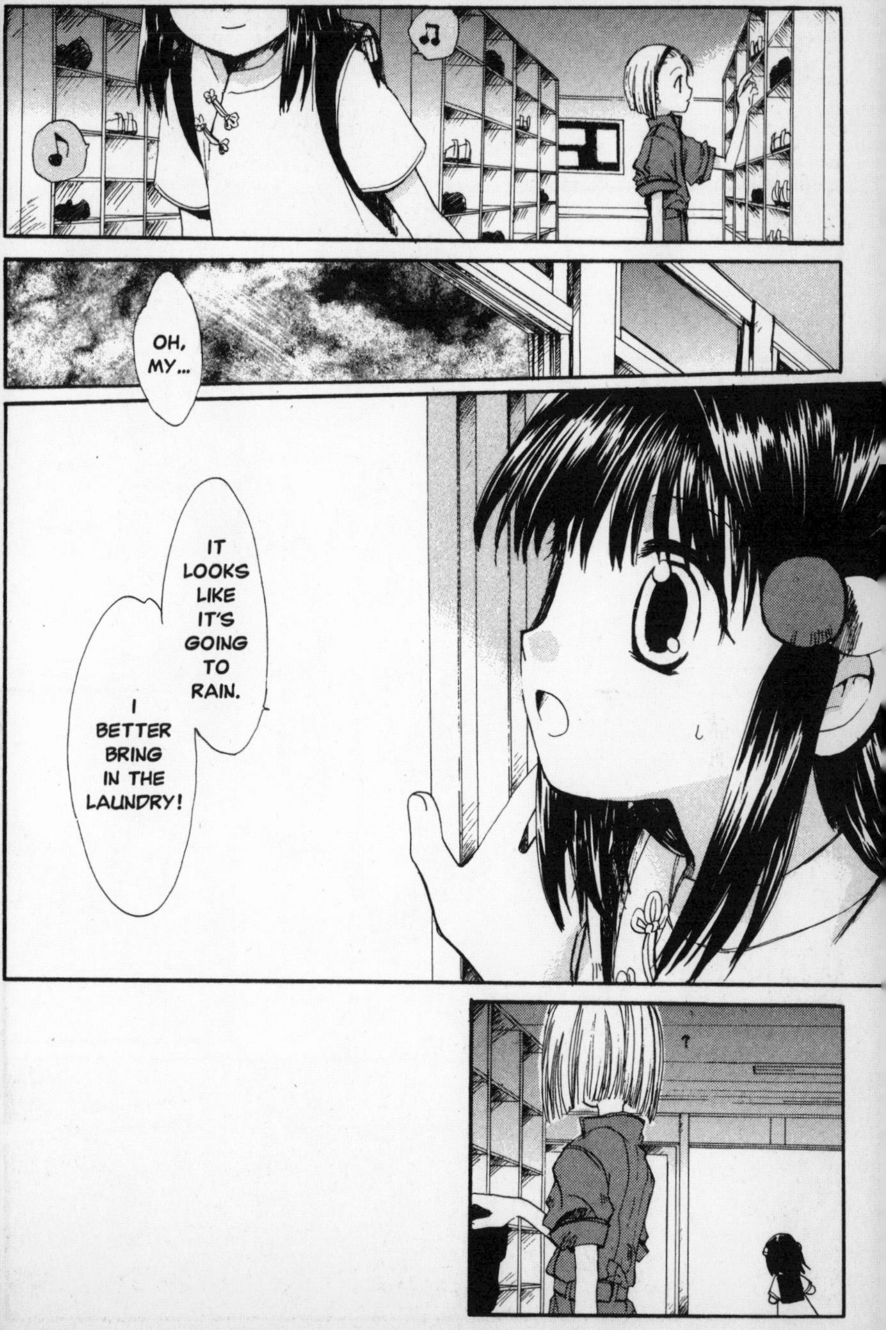

♪
♫
OH, MY...
IT LOOKS LIKE IT'S GOING TO RAIN.
I BETTER BRING IN THE LAUNDRY!

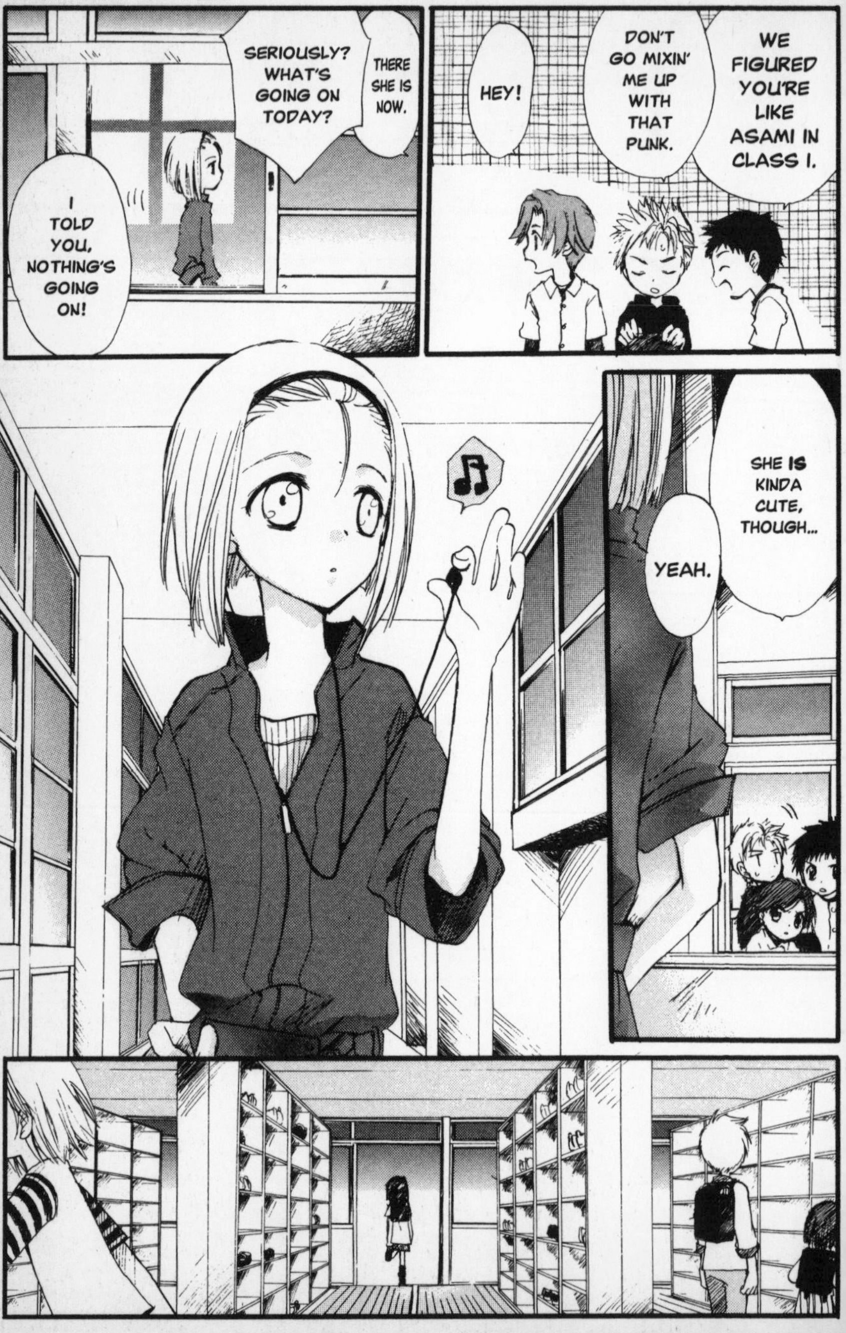
WE FIGURED YOU'RE LIKE ASAMI IN CLASS 1.
DON'T GO MIXIN' ME UP WITH THAT PUNK.
HEY!
THERE SHE IS NOW.
SERIOUSLY? WHAT'S GOING ON TODAY?
I TOLD YOU, NOTHING'S GOING ON!
SHE **IS** KINDA CUTE, THOUGH...
YEAH.

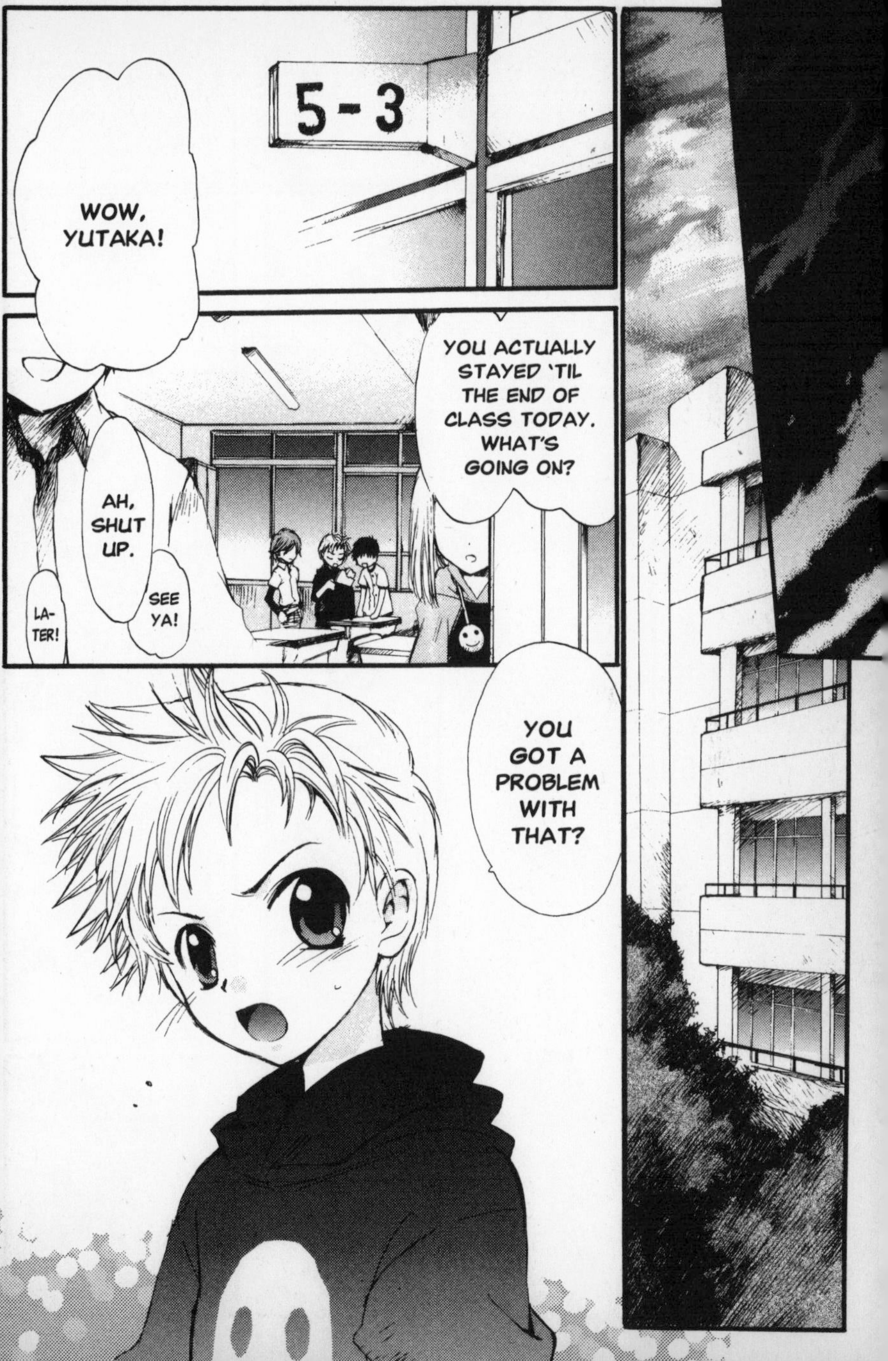
5-3
WOW, YUTAKA!
YOU ACTUALLY STAYED 'TIL THE END OF CLASS TODAY. WHAT'S GOING ON?
AH, SHUT UP.
SEE YA!
LA-TER!
YOU GOT A PROBLEM WITH THAT?

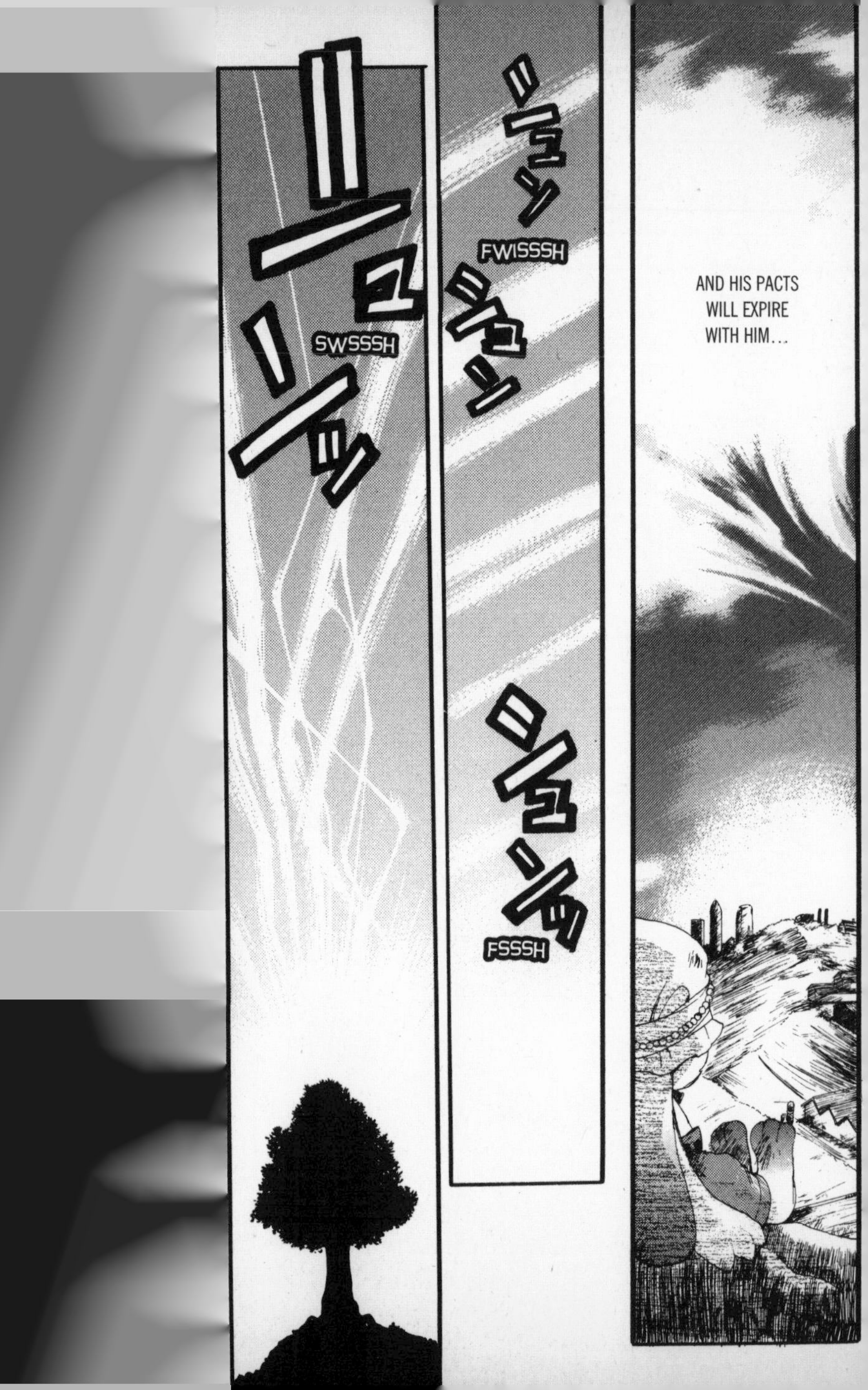
AND HIS PACTS WILL EXPIRE WITH HIM...
FWISSSH
FSSSH
SWSSSH

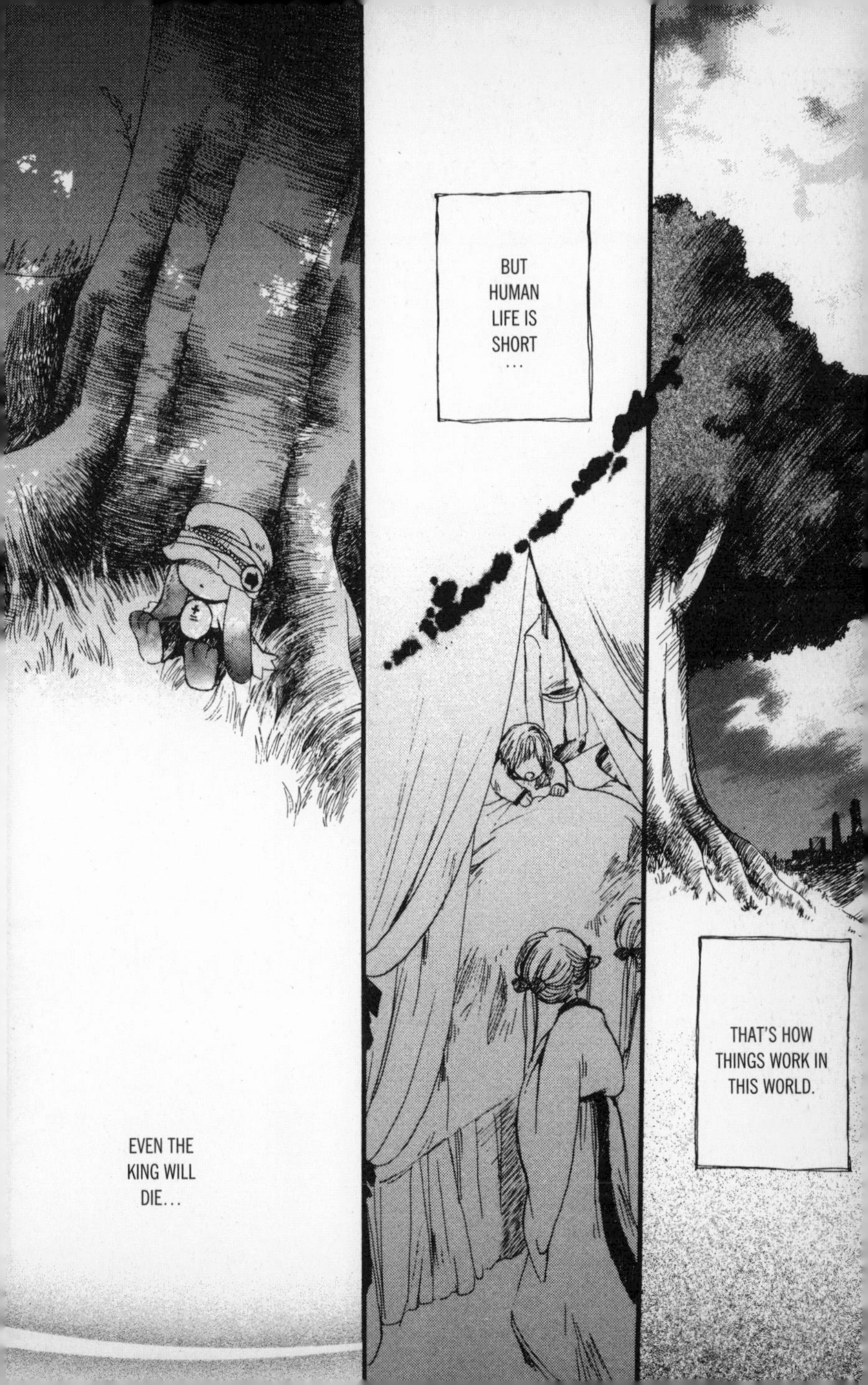
THAT'S HOW THINGS WORK IN THIS WORLD.
BUT HUMAN LIFE IS SHORT...
EVEN THE KING WILL DIE...

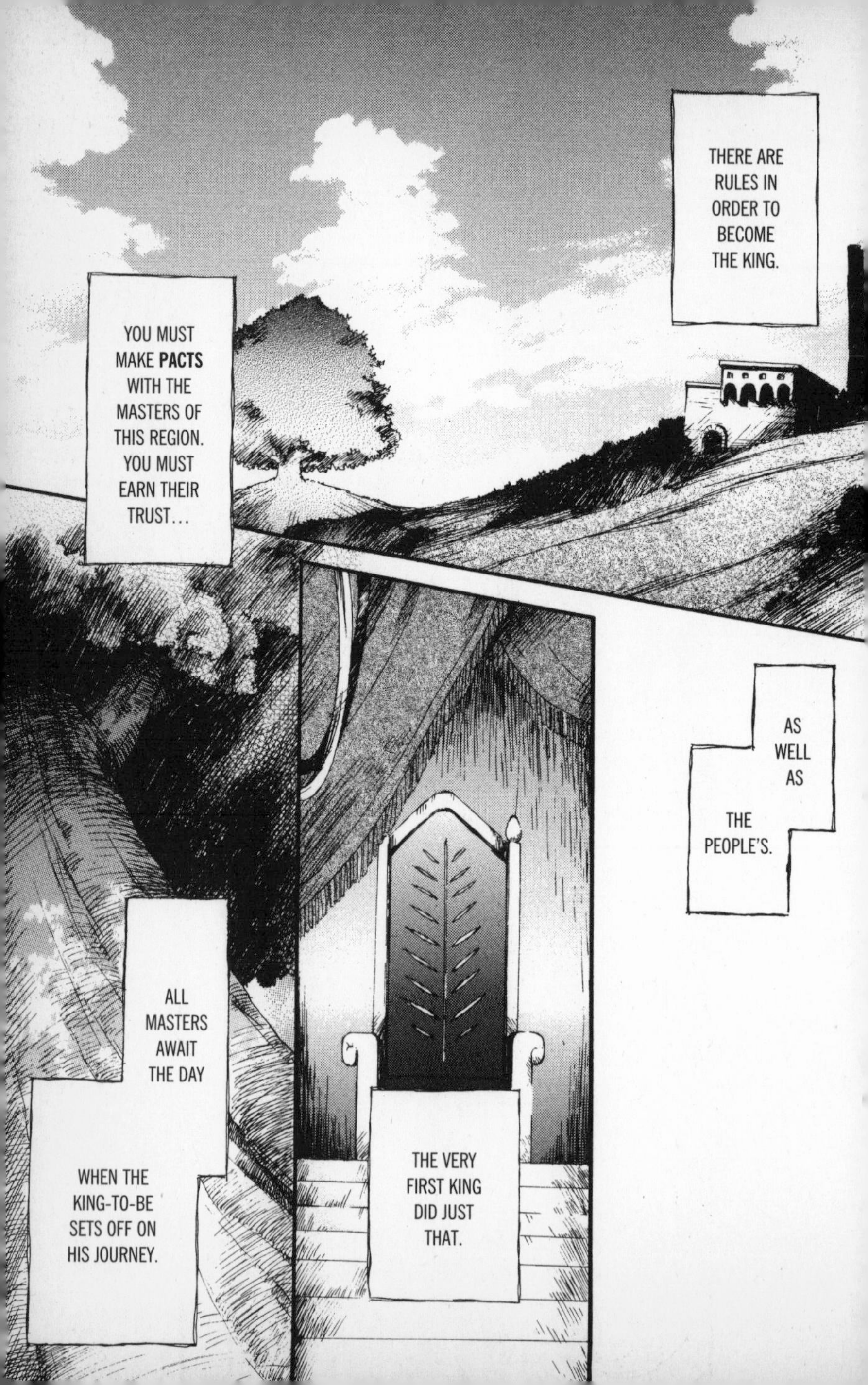
THERE ARE RULES IN ORDER TO BECOME THE KING.
YOU MUST MAKE **PACTS** WITH THE MASTERS OF THIS REGION. YOU MUST EARN THEIR TRUST…
AS WELL AS
THE PEOPLE'S.
THE VERY FIRST KING DID JUST THAT.
ALL MASTERS AWAIT THE DAY
WHEN THE KING-TO-BE SETS OFF ON HIS JOURNEY.

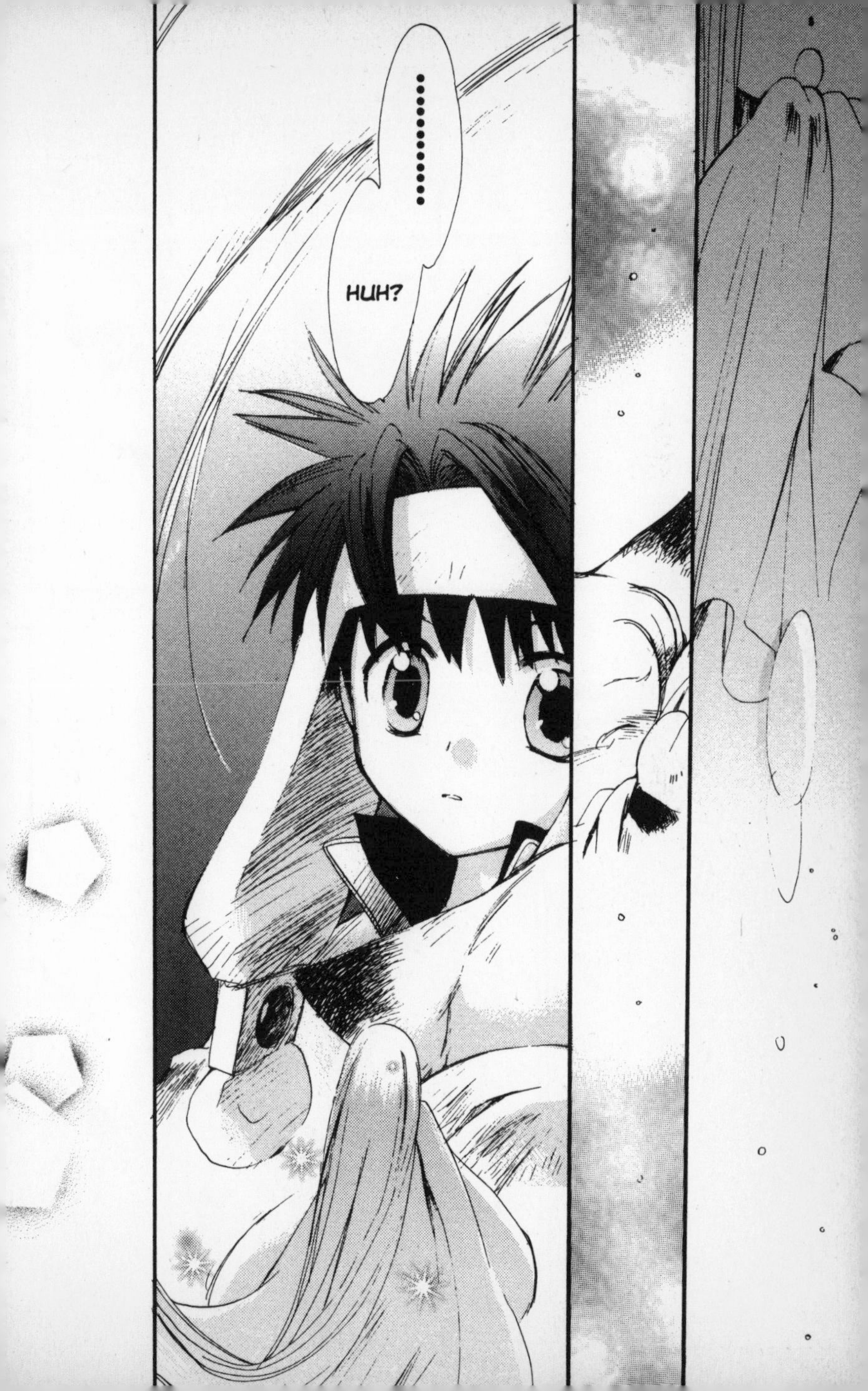
....
HUH?

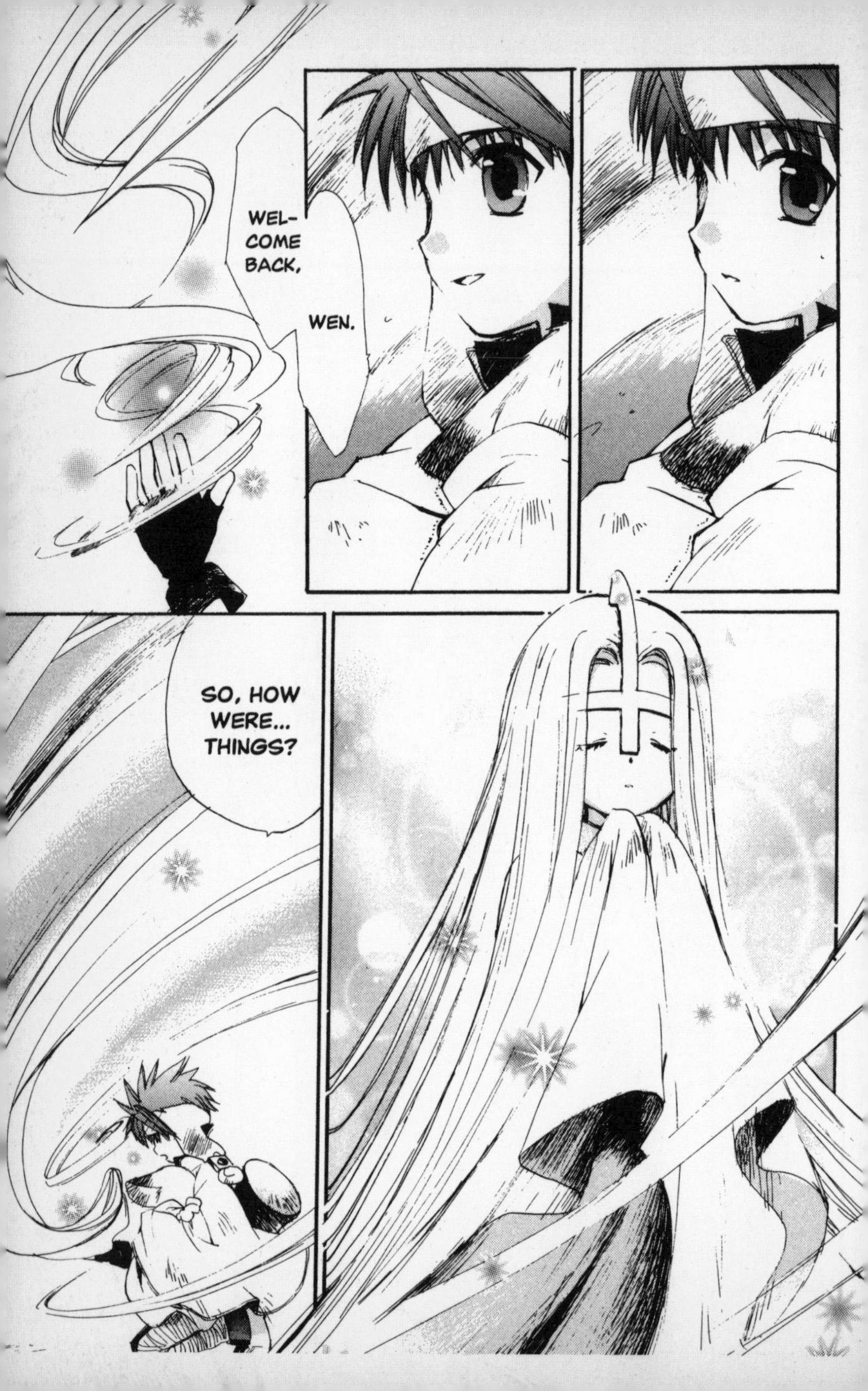
WEL-COME BACK,
WEN.
SO, HOW WERE... THINGS?

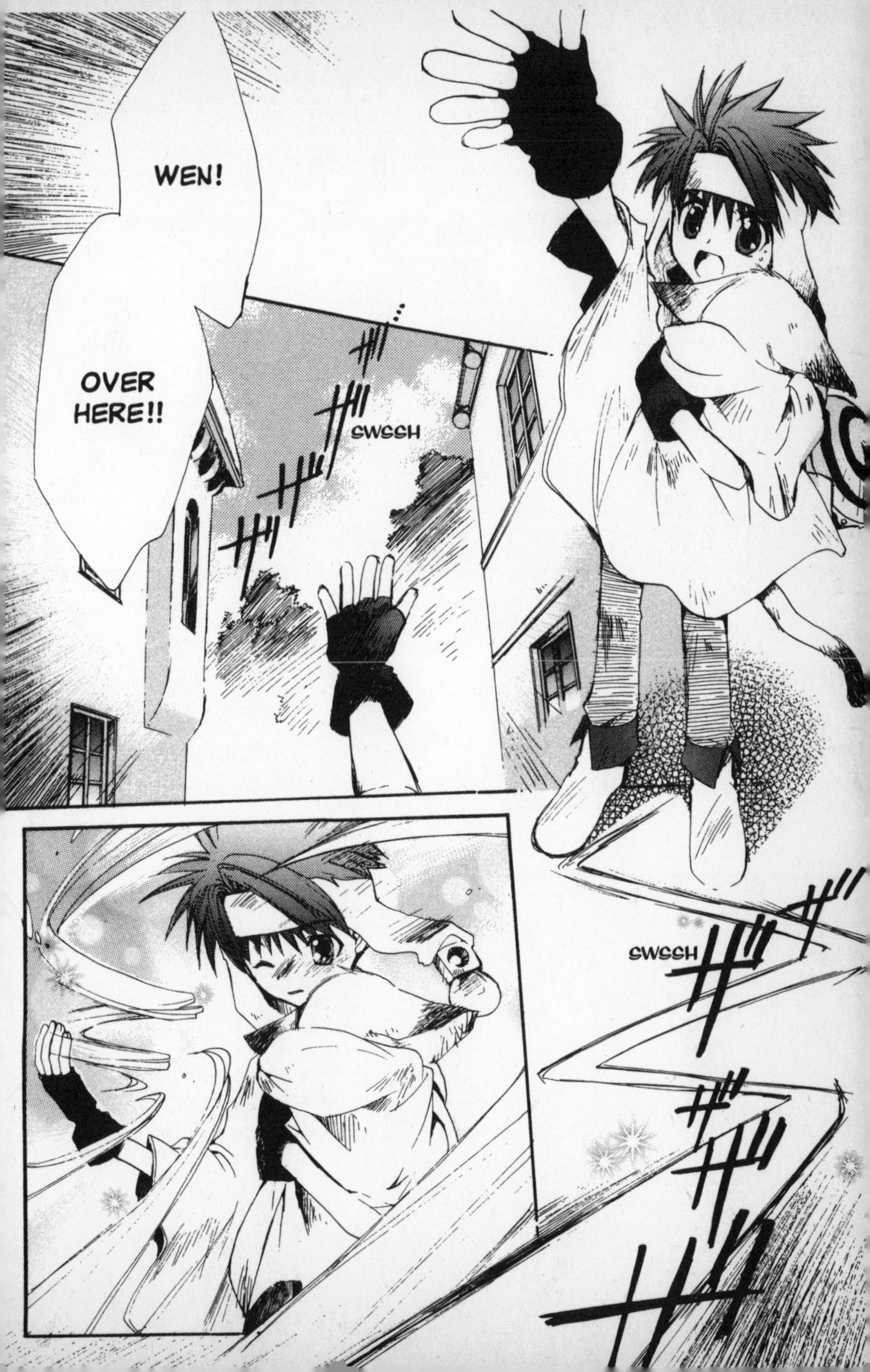
WEN!
OVER HERE!!
SWSSH
SWSSH

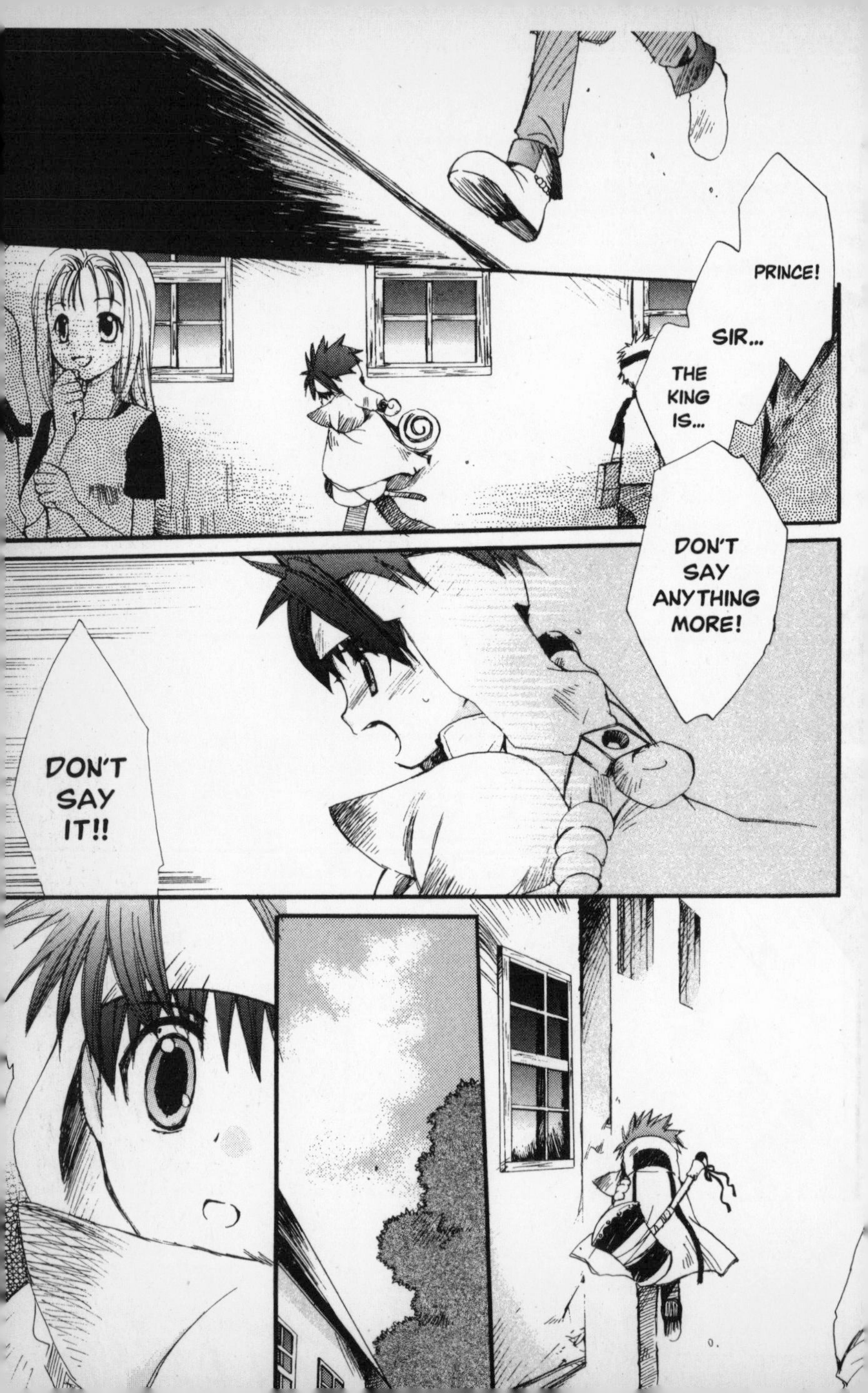
PRINCE!
SIR...
THE KING IS...
DON'T SAY ANYTHING MORE!
DON'T SAY IT!!

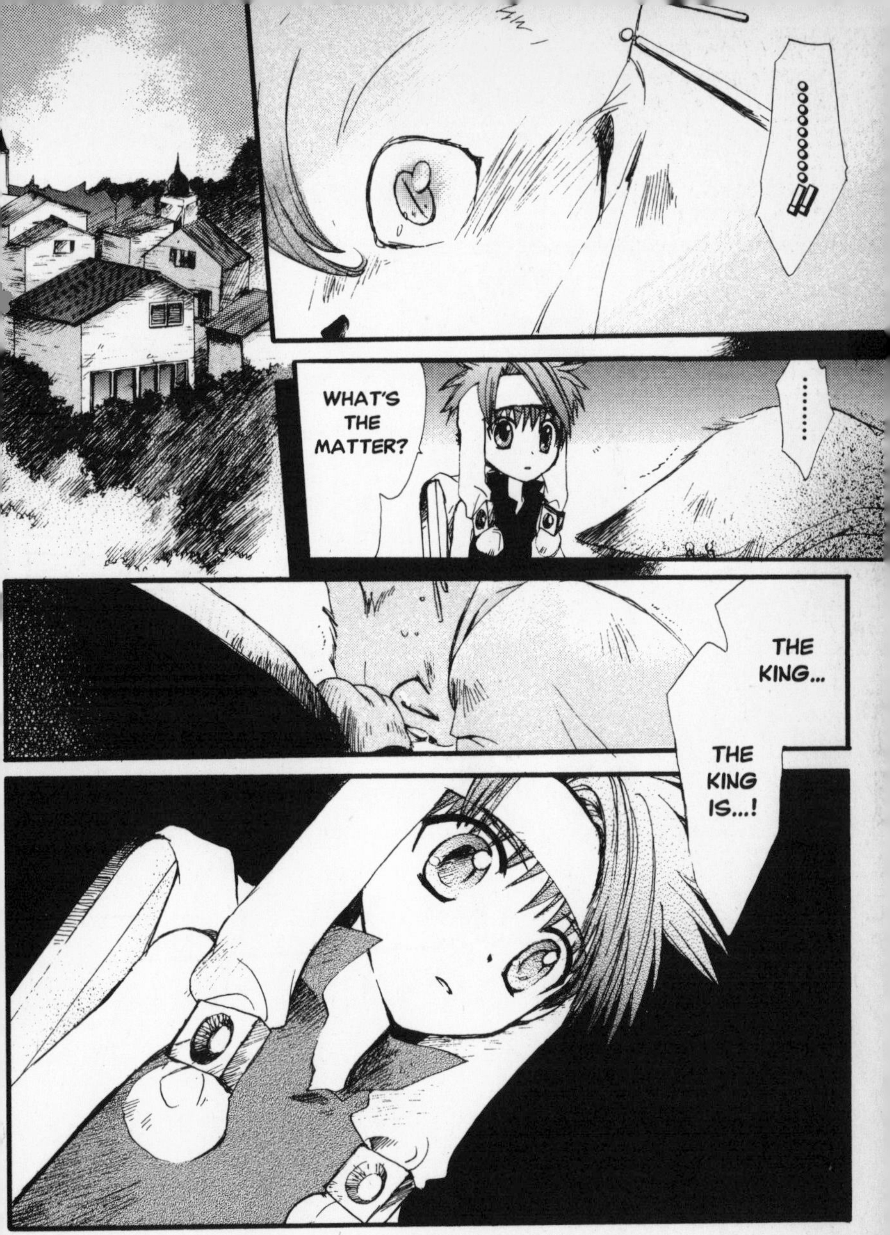

OOOOOOOOO!!
......
WHAT'S THE MATTER?
THE KING...
THE KING IS...!

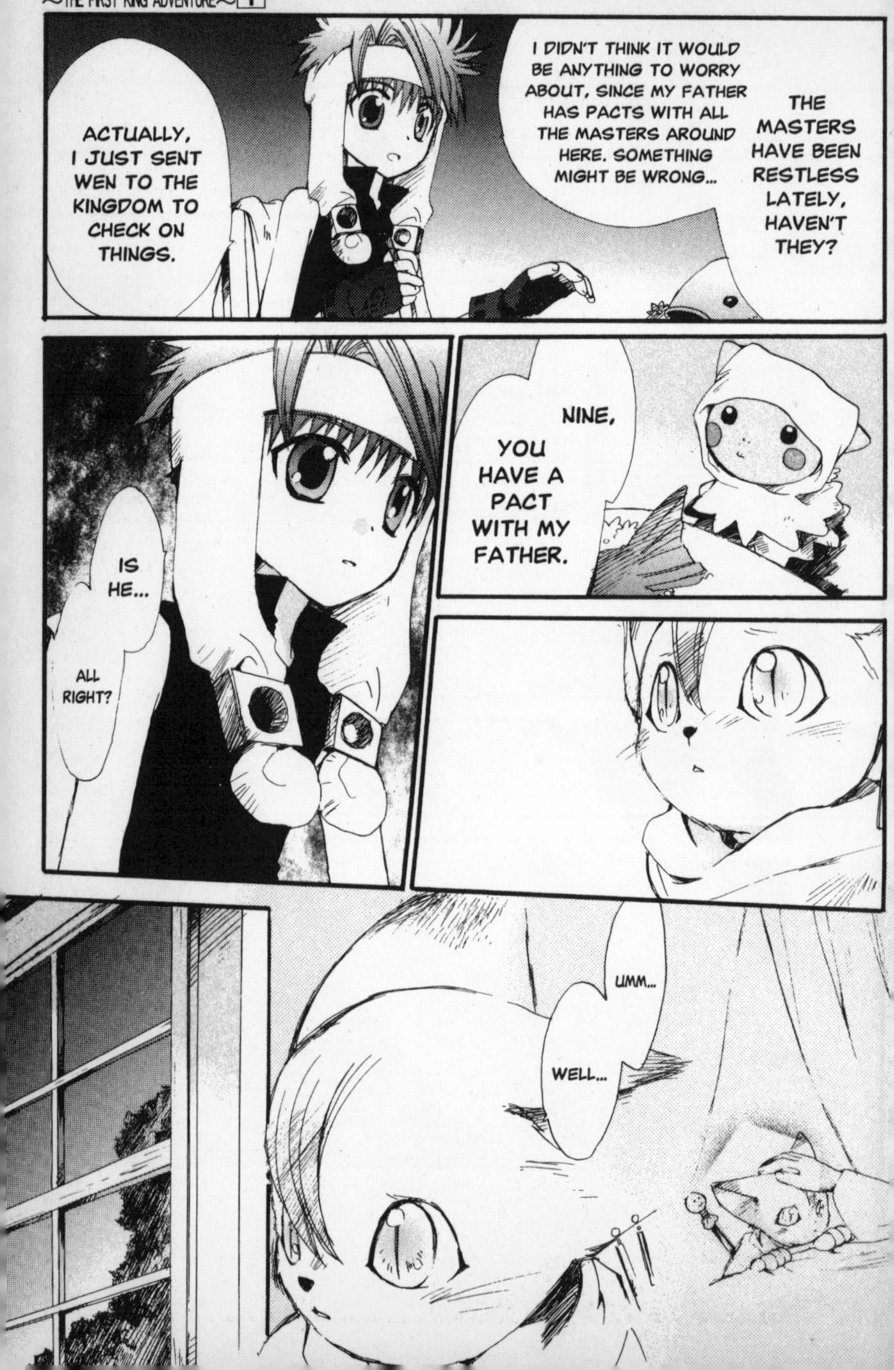
THE MASTERS HAVE BEEN RESTLESS LATELY, HAVEN'T THEY?
I DIDN'T THINK IT WOULD BE ANYTHING TO WORRY ABOUT, SINCE MY FATHER HAS PACTS WITH ALL THE MASTERS AROUND HERE. SOMETHING MIGHT BE WRONG...
ACTUALLY, I JUST SENT WEN TO THE KINGDOM TO CHECK ON THINGS.
NINE,
YOU HAVE A PACT WITH MY FATHER.
IS HE...
ALL RIGHT?
UMM...
WELL...

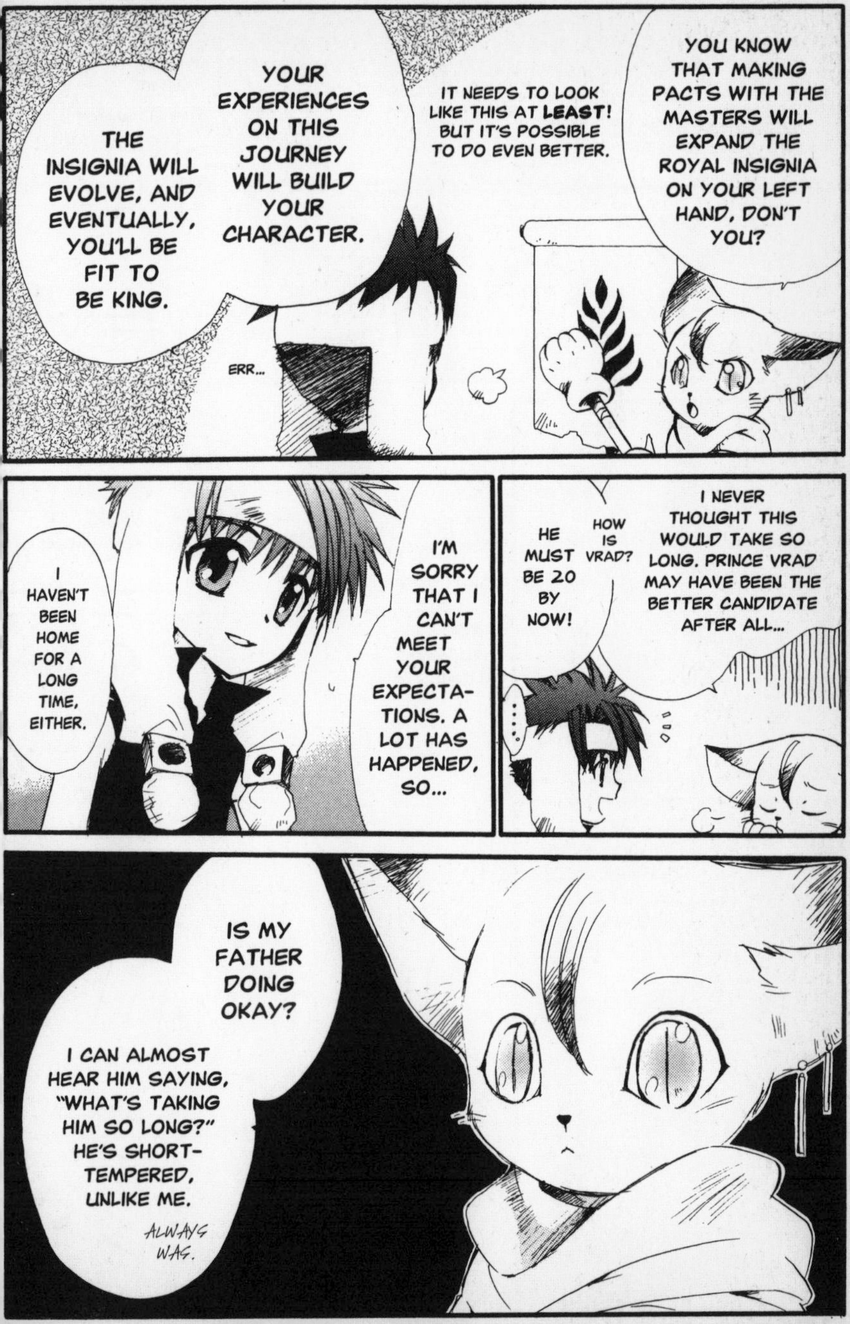
YOU KNOW THAT MAKING PACTS WITH THE MASTERS WILL EXPAND THE ROYAL INSIGNIA ON YOUR LEFT HAND, DON'T YOU?
IT NEEDS TO LOOK LIKE THIS AT **LEAST**! BUT IT'S POSSIBLE TO DO EVEN BETTER.
YOUR EXPERIENCES ON THIS JOURNEY WILL BUILD YOUR CHARACTER.
THE INSIGNIA WILL EVOLVE, AND EVENTUALLY, YOU'LL BE FIT TO BE KING.
ERR...
I NEVER THOUGHT THIS WOULD TAKE SO LONG. PRINCE VRAD MAY HAVE BEEN THE BETTER CANDIDATE AFTER ALL...
HOW IS VRAD?
HE MUST BE 20 BY NOW!
I'M SORRY THAT I CAN'T MEET YOUR EXPECTATIONS. A LOT HAS HAPPENED, SO...
I HAVEN'T BEEN HOME FOR A LONG TIME, EITHER.
IS MY FATHER DOING OKAY?
I CAN ALMOST HEAR HIM SAYING, "WHAT'S TAKING HIM SO LONG?" HE'S SHORT-TEMPERED, UNLIKE ME.
ALWAYS WAS.

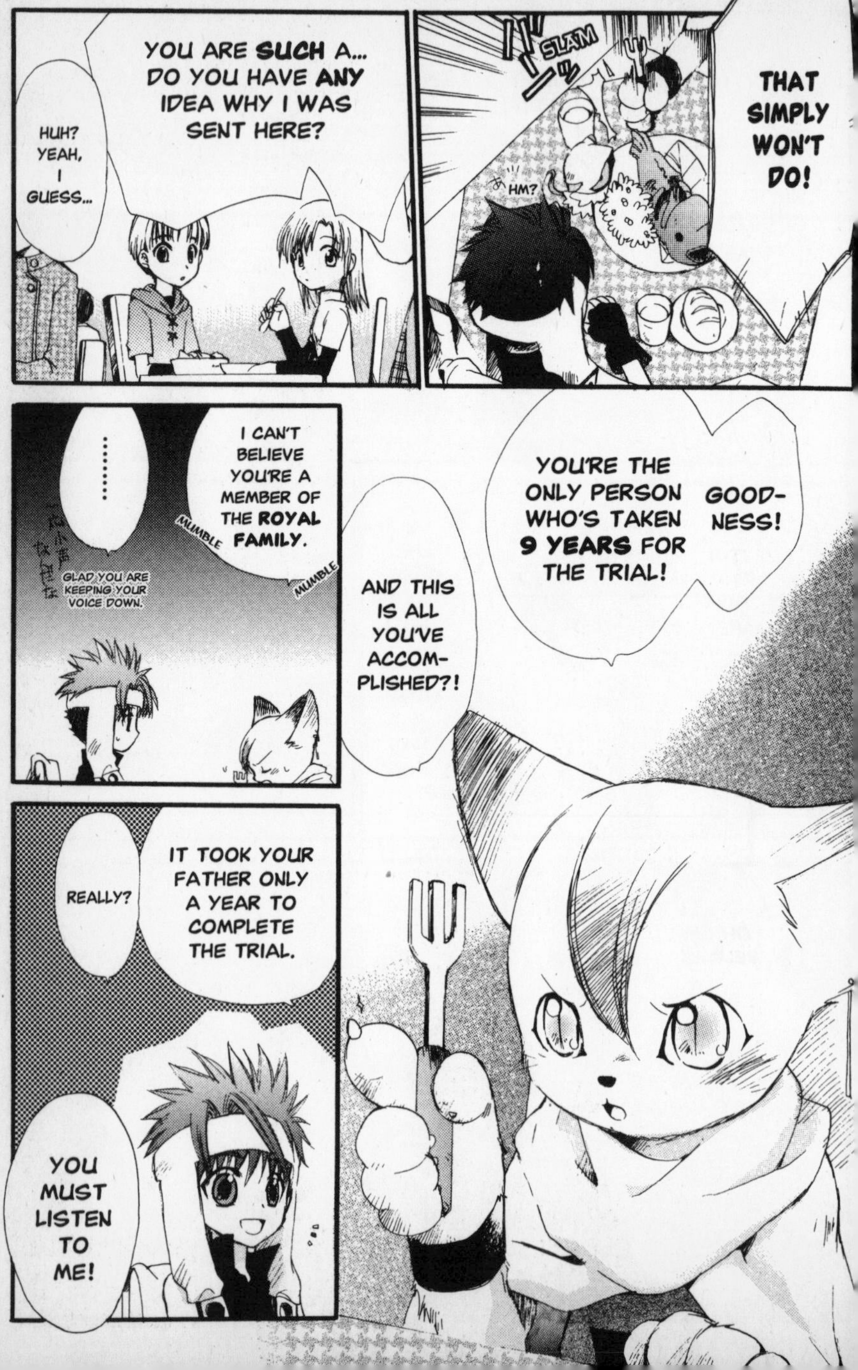

SLAM
THAT SIMPLY WON'T DO!
HM?
YOU ARE SUCH A... DO YOU HAVE ANY IDEA WHY I WAS SENT HERE?
HUH? YEAH, I GUESS...
GOODNESS!
YOU'RE THE ONLY PERSON WHO'S TAKEN 9 YEARS FOR THE TRIAL!
AND THIS IS ALL YOU'VE ACCOMPLISHED?!
I CAN'T BELIEVE YOU'RE A MEMBER OF THE ROYAL FAMILY.
MUMBLE
MUMBLE
....
GLAD YOU ARE KEEPING YOUR VOICE DOWN.
IT TOOK YOUR FATHER ONLY A YEAR TO COMPLETE THE TRIAL.
REALLY?
YOU MUST LISTEN TO ME!

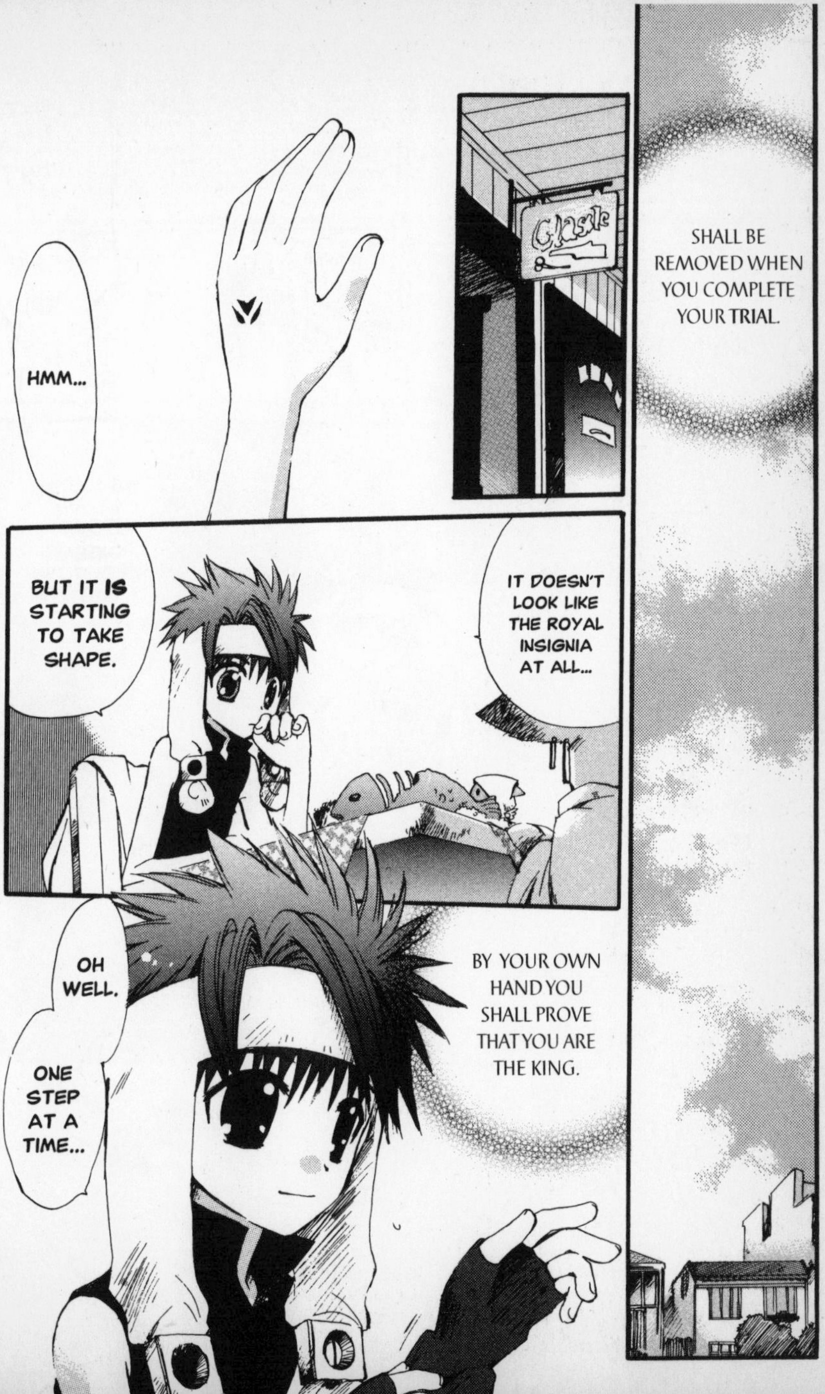
SHALL BE REMOVED WHEN YOU COMPLETE YOUR TRIAL.
HMM...
IT DOESN'T LOOK LIKE THE ROYAL INSIGNIA AT ALL...
BUT IT IS STARTING TO TAKE SHAPE.
BY YOUR OWN HAND YOU SHALL PROVE THAT YOU ARE THE KING.
OH WELL.
ONE STEP AT A TIME...

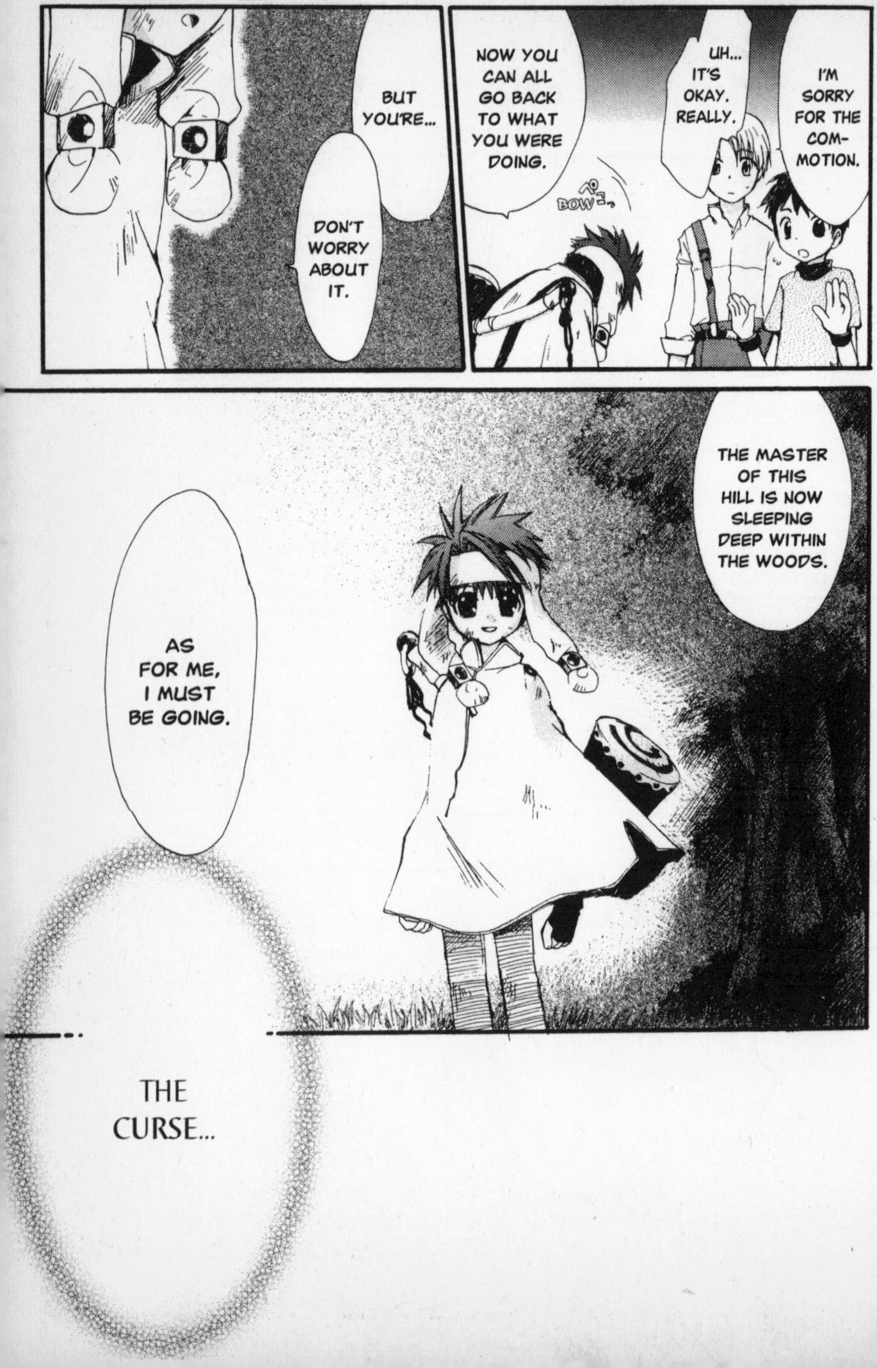
I'M SORRY FOR THE COM-MOTION.
UH... IT'S OKAY. REALLY.
NOW YOU CAN ALL GO BACK TO WHAT YOU WERE DOING.
BOW
BUT YOU'RE...
DON'T WORRY ABOUT IT.
THE MASTER OF THIS HILL IS NOW SLEEPING DEEP WITHIN THE WOODS.
AS FOR ME, I MUST BE GOING.
THE CURSE...

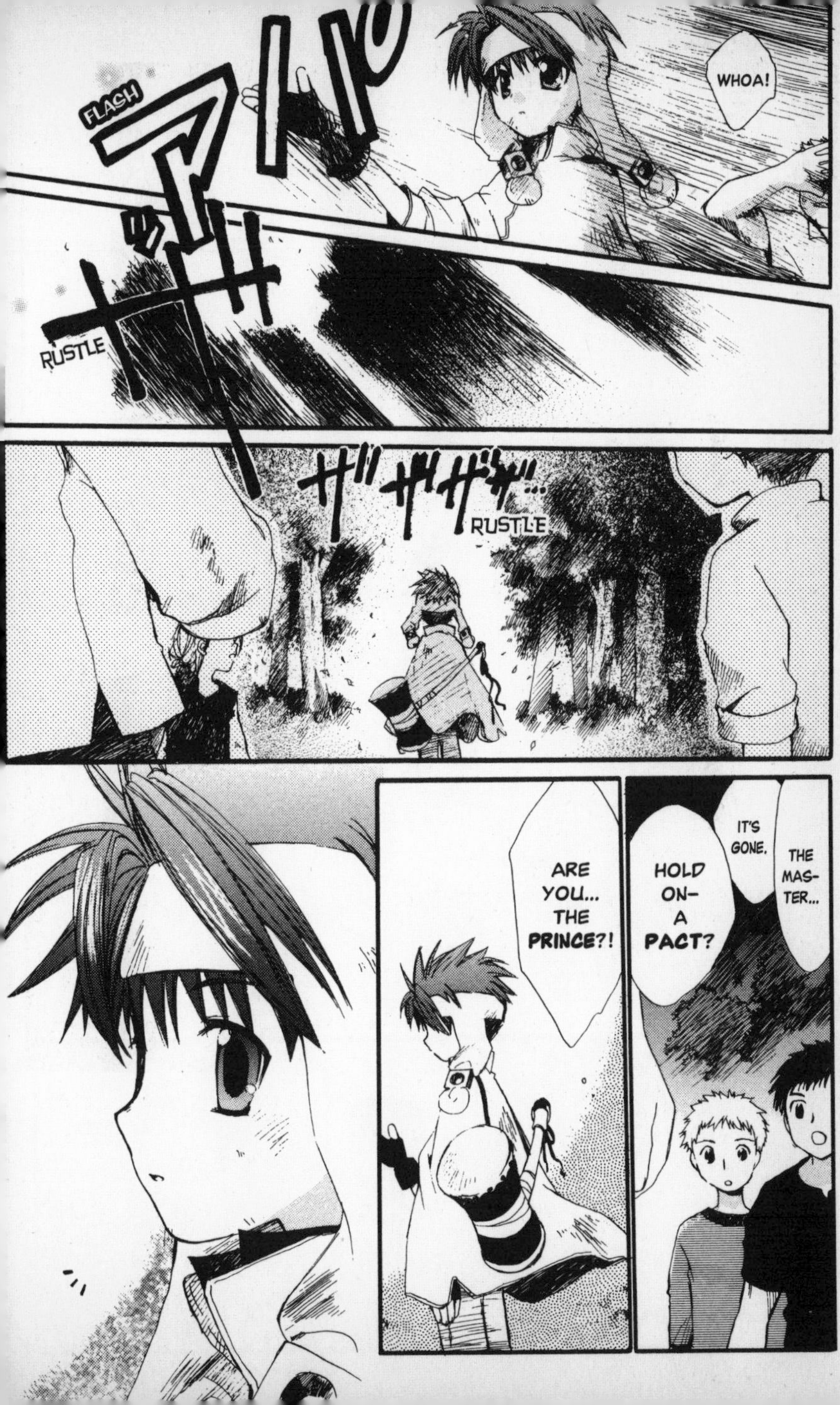

WHOA!
FLASH
RUSTLE
RUSTLE
THE MAS-TER...
IT'S GONE.
HOLD ON— A PACT?
ARE YOU... THE PRINCE?!

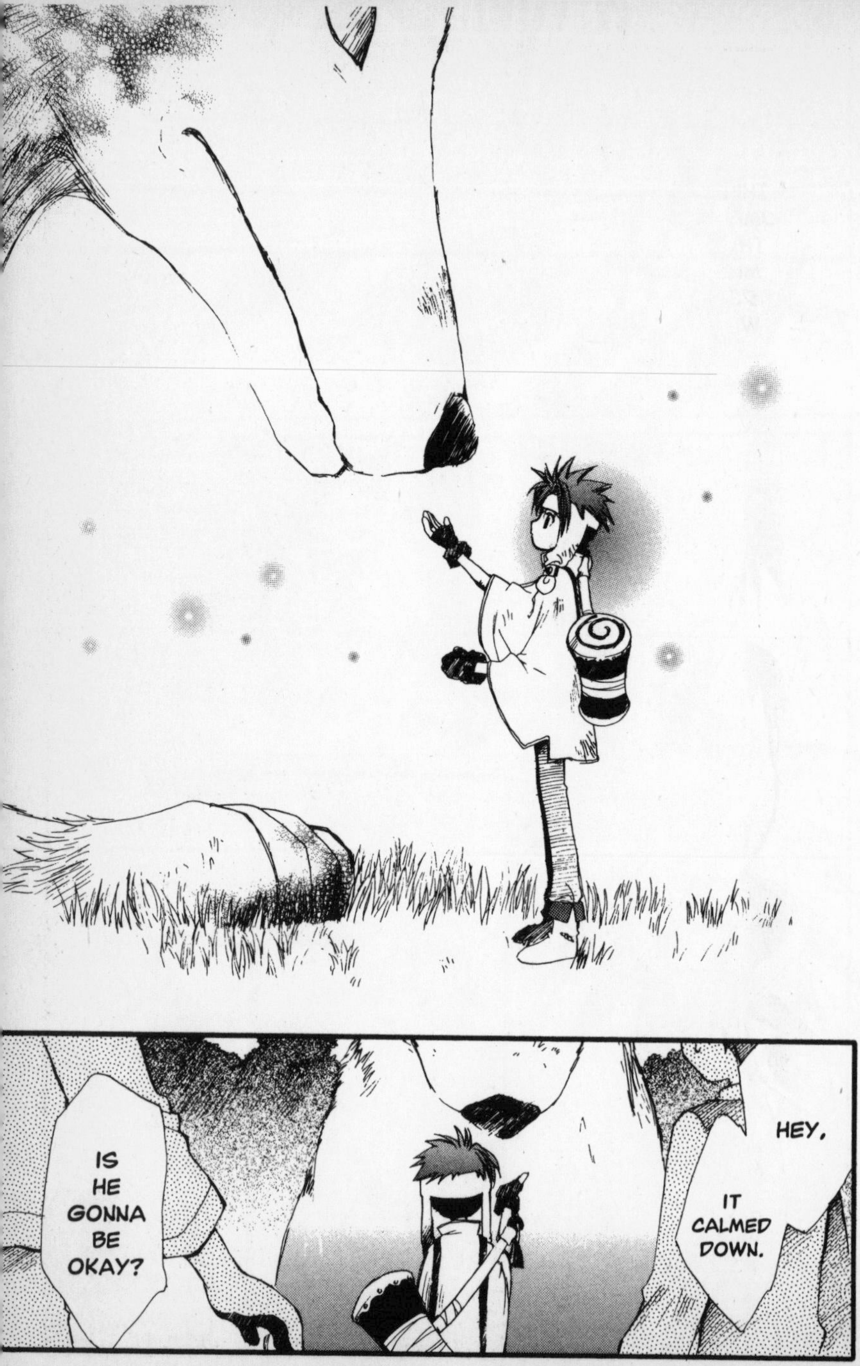
HEY,
IT CALMED DOWN.
IS HE GONNA BE OKAY?

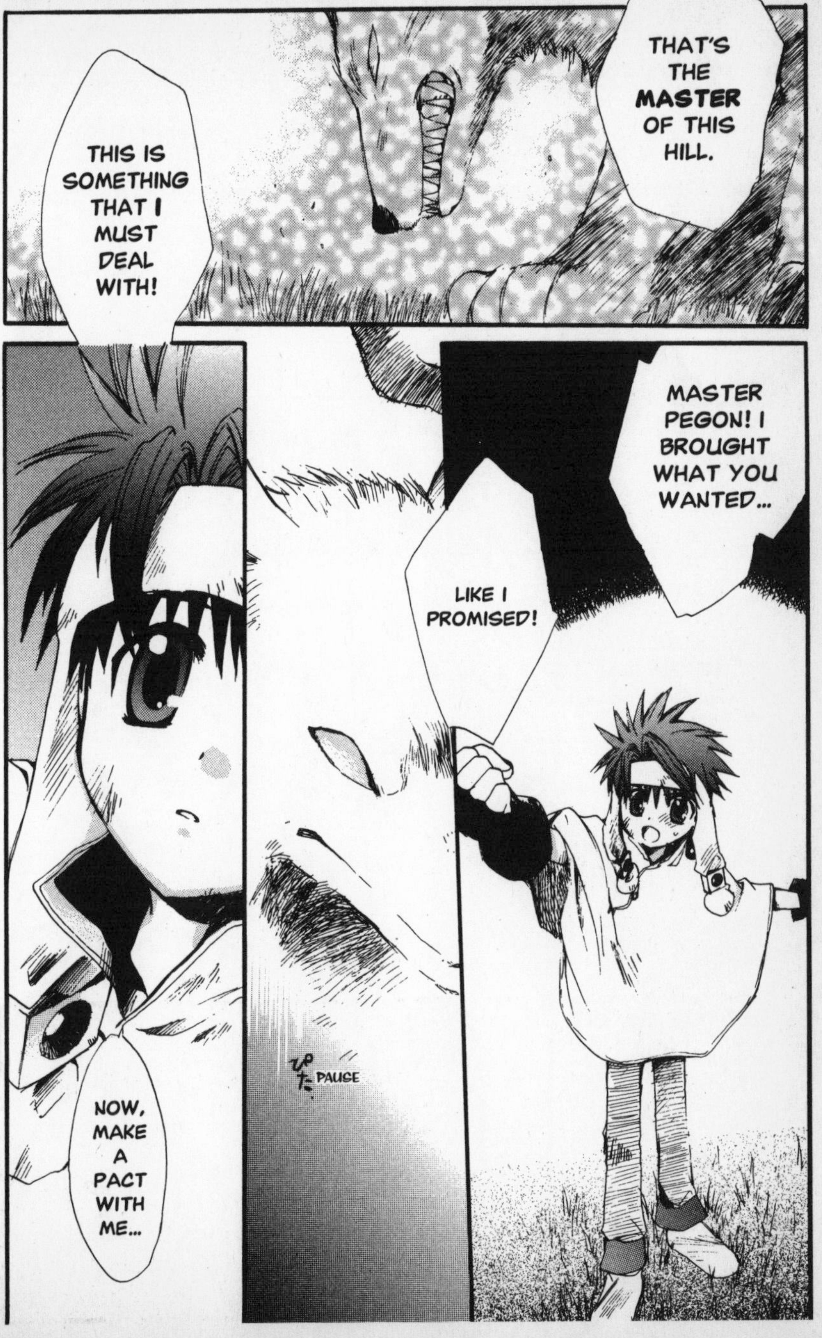
THAT'S THE **MASTER** OF THIS HILL.
THIS IS SOMETHING THAT I MUST DEAL WITH!
MASTER PEGON! I BROUGHT WHAT YOU WANTED...
LIKE I PROMISED!
PAUSE
NOW, MAKE A PACT WITH ME...

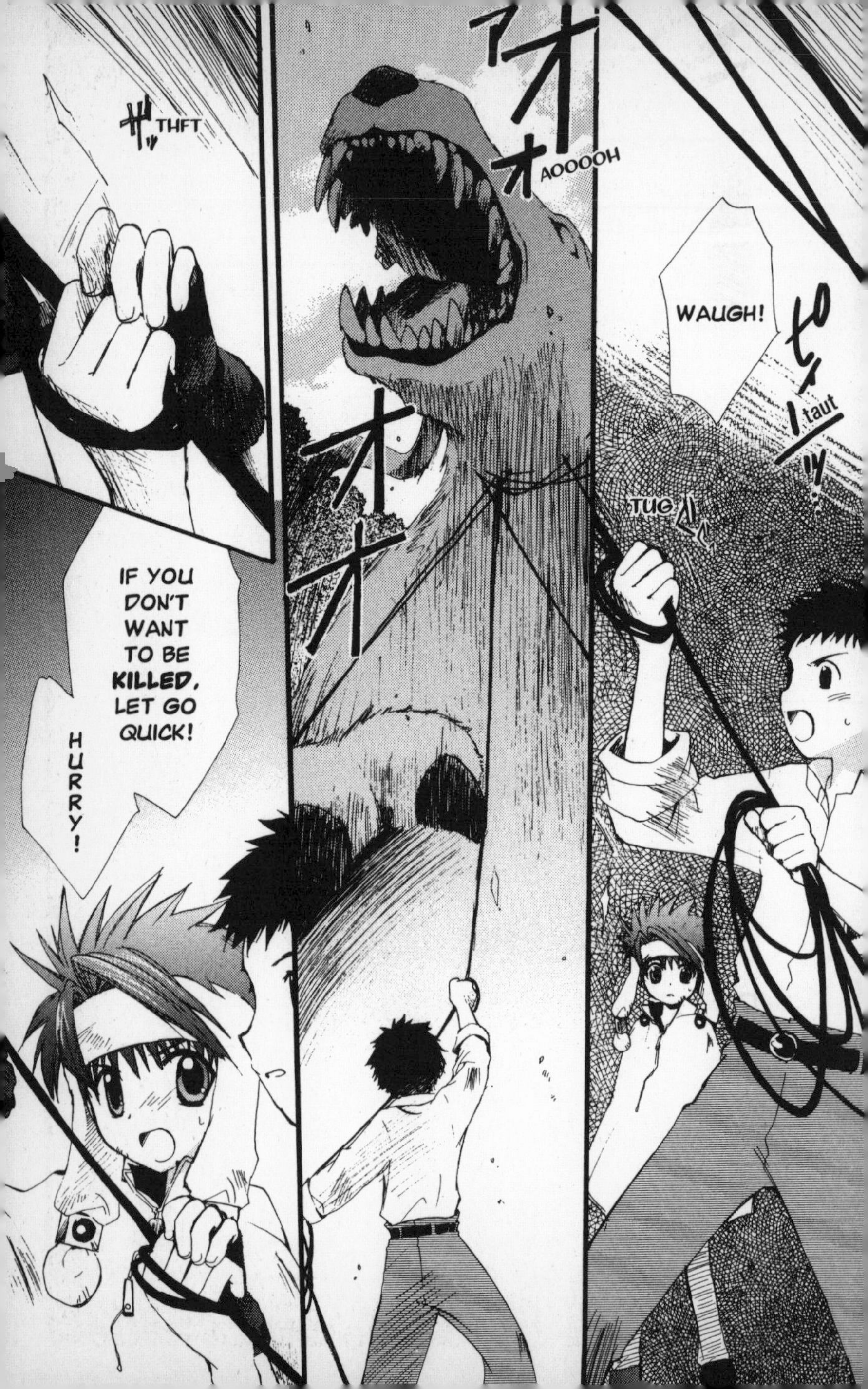

WAUGH!
taut
TUG
AOOOOH
THFT
IF YOU DON'T WANT TO BE KILLED, LET GO QUICK!
HURRY!

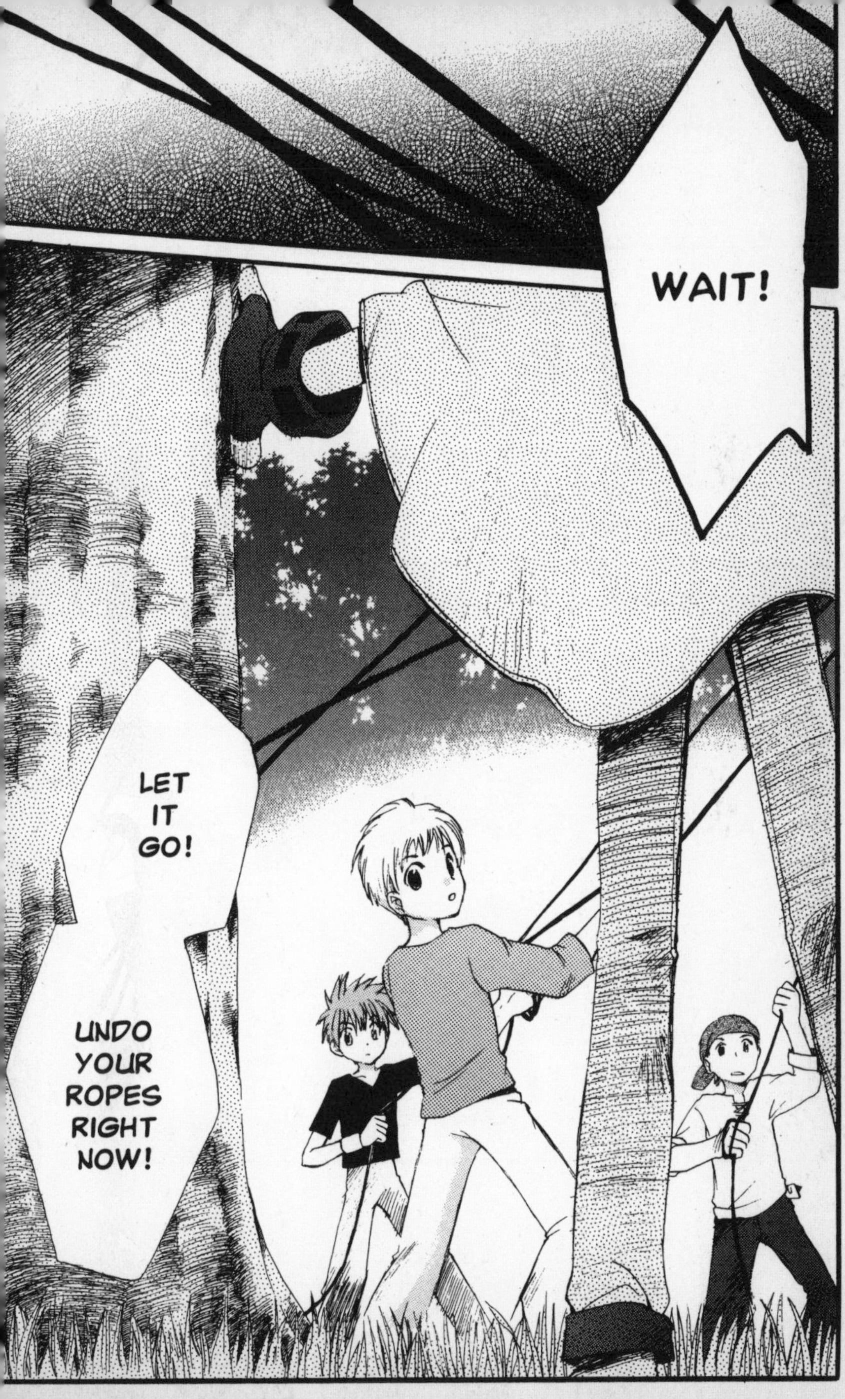
WAIT!
LET IT GO!
UNDO YOUR ROPES RIGHT NOW!

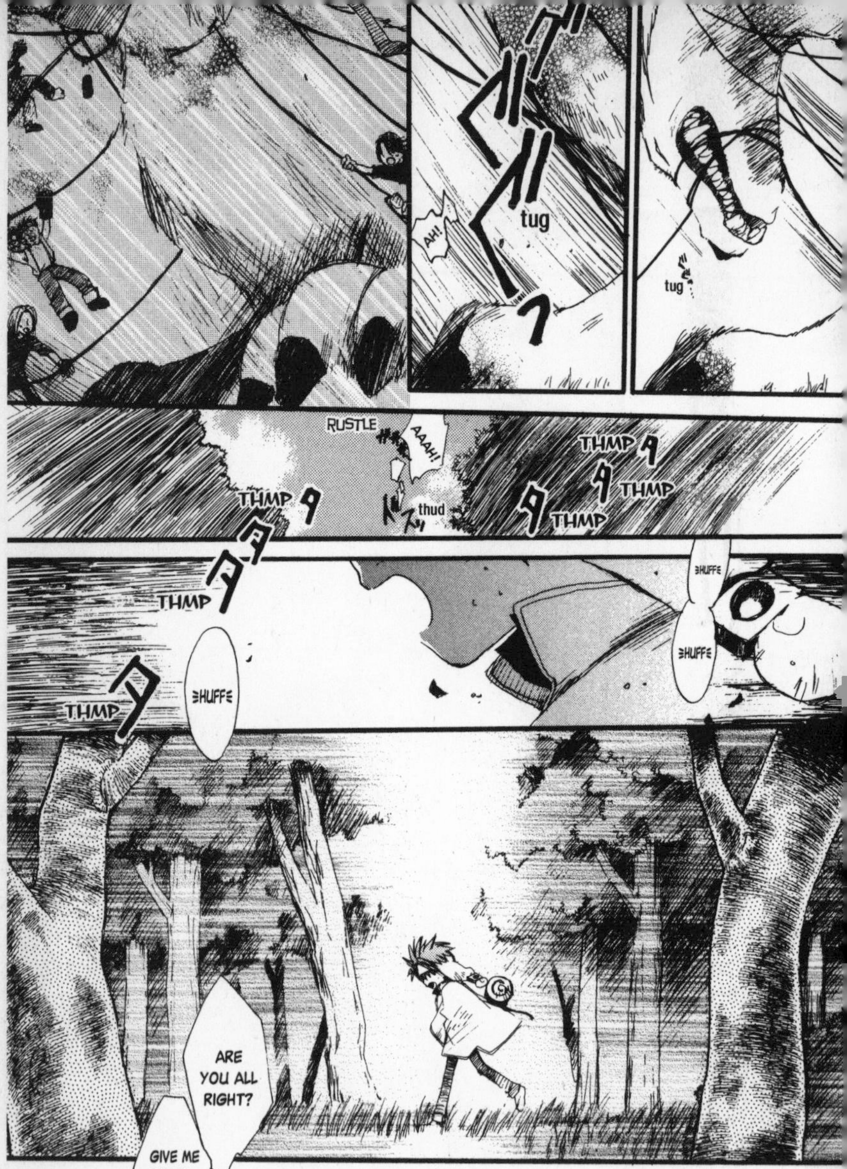
tug
AH!
tug
RUSTLE
AAAH!
thud
THMP
THMP
THMP
THMP
HUFF
HUFF
THMP
THMP
HUFF
ARE YOU ALL RIGHT?
GIVE ME YOUR HAND!
!…

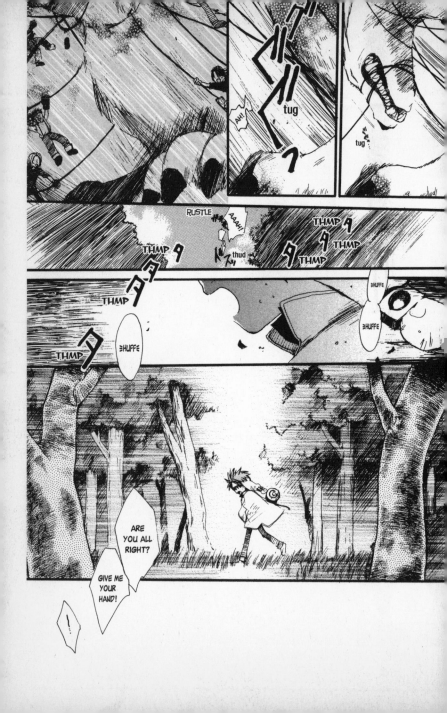

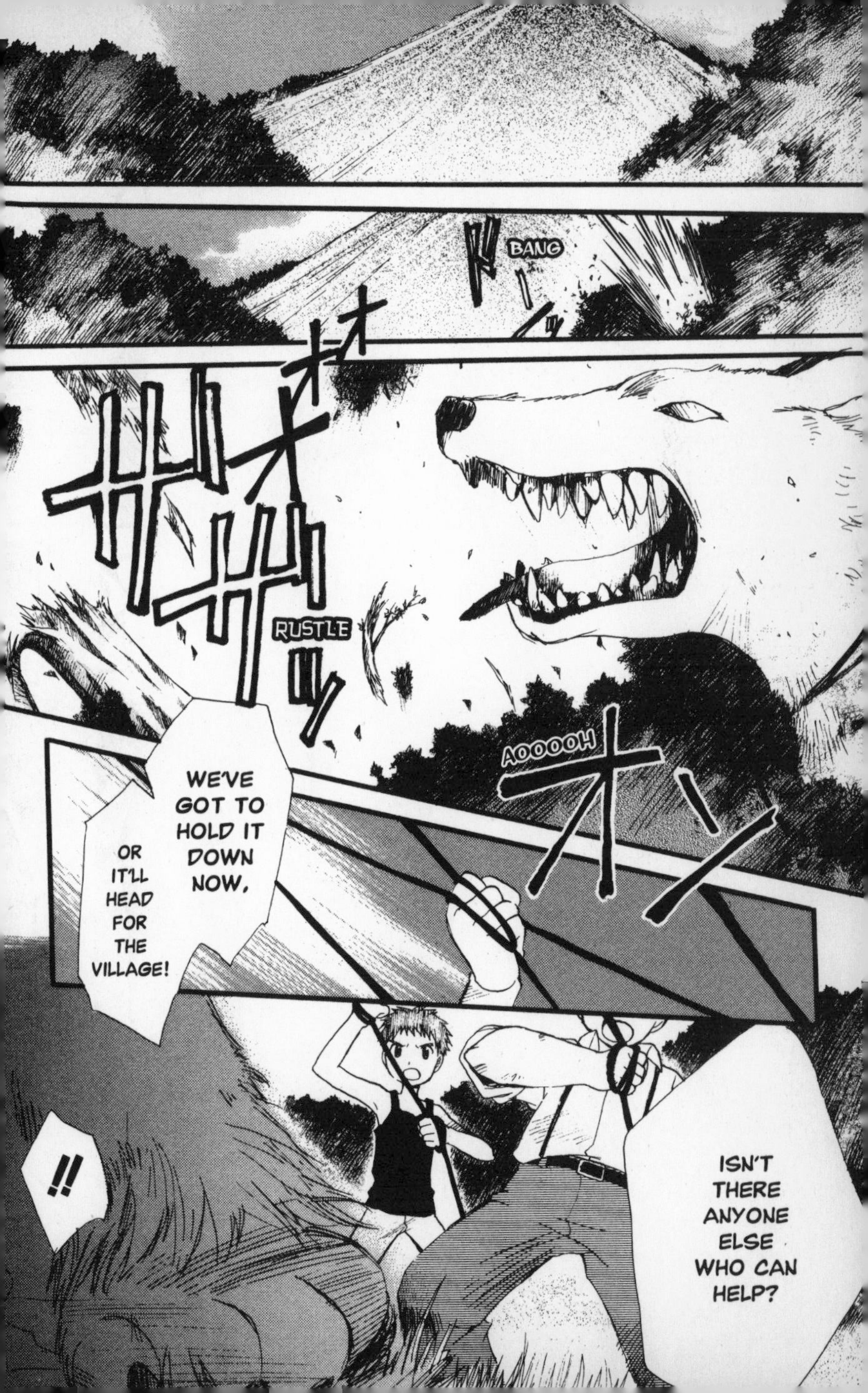

BANG
RUSTLE
AOOOOH
WE'VE GOT TO HOLD IT DOWN NOW,
OR IT'LL HEAD FOR THE VILLAGE!
!!
ISN'T THERE ANYONE ELSE WHO CAN HELP?

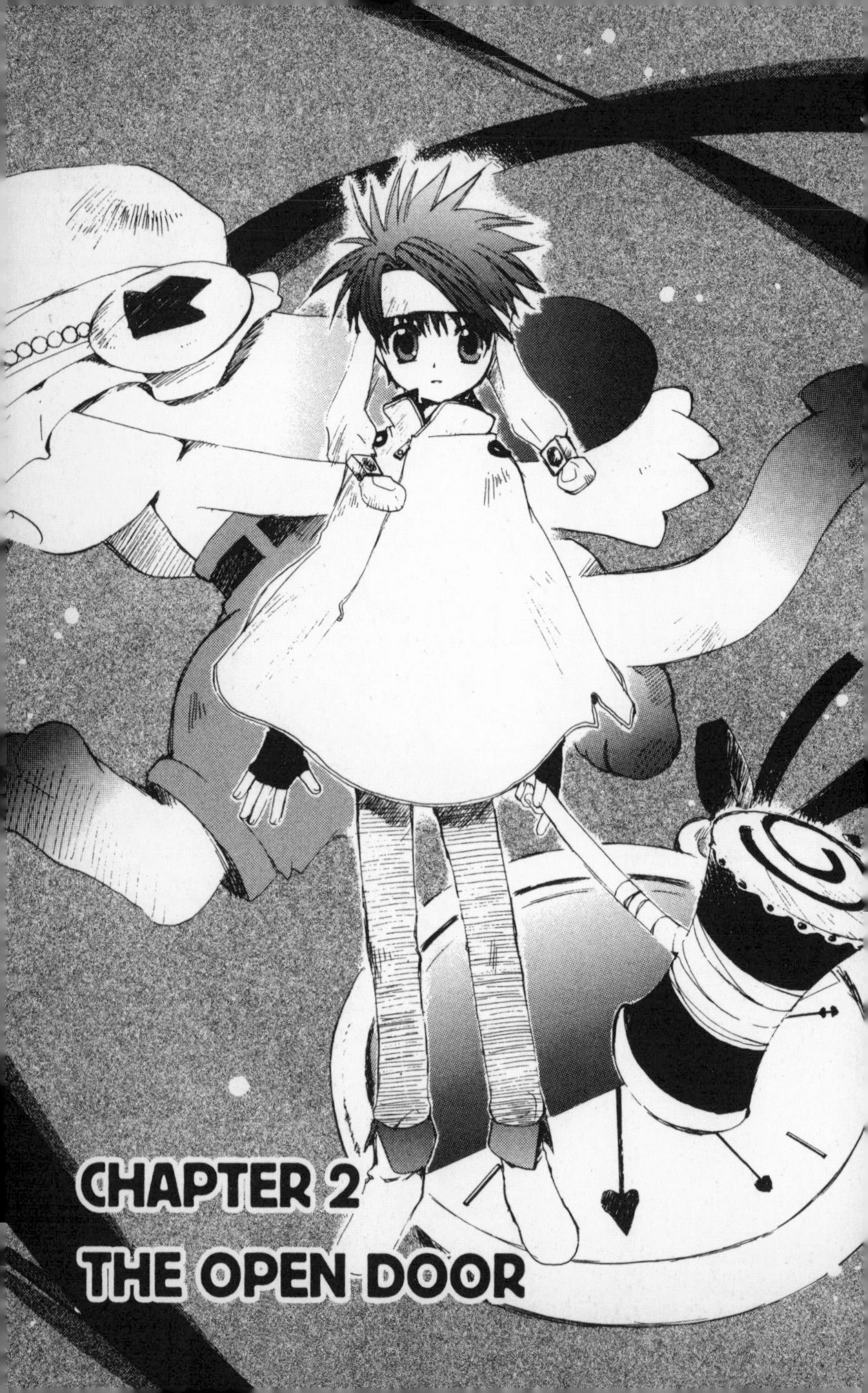
CHAPTER 2
THE OPEN DOOR

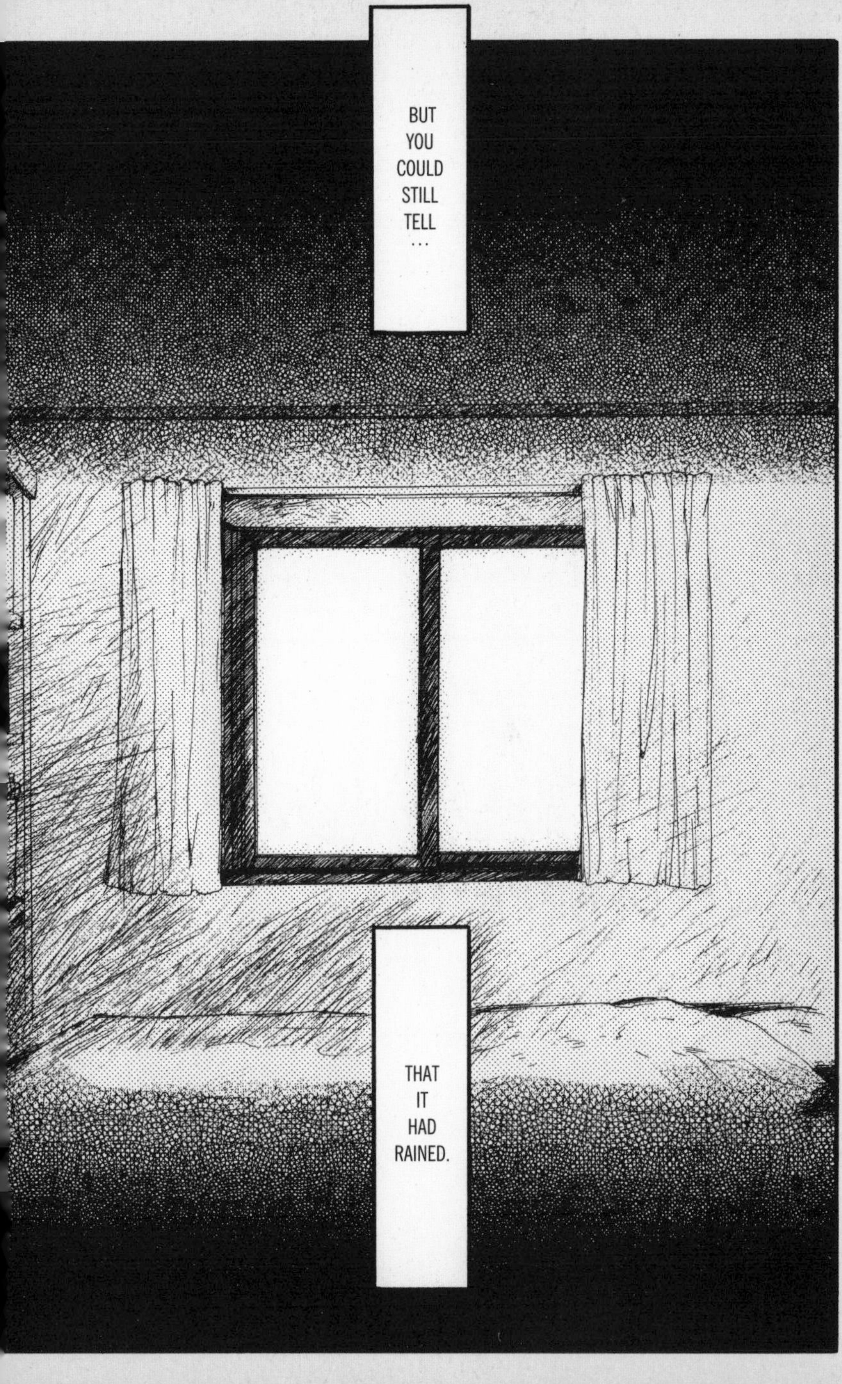
BUT YOU COULD STILL TELL ...
THAT IT HAD RAINED.

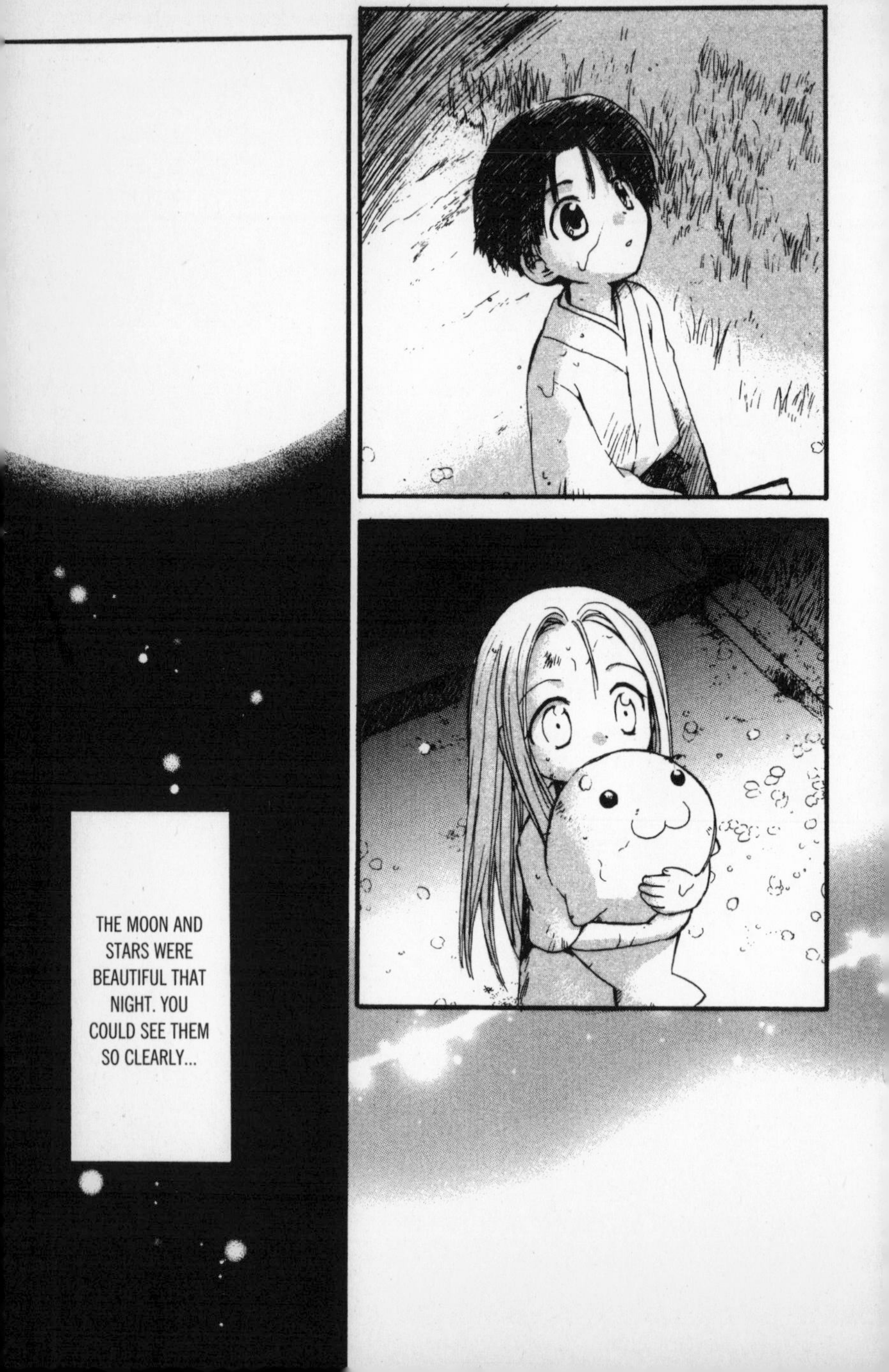
THE MOON AND STARS WERE BEAUTIFUL THAT NIGHT. YOU COULD SEE THEM SO CLEARLY...

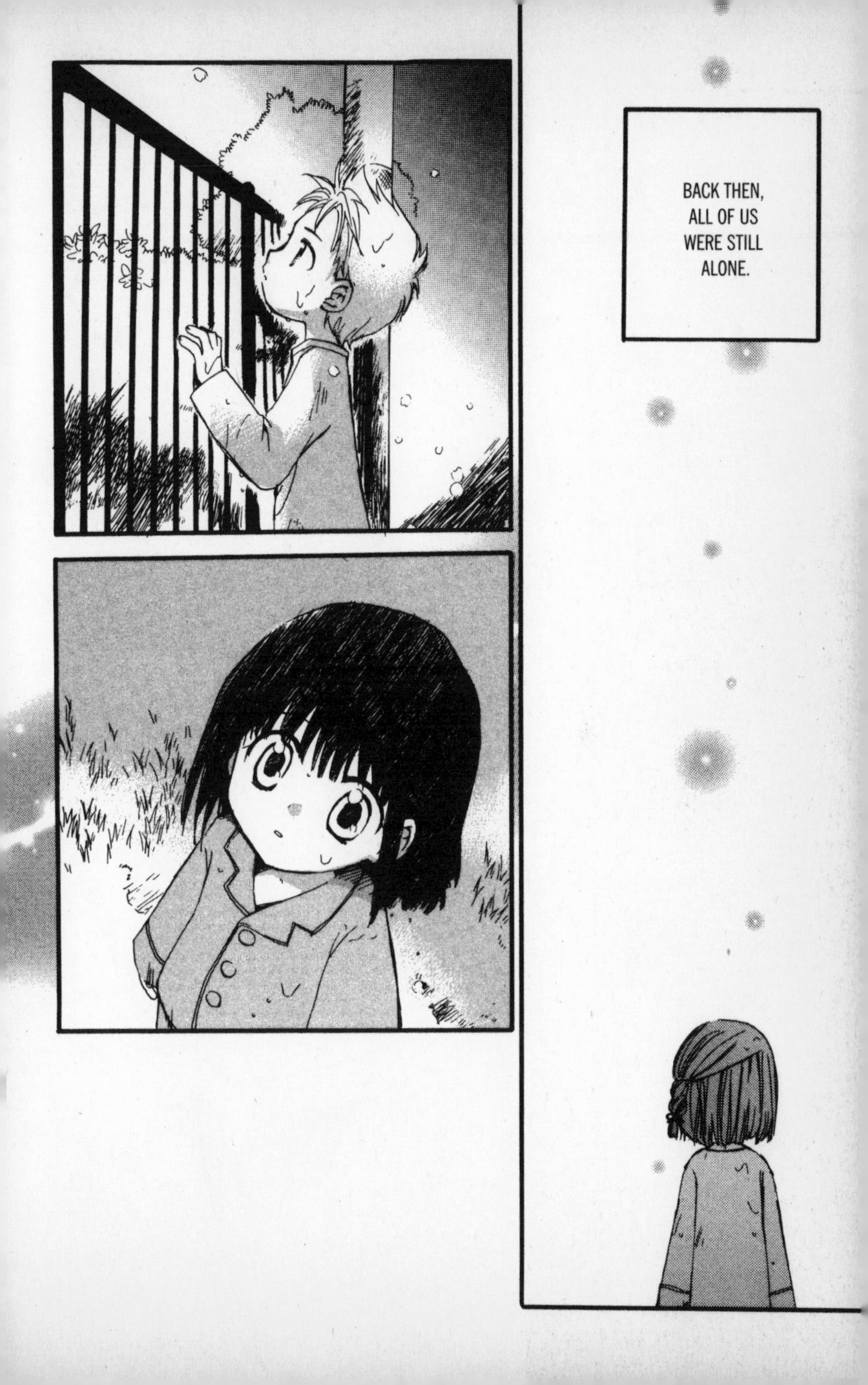
BACK THEN, ALL OF US WERE STILL ALONE.

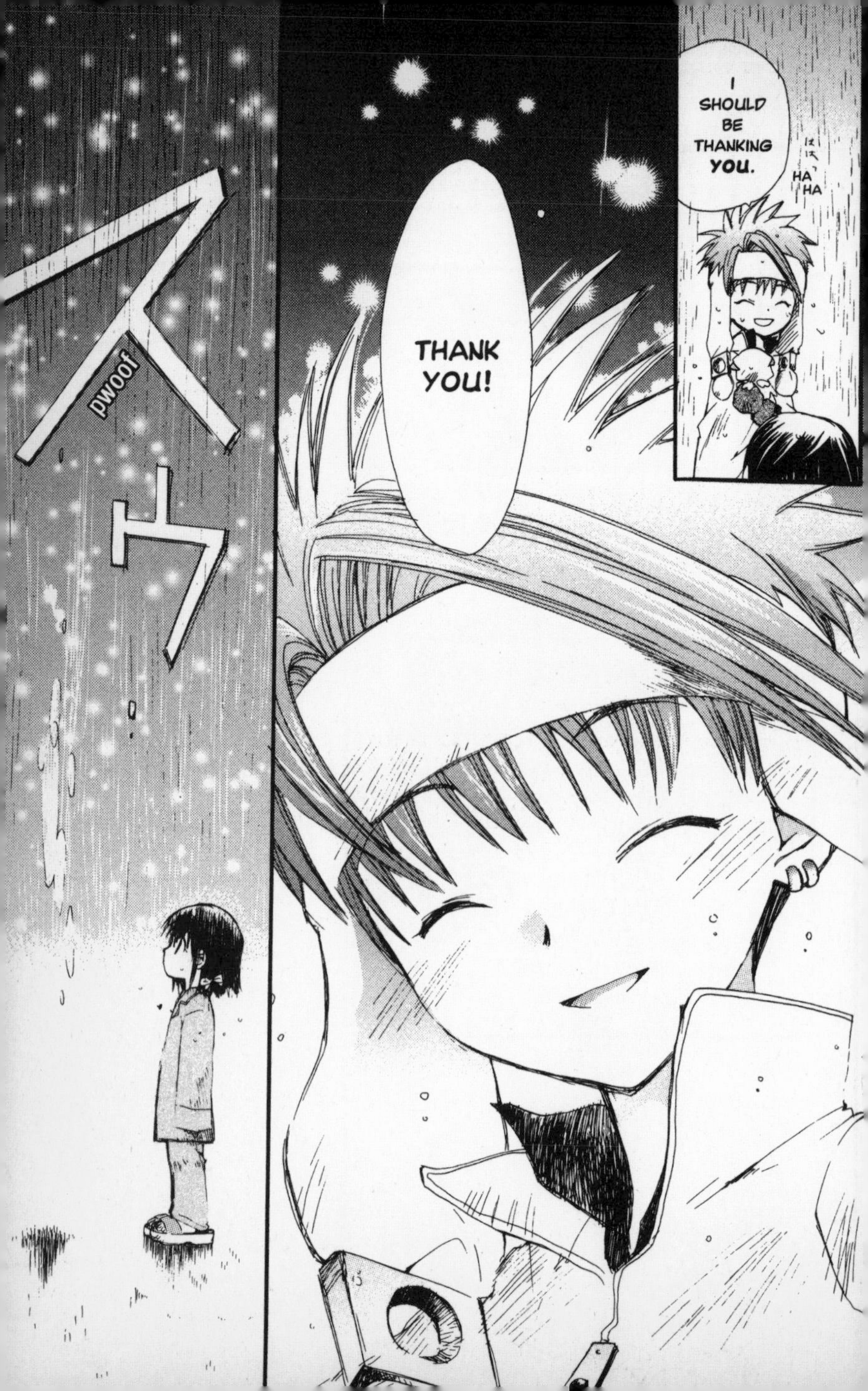
I SHOULD BE THANKING YOU.
HA HA
THANK YOU!
pwoof

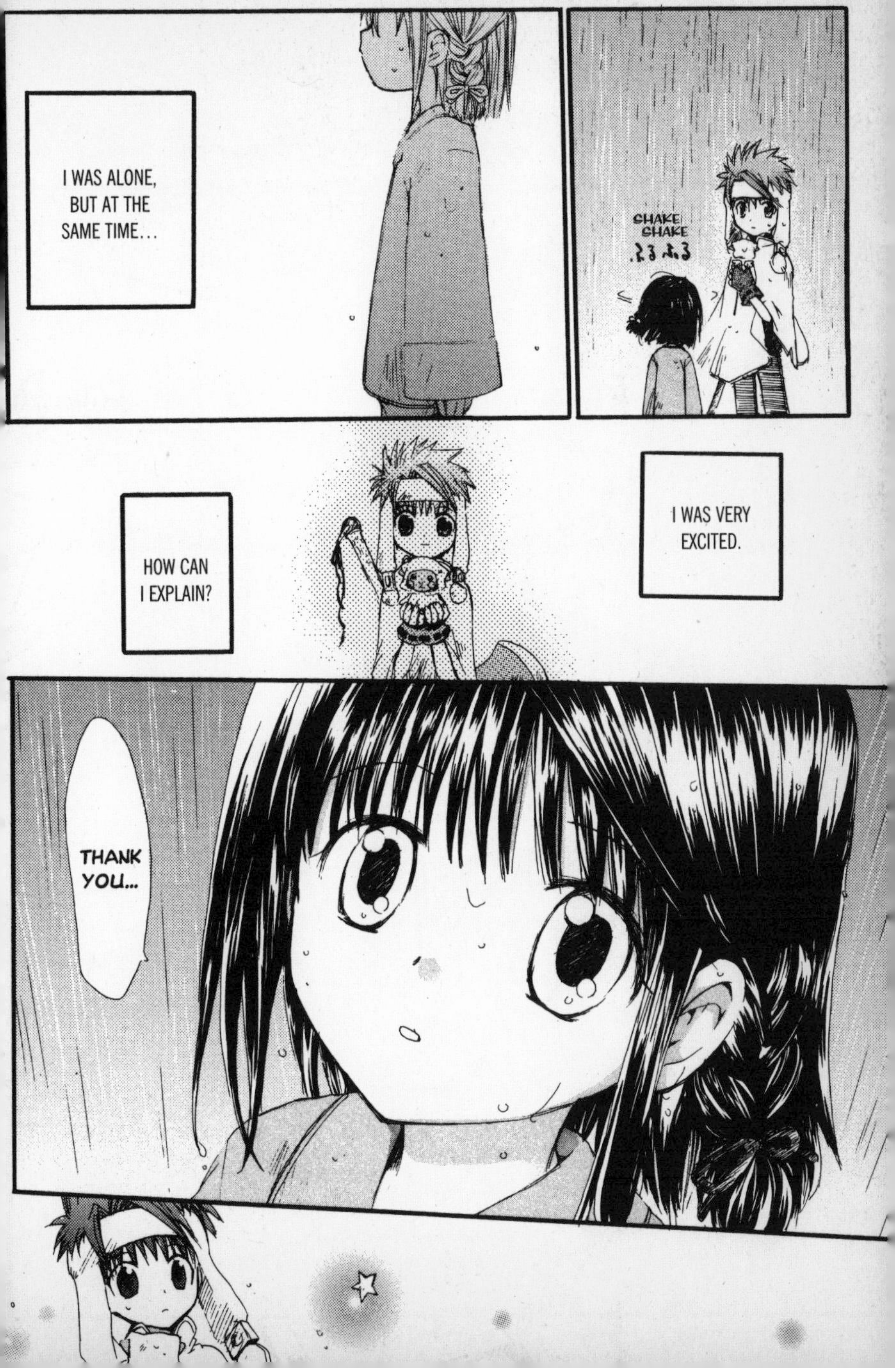
SHAKE SHAKE
ふるふる
I WAS ALONE, BUT AT THE SAME TIME…
I WAS VERY EXCITED.
HOW CAN I EXPLAIN?
THANK YOU...

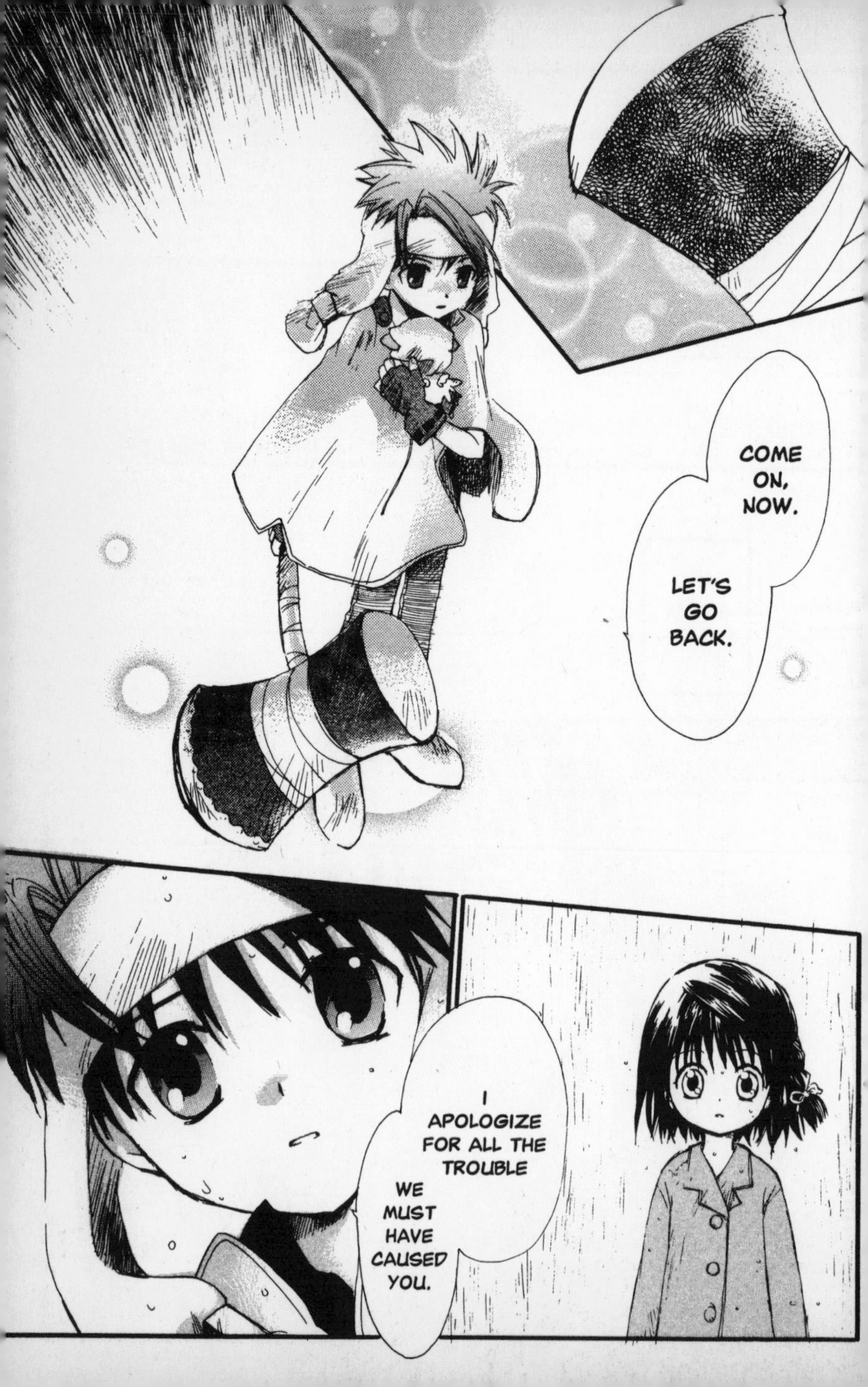
COME ON, NOW.
LET'S GO BACK.
I APOLOGIZE FOR ALL THE TROUBLE
WE MUST HAVE CAUSED YOU.

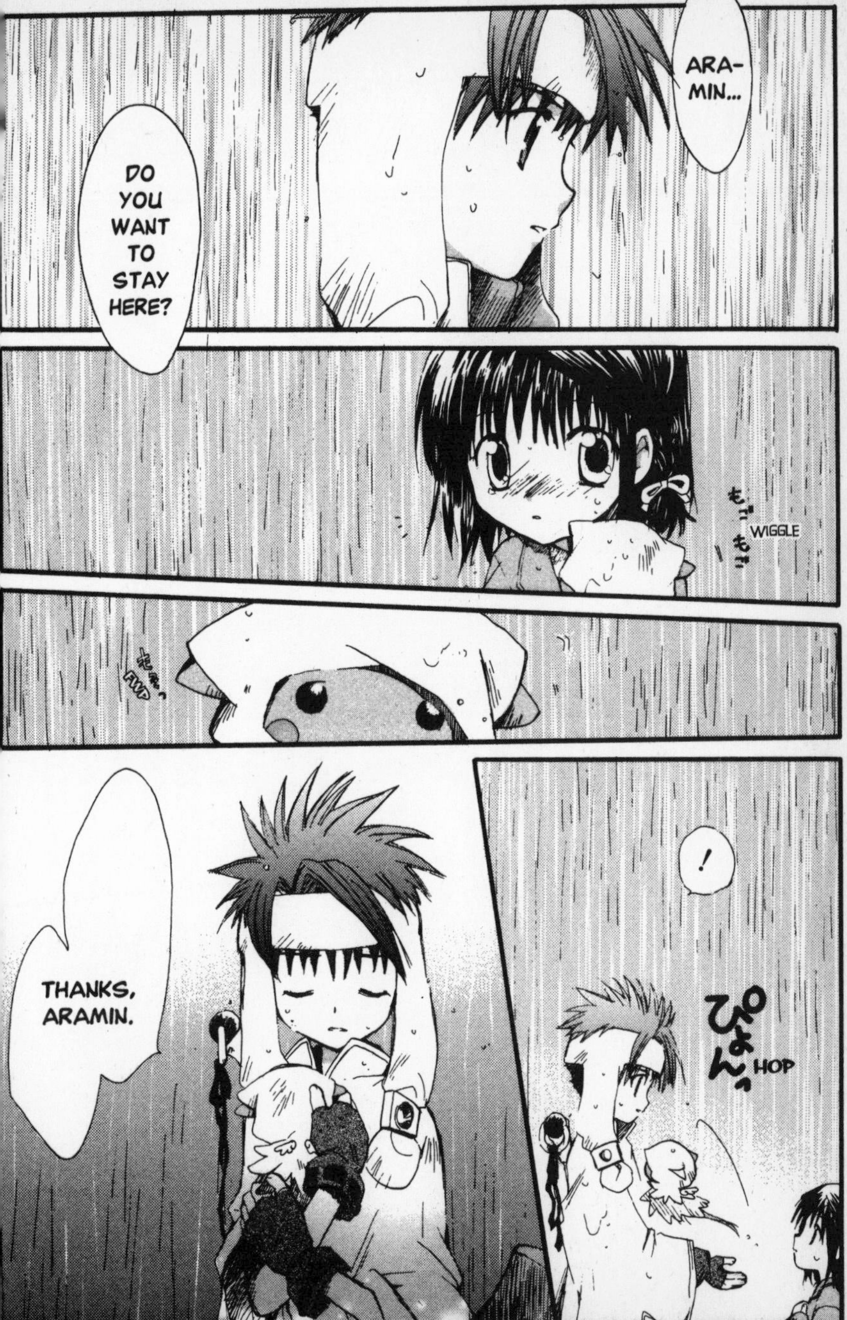
ARA-MIN...
DO YOU WANT TO STAY HERE?
もごもご WIGGLE
FWP
!
ぴょん HOP
THANKS, ARAMIN.

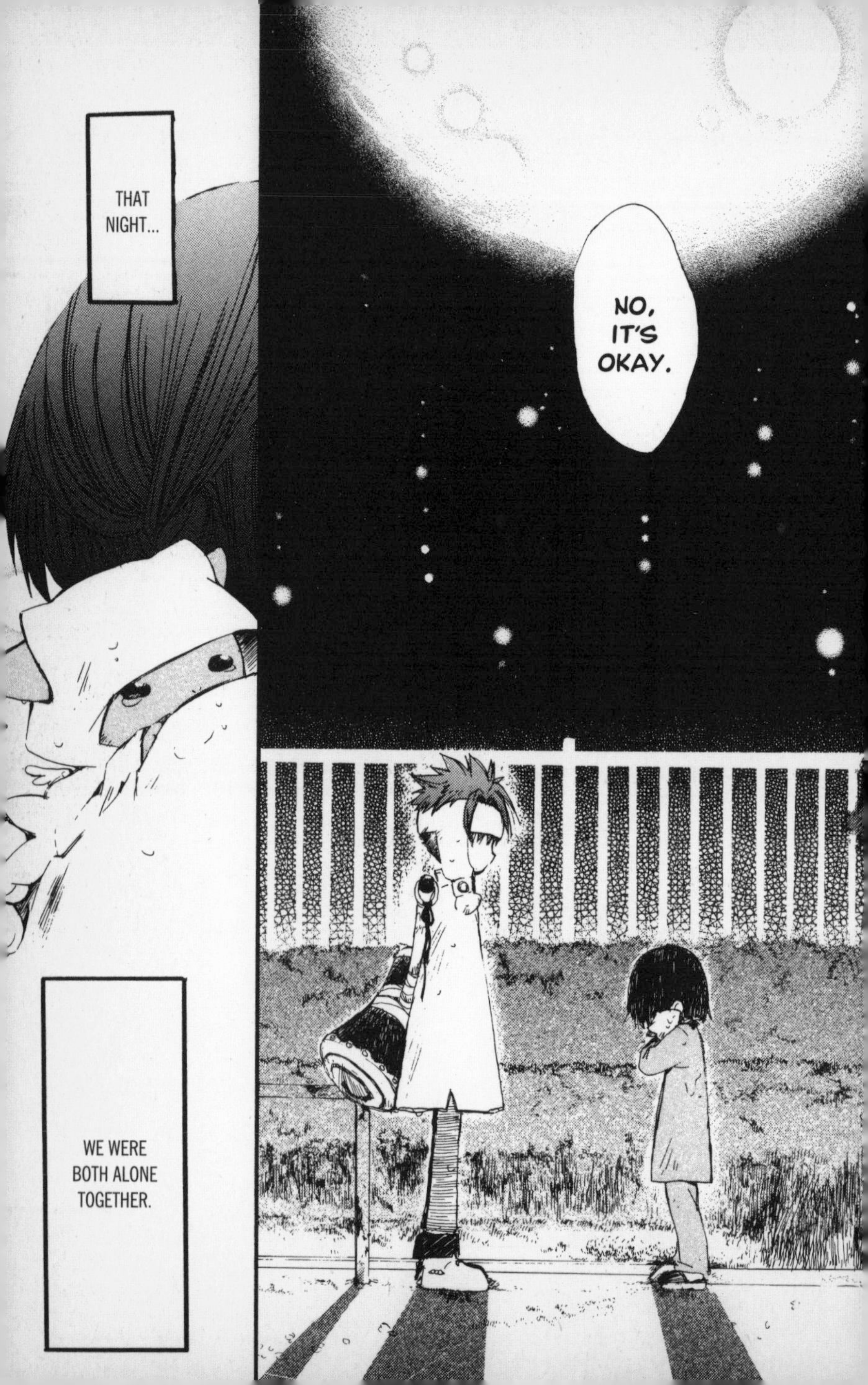
NO, IT'S OKAY.
THAT NIGHT...
WE WERE BOTH ALONE TOGETHER.

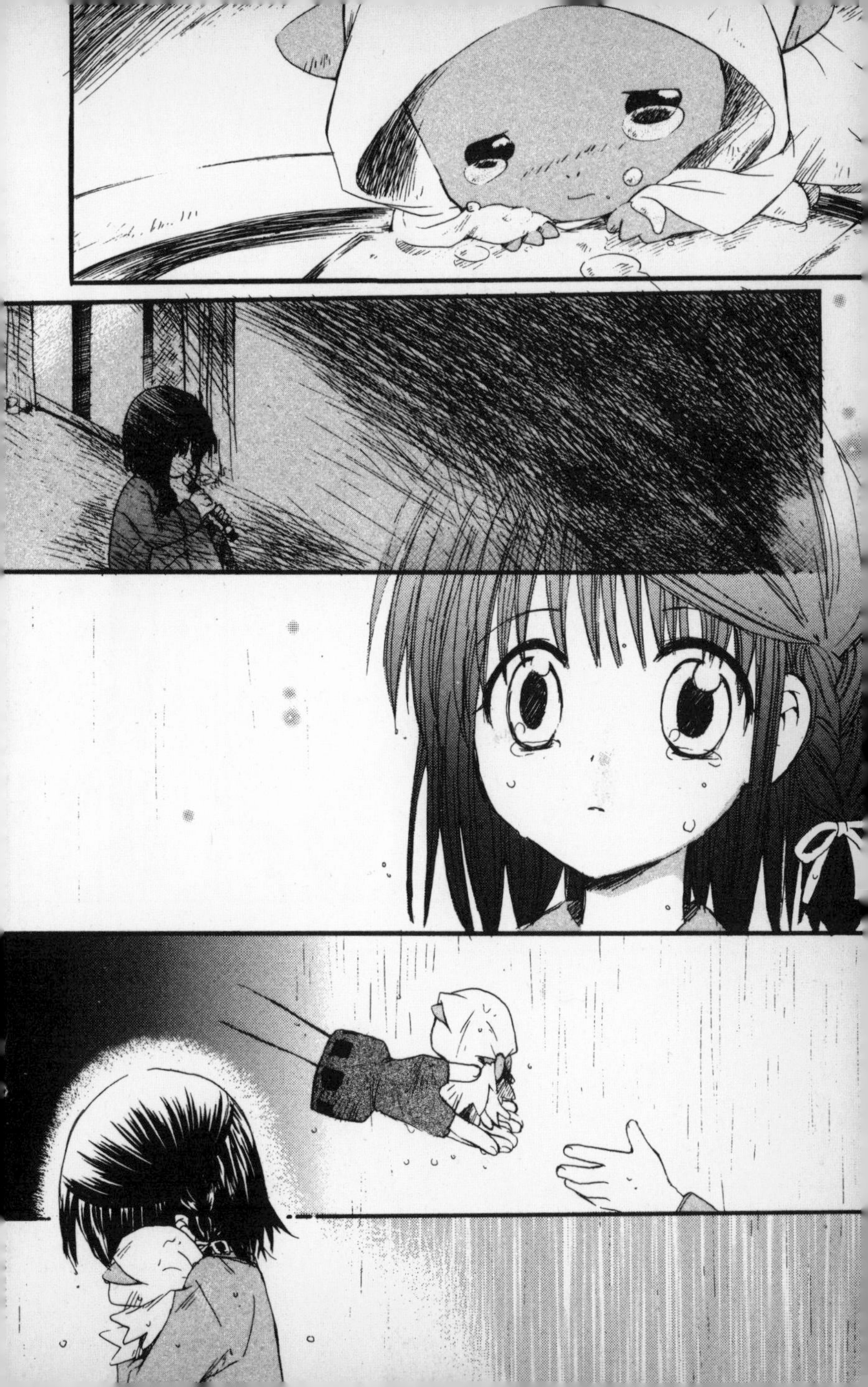

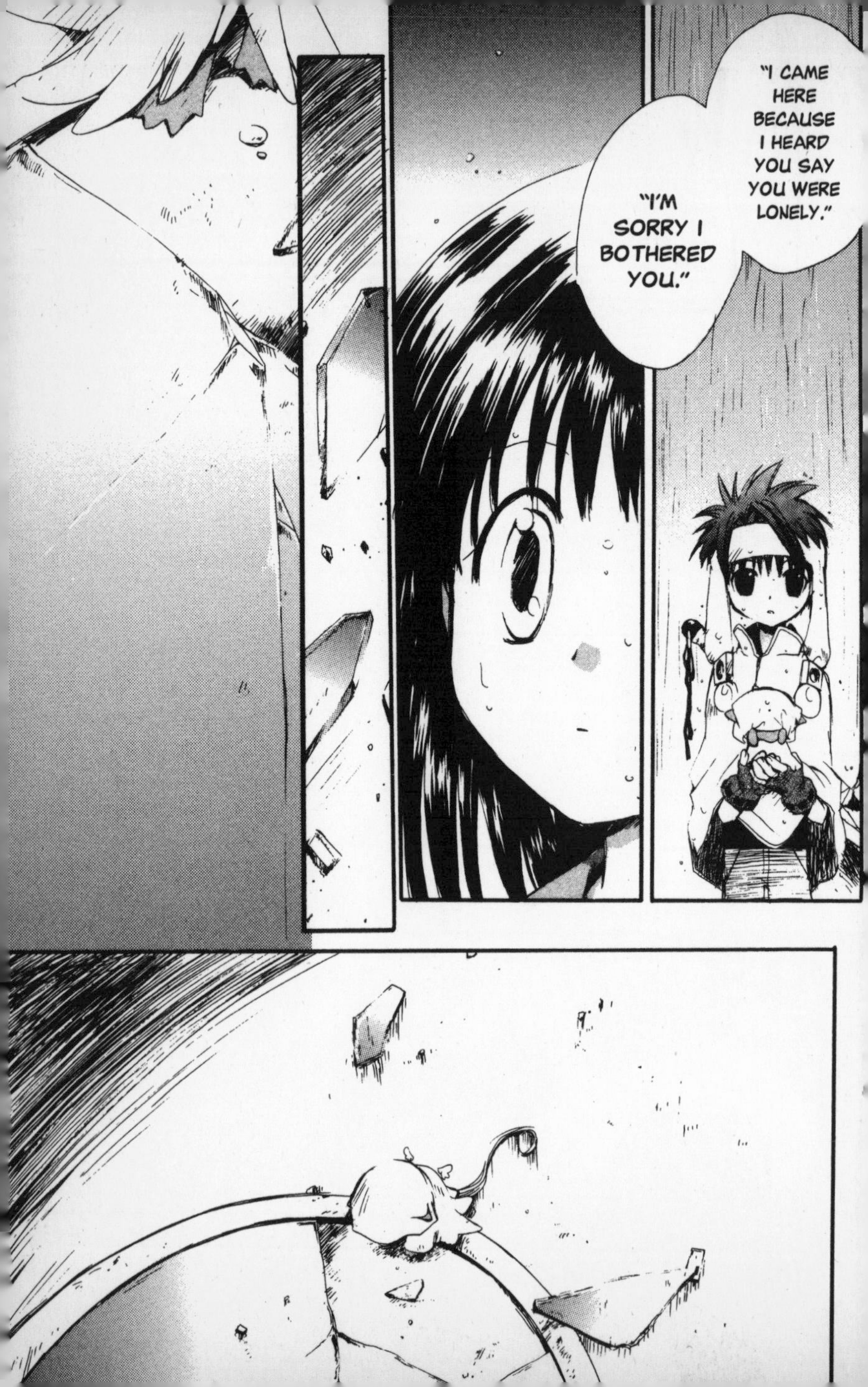
"I CAME HERE BECAUSE I HEARD YOU SAY YOU WERE LONELY."
"I'M SORRY I BOTHERED YOU."

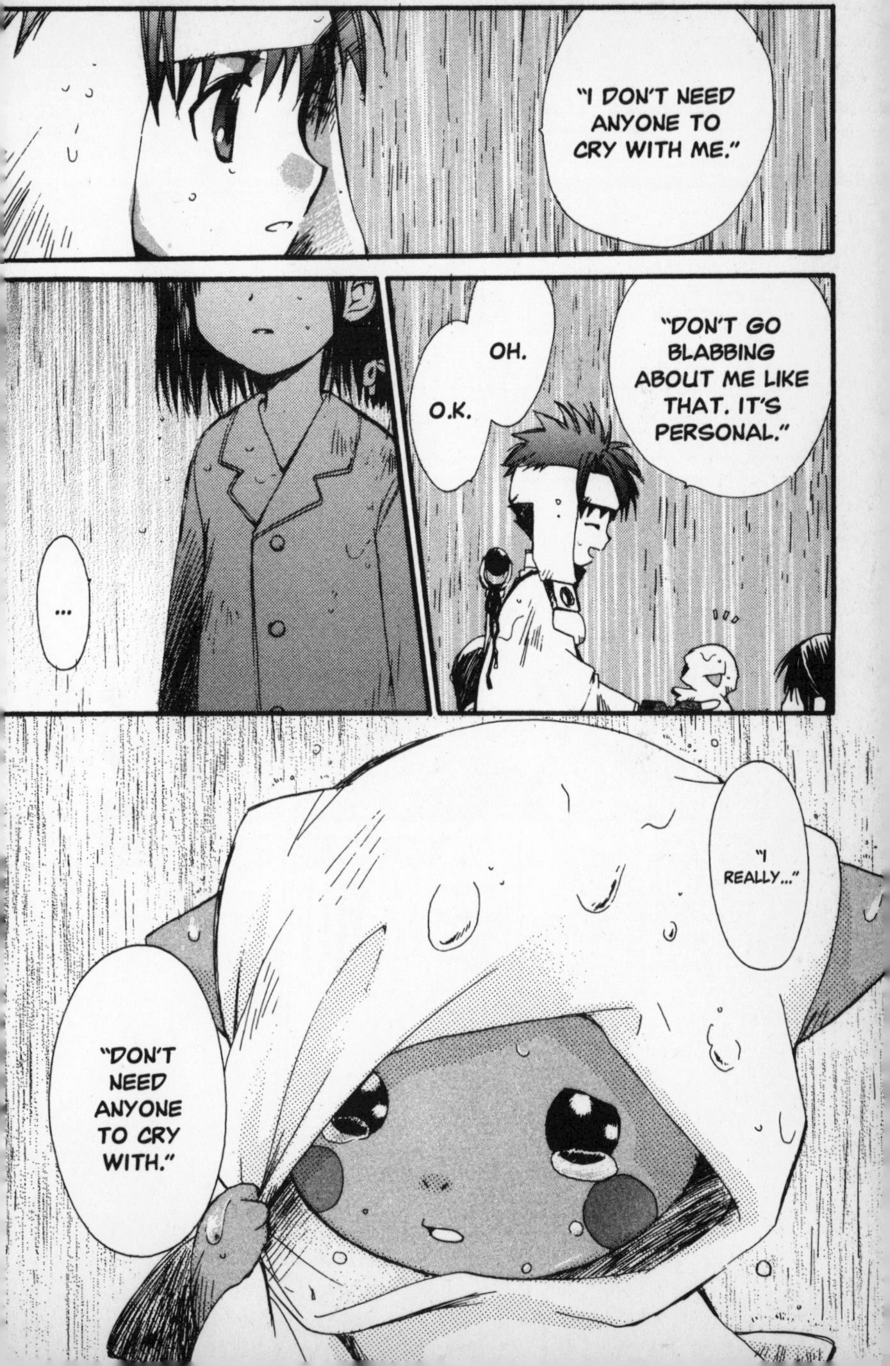
"I DON'T NEED ANYONE TO CRY WITH ME."
"DON'T GO BLABBING ABOUT ME LIKE THAT. IT'S PERSONAL."
OH.
O.K.
...
"I REALLY..."
"DON'T NEED ANYONE TO CRY WITH."

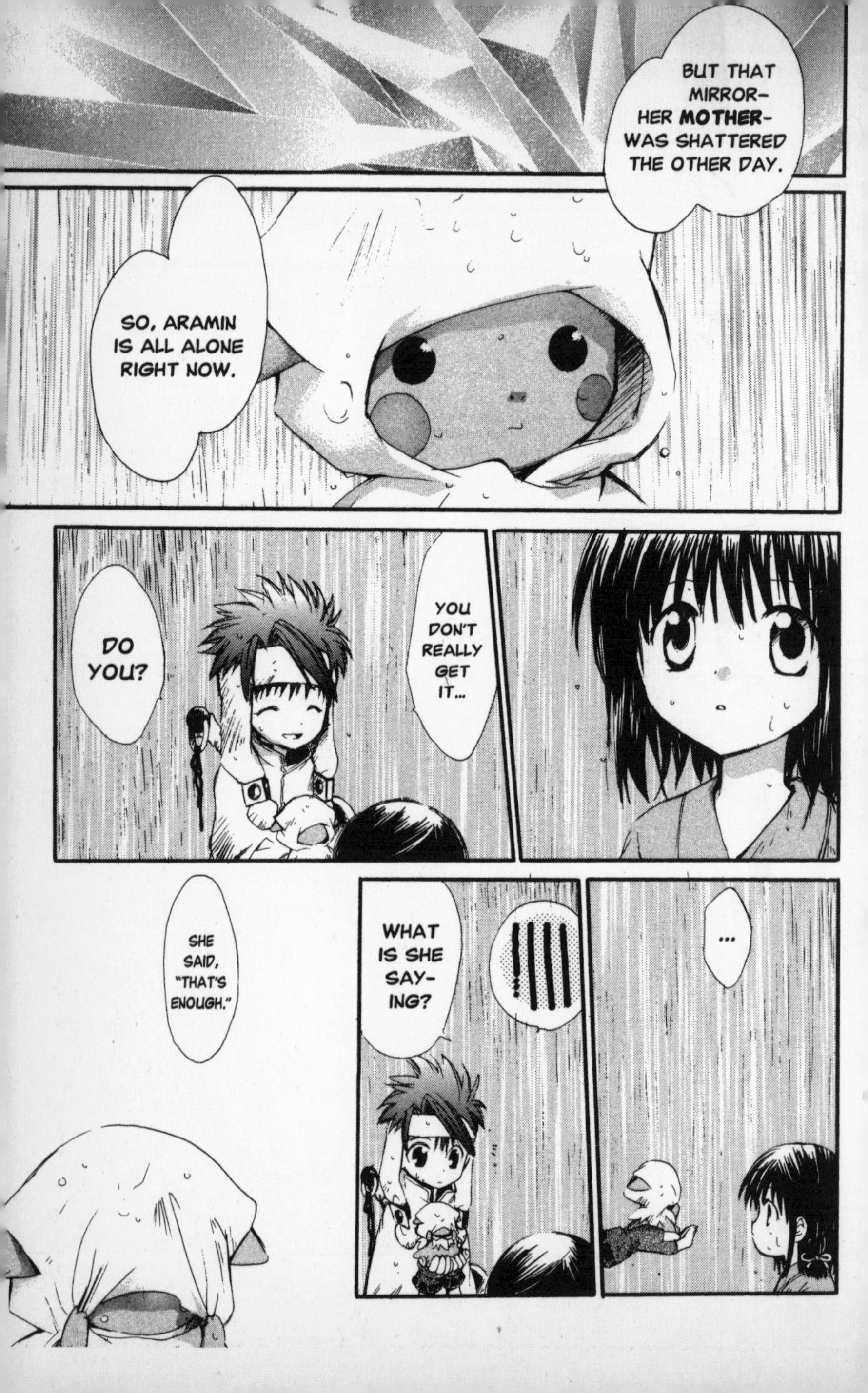
BUT THAT MIRROR– HER MOTHER– WAS SHATTERED THE OTHER DAY.
SO, ARAMIN IS ALL ALONE RIGHT NOW.
YOU DON'T REALLY GET IT...
DO YOU?
...
!!!!
WHAT IS SHE SAYING?
SHE SAID, "THAT'S ENOUGH."

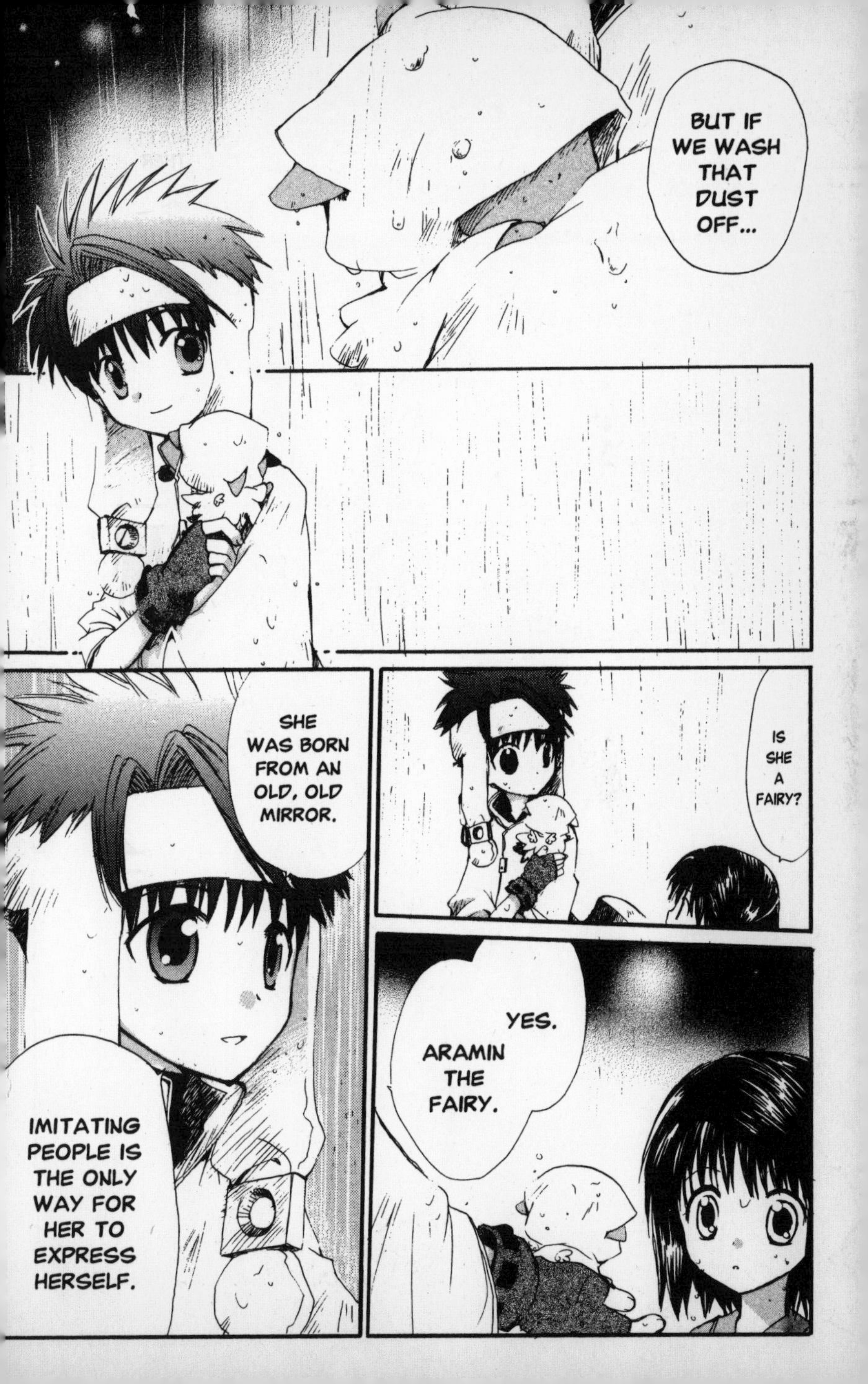
BUT IF WE WASH THAT DUST OFF...
SHE WAS BORN FROM AN OLD, OLD MIRROR.
IS SHE A FAIRY?
YES. ARAMIN THE FAIRY.
IMITATING PEOPLE IS THE ONLY WAY FOR HER TO EXPRESS HERSELF.

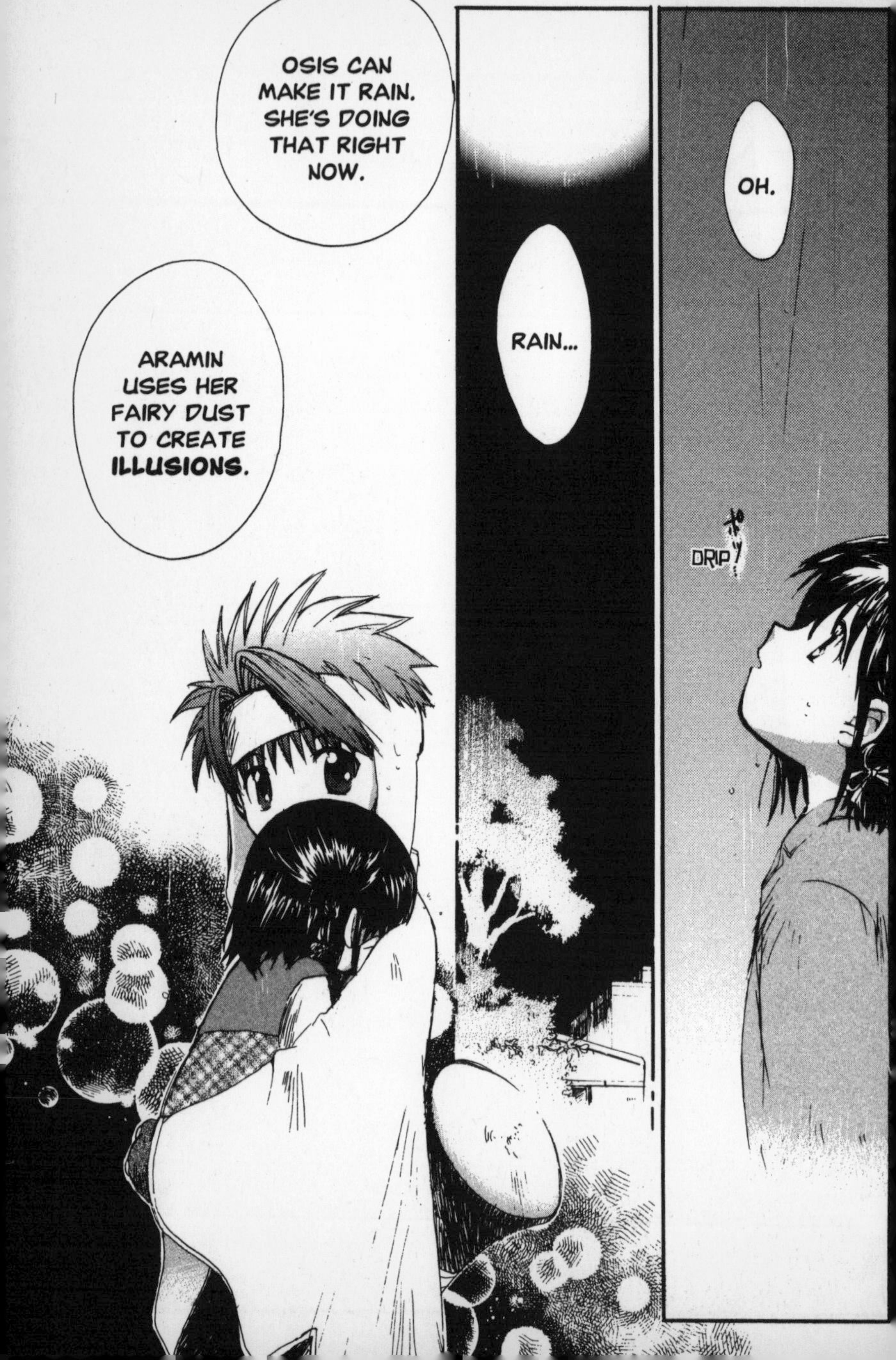
OH.
DRIP
RAIN...
OSIS CAN MAKE IT RAIN. SHE'S DOING THAT RIGHT NOW.
ARAMIN USES HER FAIRY DUST TO CREATE **ILLUSIONS.**

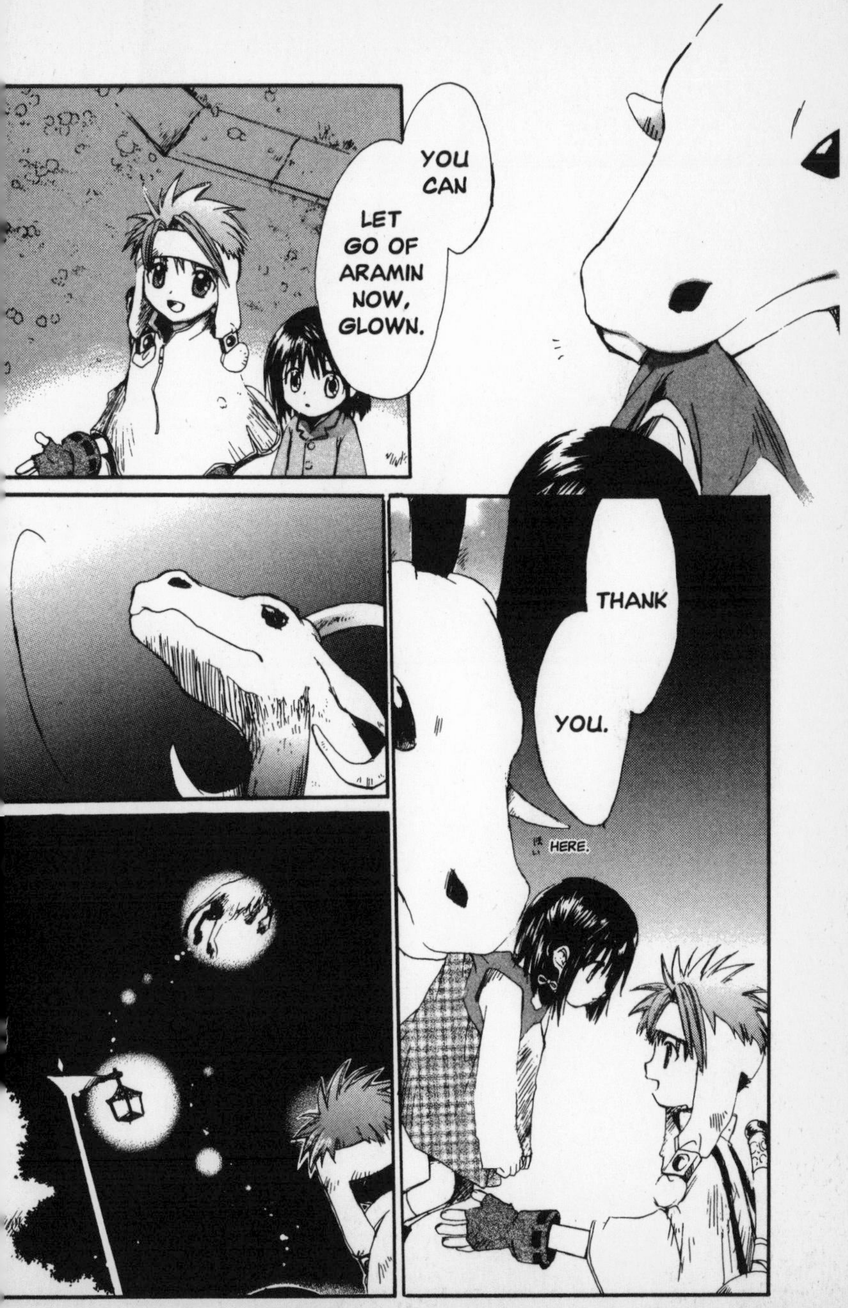
YOU CAN LET GO OF ARAMIN NOW, GLOWN.
THANK YOU.
HERE.

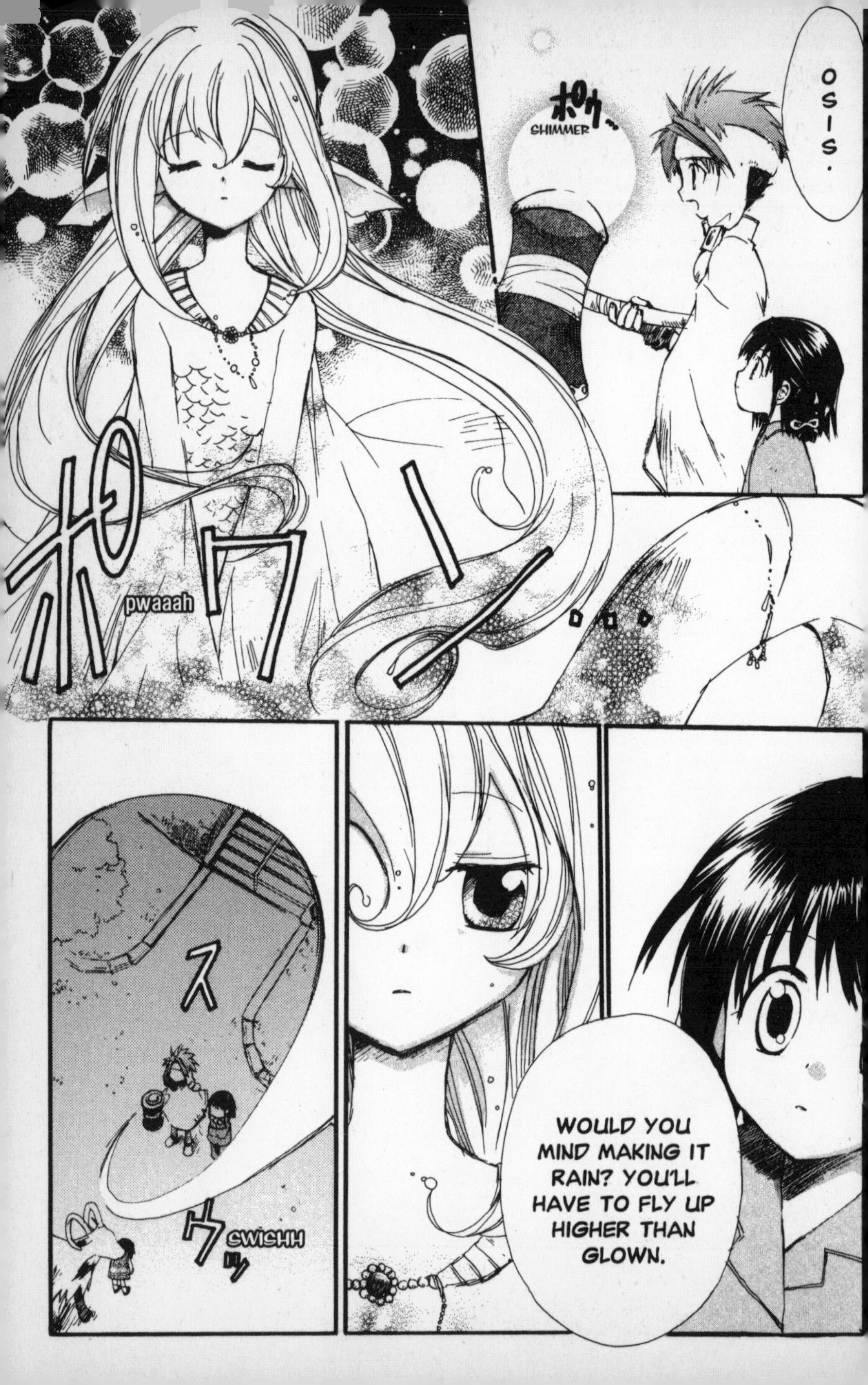
OSIS.
ホワ...
SHIMMER
ホワーン
pwaaah
...
WOULD YOU MIND MAKING IT RAIN? YOU'LL HAVE TO FLY UP HIGHER THAN GLOWN.
スウッ
SWISHH

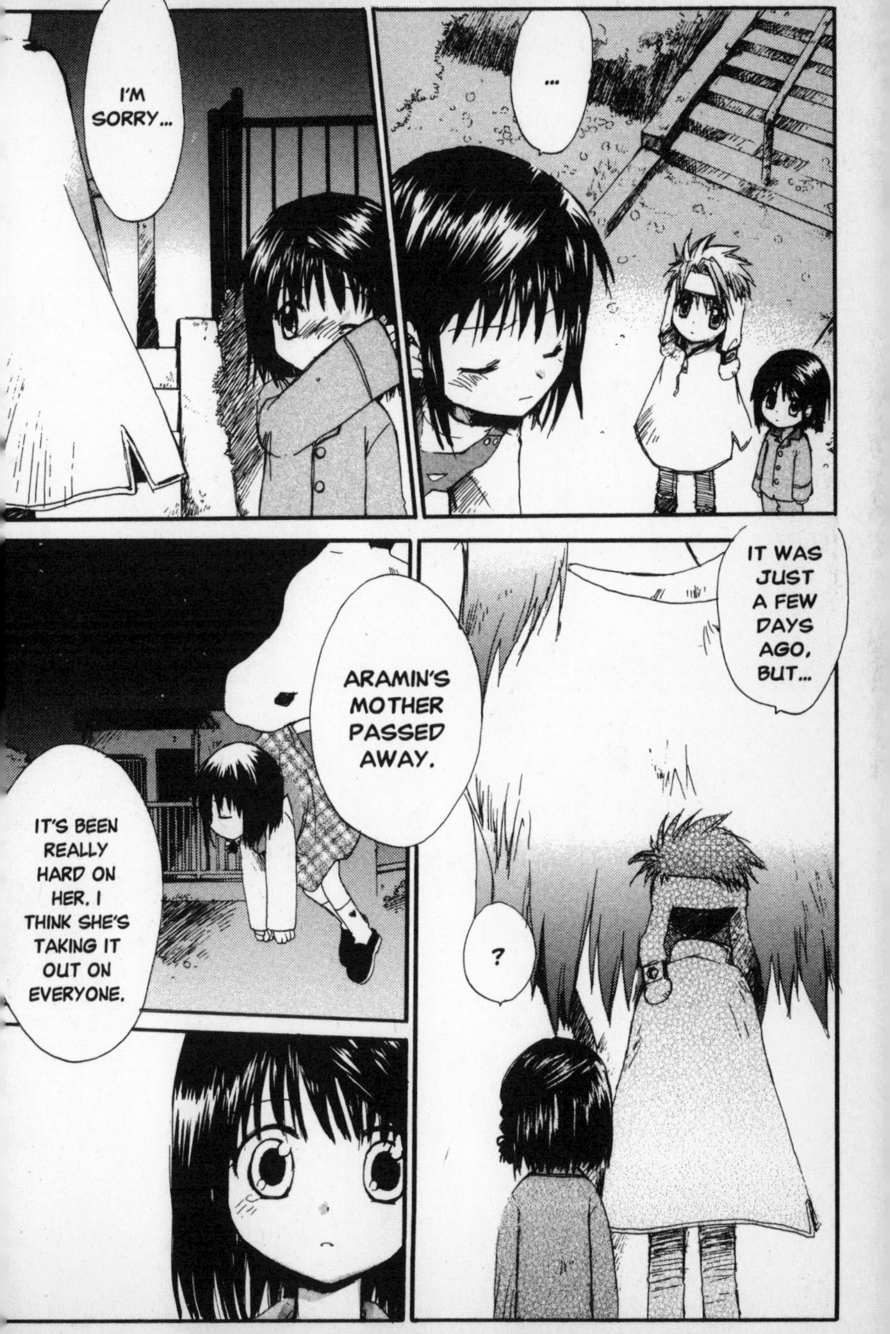
...
I'M SORRY...
IT WAS JUST A FEW DAYS AGO, BUT...
ARAMIN'S MOTHER PASSED AWAY.
?
IT'S BEEN REALLY HARD ON HER. I THINK SHE'S TAKING IT OUT ON EVERYONE.

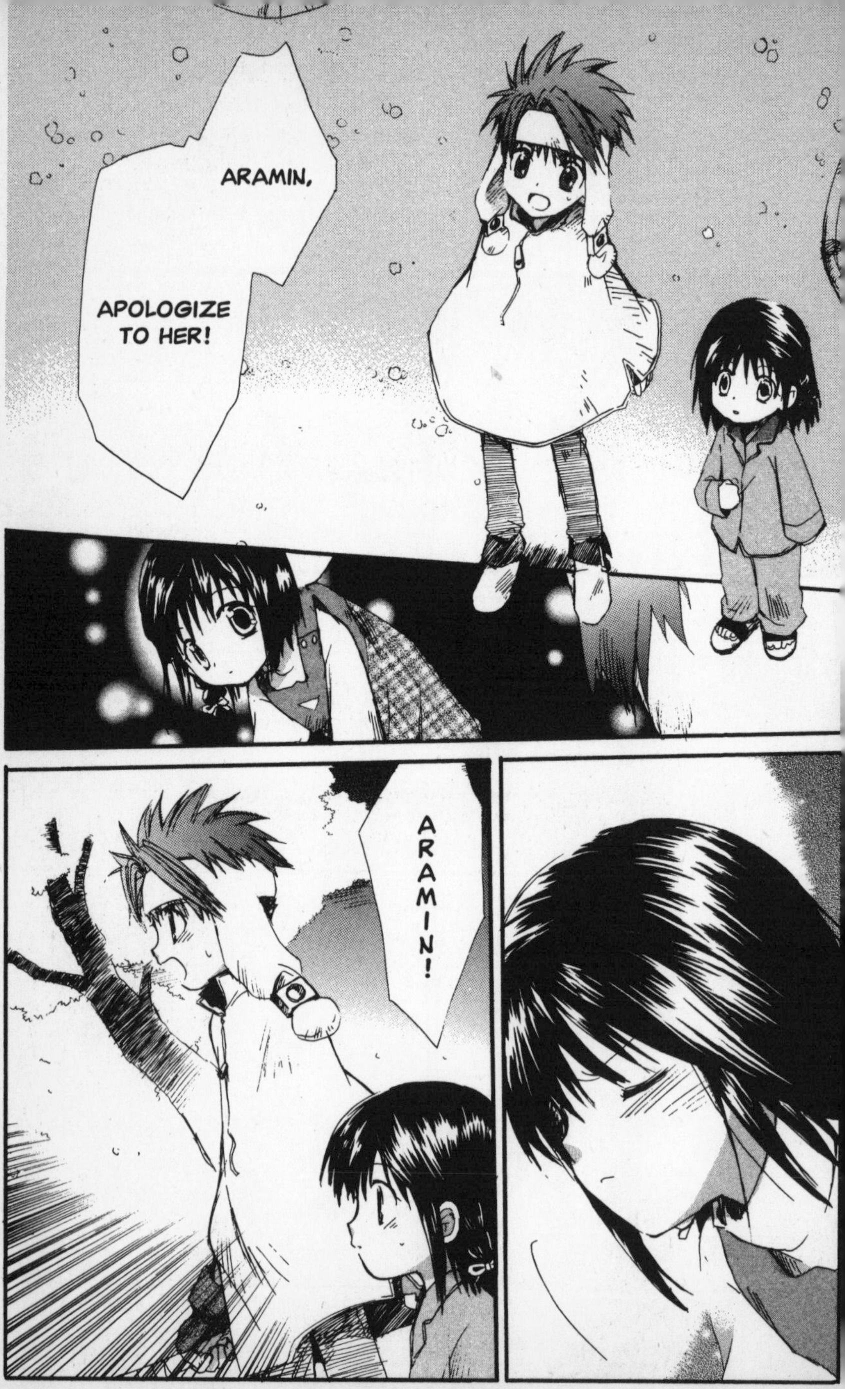
ARAMIN,
APOLOGIZE TO HER!
ARAMIN!

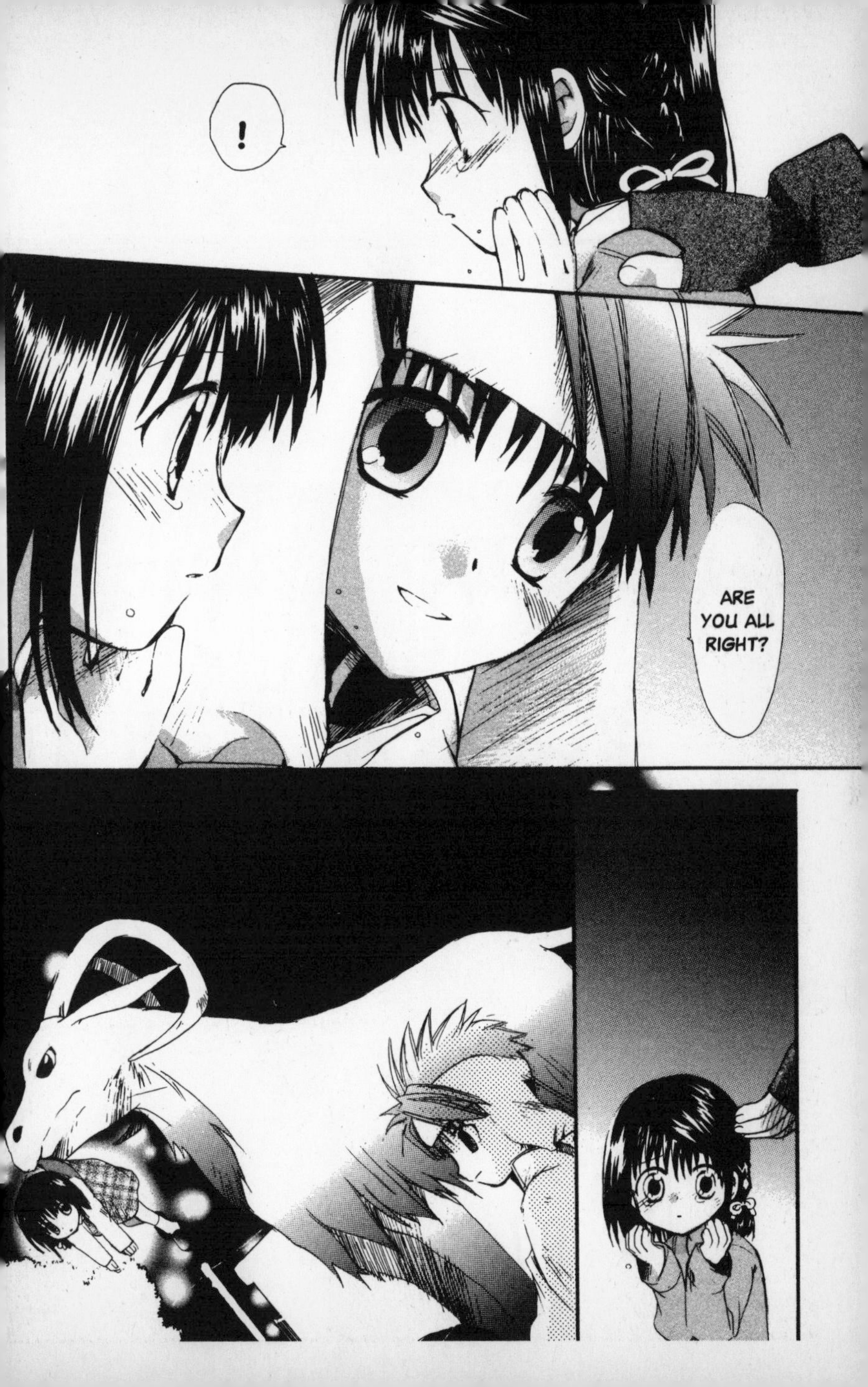
!
ARE YOU ALL RIGHT?

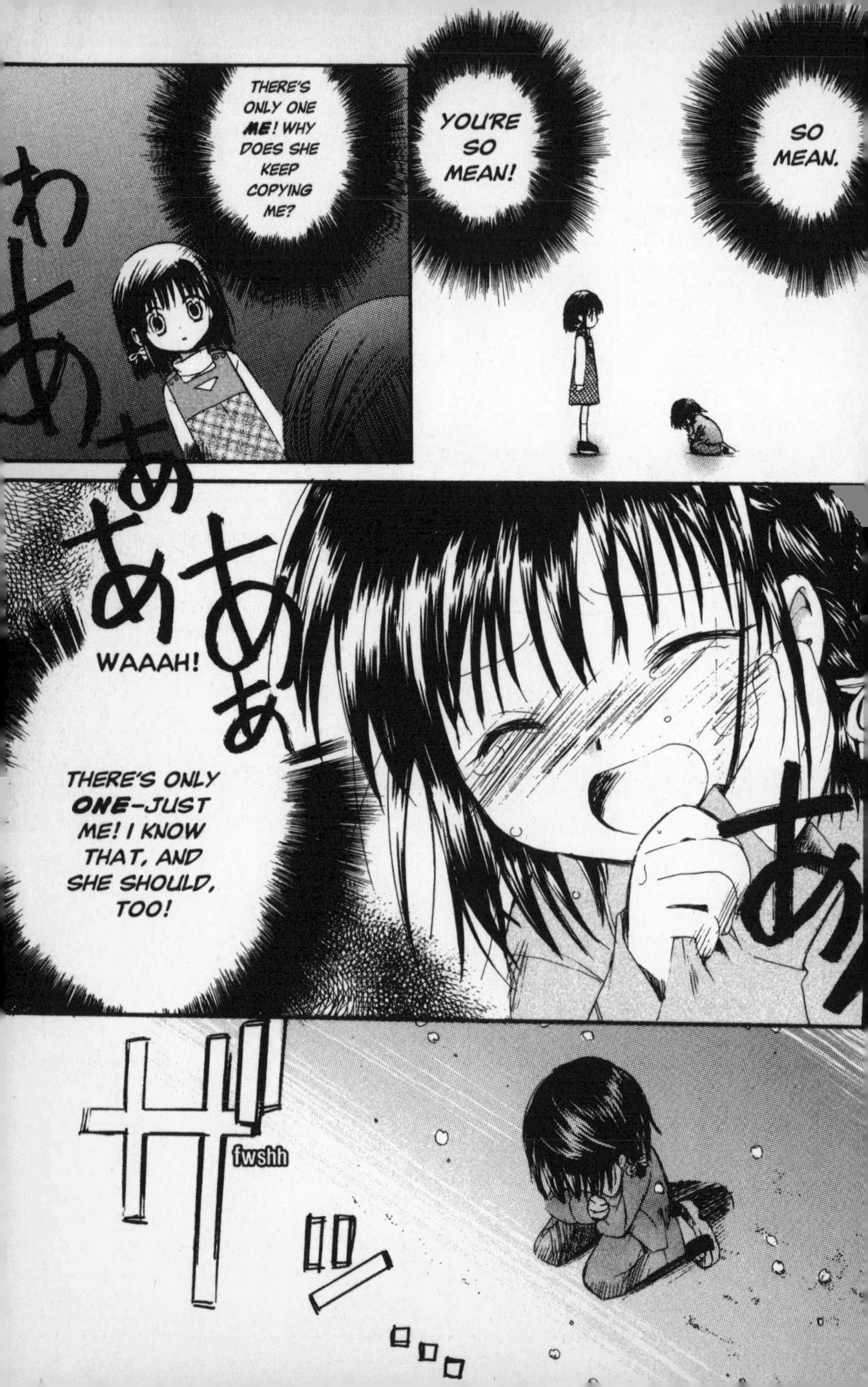
SO MEAN.
YOU'RE SO MEAN!
THERE'S ONLY ONE ME! WHY DOES SHE KEEP COPYING ME?
WAAAH!
THERE'S ONLY ONE—JUST ME! I KNOW THAT, AND SHE SHOULD, TOO!
fwshh

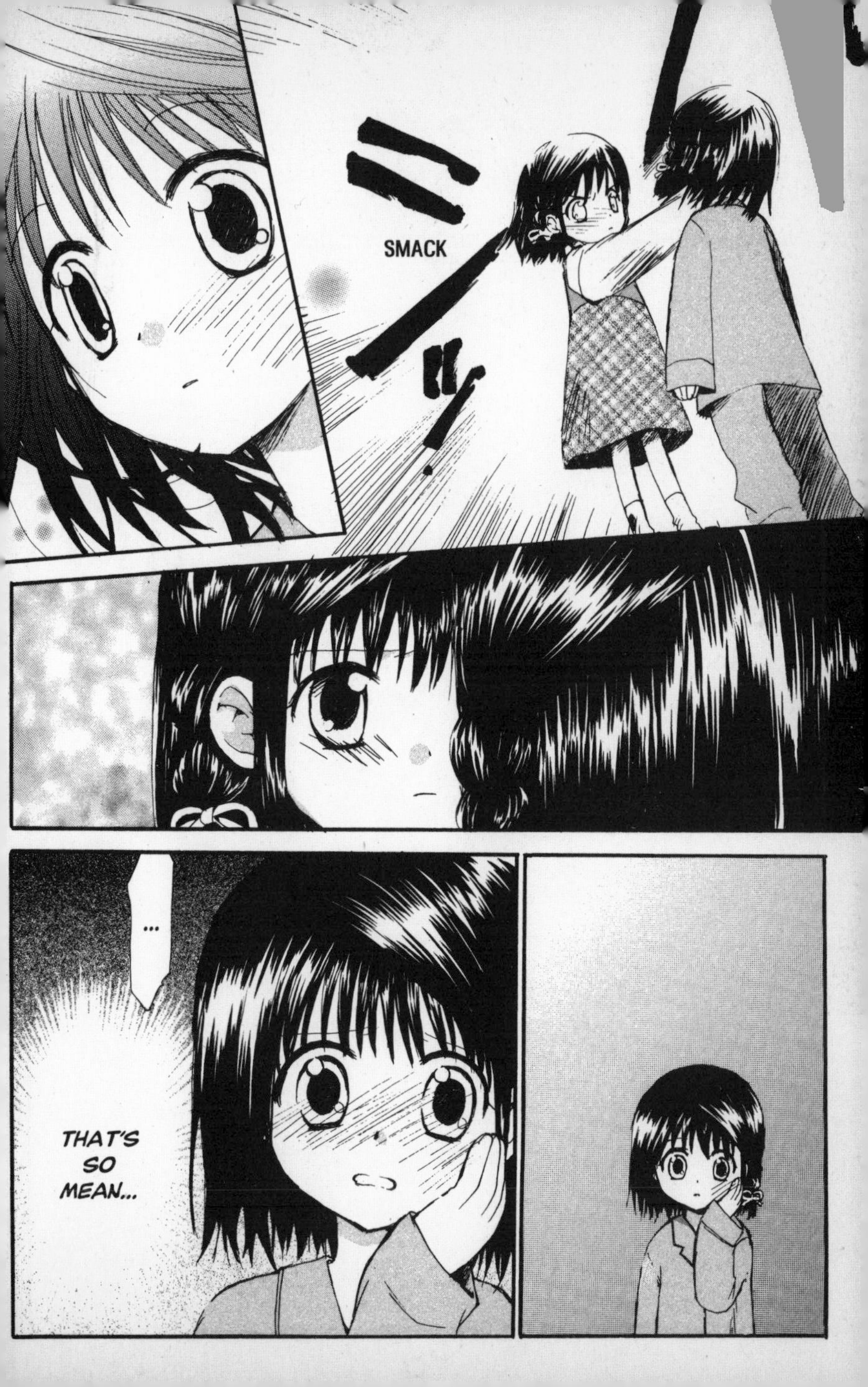

SMACK
...
THAT'S SO MEAN...

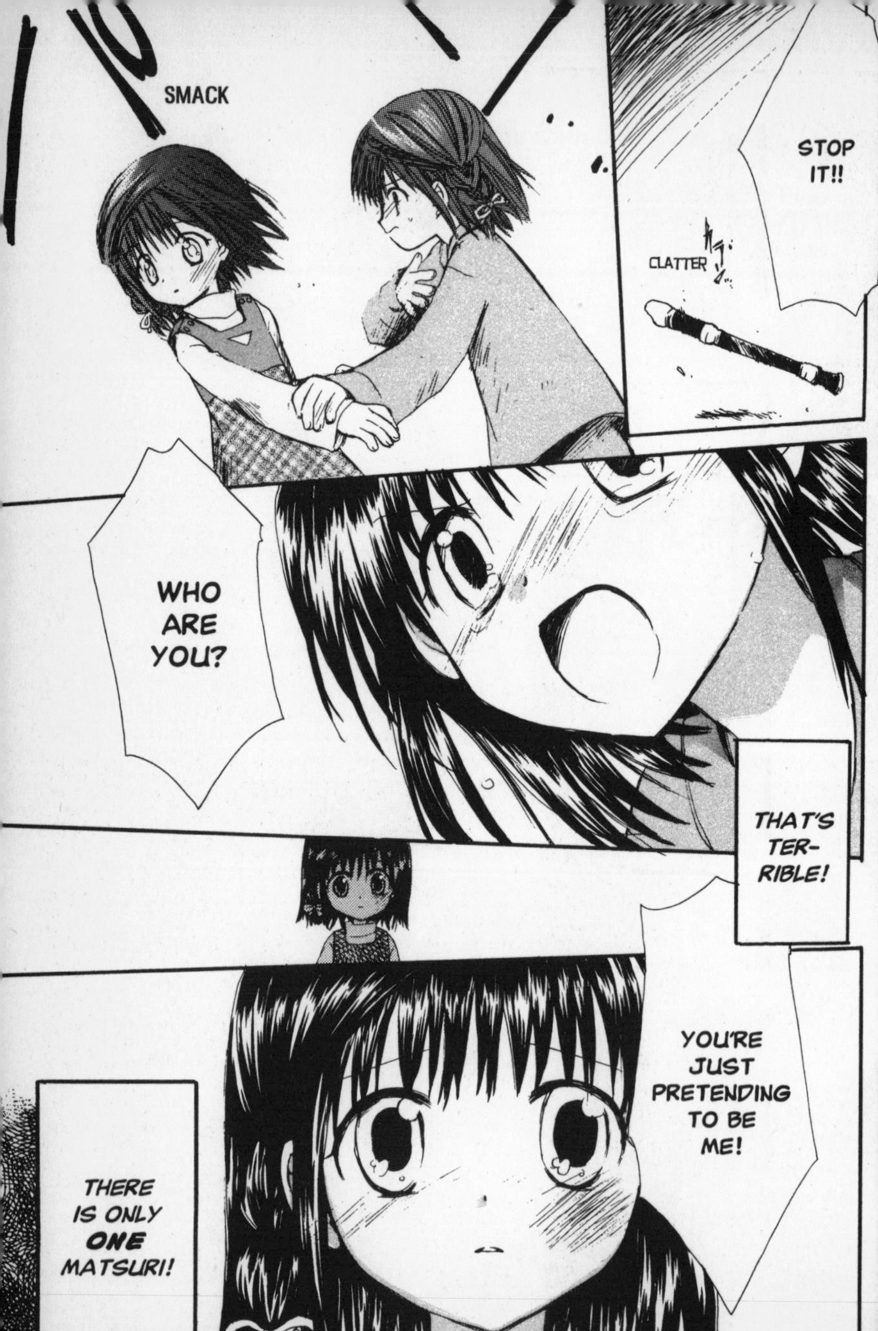
STOP IT!!
CLATTER
SMACK
WHO ARE YOU?
THAT'S TER-RIBLE!
YOU'RE JUST PRETENDING TO BE ME!
THERE IS ONLY ONE MATSURI!

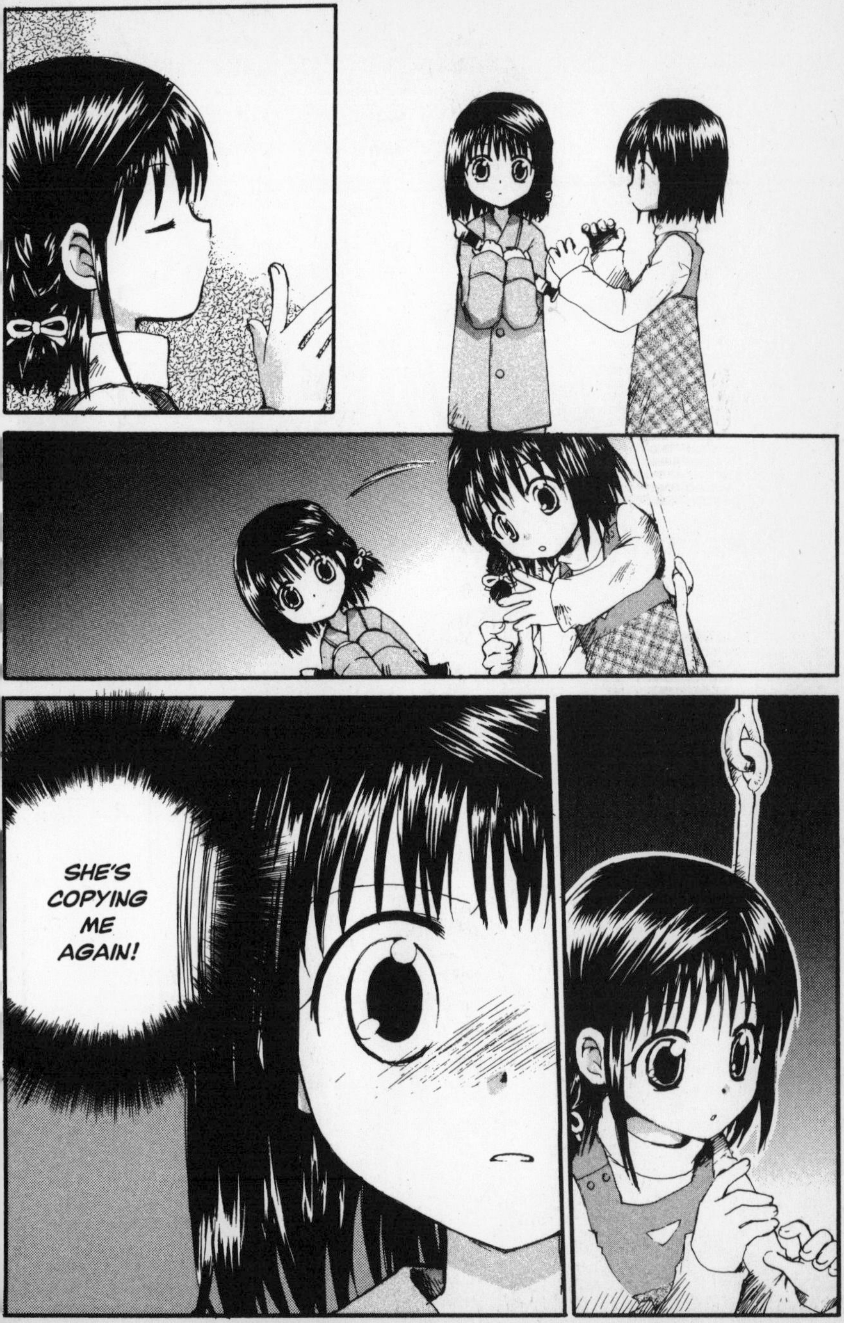
SHE'S COPYING ME AGAIN!

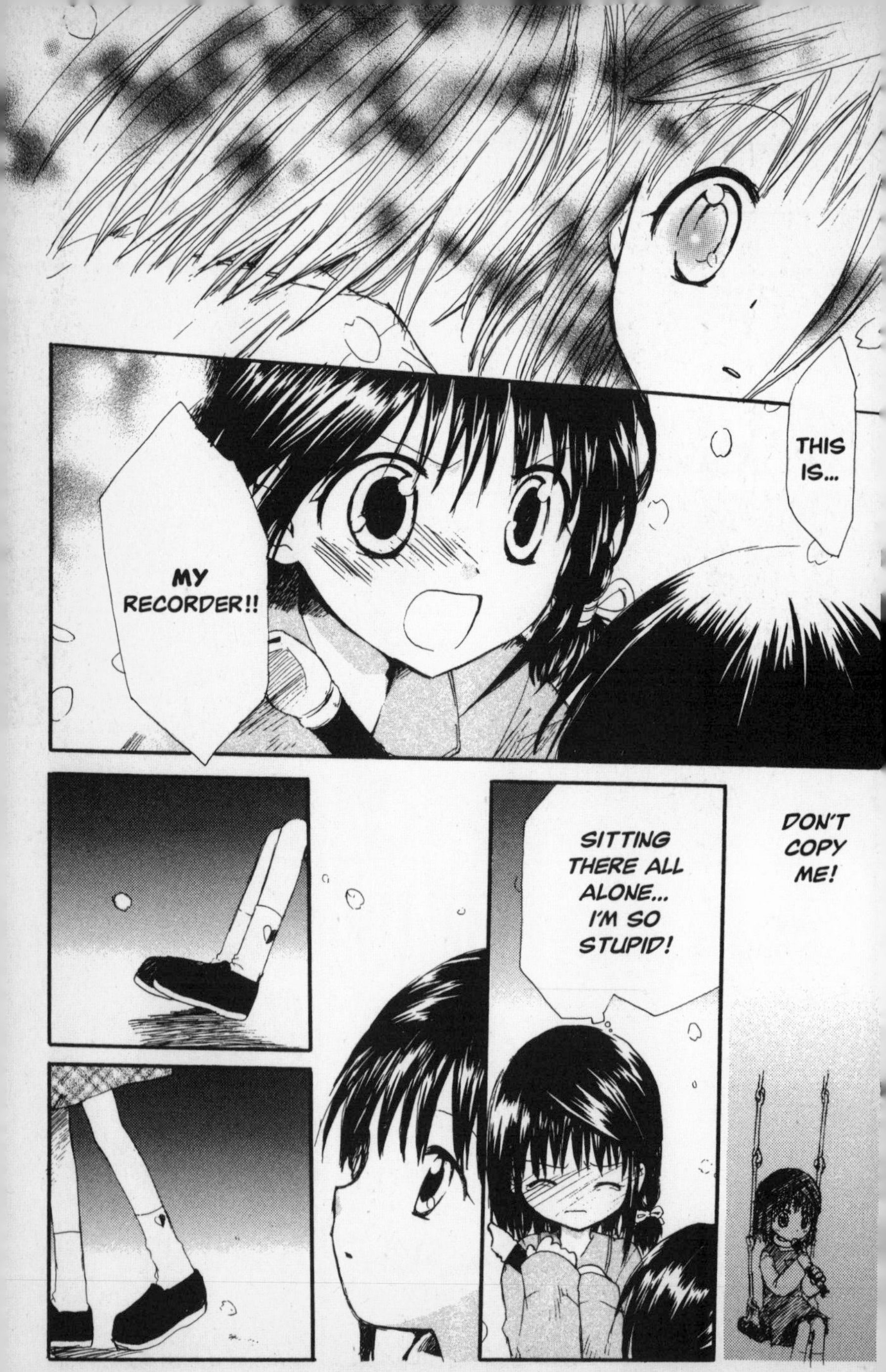
THIS IS...
MY RECORDER!!
DON'T COPY ME!
SITTING THERE ALL ALONE... I'M SO STUPID!

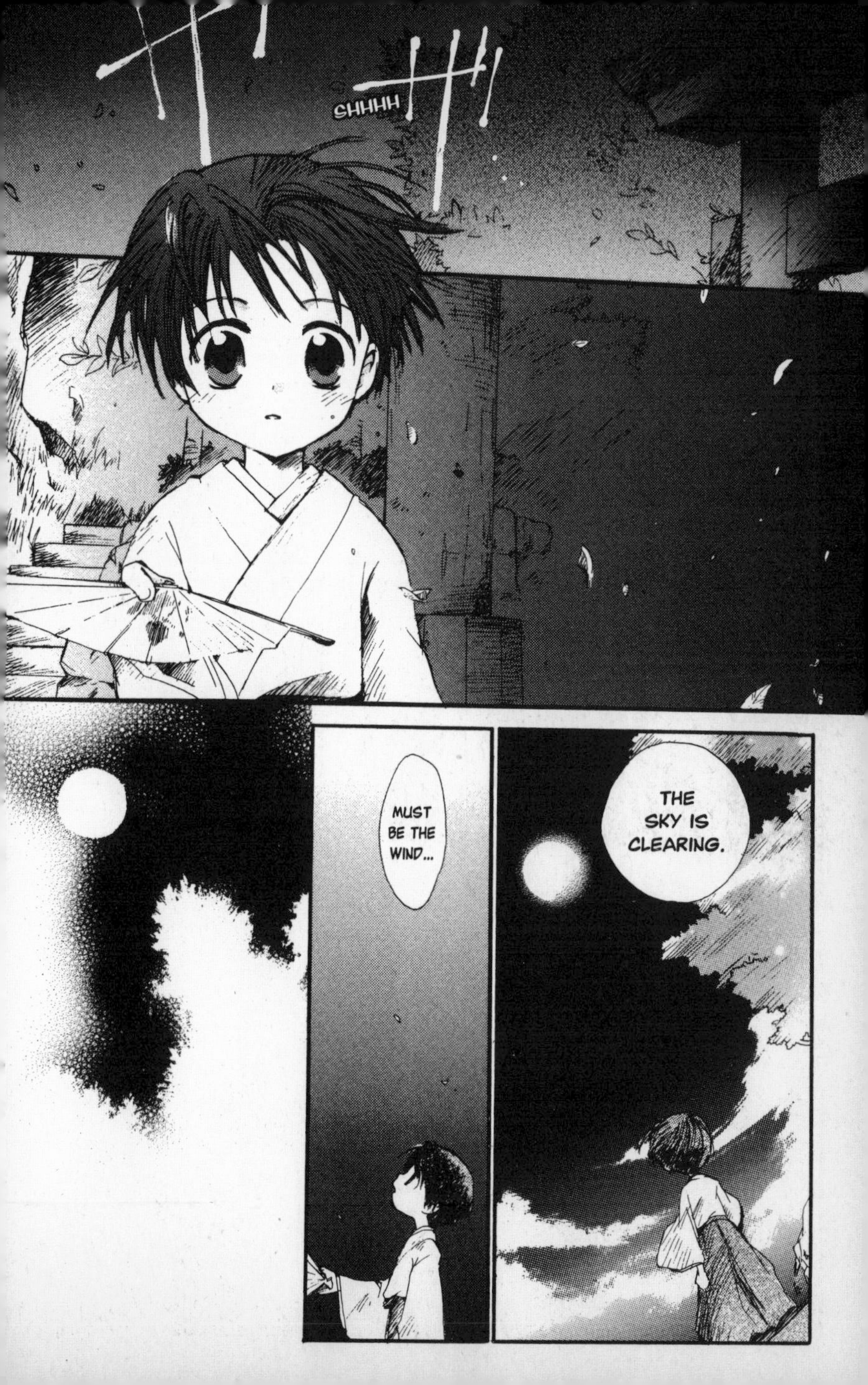
SHHHH
THE SKY IS CLEARING.
MUST BE THE WIND...

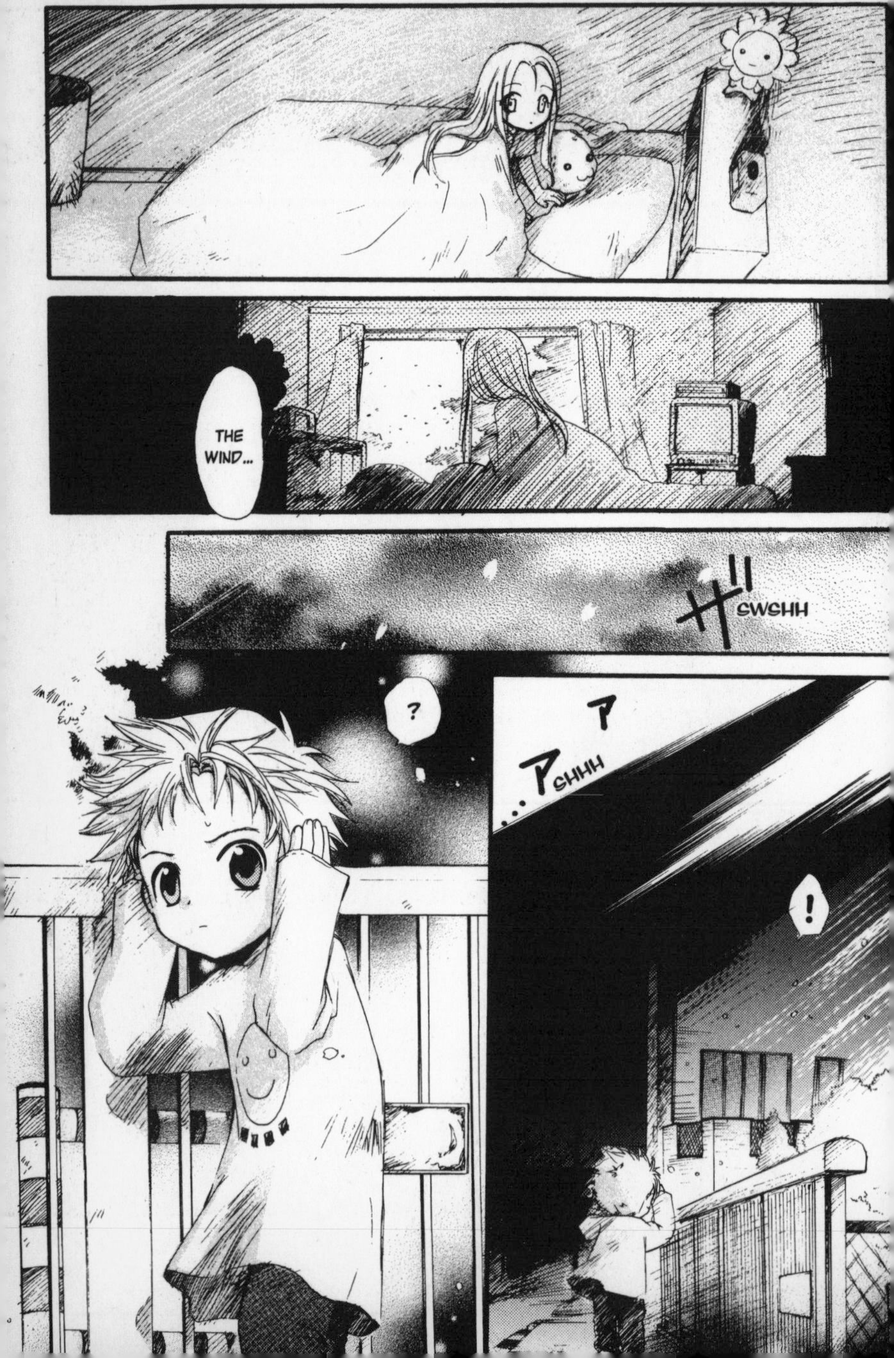
THE WIND...
SWSHH
SHHH
!
?

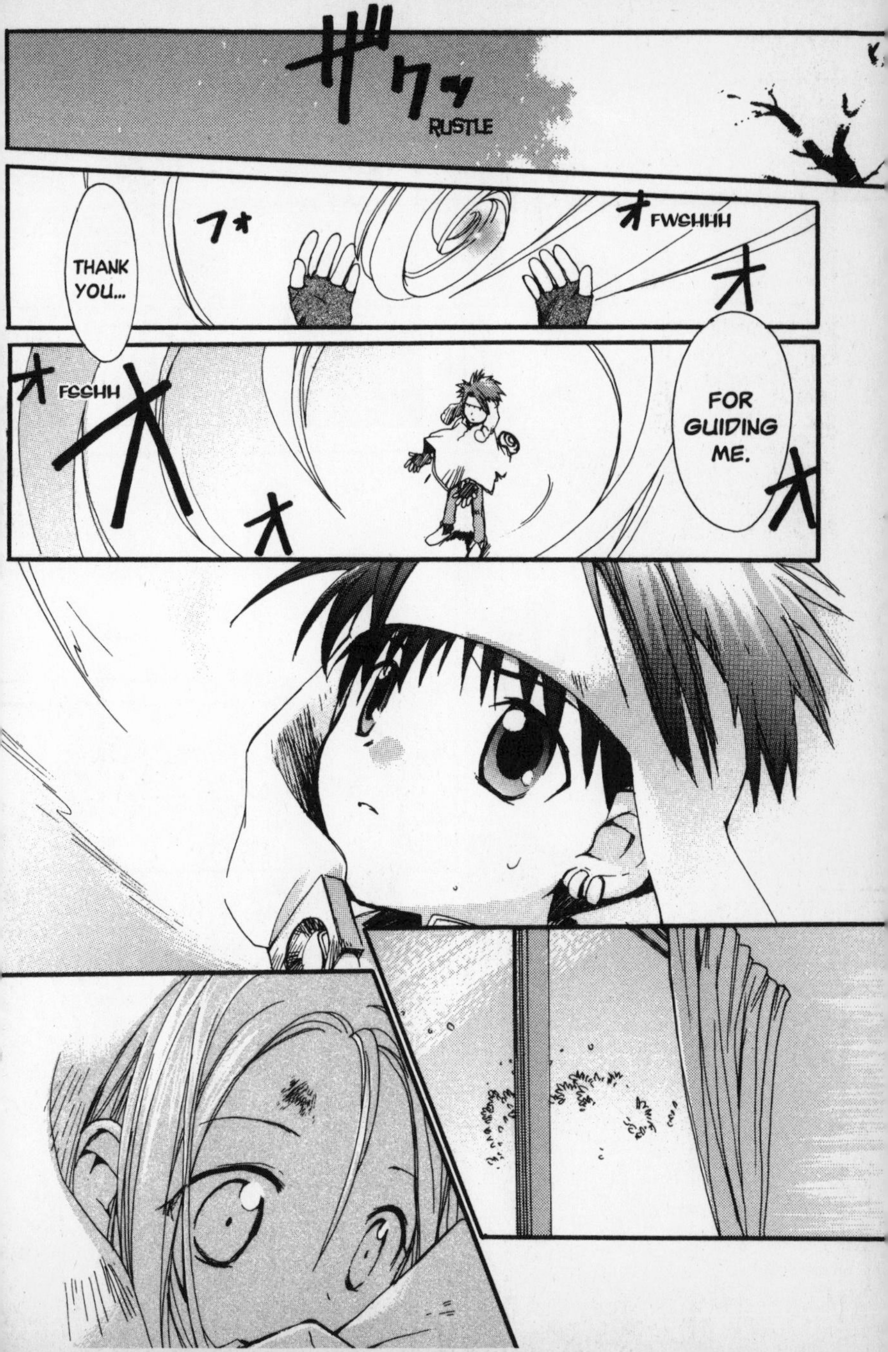
ザクッ
RUSTLE
フォ
FWSHHH
THANK YOU...
FSSHH
FOR GUIDING ME.

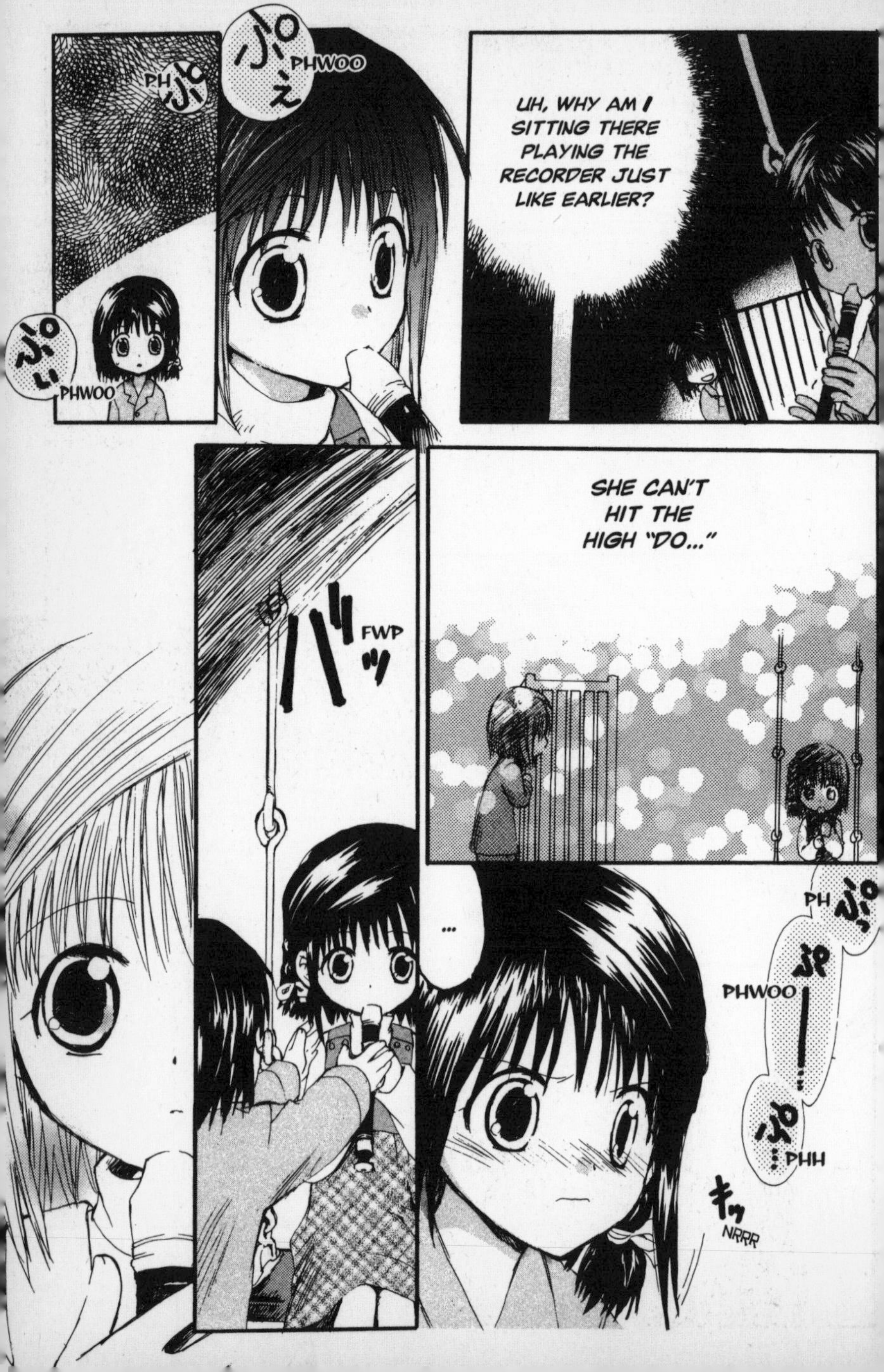
UH, WHY AM I SITTING THERE PLAYING THE RECORDER JUST LIKE EARLIER?
ぷぇ PHWOO
PH ぷ
ぷぃ PHWOO
SHE CAN'T HIT THE HIGH "DO..."
バッ FWP
...
PH ぷ
ぷー PHWOO
ぷ… PHH
キッ NRRR

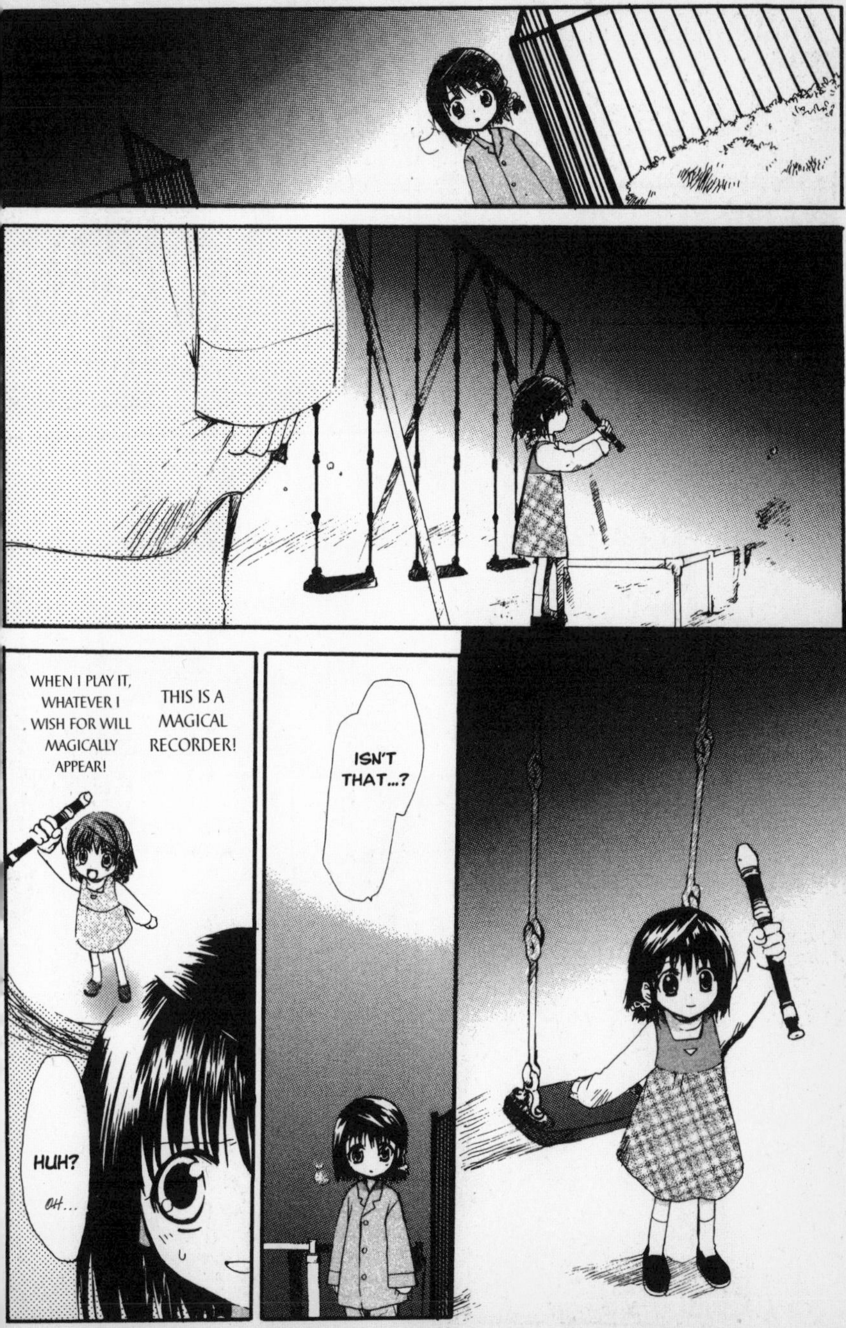
ISN'T THAT...?
THIS IS A MAGICAL RECORDER!
WHEN I PLAY IT, WHATEVER I WISH FOR WILL MAGICALLY APPEAR!
HUH?
OH...

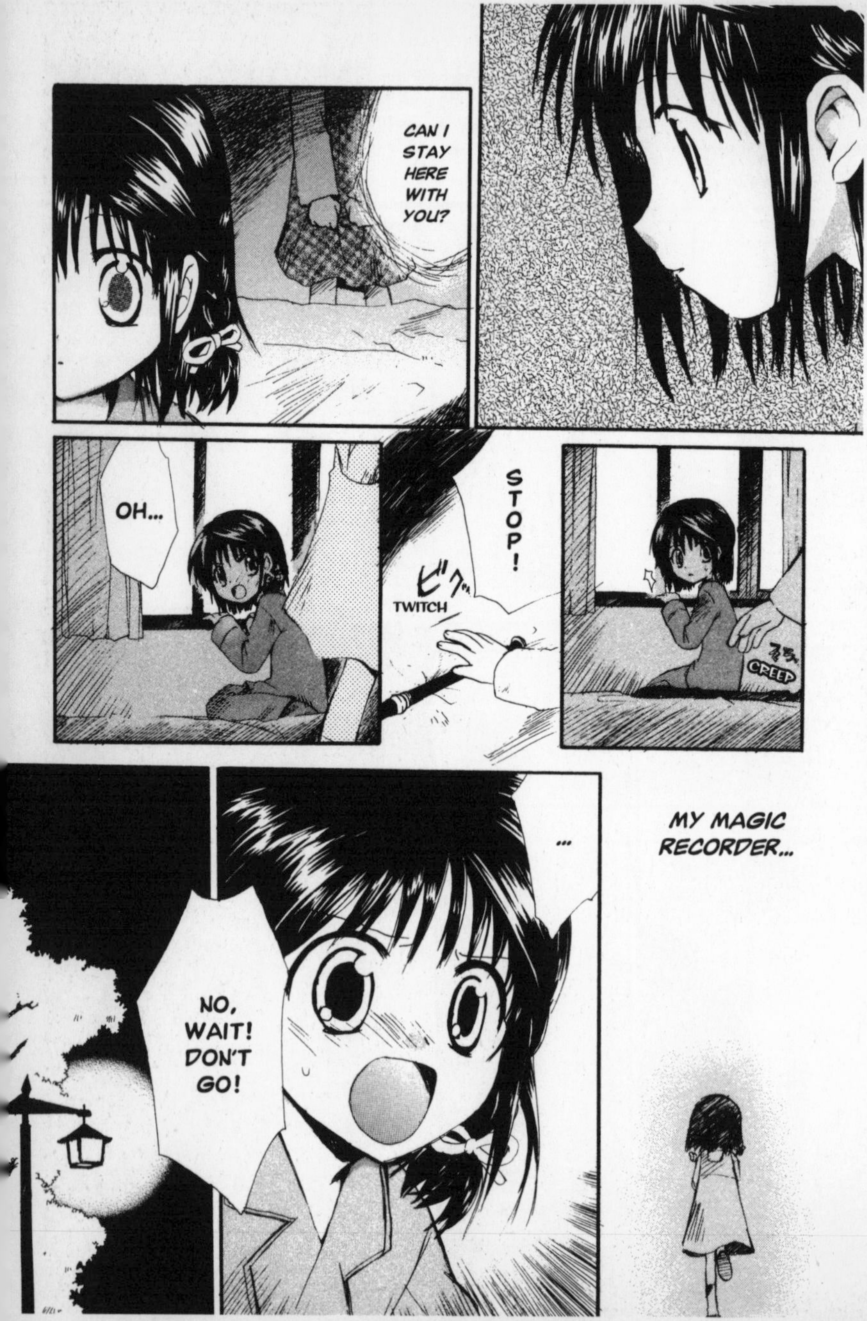

CAN I STAY HERE WITH YOU?
CREEP
STOP!
ビクッ
TWITCH
OH...
MY MAGIC RECORDER...
...
NO, WAIT! DON'T GO!

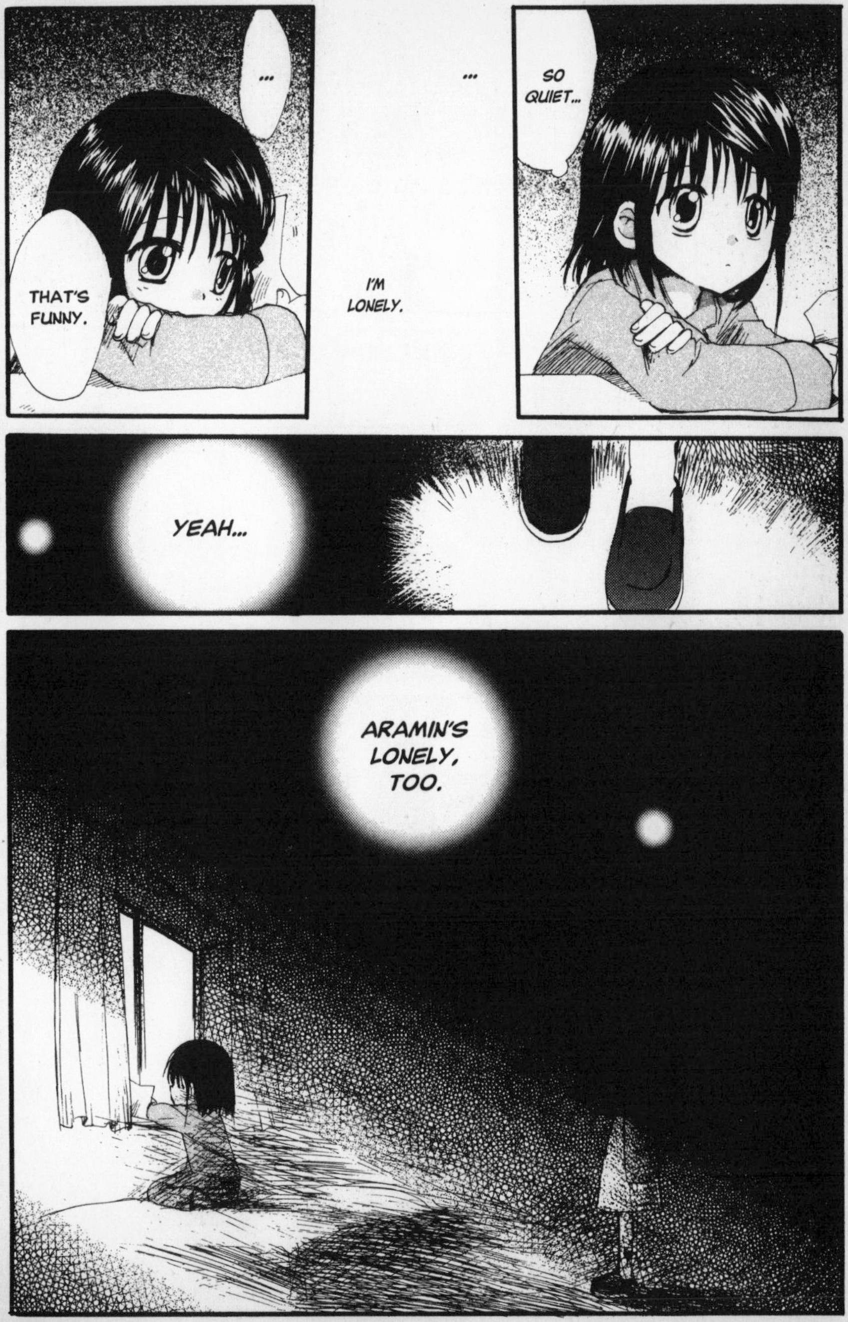
SO QUIET...
...
I'M LONELY.
...
THAT'S FUNNY.
YEAH...
ARAMIN'S LONELY, TOO.

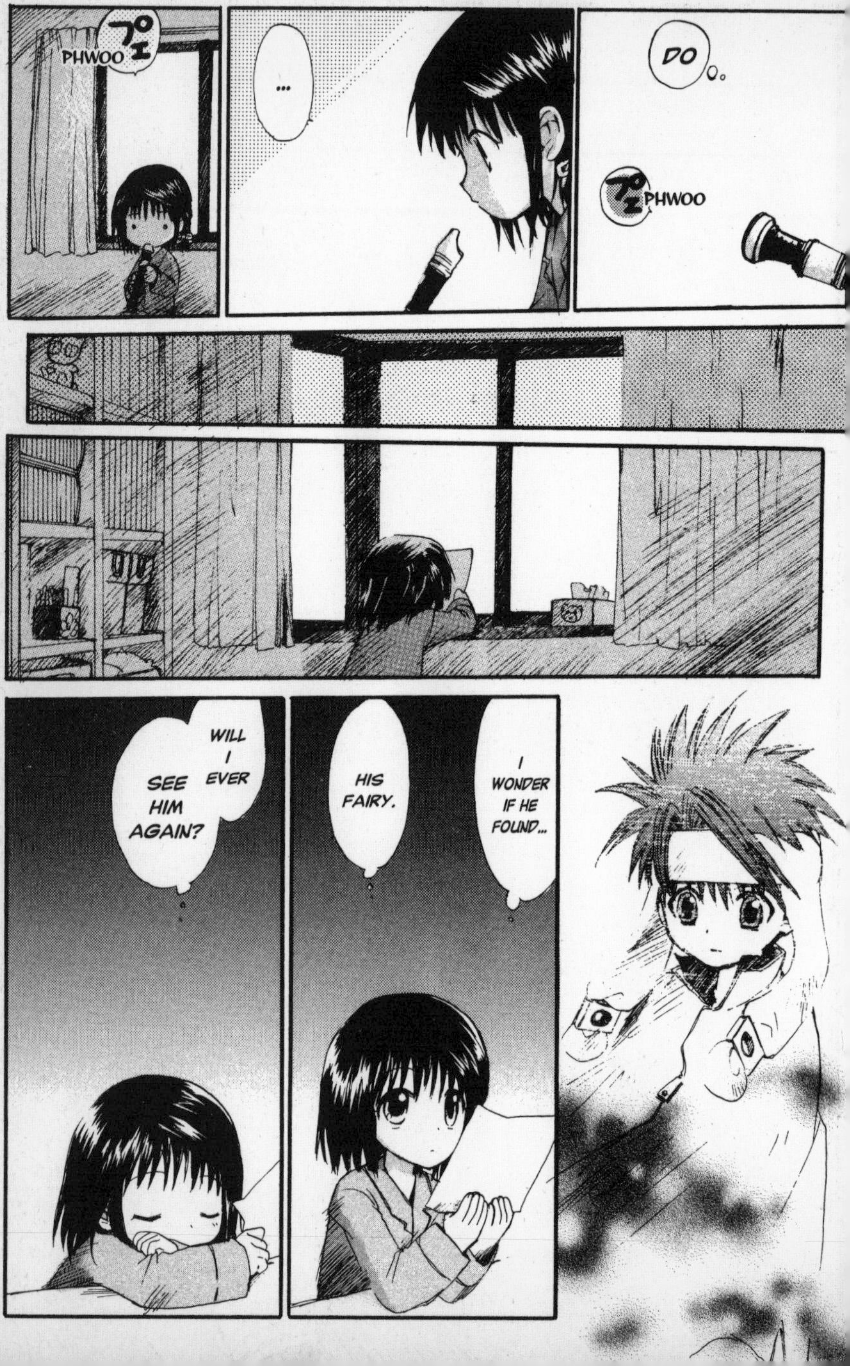
DO..
PHWOO
...
PHWOO
I WONDER IF HE FOUND...
HIS FAIRY.
WILL I EVER SEE HIM AGAIN?

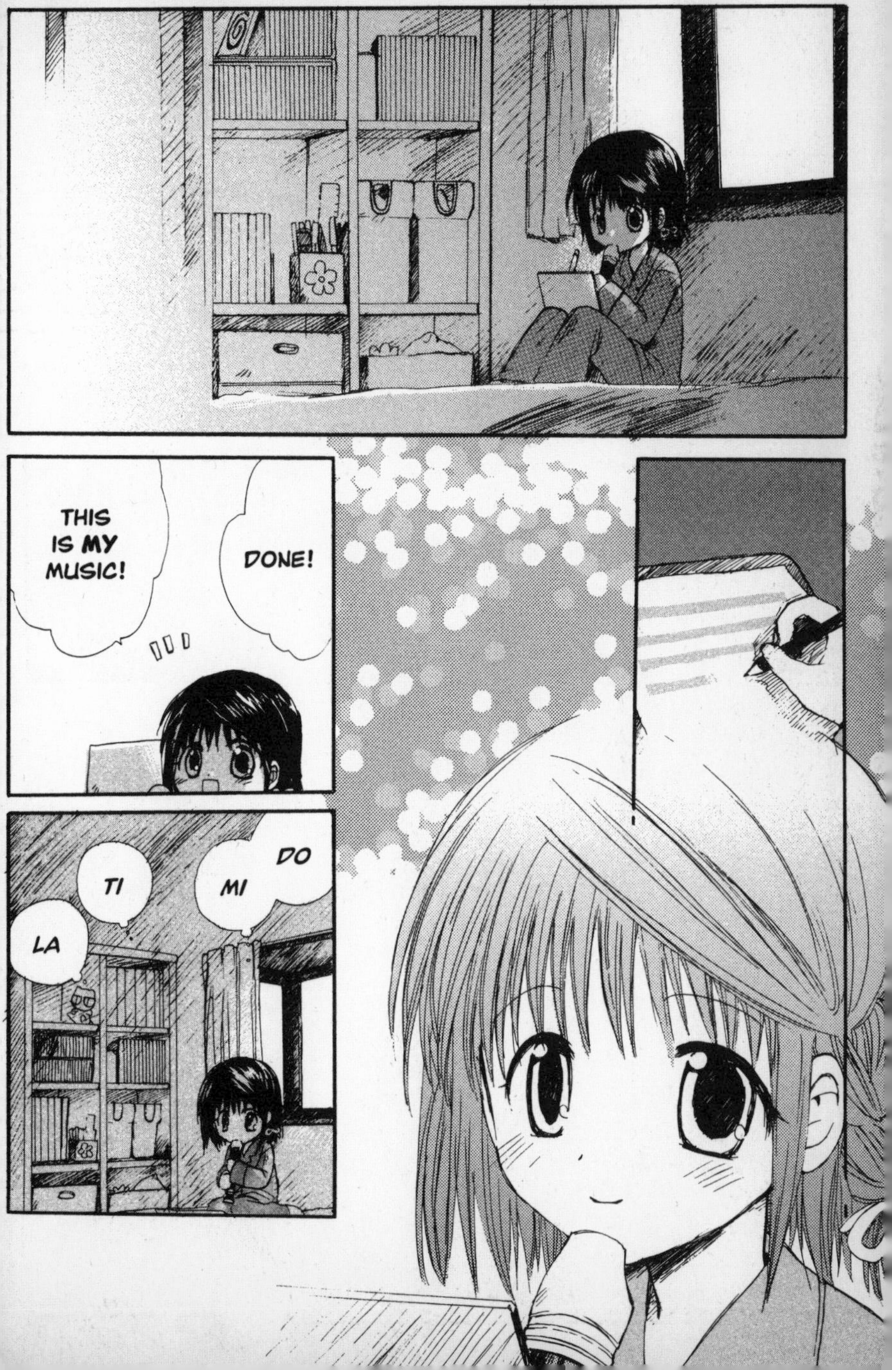
DONE!
THIS IS MY MUSIC!
DO
MI
TI
LA

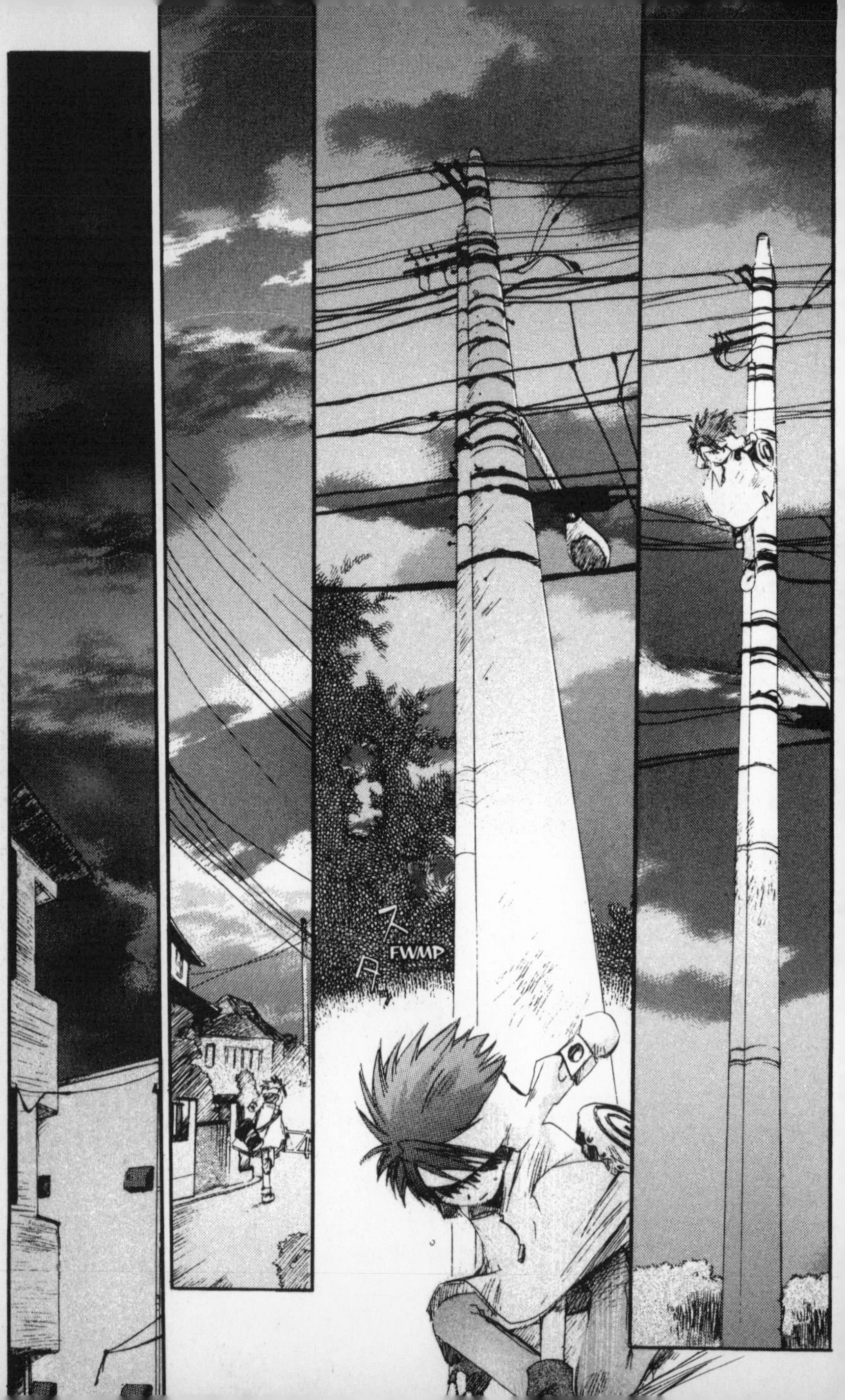

スタ
FWMP

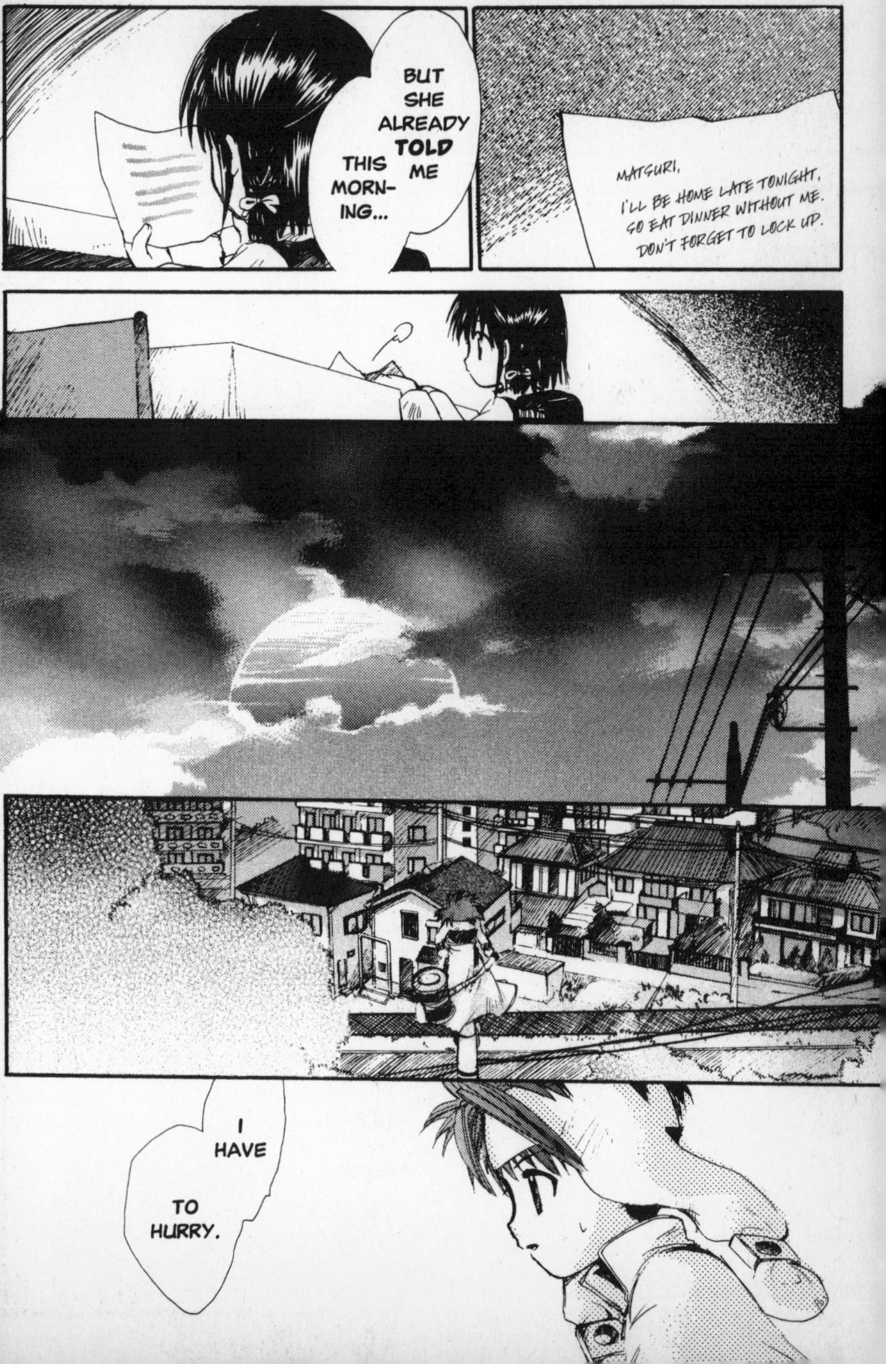
MATSURI,
I'LL BE HOME LATE TONIGHT, SO EAT DINNER WITHOUT ME. DON'T FORGET TO LOCK UP.
BUT SHE ALREADY TOLD ME THIS MORNING...
I HAVE TO HURRY.

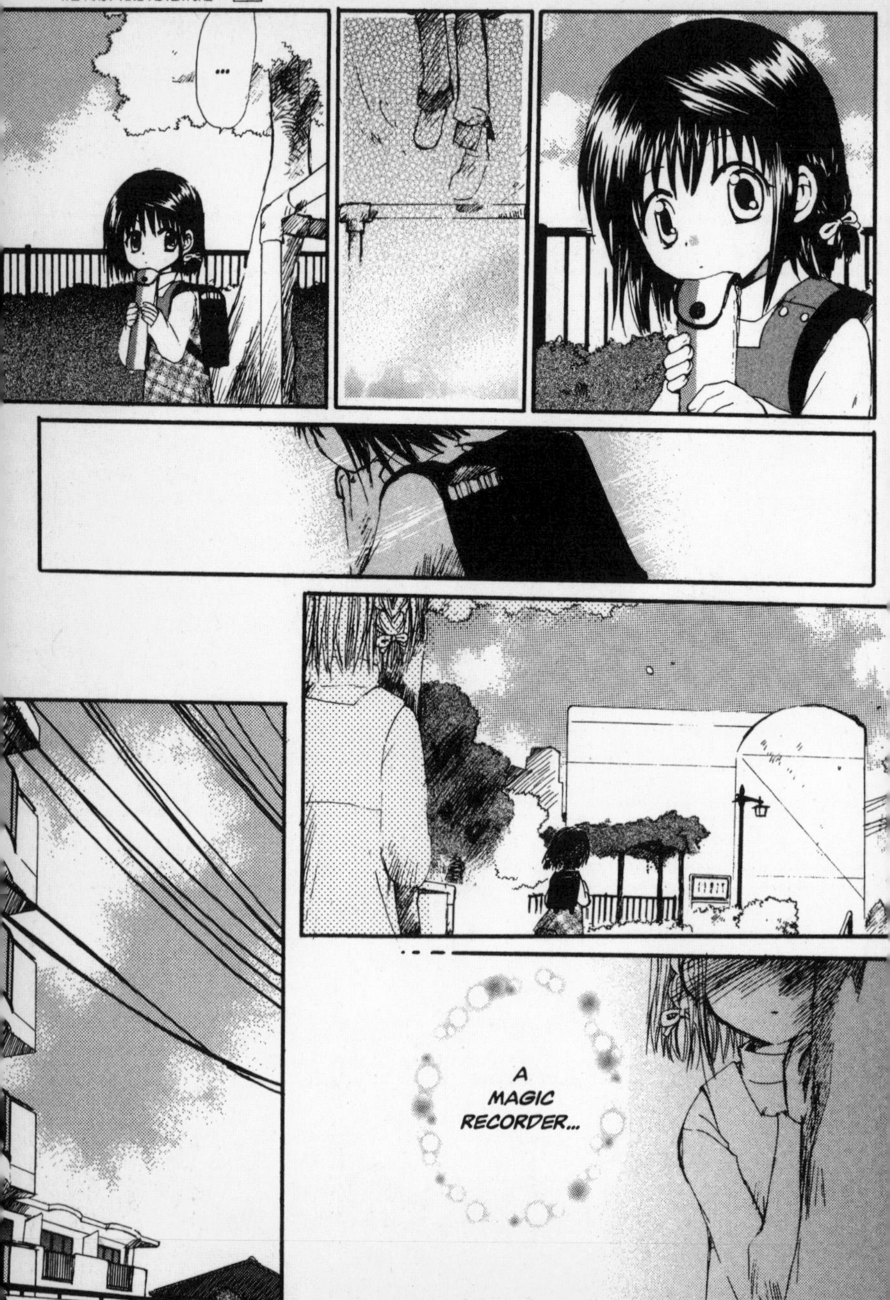
...
A MAGIC RECORDER...

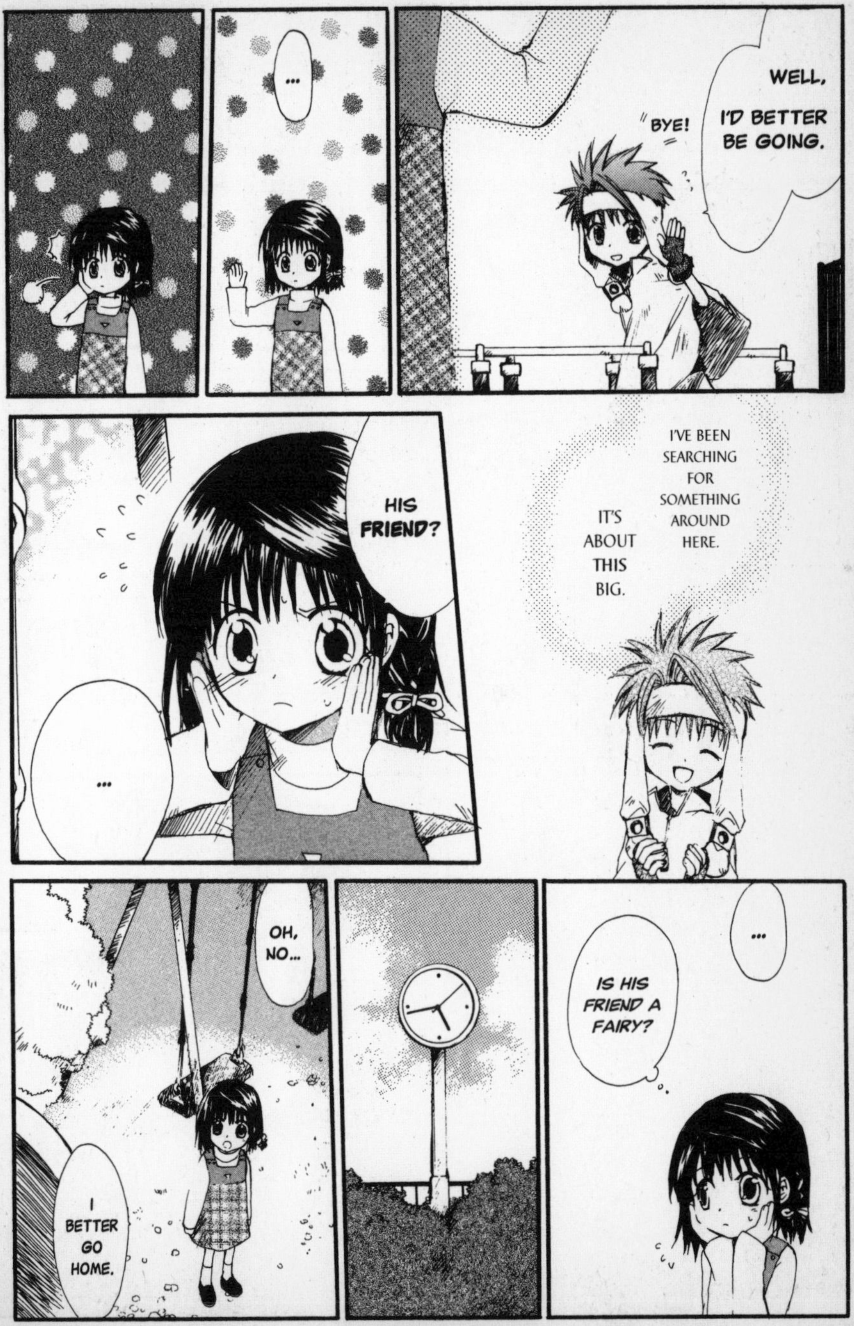

WELL, I'D BETTER BE GOING.
BYE!
...
I'VE BEEN SEARCHING FOR SOMETHING AROUND HERE.
IT'S ABOUT THIS BIG.
HIS FRIEND?
...
...
IS HIS FRIEND A FAIRY?
OH, NO...
I BETTER GO HOME.

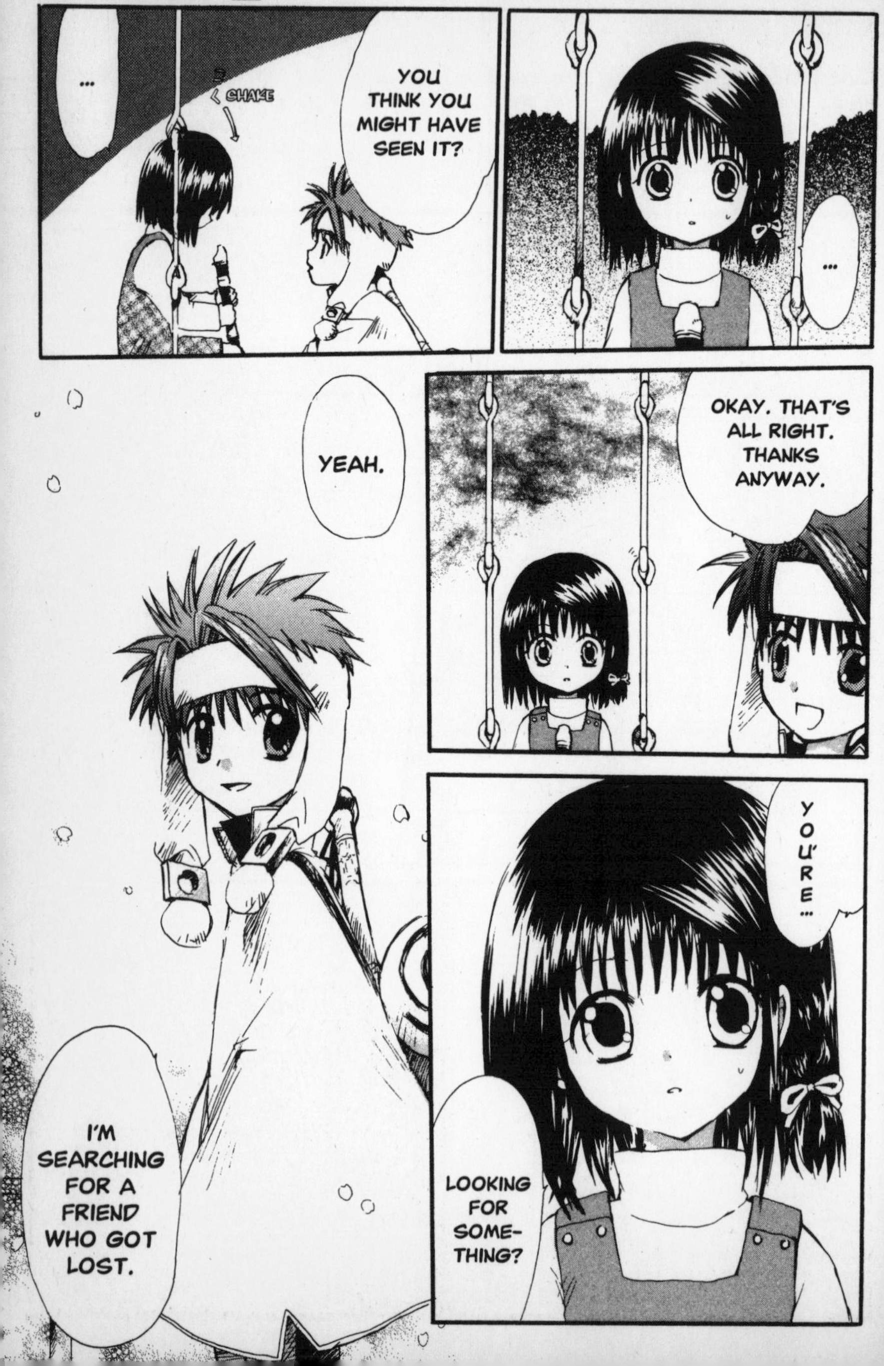
...
YOU THINK YOU MIGHT HAVE SEEN IT?
...
OKAY. THAT'S ALL RIGHT. THANKS ANYWAY.
YOU'RE...
LOOKING FOR SOME-THING?
YEAH.
I'M SEARCHING FOR A FRIEND WHO GOT LOST.

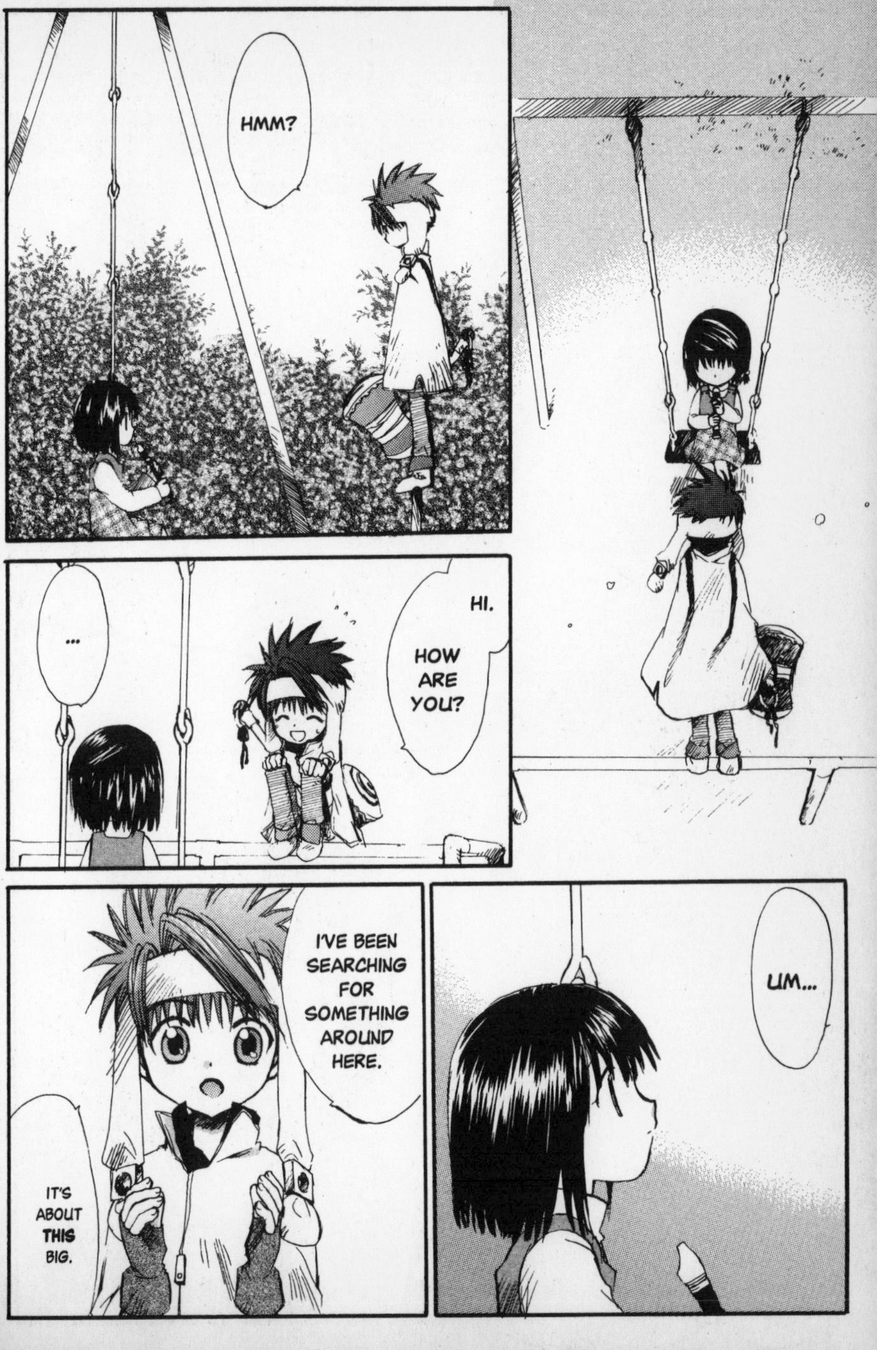
HMM?
HI.
HOW ARE YOU?
...
UM...
I'VE BEEN SEARCHING FOR SOMETHING AROUND HERE.
IT'S ABOUT THIS BIG.

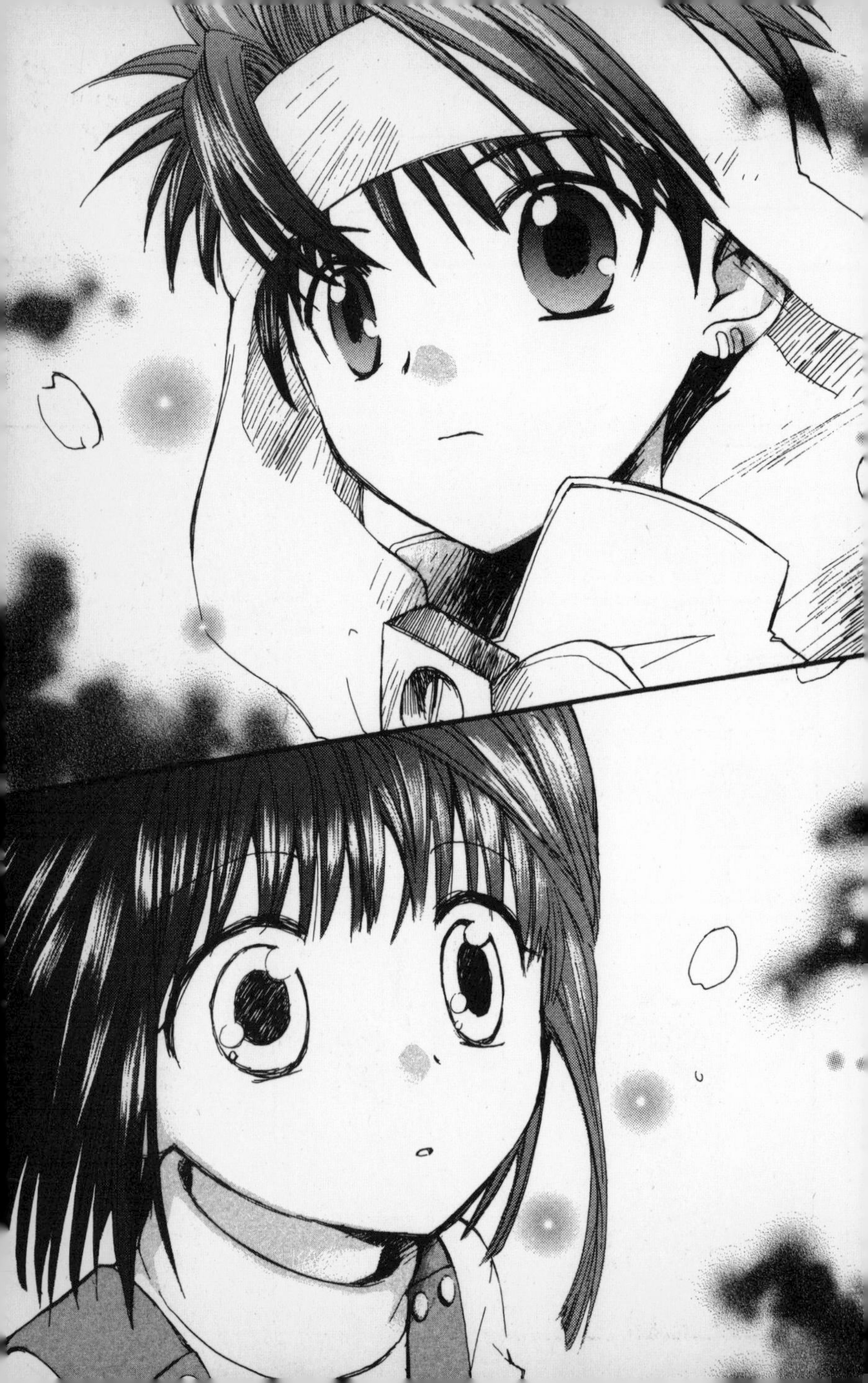

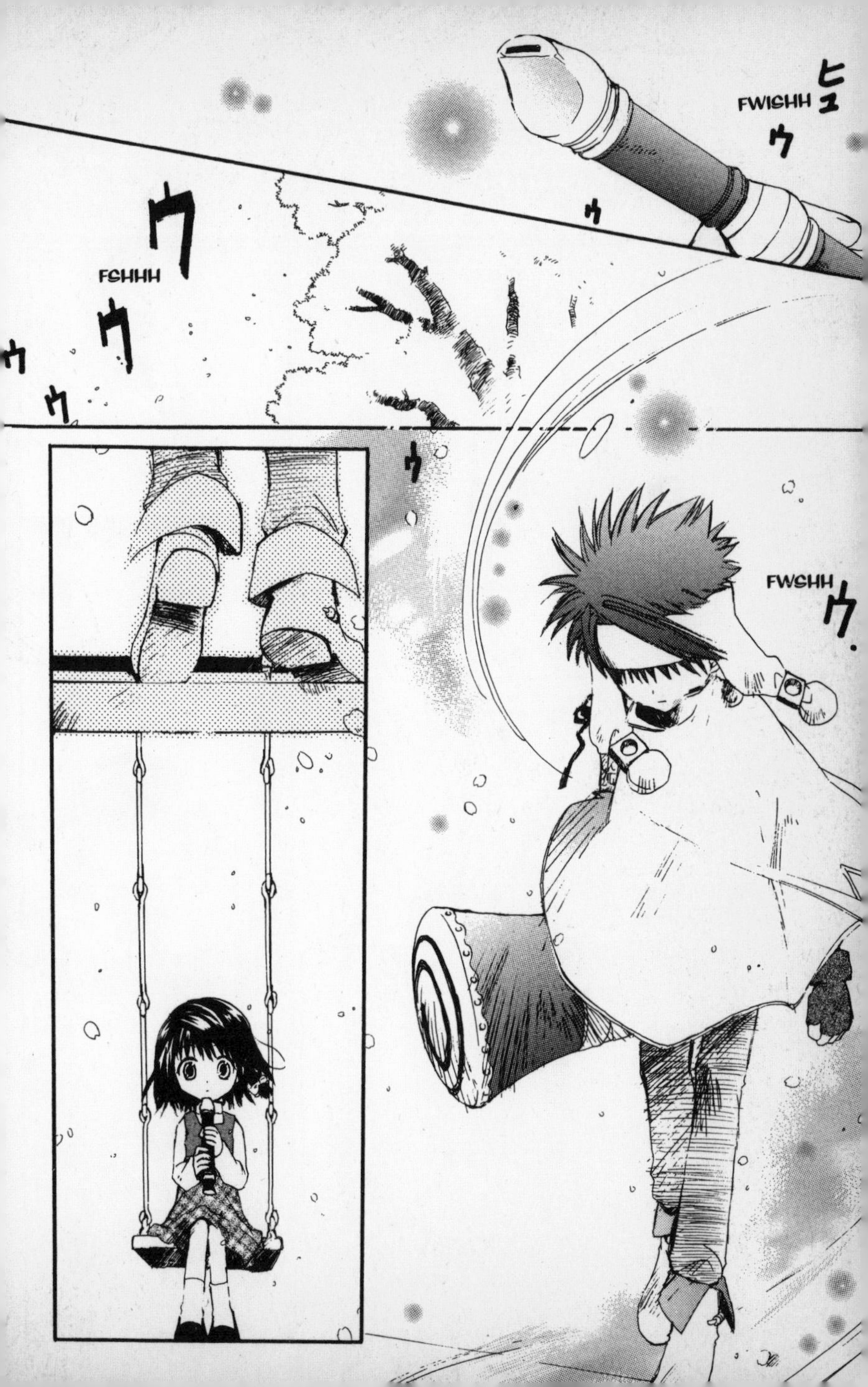
FWISHH
ヒュ
ウ
ゥ
ウ
FSHHH
ウ
ゥ
ゥ
ゥ
FWSHH
ウ.

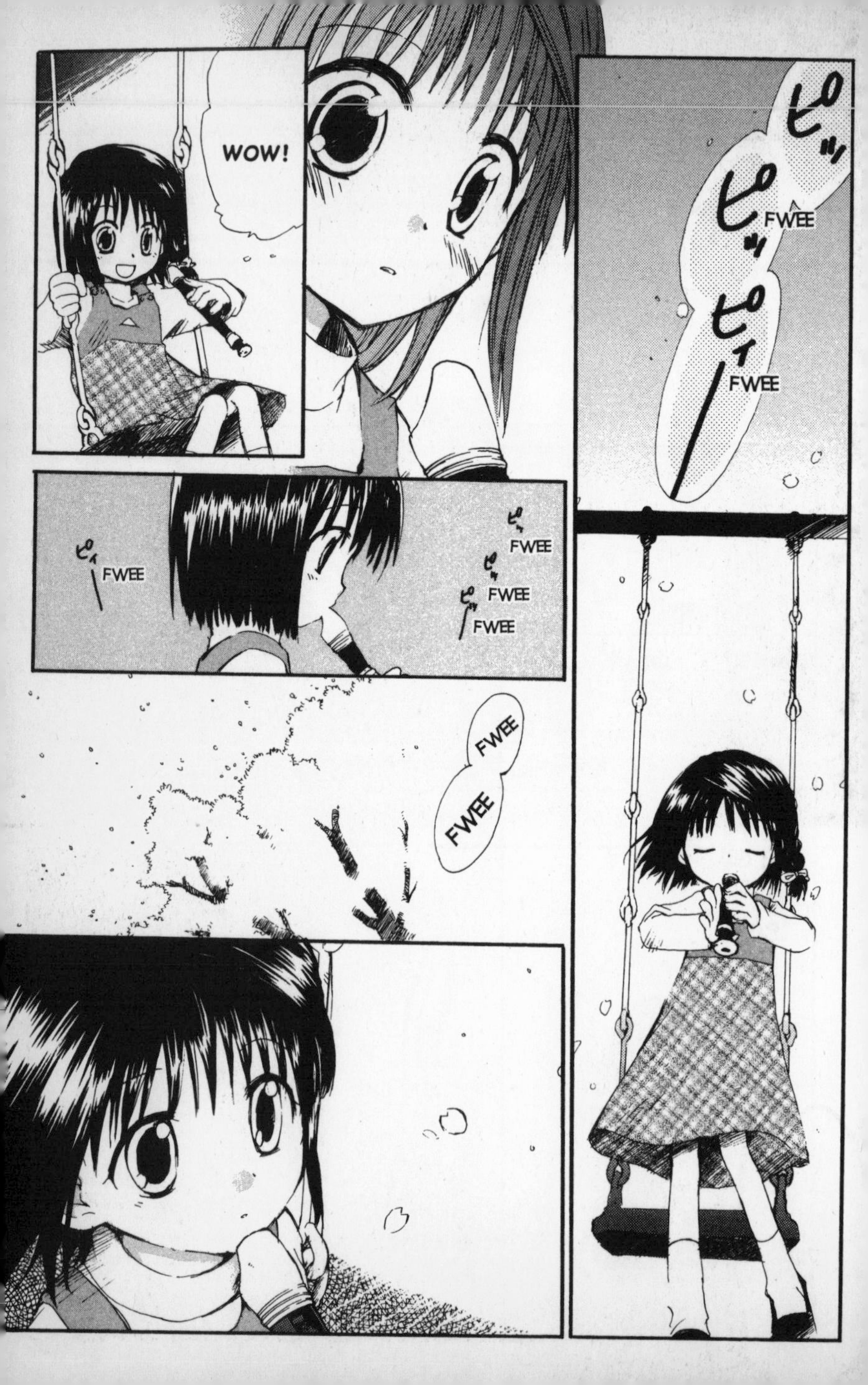
ピッ
ピッ FWEE
ピィー FWEE
WOW!
ピッ FWEE
ピッ FWEE
ピッ FWEE
ピィ FWEE
FWEE
FWEE

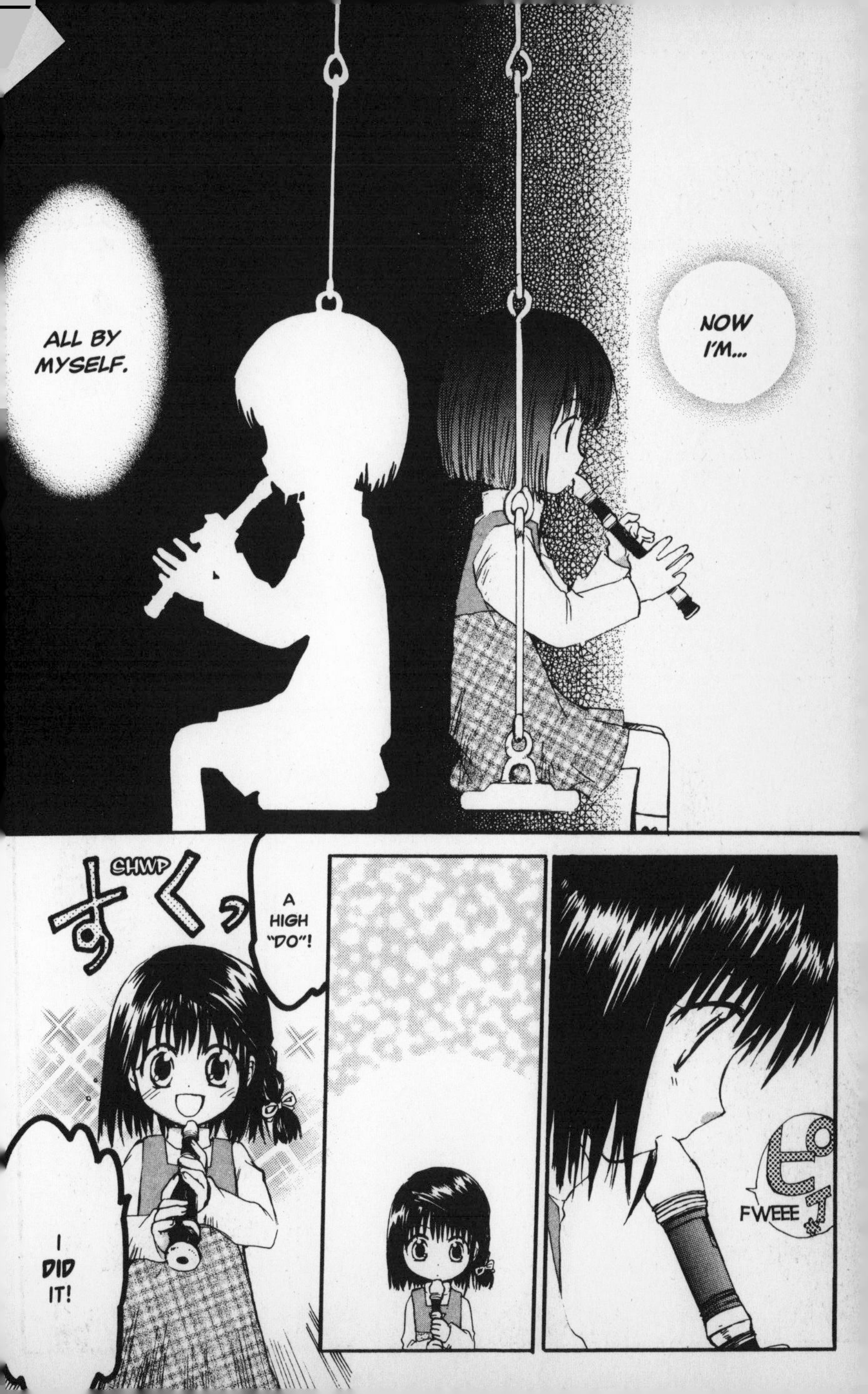
NOW I'M...
ALL BY MYSELF.
FWEEE
ピー
A HIGH "DO"!
SHWP
すくっ
I DID IT!

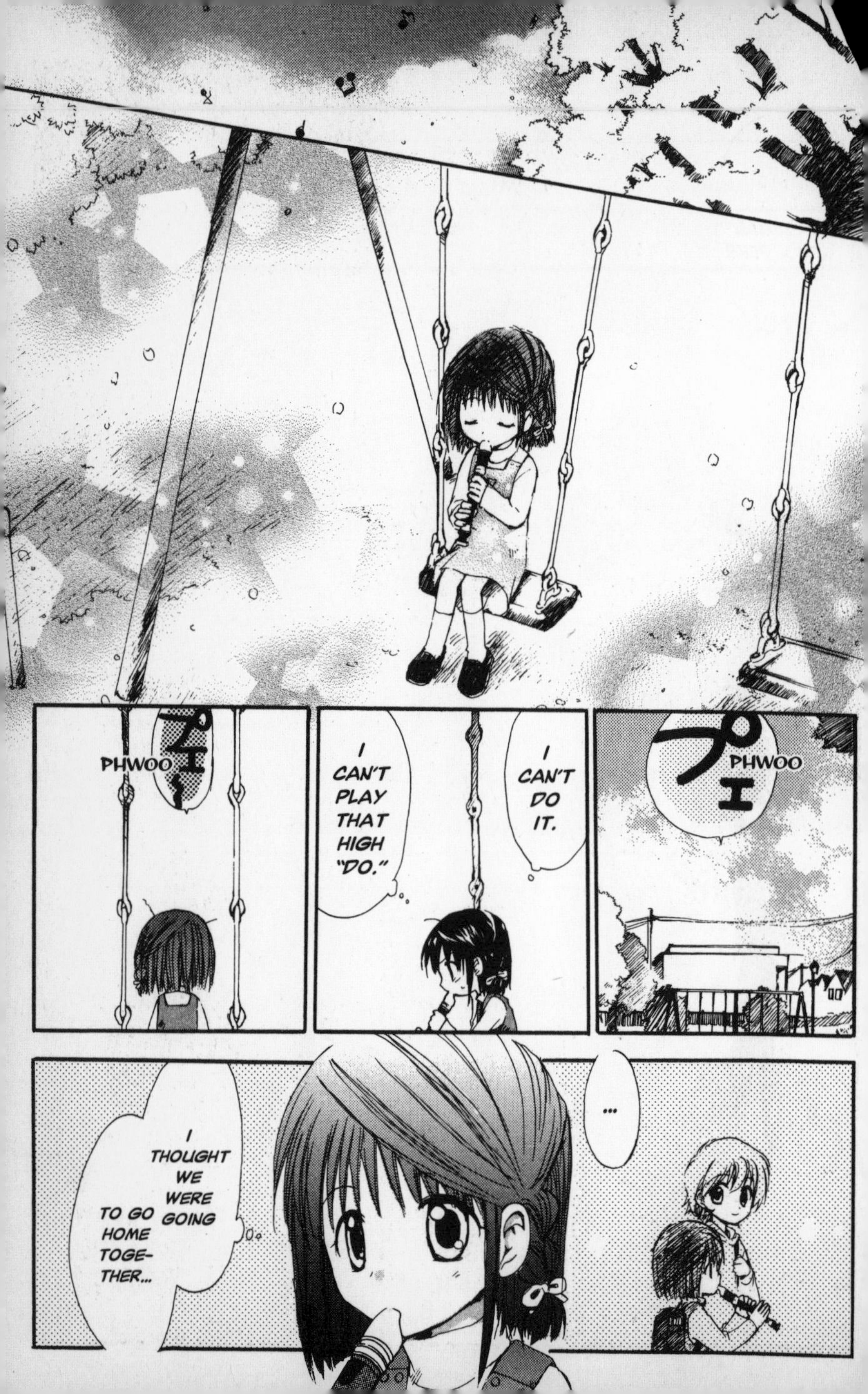

プェ
PHWOO
I CAN'T DO IT.
I CAN'T PLAY THAT HIGH "DO."
プェ〜
PHWOO
...
I THOUGHT WE WERE GOING TO GO HOME TOGETHER...

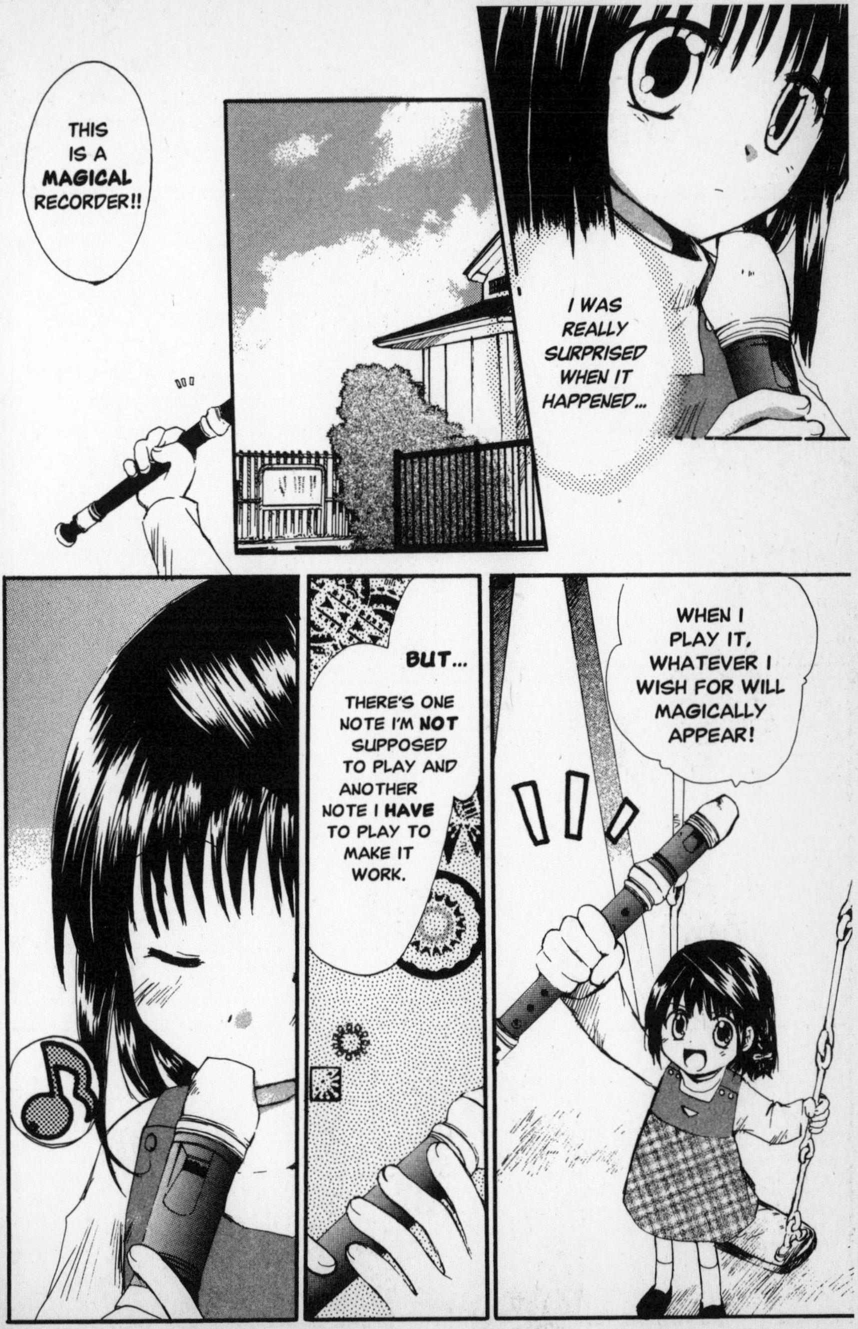
I WAS REALLY SURPRISED WHEN IT HAPPENED...
THIS IS A **MAGICAL** RECORDER!!
WHEN I PLAY IT, WHATEVER I WISH FOR WILL MAGICALLY APPEAR!
BUT...
THERE'S ONE NOTE I'M **NOT** SUPPOSED TO PLAY AND ANOTHER NOTE I **HAVE** TO PLAY TO MAKE IT WORK.

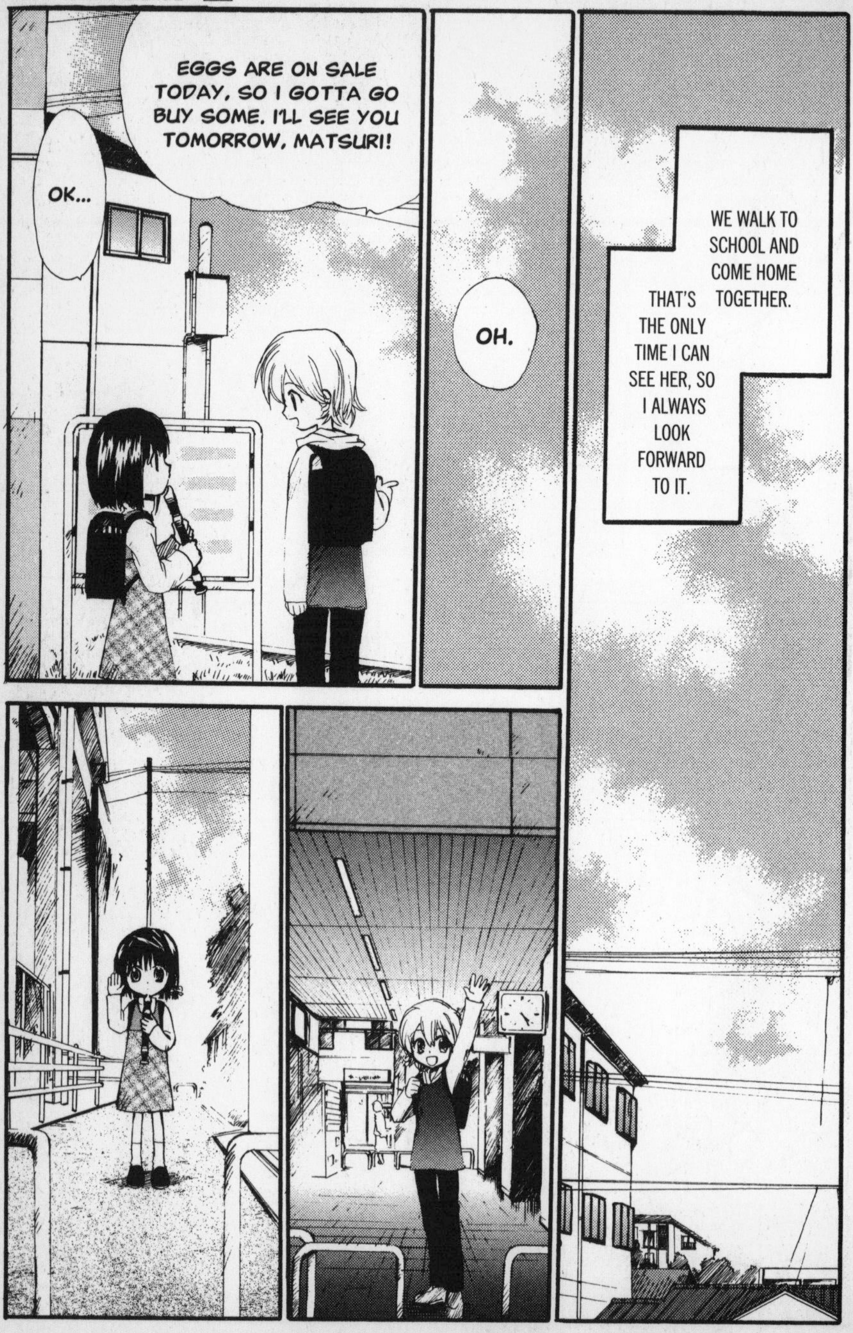
WE WALK TO SCHOOL AND COME HOME TOGETHER.
THAT'S THE ONLY TIME I CAN SEE HER, SO I ALWAYS LOOK FORWARD TO IT.
OH.
EGGS ARE ON SALE TODAY, SO I GOTTA GO BUY SOME. I'LL SEE YOU TOMORROW, MATSURI!
OK...

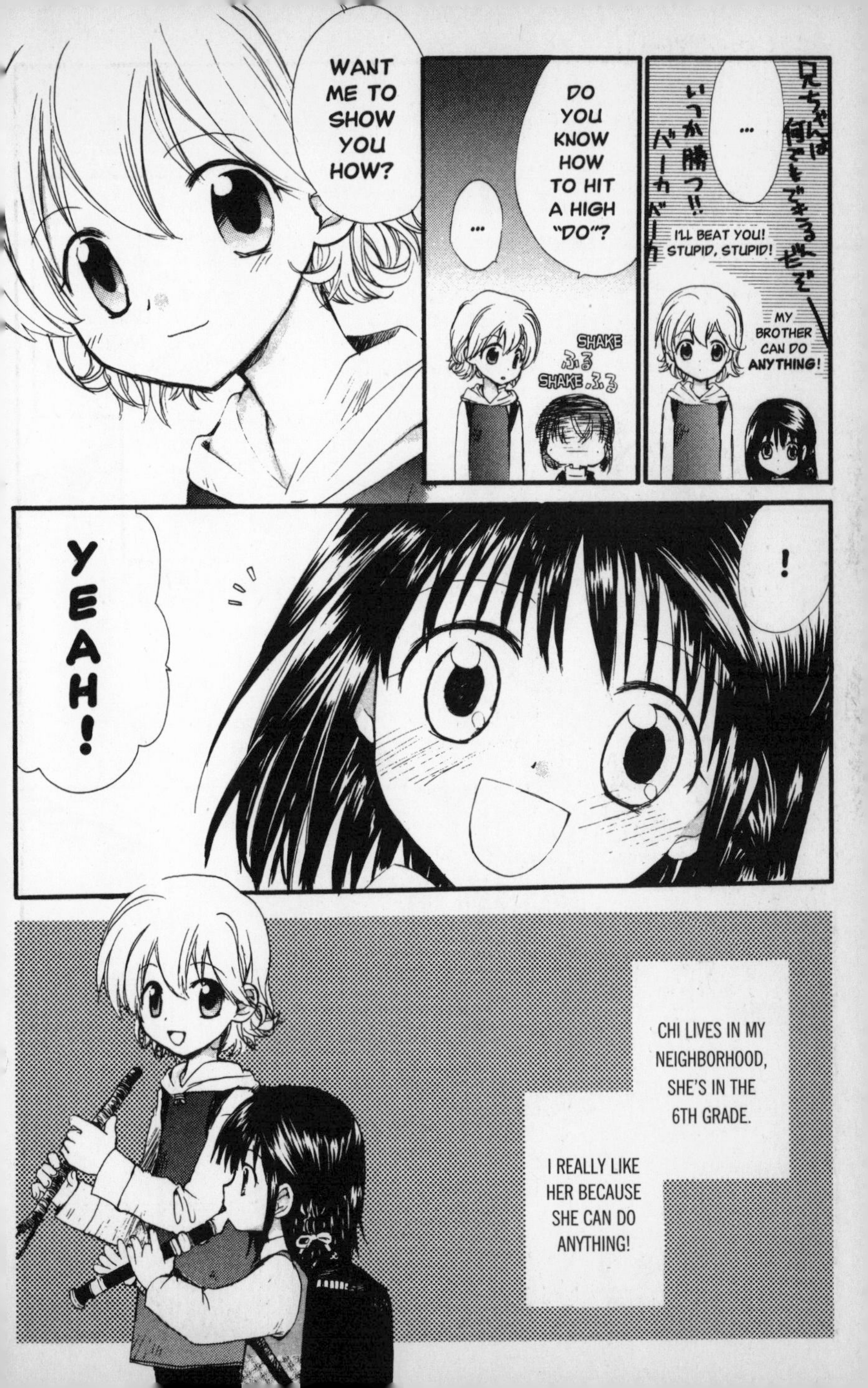

...
兄ちゃんは何でもできるんだぞ
MY BROTHER CAN DO ANYTHING!
いつか勝つ!!
バーカバーカ
I'LL BEAT YOU! STUPID, STUPID!
...
DO YOU KNOW HOW TO HIT A HIGH "DO"?
SHAKE ふる SHAKE ふる
WANT ME TO SHOW YOU HOW?
!
YEAH!
CHI LIVES IN MY NEIGHBORHOOD, SHE'S IN THE 6TH GRADE.
I REALLY LIKE HER BECAUSE SHE CAN DO ANYTHING!

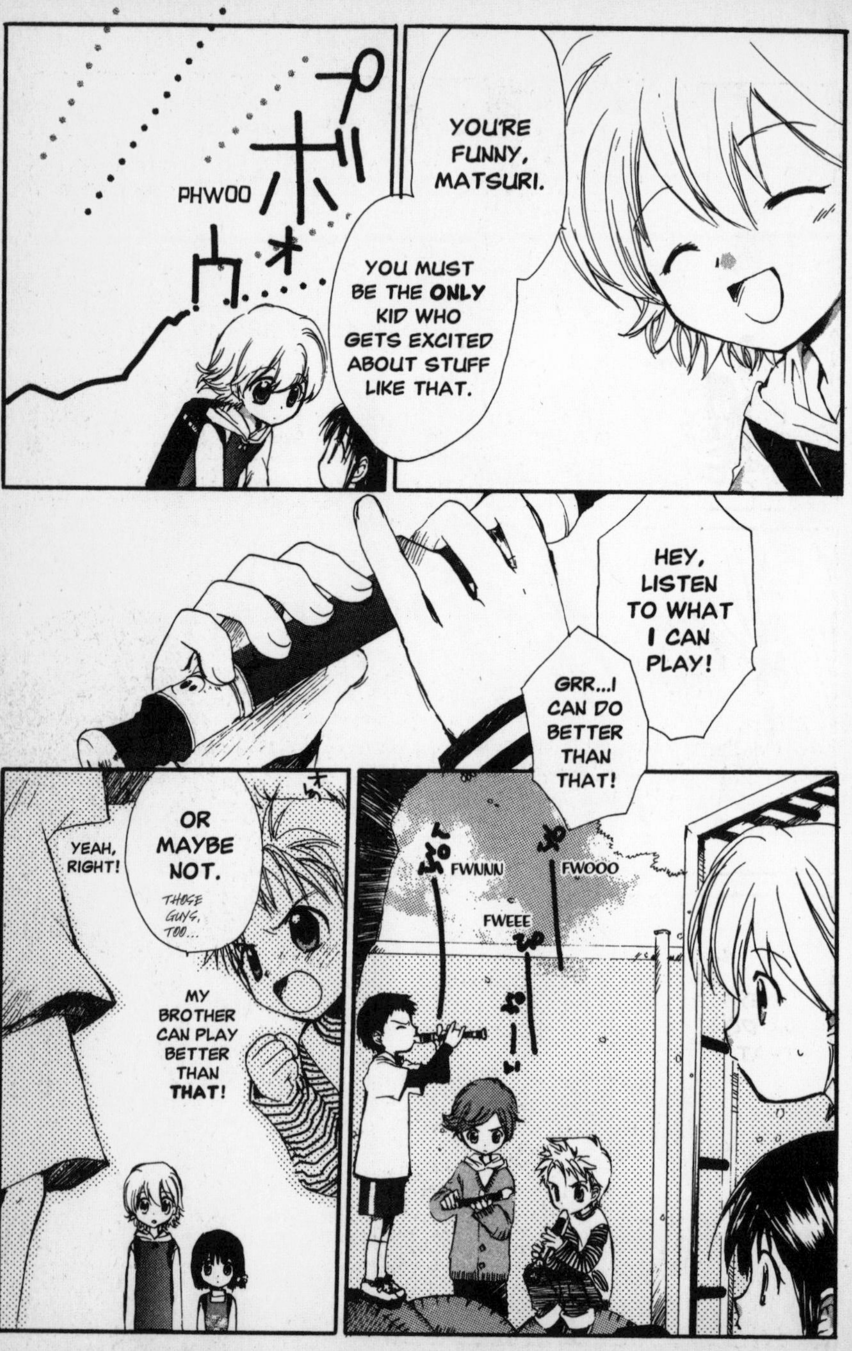
YOU'RE FUNNY, MATSURI.
YOU MUST BE THE ONLY KID WHO GETS EXCITED ABOUT STUFF LIKE THAT.
PHWOO
HEY, LISTEN TO WHAT I CAN PLAY!
GRR...I CAN DO BETTER THAN THAT!
FWOOO
FWNNN
FWEEE
OR MAYBE NOT.
THOSE GUYS, TOO...
YEAH, RIGHT!
MY BROTHER CAN PLAY BETTER THAN THAT!

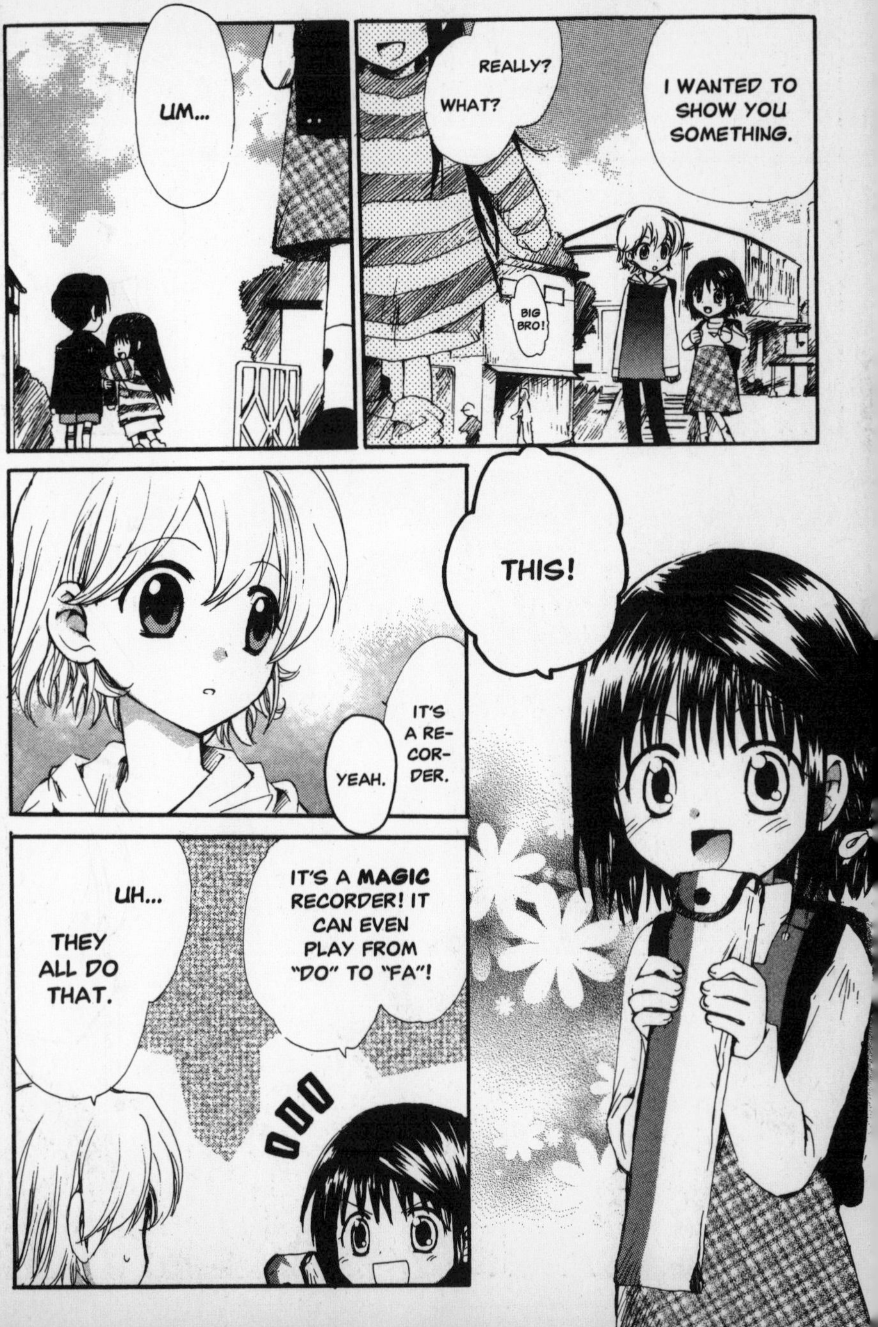

I WANTED TO SHOW YOU SOMETHING.
BIG BRO!
REALLY?
WHAT?
UM...
THIS!
IT'S A RE-COR-DER.
YEAH.
IT'S A **MAGIC** RECORDER! IT CAN EVEN PLAY FROM "DO" TO "FA"!
UH...
THEY ALL DO THAT.

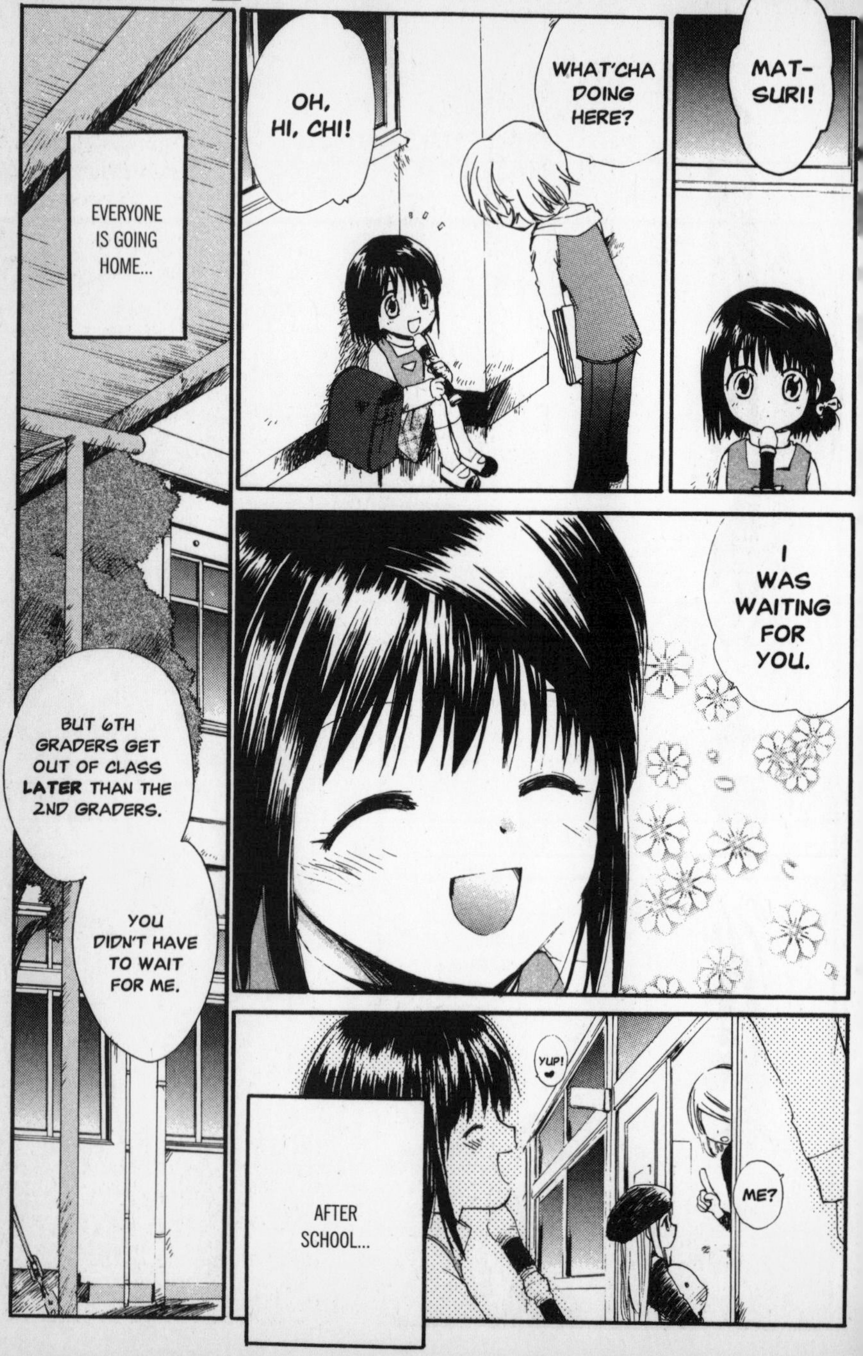
MAT-SURI!
WHAT'CHA DOING HERE?
OH, HI, CHI!
EVERYONE IS GOING HOME...
I WAS WAITING FOR YOU.
BUT 6TH GRADERS GET OUT OF CLASS LATER THAN THE 2ND GRADERS.
YOU DIDN'T HAVE TO WAIT FOR ME.
ME?
YUP!
AFTER SCHOOL...

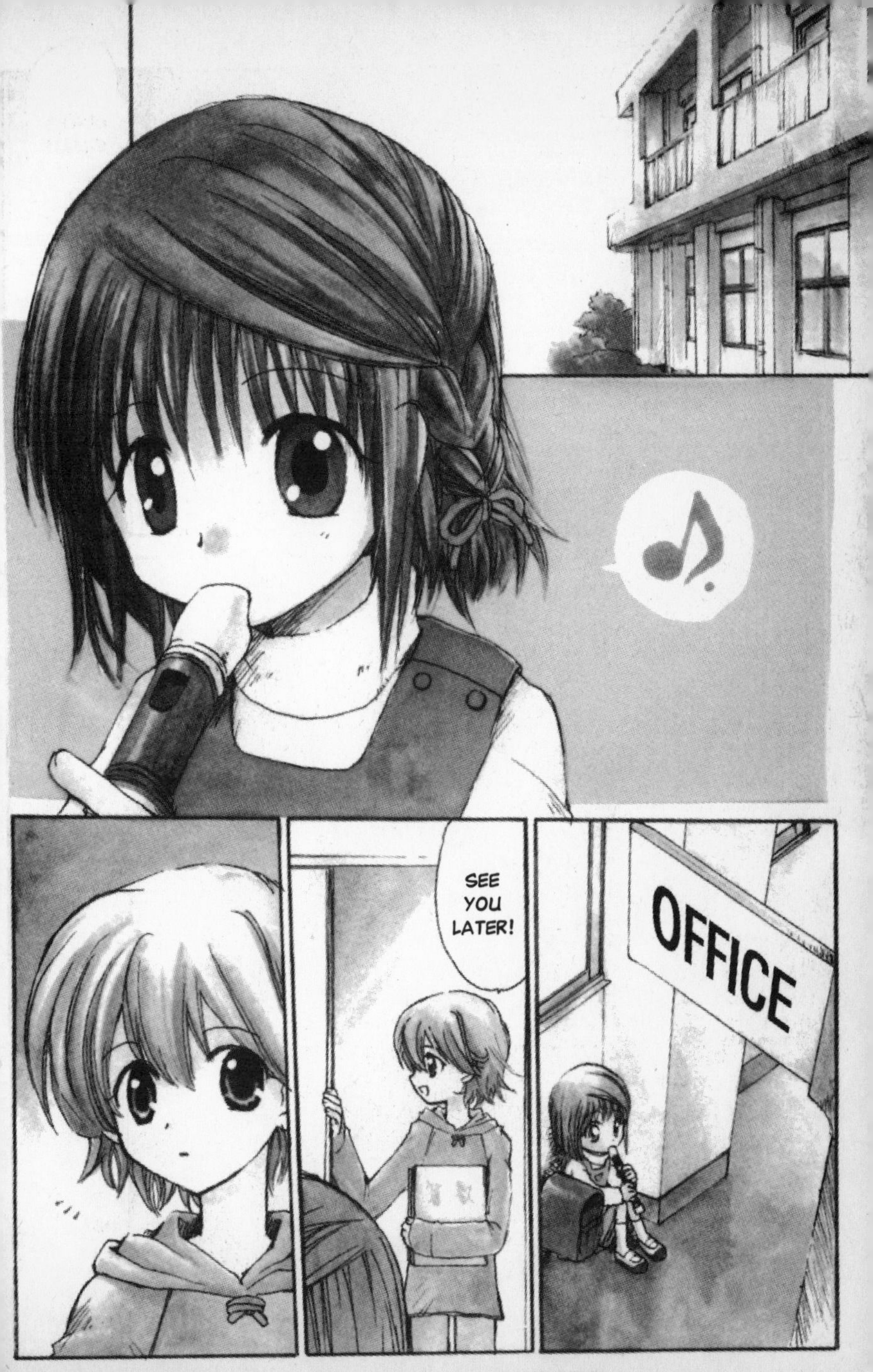

SEE YOU LATER!
OFFICE

CHAPTER 1
THE PRINCE AND THE FULL MOON

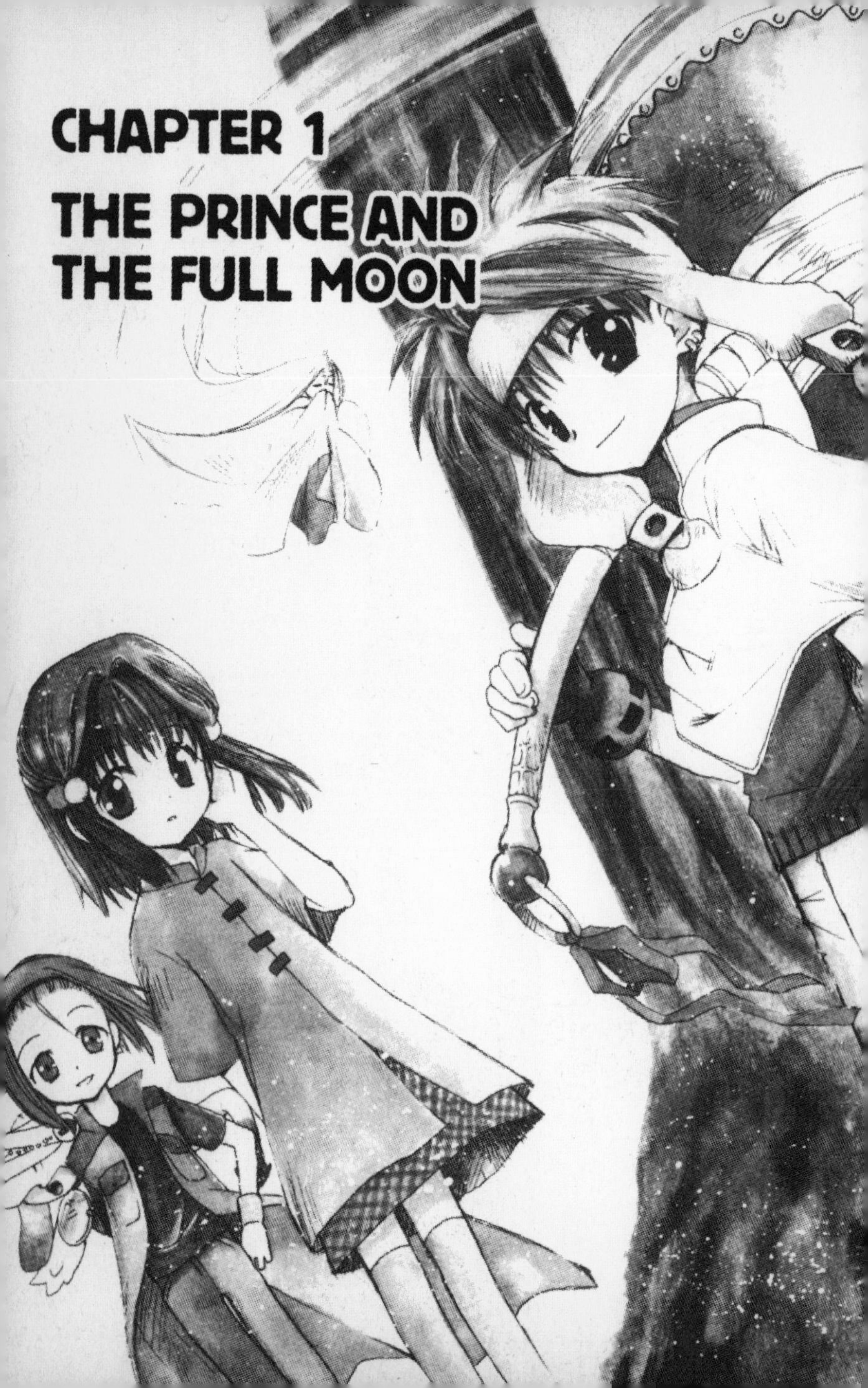

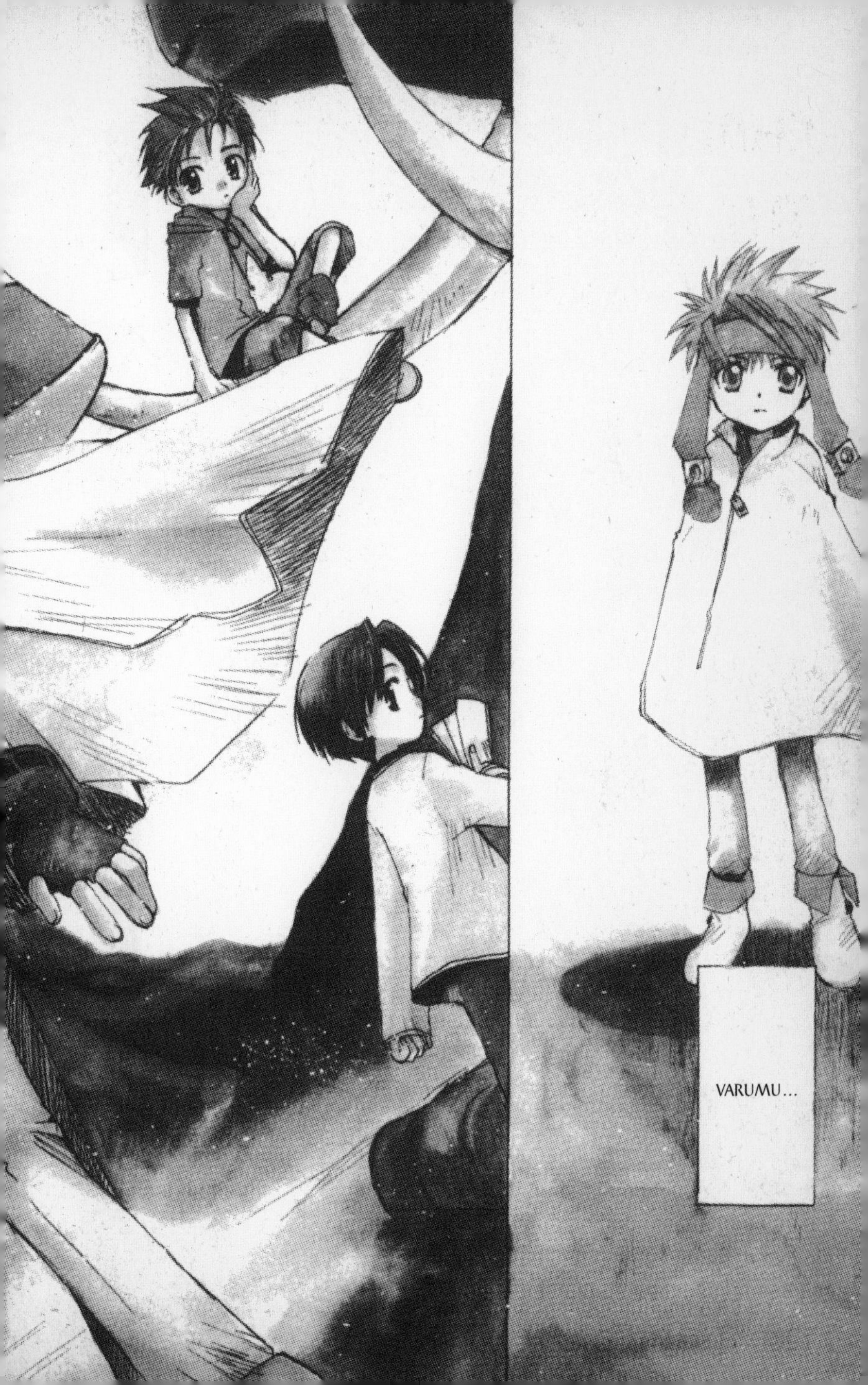
VARUMU...

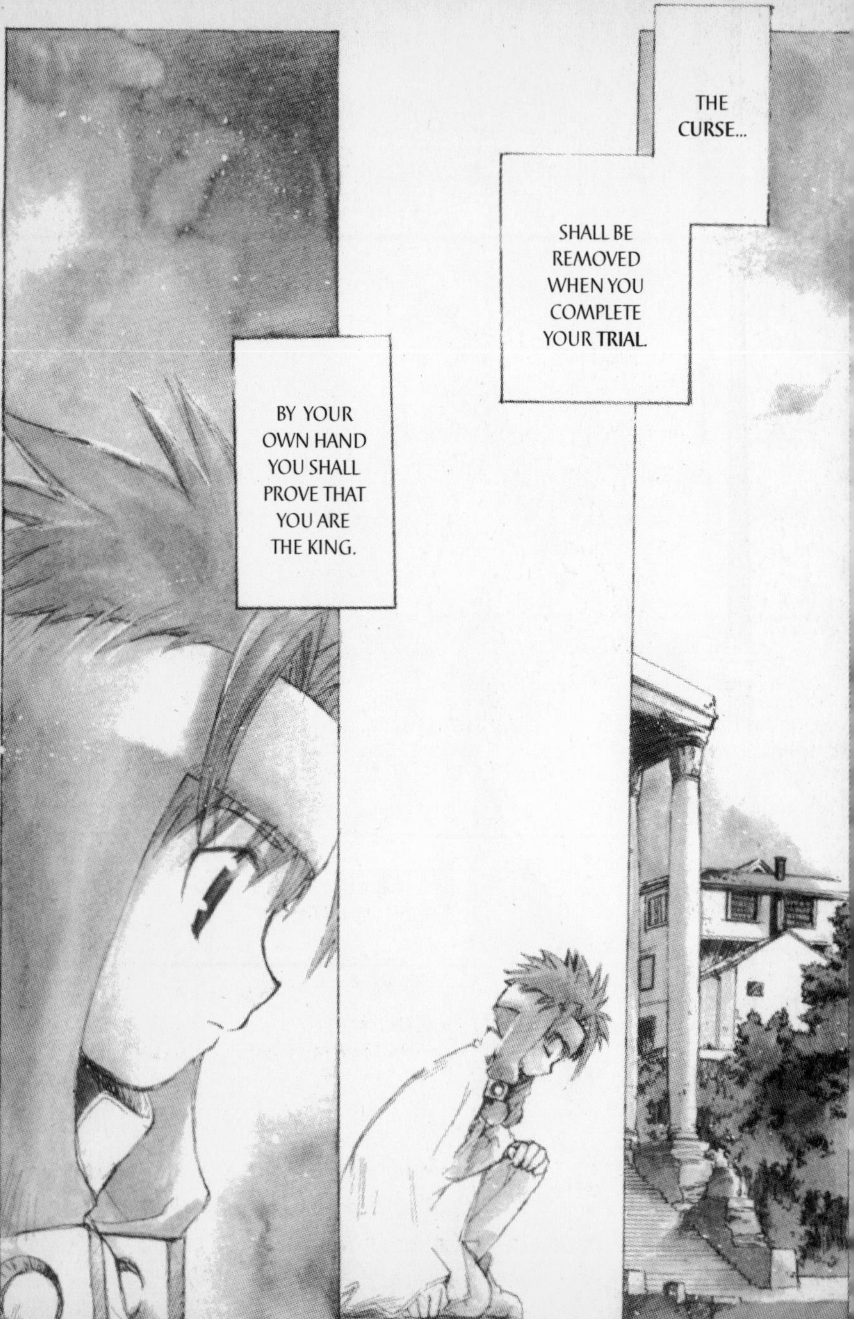
THE CURSE...
SHALL BE REMOVED WHEN YOU COMPLETE YOUR TRIAL.
BY YOUR OWN HAND YOU SHALL PROVE THAT YOU ARE THE KING.

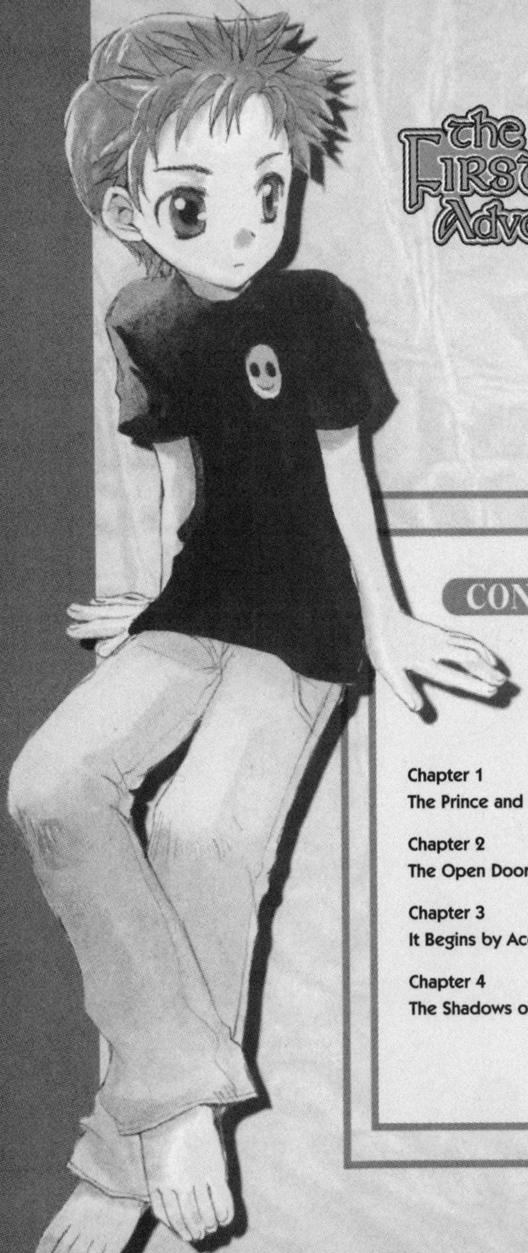

The First King Adventure

1

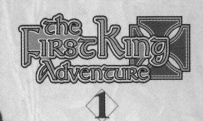

CONTENTS

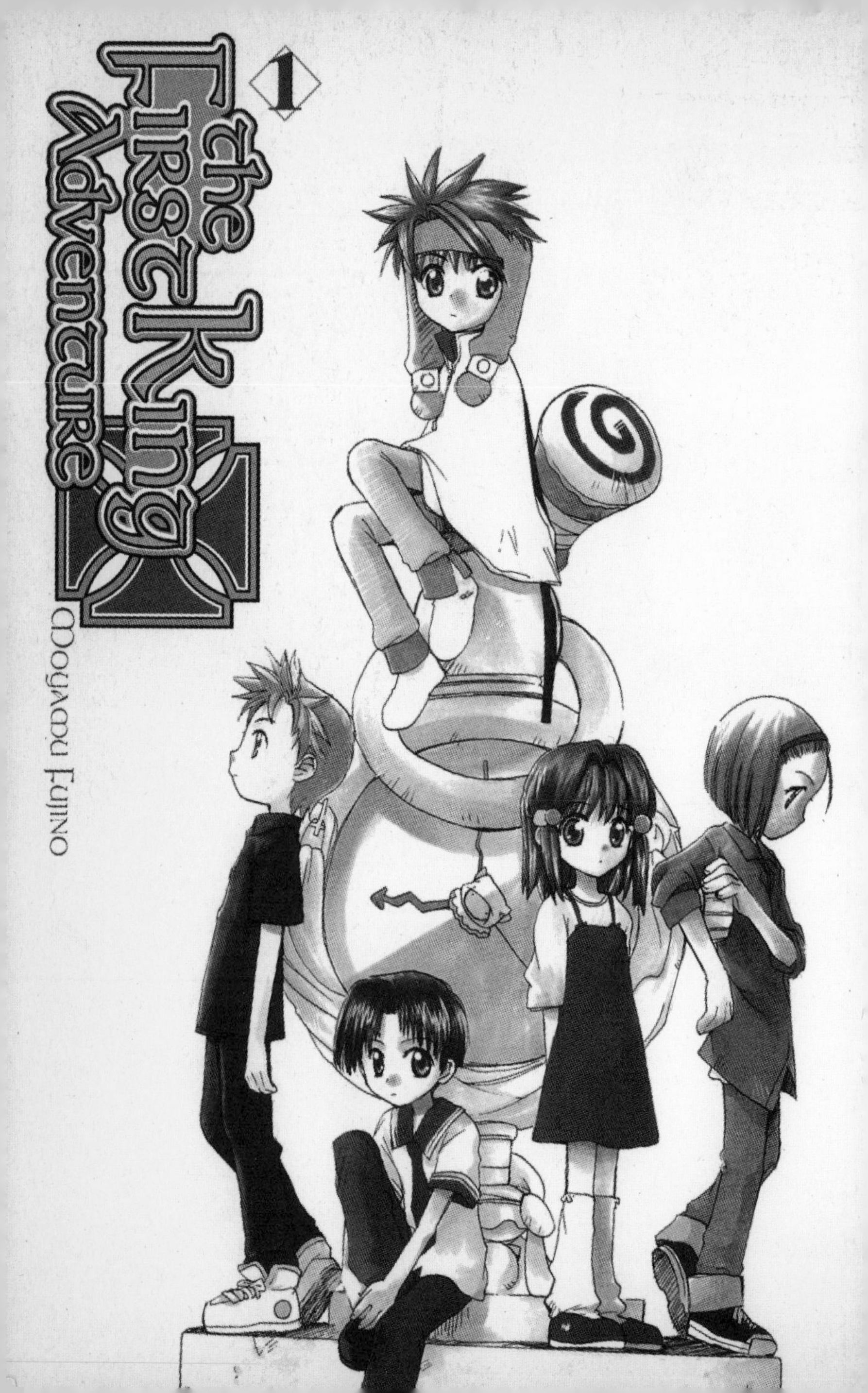

1
the First King Adventure
Moyamu Fujino